THE JOSEPH SMITH EGYPTIAN PAPYRI

The Joseph Smith Egyptian Papyri

A COMPLETE EDITION

P. JS 1–4 AND THE HYPOCEPHALUS OF SHESHONQ

ROBERT K. RITNER

WITH CONTRIBUTIONS BY

MARC COENEN
H. MICHAEL MARQUARDT
CHRISTOPHER WOODS

Signature Books
SALT LAKE CITY, 2013

www.signaturebooks.com

First published in 2011 in hardback (978-1-56085-220-9) by the Smith-Pettit Foundation, Salt Lake City.
Typography by Olaf Nelson of Chinook Design, Inc.
Cover design by Jason Francis.

The cover superimposes the preserved initial vignette of the Breathing Permit of Hôr (P. JS 1) onto the reconstructed image published as Facsimile 1 in Joseph Smith's Book of Abraham. See pp. 113-19 and plates III-IV.

17 16 15 14 13 5 4 3 2 1

Library of Congress Cataloging-in-Publication Data

The Joseph Smith Egyptian papyri : a complete edition : P. JS 1-4 and the hypocephalus of Sheshonq / Robert K. Ritner ; with contributions by Marc Coenen, H. Michael Marquardt, Christopher Woods.

pages cm

Includes bibliographical references.

ISBN 1-56085-232-2 : alk. paper 1. Book of breathings. 2. Book of the dead. 3. Hypocephalus of Sheshonq. I. Ritner, Robert Kriech, editor, translator. II. Coenen, M. (Marc). Ownership and dating of certain Joseph Smith papyri. III. Marquardt, H. Michael. Joseph Smith's Egyptian papers. IV. Woods, Christopher, 1968- Practice of Egyptian religion at "Ur of the Chaldees." V. Book of breathings. English. Selections (Ritner) VI. Book of breathings. Egyptian. Selections (Ritner) VII. Book of the dead. English. Selections (Ritner) VIII. Book of the dead. Egyptian Selections (Ritner) IX. Hypocephalus of Seshonq. English (Ritner) X. Hypocephalus of Sheshonq. Egyptian (Ritner)

PJ1559.B42J67 2012

289.3'2--dc23

2011045014

CONTENTS

PLATES

"Some writings on papirus [*sic*] found with the mummies, can also be seen, and will afford, no doubt, much satisfaction to amateurs of antiquities."

Philadelphia U.S. Gazette, 3 April 1833
(Wolfe and Singerman 2009, p. 100)

TIMES AND SEASONS.

"Truth will prevail."

Vol. III. No. 9.] CITY OF NAUVOO, ILL. MARCH, 1, 1842. [Whole No. 45.

A FAC-SIMILE FROM THE BOOK OF ABRAHAM.
NO. 1.

EXPLANATION OF THE ABOVE CUT.

FIG. 1,—The Angel of the Lord.

2. Abraham, fastened upon an Altar.

3. The Idolatrous Priest of Elkenah attempting to offer up Abraham as a sacrifice.

4. The Altar for sacrifice, by the Idolatrous Priests, standing before the Gods of Elkenah, Libnah, Mahmachrah, Korash, and Pharaoh.

5. The Idolatrous God of Elkenah.

6. The " " " Libnah.

7. The " " " Mahmachrah.

8. The " " " Korash.

9. The " " " Pharaoh.

10. Abraham in Egypt.

11. Designed to represent the pillars of Heaven, as understood by the Egyptians.

12. Raukeeyang, signifying expanse, or the firmament, over our heads; but in this case, in relation to this subject, the Egyptians meant it to signify Shamau, to be high, or the heavens: answering to the Hebrew word, Shaumahyeem.

"These old folks, who flourished perhaps when Moses and Aaron were little boys, deserve some public attention. The rolls of papyrus, the hieroglyphics, the wrappers and other appliances are all exceedingly interesting."

Philadelphia U.S. Gazette for the Country,
8 April 1833
(Wolfe and Singerman 2009, p. 101)

INTRODUCTION

On or just before July 3, 1835, a touring exhibitor named Michael H. Chandler brought to Kirtland, Ohio, four Egyptian mummies and a selection of Egyptian papyrus documents. Kirtland resident Joseph Smith, Jr., founder and prophet of the Church of Latter-day Saints,[1] who had produced The Book of Mormon five years earlier based on claimed translations from gold plates inscribed in "Reformed Egyptian," took an immediate interest in the Egyptian texts and offered preliminary translations to the exhibitor. Within the month, members of the young church ("the brethren") purchased Chandler's exhibit for $2,400.[2] Copying the texts

[1] Popularly termed "the Mormon Church" by both members and the general public, the official name of the institution (since 1851) is The Church of Jesus Christ of Latter-day Saints (hereafter abbreviated LDS). An intermediate 1838 revision had spelled "Latter-day" as "Latter Day."

[2] An overview of the Mormon purchase in the context of American interest in mummies as "artifacts," as well as possible identifications of surviving mummies, appears in Wolfe and Singerman 2009, "The Leg of Pharaoh's Daughter, the One who Saved Moses," pp. 96–131 and 136. One or more of the "lost Mormon mummies"—formerly in the Niagara Falls Museum—may now be found in the Michael C. Carlos Museum at Emory University. The date July 3 is noted in the official *History of the Church,* but correspondence suggests that the mummies arrived in Kirtland at the end of June; see ibid., p. 111. The history of Smith's Egyptian project, and its intellectual and political motivations, is recounted in Brodie 1945, pp. 168–75. Smith later claimed that his mother had bought the Egyptian materials "with her own money at a cost of six thousand dollars"; see Brodie 1945, pp. 170 and 293. The Mormon mummies were apparently first found in a pit-tomb at Gurna by the Italian adventurer Antonio Lebolo; for whom see Dawson, Uphill and Bierbrier 1995, p. 241; Herbin 2008, p. 5; John A.

with the assistance of select "scribes," Smith quickly recognized several biblically-themed compositions within the papyri, eventually including the Book of Abraham (P. Joseph Smith 1), the record of Joseph of Egypt (P. Joseph Smith 2 and 3) and a tale of an Egyptian princess Katumin or Kah tou mun (P. Joseph Smith 4). Only the first of these translations was ever published, beginning in serialized excerpts during 1842, well before Jean François Champollion's correct decipherment of Egyptian was generally known in America.[3]

Smith exhibited the mummies and papyri in his and his mother's Nauvoo (Illinois) cabins and in his "Mansion House" museum. A representative example of his banter is recorded for the May 15, 1844, visit to the museum by Josiah Quincy and Charles Francis Adams: "Opening pine presses along the wall, he disclosed four black, shrunken bodies. 'These are mummies,' he said. 'I want you to look at that little runt of a fellow over there. He was a great man in his day. Why that was Pharaoh Necho, King of Egypt!' He pointed to various hieroglyphs on the papyri, which were preserved under glass. 'That is the handwriting of Abraham, the Father of the Faithful; this is the autograph of Moses, and these lines were written by his brother Aaron. Here we have the earliest accounts of the Creation, from which Moses composed the first Book of Genesis.'"[4] In the same year, he made his last attempt at Egyptian translation (among seventeen foreign languages): "Egyptian, Su-e-eh-ni (What other persons are those?)."[5]

Larson 1994, and the chapter by Marquardt, below. For Lebolo's presence at Thebes, see his graffiti at the Ramesseum ("Lebolo 1820") and Theban Tomb 32 ("Lebolo") in De Keersmaecker 2010, pp. 35–36.

[3] For Smith's conflation of Egyptian and Greek, see Brodie 1945, p. 290. Champollion's discovery was reported in the United States in the *New York Herald,* December 28, 1842. For its potential restraint on Smith's future translations, see Brodie 1945, pp. 291–92 (regarding the falsified "Kinderhook plates" supposedly found in an Indian mound). Smith noted in his journal that he "translated a portion" of the plates, which he thought recounted the history of a person buried in the mound, "a descendant of Ham, through the loins of Pharaoh, king of Egypt." The translations of this hoax were not published.

[4] Quotation in Brodie 1945, p. 293. See also Adams 1952 for the visit.

[5] *The Voice of Truth* (1844), pp. 16–17; quotation in Brodie 1945, p. 292. Gee's interpretation (1992, p. 114, n. 58) of Sue-e-eh-ni as s nỉm ("who is the man?") is untenable phonetically (Sue-e-eh cannot represent s/ⲥⲁ-, and the final m of nỉm is preserved in

Following Smith's arrest and death in June 1844, the church divided, with most (but not all) of the Egyptian materials left behind by the dominant faction led by Brigham Young to Utah. As part of the collection *The Pearl of Great Price,* the full text of the Book of Abraham was published in pamphlet form in 1851 in Liverpool and reissued by the church in Utah in 1878. In 1880, it was adopted as canonical scripture by what is now the Church of Jesus Christ of Latter-day Saints. In contrast, the Reorganized Church of Jesus Christ of Latter Day Saints (based in Independence, Missouri, and since 2001 the Community of Christ) treats the Book of Abraham as mere speculative writing by Smith with no formal scriptural status.

The brief tale of Abraham, only fifteen printed pages including woodcut illustrations explicitly said to be part of the book, presents a curious narrative. Abraham is miraculously rescued from Chaldean priests in Ur, who commit human sacrifice "unto the god of Pharaoh ... after the manner of the Egyptians"(!) on a hill named after the Egyptian Potiphar (1:6–15 and 20). The name Potiphar, taken from the Bible, employs a Late Egyptian grammatical construction ("The one whom Pre has given")[6] and the late form of the sun god Re's name with the definite article ("Pre"), so that it cannot be contemporary with any date typically assigned to Abraham. The anglicized Latin term "Egyptus" is said to be Chaldean for "that which is forbidden" in reference to the cursed race of Ham who are denied the "right of priesthood" (1:23–27), a statement that served as the basis for Mormon racial discrimination[7] until a "revelation" during the modern

all dialects) and grammatically (the proper sequence should be nỉm pw s > nỉm pꜣy pꜣ s). In the same appeal to the "Brave Green Mountain Boys" (Brodie 1945, p. 292), Smith attempted an extensive passage in Chaldean (a dialect of Aramaic). His rendition and translation are described by my colleague Gene B. Gragg, Professor Emeritus of Near Eastern Languages at the Oriental Institute, as incompetent and based on sources misunderstood or misrepresented; personal communication, September 14, 2010. Similarly, Rebecca Hasselbach, Asst. Professor of Comparative Semitics at the Oriental Institute, noted that the Chaldean "is Aramaic, but a pretty butchered version," perhaps "because he (or his source) transliterated the gutturals as vowels instead of consonants and some of the forms seem to be made up"; personal communication September 17, 2010.

[6] Ranke 1935, p. 123, no. 11. For the late date of the name, see Vergote 1959, pp. 146–48. Examples survive from Dynasty 21, and the form is not grammatically possible before Dynasty 18.

[7] See Brodie 1945, pp. 172–74. The translated Book of Abraham conveniently served

era of civil rights legislation reversed the policy (but not the "scripture") in 1978. A famine takes Abraham to Egypt, where he is ultimately shown "sitting upon Pharaoh's throne, by the politeness of the king," "reasoning upon the principles of Astronomy."[8] The three woodcut illustrations purport to depict: (1) the "sacrifice" on an "altar" (wrongly restored from a scene of Anubis tending Osiris on the funerary bier), (2) an astronomical scene of planets (actually a hypocephalus), and (3) enthroned Abraham lecturing the male Pharaoh (actually enthroned Osiris with the female Isis). In the last image alone, Smith's interpretation turns the goddess Maat into a male prince, the papyrus owner into a "waiter," and the black jackal Anubis into a "slave." As true ancient history, the Book of Abraham has no validity, yet the tale and the papyri that inspired it were to become a minor, if protracted, chapter in the history of American Egyptology.[9]

By 1861, Théodule Devéria had noted a series of anachronisms and absurdities in the supposed translation and woodcut vignettes, and in 1912 a solicitation for professional opinions on the matter of "Joseph Smith, Jr., as a Translator" by F. S. Spalding, Episcopal Bishop of Utah, drew uniformly derisive assessments from A. H. Sayce, W. M. F. Petrie, J. H. Breasted, A. C. Mace, J. Peters, S. A. B. Mercer, E. Meyer, and F. W. von Bissing.[10] Apologetic response was muted, as the papyri no longer belonged to the church when it migrated west to Utah, and they were thought to have been lost, perhaps in the great Chicago fire of 1871. Aside from *ad hominem* attacks on the Egyptologists themselves,[11] the

to resolve an abolitionist dispute within the developing Mormon community.

[8] Facsimile No. 3, Explanation.

[9] See the brief discussion accorded Joseph Smith in Trigger 1995, p. 22, in an article on Egypt and "the American Imagination." The longest Egyptological treatment to date is John A. Larson 1994.

[10] Spalding 1912. Reaction to the Egyptologists' condemnation is found in "Helping Out the Mormon," *Life* (February 10, 1916), vol. 67, issue 1737, p. 265: "The papers say the younger Mormons have taken notice of this discrepancy to the dismay of their elders, and that it is one thing that led to the recent flare-up in the University of Utah, when four Gentile professors were dismissed and fourteen members of the faculty resigned in protest." See also "Are the Mormon Scriptures Based on Fraud?," *Current Opinion* (February 1913), vol. LIV, no. 2, pp. 134–35.

[11] Cf. Nelson 1913, pp. 606 ff: "... a jury of Gentiles, prejudiced, ill-tempered and mad with the pride of human learning" (as cited in Nibley 1968–70 [January 1968], p. 24, n. 6).

matter generated little further discussion. "Faced by a solid phalanx of PhD's, the Mormons were properly overawed."[12] A rebuttal of sorts did come from a certain "Robert C. Webb" in a series of LDS publications beginning in 1913 and in "The Case Against Mormonism" published in 1915.[13] Although posing as an unbiased "Non-'Mormon'" and a PhD, "Webb" was in fact a non-degreed writer for hire named J. E. Homans.[14]

[12] Nibley 1968–70 (January 1968), p. 23. Within this and continuing installments, Nibley undercuts this "appeal to authority" by a series of personal attacks: Mercer, "a hustling young clergyman" (ibid., p. 21), is extensively attacked in May 1968, pp. 55–57, and June 1968, 18–22, not "primarily to discredit the authority" of the scholar, but to illustrate "the limitations and pitfalls of Egyptology in general" (June 1968, p. 22). Presumably for the same reason, Nibley notes that Sayce was a "spoiled dilettante" (July 1968, p. 50), that Petrie "never went to a theatre" (ibid.), that Meyer "lacked aesthetic sense" (ibid, p. 51) but had a rationalistic bent that "ineffectively [!!] disqualifies himself from the jury" (p. 52), that Breasted was "pro-German" (p. 54), and that von Bissing had "an uncompromising loyalty to a feudal society and *feudal religion*—hardly the man to look with a kindly eye on the *supernaturalism* ... of a Joseph Smith" (p. 54, emphasis added). European "feudal religion," of course, presupposed the reality of supernatural intervention, but Nibley's logic is peculiar in these tracts circulated only among the faithful. The Egyptologists are stigmatized as being idiosyncratic and aloof, which should make their unified assessment even more compelling. In any case, Nibley wanted a sympathetic audience, not Egyptological fact. The August 1968 continuation derides the careers of T. Devéria, J. Peters, A. C. Mace, A. M. Lythgoe, G. Barton, E. Banks and E. A. W. Budge. Nibley's tactic has been adopted by his followers. In 2002, however, the *New Yorker* signaled exhaustion with the topic: "Today, even Nibley seems weary of the effort to authenticate the Book of Abraham" (Lawrence Wright 2002, p. 53). Nibley's zealous involvement with the Smith papyri would later be blamed in a family tragedy; see Scott Gordon's LDS review (2005) of Martha Nibley Beck's 2005 biography, *Leaving the Saints:* "Beck accuses her father of putting on an Egyptian costume and ritually abusing her, something all seven of her siblings deny ... Martha claims (p. 147) that her father dressed up as the Egyptian god Amut the Destroyer by putting on a costume with an alligator head and a lion's body and molesting her between the ages of 5 and 7 ... Martha blames the whole incident on the stress of having to defend the Book of Abraham when Nibley knew it was a fraud."

[13] The Spalding volume is disputed in Webb 1915, pp. 26–34. For a list of contemporary Mormon responses to the Spalding publication, see Kevin L. Barney 2005, pp. 109–10, n. 9.

[14] His true identity was revealed in Brodie 1945, p. 175n: "Webb, whose real name is J. E. Homans, is neither an Egyptologist nor a PhD." For the Spalding episode and its aftermath, see Charles M. Larson 1992, pp. 27–30. In his 1915 book, "Webb" consistently misspells Spalding's name as Spaulding, and this has influenced Larson on p. 30 (only).

"Webb"'s fraudulent expertise would be revived by Nibley in his attacks on professional Egyptology following the next major event in the saga of the Joseph Smith papyri.[15]

The state of affairs changed dramatically on November 27, 1967, when the Metropolitan Museum of Art in New York made a gift to the Church of Jesus Christ of Latter-day Saints of eleven papyrus fragments that had passed from the mother of Joseph Smith to an employee's family before acquisition by the museum in 1947.[16] Comparison of the papyrus illustrations with the woodcuts in the *Pearl of Great Price* confirmed that these fragments were those once owned by Joseph Smith and employed as the basis for the Book of Abraham.[17] In January and February of the following year, sepia-toned photographs of the fragments were published in the official LDS magazine *The Improvement Era,*[18] and on the basis of these photographs, the independent publication *Dialogue: A Journal of Mormon Thought* commissioned translations and commentaries on the texts, now designated as "The Joseph Smith Papyri." In the summer issue of 1968, Egyptologists John A. Wilson and Richard A. Parker identified fragments within Smith's original collection as sections of a late mortuary text known as a "Book of Breathings," copied for a Theban priest named Hôr, as well as portions from additional Books of the Dead.[19]

The rediscovery of the primary documents that inspired, but in no way corroborate, a canonical book of Mormon theology has resulted in more than a generation of confrontation between Egyptological scholars and Mormon traditionalists. Whereas earlier apologists had condemned

[15] See Nibley 1968–1970 (January 1968), p. 24, nn. 2 (equating Webb with J. C. Homans), 5, 11, 16 and 22; (February 1968), p. 21, nn. 45, 47, 52, 56, 58, 68, 80 and 94.

[16] MMA 47.102.1–11 (acquired through the Rogers Fund). The papyri were accompanied by documents of sale, indicating that they had formally passed from church ownership; see Howard 1968, p. 91, with reference to *Dialogue* 2/4 (1967): 57 note. For the early history of the papyri, see n. 2, above.

[17] The Book of Abraham is subtitled: "Translated from the Papyrus by Joseph Smith," and the initial vignette of P. Joseph Smith 1 reappears (in altered form) in the Book of Abraham as "A Facsimile From the Book of Abraham. No. 1."

[18] Subtitled "The Voice of the Church" and described as the "Official organ of the Priesthood Quorums, Mutual Improvement Associations, Home Teaching Committee, Music Committee, Church School System, and other agencies of The Church of Jesus Christ of Latter-day Saints" (p. 1).

[19] John Wilson 1968, and Parker 1968a and 1968b (partial translation).

Egyptologists for not translating the defectively copied hieroglyphs of the woodcuts, new translations of the actual documents were even more disturbing.[20] Some religious Mormons have sought Egyptological degrees merely to pursue the argument with scholarly status. Attempts to salvage the Book of Abraham over the years have been varied, creative and ultimately desperate: 1) Egyptian hieroglyphs had multiple readings, unknown to modern Egyptologists,[21] 2) Smith used the Hôr papyrus merely as a "mnemonic device" for channeling inspiration, not as a true source of translation,[22] and 3) the portion of the Hôr papyrus containing the original Book of Abraham is now lost, with only the words "Beginning of the Book of ..." surviving.[23]

While recent disputes over this or that feature of Smith's interpretation typically dominate these exchanges, often lost in the greater picture is the simple fact that the Mormon defense of the Book of Abraham has been lost for well over a century. Long past are the days when any speculation could be attributed to the Egyptian language or history; such fantasies are intellectual casualties from Napoleon's Egyptian expedition and the

[20] See Nibley 1968–70 (March 1968): 20, for Mormon complaints that the 1912 reviewers did not translate the (hand copy) inscriptions. For an overview of the negative reactions to the papyrus translations of 1968, see the quotations selected in Mormon Quotes, "Book of Abraham," http://www.ils.unc.edu/~unsworth/mormon/bookofabraham.html.

[21] So George Reynolds 1879, p. 44: "Egyptian hieroglyphics had at least two (but more probably three) meanings, the one understood by the masses—the other comprehended by the initiated, the priesthood." Quotation also in Brodie 1945, p. 175n. The argument was revived by Nibley in 1968; see Charles M. Larson 1992, pp. 114–16.

[22] So Crapo and Tvedtnes 1968 and 1969; Tvedtnes 1970; and Urrutia 1969. The argument (disputed in correspondence by Baer with Jay Todd) was adopted by Nibley later in 1968; see Charles M. Larson 1992, pp. 116–19. Tvedtnes complained about his "unfair treatment" in Baer's correspondence in Gee 1992, pp. 109–10, n. 48, but admitted that Baer remained unconvinced by the mnemonic theory. Crapo and Tvedtnes 1968 and 1969 are cited in Charles M. Larson 1992, p. 233, nn. 4–5, *contra* Gee 1992, p. 109, n. 48.

[23] So Gee 2000a, p. 10, 2000b, p. 212, n. 57, and 2005, p. 96. For discussion of Gee's reasoning and "sources," see the description of the size of the P. JS 1 manuscript in the relevant chapter on "Comparative Transliterations and Translations," below. A variant of this theory, that the Book of Abraham was on another, now-missing scroll, was adopted by Nibley in 1975 (p. 2); for this and other defenses, see Ritner 2003a, p. 166, n. 31; and Charles M. Larson 1992, pp. 119–40.

decipherment of hieroglyphs by Champollion. As noted in the included essay by Christopher Woods, the depiction of Mesopotamian society in the Book of Abraham is no less problematic. The basic events of Smith's romance do not correspond with either Mesopotamian or Egyptian history, and outside of Mormon confessional institutions, the Book of Abraham is not taught—or usually even noted—in studies of ancient history, religion or society.

If the Egyptian documents used by Smith in his composition of the Book of Abraham have been discussed and translated on several occasions (Papyrus Joseph Smith 1 and the Hypocephalus of Sheshonq), the remainder of Smith's papyri continues to be unedited, aside from the initial comments of Wilson and Parker in 1968. It is the purpose of this volume to provide the first, comprehensive edition of the papyri of Joseph Smith.

The impetus for the current volume derives from two sources: 1) an initial invitation in February 2004 by Gary James Bergera of the Smith-Pettit Foundation to produce a complete translation and transliteration of the Joseph Smith Papyri, with footnotes providing a synoptic comparison of all the varying published readings of the texts (Smith, Nibley, Baer, Rhodes, et al.),[24] and 2) a steady stream of emails from both scholars and laymen requesting further information on the true nature of the Smith Egyptian papyri and their contents following my publications of "The Breathing Permit of Hôr" (2002–2003a). In 2004, Bergera also solicited discussions of the acquisition history of Smith's papyri from H. Michael Marquardt and of the ancient ownership and dating of the papyri from Marc Coenen. The original proposal from the Smith-Pettit Foundation was not realized, but the current volume of studies is a direct result of that undertaking, and the contributions by Marquardt and Coenen are included here with sincere gratitude to Bergera and to the authors.[25] Although the authors consulted in 1912 included the Assyriologist A. H. Sayce, comments on the Book of Abraham from a Mesopotamian

---

[24] A new volume by Michael D. Rhodes, *Books of the Dead Belonging to Tshemmin and Neferirnub* (Provo: Neal A. Maxwell Institute, 2010), reached me (February 25, 2011) while my manuscript was in press, too late to be incorporated in my study.

[25] I am particularly indebted to Bergera, Brent Lee Metcalfe and Edward H. Ashment, whose forwarded encouragement, articles and photographs have benefited this volume greatly.

perspective have been few, and I am indebted to Christopher Woods for revisiting this issue. Thus even the location of Abraham's home, "Ur of the Chaldees" (Genesis 11.28–31; 15.7; Nehemiah 9.7; Book of Abraham 2.4), is disputed, with sites identified at Uri (Mugheir/Tell el-Muqayyar) in southern Babylon or near Harran/Haran in modern Turkey.[26] In neither area, however, were (supposed) Egyptian sacrificial rites locally dominant.

Clearly, the need for a full edition of these texts is both justified and long past-due, and, given their importance in American religious and social history, the publication must be accessible not merely to Egyptologists but to non-specialists within and outside of the LDS religious community for whom the Book of Abraham was produced. This dual focus necessarily repeats older, and obsolete, translations of minor value for modern Egyptologists, but of great significance for the historiography of the papyri and for demonstrating to non-Egyptologists the evolving process of deciphering the fragmented documents. Rather than restricting these variant translations to footnotes, as originally suggested, the variants are provided in the body of the text for easy comparison. In return, the editions contain specialized transliterations and often complex notes establishing major or minor differences in the Egyptian readings and interpretations. Such minutiae have been largely confined to the footnotes so that the non-specialist reader need not be detained.

The commentary on the accuracy of readings and interpretations of the Smith Papyri is a necessary feature of this volume provided in direct response to over seven years of (often anguished) requests. As such, these assessments are neither equivocal nor muted, but have no partisan basis originating in any religious camp, financial incentive or personal animus. Published criticism by Mormon apologists (often vituperative) is further treated in the notes (often bluntly), where they may be ignored by Egyptologists, who have little interest in such parochial matters. The footnotes thus contain specialized materials for either set of readers. It must be stressed that all opinions in the volume are those of the individual authors and not necessarily those of the publisher or co-authors.

[26] For "Ur of the Chaldees," see Pinches 1909; Hastings, Grant and Rowley 1963, p. 1019; Margueron 1992; and Kobayashi 1992. Gee 1992, p. 116, prefers a northern location, but this cannot justify the supposed Egyptian sacrificial rites practiced in the area. See further the chapter by Christopher Woods in this volume.

Attentive readers may notice some minor inconsistencies in grammar, punctuation, citations, etc., in the essays that follow. Each of the essays was written more or less independently and so tends to reflect each author's stylistic approach to such matters.

Robert K. Ritner
The Oriental Institute
The University of Chicago
Chicago, 2010

H. Michael Marquardt

JOSEPH SMITH'S EGYPTIAN PAPERS: A HISTORY

During the years 1817 to 1822, an unspecified number of Egyptian mummies and other artifacts came into the possession of Giovanni Pietro Antonio Lebolo (b. 1781). Lebolo was an associate of Bernardino Drovetti (1776–1852), France's Consul General to Egypt from 1803 to 1814. For several years, Lebolo had assisted Drovetti in looking for ancient Egyptian relics. When Lebolo returned to Italy in 1822, he took with him a collection of at least eleven mummies and some additional artifacts. The mummies had been found in catacombs near Thebes, about 400 miles south of the Mediterranean Sea on the Nile River. In 1830, Lebolo died in Castellamonte, Piedmont (now Italy). The eleven mummies and various antique objects were subsequently sent to New York City with instructions that they be sold and that the proceeds benefit Lebolo's heirs.[1]

Lebolo's eleven mummies may constitute the largest shipment of Egyptian mummies to America up to that time. Only a small number of public exhibits of mummies had been previously reported in major American cities. A man named Michael H. Chandler (1797–1866)

H. Michael Marquardt is an independent historian. He is the author of, among other works, *The Joseph Smith Revelations: Text and Commentary, The Rise of Mormonism: 1816–1844, The Book of Abraham Revisited, The Joseph Smith Egyptian Papers,* and (as co-author) *Inventing Mormonism: Tradition and the Historical Record.* He lives in Sandy, Utah. For their suggestions and advice, he thanks Edgar C. Snow and Gary James Bergera.

[1] H. Donl Peterson, *The Story of the Book of Abraham: Mummies, Manuscripts, and Mormonism* (Salt Lake City: Deseret Book Co., 1995), 78–79, 83. Peterson's book—part history, part autobiography—is a good introduction to the topic.

reportedly secured Lebolo's mummies in early 1833 and started to exhibit them, beginning in Philadelphia, Pennsylvania, though to date there has been no independent confirmation of this.[2] What can be documented is that from early April to June 1833, the mummies and some papyri were displayed in the Masonic Hall and the Philadelphia Arcade. Adults were charged 25 cents, children 12½ cents. An early advertisement read:

> The largest collection of EGYPTIAN MUMMIES ever exhibited in this city, is now to be seen at the Masonic Hall, in the Ches[t]nut Street above Seventh. They were found in the vicinity of Thebes, by the celebrated traveler Antonio Lebolo and Chevalier Drovetti, General Council of France in Egypt. Some writings on Papirus [Papyrus] with the Mummies, can also be seen, and will afford, no doubt, much satisfaction to Amateurs of Antiquities.[3]

Next on the mummies' tour was Baltimore, Maryland, from mid-July to mid-August 1833. By this time, however, the eleven mummies had been reduced to six. Two had been sold to the Academy of Natural Sciences of Philadelphia; another was reported to have been stripped of its wrappings in New York.[4] In December 1833, Dr. Samuel George Morton conducted a dissection of the two mummies sold to Philadelphia's Academy of Natural Sciences. The following certificate was issued by a group of medical doctors:

> Having examined with considerable attention and deep interest, a number of Mummies from the catacombs, near Thebes, in Egypt, and now exhibited in the Arcade, we beg leave to recommend them to the observation of the curious inquirer on subjects of a period so long elapsed; probably not less than three thousand years ago. The features of some of these Mummies are in perfect expression.—The papyrus, covered with black or red ink, or paint, in excellent preservation, are very interesting. The undersigned, unsolicited by any person connected by interest with this exhibition, have

[2] See "Mystery of the Mummies: An Update on the Joseph Smith Collection[:] Interview with Brian L. Smith by Philip R. Webb," *Religious Studies Center Newsletter* (Brigham Young University), 20/2 (2005): 3.

[3] *U.S. Gazette,* Apr. 3, 1833, Philadelphia, in Peterson 1995, p. 89.

[4] Ibid., 92.

voluntarily set their names hereunto, for the simple purpose of calling the attention of the public to an interesting collection, not sufficiently known in this city.

JOHN REDMAN COXE, M.D.
RICHARD HARLAN, M.D.
J. PANCOAST, M.D.
WILLIAM P. C. BARTON, M.D.
E. F. RIVINUS, M.D.
SAMUEL G. MORGAN [MORTON], M.D.

I concur in the above sentiments, concerning the collection of Mummies in the Philadelphia Arcade, and consider them highly deserving the attention of the curious.

W. E. HORNER, M.D.[5]

The traveling exhibition, featuring the remaining six Lebolo mummies—by now, clearly in Chandler's possession—continued to Lancaster, then to Harrisburg, and on to Pittsburgh, Pennsylvania. By the end of 1833 and into 1834, the relics were on display in Cincinnati, and in January and February 1834 they were at the Louisville Museum in Kentucky. Before leaving Louisville, Chandler sold two more of the mummies, this time to the Louisville Museum.[6]

Early the next year, Chandler was in Ohio. In February 1835, his exhibit was in Hudson, and by March had reached Cleveland, some twenty miles north. A description of Chandler's remaining four mummies appeared in the nearby Painesville, Ohio, *Telegraph*. There were three female mummies and one male mummy. Rolls of writings were associated with three of them. Of particular interest is the male mummy: "No. 3.—Height 4 ft. 4½.—Male, very old, say 80; arms crossing on the breast, each hand on its opposite shoulder; had a roll of writing as No. 1 & 2; superior head, it will compare in the region of the sentiments with any in our land; passions mild."[7]

---

[5] "Egyptian Antiquities," *Times and Seasons* 3 (May 2, 1842): 774, Nauvoo, Illinois. See also "Egyptian Mummies—Ancient Records," *Latter Day Saints' Messenger and Advocate* 2 (Dec. 1835): 235, Kirtland, Ohio.

[6] See Brian L. Smith, "A Book of Abraham Research Update," *Religious Studies Center Newsletter* (Brigham Young University), May 1997, 5–8; and Webb 2005, p. 1–5.

[7] "Mummies," *Telegraph* 13 (Mar. 27, 1835), Painesville, Ohio. See Jay M. Todd, *The*

A Cleveland newspaper—reporting that the mummies were three males and one female—described the writing found in "the arms of the old man" to measure in length "10 or 12 inches, and 3 or 4 [inches] in width." Continuing, the article said, "The characters are the Egyptian hyeroglyphics; but of what it discourses none can tell."[8] The publication of these two newspapers' accounts shows the difficulty in identifying the gender, age, and condition of the four mummies. This problem continued throughout the years by those who examined the mummies.

As the Cleveland newspaper noted, no one in America at this time could provide a reliable English translation of these or any other Egyptian hieroglyphs. Books such as J. G. H. Greppo's *Essay on the Hieroglyphic System of M. Champollion, Jun.* (Boston, 1830) contained some rudimentary ideas. Jean-François Champollion (1790–1832), a young French scholar, helped to decipher the Rosetta stone, which contained the same text written in hieroglyphs, Demotic, and Classical Greek.[9] But at his death, he left his important works on translation to be published posthumously in Paris. His ground-breaking books *Grammaire égyptienne* [*Egyptian Grammar*] (1836) and *Dictionnaire égyptienne* [*Egyptian Dictionary*] (1841) together with the studies of other scholars led eventually to the successful decipherment of Egyptian hieroglyphs.

ACQUIRING THE EGYPTIAN PAPERS

On June 30, 1835, Chandler's tour arrived with its four mummies and rolls of papyri in Kirtland, Ohio, headquarters of the Church of the Latter Day Saints (later Church of Jesus Christ of Latter-day Saints). Joseph Smith Jr. (1805–44), the twenty-nine-year-old prophet-president of the five-year-old Church, was shown the Egyptian artifacts. According to a promotional flyer Chandler had prepared, the mummies "may have lived in the days of

---

Saga of the Book of Abraham (Salt Lake City: Deseret Book Co., 1969), 134; and Peterson 1995, p. 117. The comments regarding the head of the mummy reflect an awareness of phrenology.

[8] "A Rare Exhibition," *Cleveland Whig*, Mar. 25, 1835, Cleveland, Ohio, in Peterson 1995, p. 112. In fact, the writing is both Egyptian hieroglyphs and hieratic.

[9] Egyptian hieroglyphs feature pictures that represent meaning(s) or sound(s) or combination(s) of both. They were used during the period 3100 B.C.E. to 400 C.E. Hieratic writing emerged in tandem with hieroglyphs and features a simplified cursive script used primarily by priests. Demotic texts (beginning about 650 B.C.E.) are written in a simplified form of hieratic.

Jacob, Moses, or David" and the papyri with their ancient writing "will be exhibited with the Mummies."[10]

Five years earlier, in March 1830, Smith had published the Book of Mormon, an account of the immigration of a Hebrew family to the Americas circa 600 B.C.E., which, according to Smith, had originally been engraved upon golden plates in a language said to be "reformed Egyptian."[11] Having seen Chandler's relics, Smith was especially interested in the papyri—extant in two rolls and some fragments. He took some of the papyri home and, examining them, believed he knew who had written them. William W. Phelps (1792–1872), a scribe for Smith, reported that the Mormon prophet considered some of these records to relate to the lives of the legendary Old Testament patriarchs Joseph of Egypt and his forebear Abraham who, according to Genesis, also had lived for a time in Egypt.[12] Chandler asserted that he had previously been able to obtain "in a small degree, the translation of a few characters."

John Whitmer, to whom Smith had dictated some of the Book of Mormon text as well as his subsequent revision of the Bible, recorded that "Joseph the Seer saw these Record[s] and by the revelation of Jesus Christ could translate these records, which gave an account of our forefathers, ~~even abraham~~ Much of which was written by Joseph of Egypt who was sold by his brethren Which when all translated will be a pleasing history and of great value to the saints."[13]

In mid-July 1835, Phelps explained to his wife:

> Last evening we received your first letter after an absence of twelve weeks and twelve hours.... Brother Joseph [Smith] remarked that it was as easy to shed tears while reading that letter as it was when reading the History of Joseph in Egypt. ...

[10] "Egyptian Antiquities," *Times and Seasons* 3 (May 2, 1842): 774.

[11] See 1830 Book of Mormon, 538; LDS Mormon 9:32.

[12] It would be a major discovery if the papyri contained mention of the patriarch Abraham and Joseph of Egypt. In fact, they would constitute the oldest authentic documents ever found regarding them.

[13] "The Book of John Whitmer Kept by Commandment," 76, Community of Christ Archives, Independence, Missouri; also Bruce N. Westergren, ed., *From Historian to Dissident: The Book of John Whitmer* (Salt Lake City: Signature Books, 1995), 167.

> The last of June [1835] four Egyptian mummies were brought here; there were two papyrus rolls, besides some other ancient Egyptian writings with them. As no one could translate these writings, they were presented to President [Joseph] Smith. He soon knew what they were and said they, the "rolls of papyrus," contained the sacred record kept of Joseph in Pharaoh's Court in Egypt, and the teachings of Father Abraham. God has so ordered it that these mummies and writings have been brought in the Church, and the sacred writing I had just locked up in Brother Joseph's house when your letter came, so I had two consolations of good things in one day. These records of old times, when we translate and print them in a book, will make a good witness for the Book of Mormon. There is nothing secret or hidden that shall not be revealed, and they come to the Saints.[14]

Smith believed that one of the papyrus rolls contained the writings of Abraham and the other the writings of Joseph. He also showed Chandler some characters on the papyrus he said were similar to the characters found on the Book of Mormon golden plates.[15] For these reasons, Smith decided to purchase the relics. Chandler presented the following certificate to Smith before the purchase was made:

> Kirtland, July 6th, 1835.
>
> This is to make known to all who may be desirous, concerning the knowledge of Mr. Joseph Smith, jr. in deciphering the ancient Egyptian hieroglyphic characters, in my possession, which I have, in many eminent cities, shown to the most learned: And, from the information that I could learn, or meet with, I find that [i.e., the translation] of Mr. Joseph Smith, jr. to correspond in the most minute matters.
> (Signed) Michael H. Chandler.
> Travelling with, and proprietor of Egyptian Mummies.[16]

---

[14] William W. Phelps, Letter to Sally Phelps, July 19–20, 1835, in Leah Y. Phelps, "Letters of Faith from Kirtland," *Improvement Era* 45 (Aug. 1942): 529. See Bruce A. Van Orden, ed., "Writing to Zion: The William W. Phelps Kirtland Letters (1835–1836)," *BYU Studies* 33 (1993): 554–56.

[15] Oliver Cowdery, Letter to William Frye, Dec. 22, 1835, Oliver Cowdery Letterbook, 72, Henry E. Huntington Library, San Marino, California; published in *Messenger and Advocate* 2 (Dec. 1835): 235.

[16] Ibid.

Chandler's asking price for the items was $2,400, a substantial amount considering the expenditures Smith's church was incurring in constructing the large meetinghouse to be known as the Kirtland House of the Lord, or Kirtland Temple. According to Joseph Coe, arrangements were made to make the purchase before Chandler left Kirtland. Coe said eight years later, in 1844, that Chandler was merely the agent for the real owners of the relics: "Previous t[o] closing the contra[c]t with Chandler I made ar[r]-angements with S[imeon]. Andrews for to take one third part and your self [Joseph Smith] & Co. one third leaving one third to be borne by myself.... Chandler was only an agent acting for some men in Philadelphia."[17]

As noted, Smith believed the papyri were the records of Joseph and Abraham. Oliver Cowdery (1806–50), another of Smith's early confidantes, related that the "beautifully written" papyrus, which included writing in red ink, was that of Joseph.[18] The more damaged record was of Abraham, father of the Hebrew nation.

An emphasis on priesthood authority was an important topic in the LDS Church in 1835. Smith's father, Joseph Sr., had been appointed as the Church's first patriarch by December 1834 to give patriarchal blessings to Church members. Smith wanted to trace the Church's new office of patriarch back to biblical times. He taught that the patriarchal priesthood "was confirmed to be handed down from father to son, and rightly belongs to the literal descendants of the chosen seed, to whom the promises were made."[19] A listing, including the line of this heavenly authority from Adam to Noah, was reportedly "written in the book of Enoch."[20]

---

[17] Coe, Letter to Joseph Smith, Jan. 1, 1844, Joseph Smith Collection, Archives, Family and Church History Department, Church of Jesus Christ of Latter-day Saints, Salt Lake City, Utah; hereafter LDS Archives. It is not known how the one-third share was finally disposed of and how the Smith family retained the mummies and papyri. Joseph Smith replied to Coe, "I have got your Deed ... for all the interest you ever held in the Mummies" (Smith, Copy of letter to Coe, Jan. 18, 1844, LDS Archives; see Dean C. Jessee, comp. and ed., *Personal Writings of Joseph Smith,* Rev. Ed. [Salt Lake City: Deseret Book Co./Provo, UT: Brigham Young University Press, 2002], 593).

[18] Cowdery, Letter to William Frye, Dec. 22, 1835, Oliver Cowdery Letterbook, 69; *Messenger and Advocate* 2 (Dec. 1835): 234.

[19] H. Michael Marquardt, *The Joseph Smith Revelations: Text and Commentary* (Salt Lake City: Signature Books, 1999), 269; LDS D&C 107:40.

[20] Marquardt 1999, p. 270; LDS D&C 107:39–57. Joseph Smith was said to recover, while revising Genesis, the lost book of Enoch mentioned in Jude 1:14. He now

In addition, since 1830, Smith had been working on a new "translation" of the King James Version of the Bible. By June 1835, he had edited his revision of Genesis to adjust the ages of some of the Old Testament patriarchs who lived before Noah, and was preparing to "print the New Translation [of the Bible]."[21] In fact, on June 21, shortly before Chandler's arrival, Smith publicly "preached in Kirtland on the evangelical [i.e., patriarchal] order."[22] Given Smith's interest in priesthood, patriarchs, and the translation of ancient texts, the arrival in Kirtland of Chandler's traveling exhibit of ancient Egyptian artifacts was fortuitous.

AN "EGYPTIAN ALPHABET"

Shortly after acquiring Chandler's mummies, papyri, and other ancient Egyptian writings, Smith embarked upon preparing an alphabet of the Egyptian characters to help him translate what he believed was the Abraham papyrus. The end result of this so-called "Egyptian Alphabet" is contained in a bound book used by Smith to record his translation and interpretation of Egyptian characters and other symbols. Only thirty-four pages of Smith's "Egyptian Alphabet" Ms. 1 have writing on them. The majority of the handwritten pages was recorded in July 1835. The original book is preserved today in the archives of the LDS Church.[23]

Smith worked closely with Cowdery and Phelps on this Alphabet. Smith regularly used scribes to help him write important records. These include the Book of Mormon, his revelations, his revision of the Bible, many of his letters, and his personal journal entries. While Smith's own handwriting sometimes appears in texts produced by him, the majority of his writings was dictated to and/or recorded by scribes. That a document is not in Smith's hand does not mean that it was not produced by him. Smith's translation of the papyri, the "Book of Abraham," was dictated to scribes.

provided the line of patriarchal authority.

[21] Smith, Letter to "Dear brethren in the Lord," June 15, 1835, LDS Archives. See Jessee 2002, p. 363.

[22] Manuscript History, Book B-1:595, LDS Archives; Joseph Smith Jr. et al., *History of the Church of Jesus Christ of Latter-day Saints. Period 1,* Brigham H. Roberts, ed., revised and enlarged, 6 vols. (Salt Lake City: Deseret Book, 1978), 2:234, hereafter *History of the Church.*

[23] See Church Historian's Office Journal, Oct. 17, 1855. See also Todd 1969, p. 286.

The "Manuscript History of the Church," also known as the "History of Joseph Smith" or *History of the Church,* contains the following two entries for the month of July 1835:

> I [Joseph Smith], with W. W. Phelps and O. Cowdery, as scribes, commenced the translation of some of the characters or hieroglyphics.[24]
>
> The remainder of this month, I [Joseph Smith] was continually engaged in translating an alphabet to the Book of Abraham, and arranging a grammar of the Egyptian language as practiced by the ancients.[25]

The surviving manuscripts of this Alphabet (see below) contain the Egyptian characters copied by Smith, Cowdery, Phelps, and later in November 1835 by a third scribe, Warren Parrish (1803–77). Some of the characters were copied directly from the original papyrus—from the vignette (or illustration) of what Smith published in 1842 as Facsimile No. 1 of his "Book of Abraham" translation. Smith, Phelps, and Cowdery first worked together on manuscripts 3 to 5. Phelps then recorded Smith's interpretations for each degree on manuscript 1. Later, Parrish briefly wrote in manuscript 1 for Smith. While Smith's Alphabet does not provide accurate English translations of the Egyptian characters, it does offer insight into the way Smith approached the papyri prior to dictating the "Book of Abraham" text.[26]

JOSEPH SMITH'S "EGYPTIAN ALPHABET" MANUSCRIPTS

Ms. 1: "EGYPTIAN ALPHABET" on outside spine; also labeled at top of 1st to 4th degree "Egyptian Alphabet"; inserted on first page of

---

[24] Manuscript History, Book B-1:596; *History of the Church,* 2:236. In January 1843, Smith "gave some instructions about Phelps & [Willard] Richards uniting in writing the history of the church" (Joseph Smith, Journal, Jan. 20, 1843, LDS Archives). These scribes wrote in Smith's name and with his authorization. The information was based upon Phelps's recollection as he was in Kirtland at the time working with Smith. The two entries for July 1835 were actually written in September 1843.

[25] Manuscript History, Book B-1:597; *History of the Church,* 2:238.

[26] I retain the numbering of the manuscripts as found in Hugh Nibley, "The Meaning of the Kirtland Egyptian Papers," *BYU Studies* 11 (Summer 1971): 351. The original manuscripts are in LDS Archives.

5th degree above first line is “Grammar & A[l]phabet of the Egyptian Language”; Egyptian characters with English interpretations; in Phelps’s handwriting, with additional entries by Parrish; bound book with handwriting on 34 pages, 184 blank pages remaining. No date on manuscript, progressive order: 1st to 5th degree. Approximate division: pp. 1–22 (first part) written July 1835; pp. 23–34 (second part) written October–November 1835.

Ms. 3: “Egyptian Alphabet”; in Phelps’s handwriting, with an entry by Parrish; 4 pp., lettered C, D, E, and F. No date, written July, October–November 1835.

Ms. 4: “Egyptian Alphabet” labeled at top of four pages; in Smith’s handwriting, with additions by Cowdery; 5 pp. lettered B, T, U, V, and W (9 leaves). No date, written July, October–November 1835.

Ms. 5: Untitled (but probably “Egyptian Alphabet”); in Cowdery’s handwriting; 4 pp., lettered A, X, I, and unlettered p. 4. No date, written July, October 1835.

Smith and his scribes also produced some additional working papers in conjunction with his “Book of Abraham” project.[27] These are:

OTHER EGYPTIAN MATERIALS IN JOSEPH SMITH’S POSSESSION

Ms. 2: “Egyptian Counting”; characters with English interpretations; in Phelps’s handwriting; 2 pp., lettered G and H. No date, written July–November 1835.

Ms. 6: “Valuable Discovery of hid[d]en records that have been obtained from the ancient bur[y]ing place of the Egyptiens [Egyptians] Joseph Smith Jr”; title probably in handwriting of Frederick G. Williams (a fourth scribe), with Smith’s signature; English contents in Cowdery’s handwriting; 4 pp.: title, pp. 1–3 (hieratic characters copied from Amenhotep papyrus, with translation on p. 3), remaining 9 pages blank; small notebook. No date, written July–October 1835.

Ms. 7: Untitled; cover reads “FGW” and “Williams” (for Frederick G. Williams); English contents in Phelps’s handwriting; 3 pp. (pp. 1–3, with

[27] At one time, there was a sample of some Arabic writing (provenance unknown) with the manuscripts.

remaining 9 pages blank); small notebook. P. 1: "A Translation of the next page" with "in part" added; p. 2 contains hieratic characters copied from Amenhotep papyrus and drawings from other vignettes; p. 3 contains characters also copied, but upside down. No date, written July–November 1835.

Ms. 8: Untitled; hieratic characters copied from what is now known to be the "Book of the Dead" (of Ta-sherit-Min); one page folded.

Ms. 9: Untitled; hieratic characters copied from what is now known to be the "Book of the Dead" (of Ta-sherit-Min); partially copied from Joseph Smith Papyrus IX.

Ms. 10: Untitled; loose pieces of Egyptian papyrus adhered to sheet of paper; same as Joseph Smith Papyrus IX; known as "Church Historian's Fragment."

The English text of the majority of the thirty-four-page "Egyptian Alphabet" Ms. 1 clearly reflects Smith's dictation to Phelps and Parrish. On page 1, there is mention of "In translating this character," showing that Smith was giving his interpretation. The book is divided into two sections. In the first, the Egyptian characters are interpreted as relating to ancient Egypt. The second section continues the same general topic, but also mentions a type of astronomy said to have been practiced by the Egyptians.

The English "translation" of each Egyptian character is presented according to five "degrees" of interpretation. Each degree represents a level of interpretation. In some cases, the interpretation relates to grammar, such as parts of speech. Below are some examples of how Smith studied the Egyptian characters. First, the characters were copied by his scribe onto the left side of the previously blank page in the record book. Next appears in English the presumed sound of the word-symbol, followed by the English interpretation, appearing at the right. Sometimes a character is dissected into its smaller constituent pen strokes and each stroke is then interpreted. (In the examples cited below, page numbers of Smith's "Egyptian Alphabet" Ms. 1 are given in parentheses.)

A number of Smith's interpretations relate to how he believed Abraham's record had been preserved with an Egyptian mummy since the time of Genesis. Smith believed the records had been hidden in Egypt according to the "tradition of Ham and according to the tradition of their elders: by whom also the art of embalming was kept" (4). Years later, the records were deposited with one of the royal Egyptian families, being placed with those embalmed individuals and buried in Egypt, like Joseph, son of Jacob/Israel, who was first buried in Egypt (Gen. 50:26).

That Smith believed the records were preserved among the Egyptians is further referred to in the Alphabet's 5th Degree. The sound "Kah tou mun" is interpreted to mean: "a lineage with whom a record of the fathers was intrusted [*sic*] by the tradition of Ham, and according to the tradition of their elders, by whom also the tradition of the art of of [*sic*] embalming was kept" (4). The sound "Toan tau ee tahee tahes toues" is explained: "Under the Sun; under heaven; downward; pointing downward going downward; stooping down going down into another place, = any place: going down into the grave—going down into misery = even Hell; coming down in lineage by royal descent; in a line by onitas one of the royal families of the Kings of Egypt" (5).

An interpretation from the 3rd Degree for the sound "Zub zool" means, according to Smith, "pointing to the end of a fixed period[.] A road which leads to some particular place for instance: from Chaldea I travelled to dwell in the land of Canaan" (14). Another character sounding "Ho-oop hah" is shown in each of the five degrees to mean:

> **1st Degree:** "Crown of a princess, or unmarried queen" (21).
> **2nd Degree:** "Corwn [Crown] of a married Queen" (17).
> **3rd Degree:** "Crown of a widowed queen" (13).
> **4th Degree:** "Queen who has been married the second time" (9).
> **5th Degree:** "Queen Kah tou mun, a distinction of Royal <female> lineage or descent, from her whom Egypt was discovered while it was under water, who was the daughter of Ham—a lineage with whom a record of the fathers was intrusted [*sic*] by the tradition of Ham and according to the tradition of their elders: by whom also the tradition of the art of embalming was kept" (3–4).[28]

Smith did not work every day on the Egyptian records. In fact, except for the later additions by Parrish, and because of the small number of pages of the four Alphabet manuscripts (Mss. 1, 3–5), one concludes that only a short time period was involved. The first part of each of the five

[28] Angled brackets here and elsewhere indicate interlinear insertions in the original.

degrees on all of these documents was recorded in July 1835 prior to and in connection with the bound "Egyptian Alphabet" Ms. 1.

Even before September 1835, work on the "Egyptian Alphabet" had come to a standstill. Phelps wrote to his wife, Sally, on September 11: "Nothing has been doing in translation of the Egyptian Record for a long time, and probably will not for some time to come."[29] Smith's personal journal for 1835 begins on September 22. The first entry was recorded by Cowdery; entries for the next two days were written by Smith himself. Cowdery started recording again on September 25. On October 1, Cowdery wrote: "This after noon labored on the Egyptian alphabet, in company with brsr [brothers] O. Cowdery and W. W. Phelps: The System of astronomy was unfolded."[30] This "unfolding" is contained in the second part of the Alphabet. The last symbols in each of the five degrees contain Smith's description of the system of ancient Egyptian astronomy, including the relationship between the Earth, moon, sun, and fixed stars or planets.

For example, the symbol ⊕ (meaning the Earth) is given the sound "Jah-oh-eh." The beginning of its explanation according to the 5th Degree includes these words: "The earth under the governing <powers> of oliblish, Enish go on dosh, and Kai-e van rash, which are the grand ~~governing~~ Key or in other words, the governing power, which governs the fifteen fixed stars...that ~~belong~~ governs the earth, sun & moon, (which have their power <in> one) with the other twelve moving planets of this system (24)."

This "System of astronomy" is what Phelps recorded in the "Egyptian Alphabet" on October 1, 1835, under Smith's dictation. Six days later, on October 7, Frederick Williams (1787–1842) wrote: "this afternoon

---

[29] W. W. Phelps, Letter to Sally Phelps, Sept. 11, 1835, William Wines Phelps Papers, L. Tom Perry Special Collections, Harold B. Lee Library, Brigham Young University, Provo, Utah. See Van Orden 1993, p. 563.

[30] Joseph Smith, Journal, 3, LDS Archives; Dean C. Jessee, ed., *The Papers of Joseph Smith: Journal, 1832–1842,* Vol. 2 (Salt Lake City: Deseret Book Co., 1992), 45; Dean C. Jessee, Mark Ashurst-McGee, and Richard L. Jensen, eds., *The Joseph Smith Papers: Journals, Volume 1: 1832–1839* (Salt Lake City: Church Historian's Press, 2008), 67 (hereafter *Joseph Smith Papers: Journals).* In 1843, the following clarifying words were added at the end of the journal entry: "and during the research, the principles of astronomy as understood by Father Abraham and the ancients, unfolded to our understanding; the particulars of which will appear hereafter" (Manuscript History, Book B-1:622; *History of the Church,* 2:286).

recommenced translating th[e] ancient reccords."[31] This was Smith's first opportunity to return to work on the "Egyptian Alphabet" and related pages since the afternoon of October 1.

One scholar has suggested that Smith's diary entry for October 1 "provides a date for the progress achieved to that point in the translation of the Book of Abraham, a point further along in the Book of Abraham than was ever published."[32] In fact, what we find is that "Egyptian Alphabet" Mss. 3–5 contain characters and symbols recorded on each document. Cowdery and Phelps were clearly working closely with Smith. Phelps then records the fuller explanation of astronomy onto the pages of the bound "Egyptian Alphabet" volume (Ms. 1).

The following comparison indicates the close relationship between Ms. 3 (written by Phelps) and the final recording (also by Phelps) on October 1, 1835, as the system of astronomy was unfolded to Smith. The Egyptian-like symbol in this case is nowhere found on the original papyrus, now labeled as Joseph Smith Papyri I (hereafter JSP followed by Roman numeral[s]).[33] The example that follows shows that Phelps wrote "Moh nit tish" on both Mss. 3 and 1, then crossed it out on both and subsequently added "Flo-ees" with the interpretation expanded according to the five degrees in Ms. 1.

Ms. 3 (Phelps scribe): ~~Moh nit tish~~ Flo-ees

"Egyptian Alphabet" Ms. 1
1st Degree, 2nd part: ~~Moh nit tish~~ Flo ees: The moon in its affinity with the sun, and the earth (34)
2nd Degree: Flo-ees[:] The moon, signifying that which borroweth light, lendeth light, it being the lesser light (31)
3rd Degree: Flo-ees: The moon—signifying its revolutions, also going between, thereby forming an eclipse (30)

[31] Joseph Smith, Journal, 7, LDS Archives; Jessee 1992, p. 50; *Joseph Smith Papers: Journals,* 71.

[32] John Gee, "Eyewitness, Hearsay, and Physical Evidence of the Joseph Smith Papyri," in Stephen D. Ricks, Donald W. Parry, and Andrew H. Hedges, eds., *The Disciple as Witness: Essays on Latter-day Saint History and Doctrine in Honor of Richard Lloyd Anderson* (Provo, UT: Foundation for Ancient Research and Mormon Studies, Brigham Young University, 2000), p. 200.

[33] See Klaus Baer, "The Breathing Permit of Hôr: A Translation of the Apparent Source of the Book of Abraham," *Dialogue: A Journal of Mormon Thought* 3 (Autumn 1968): 128.

> **4th Degree:** Flo-ees. The moon in its revolutions with earth, showing or signifying the earth going between, thereby forming an eclipse (27)
> **5th Degree:** Flo-ees[:] The moon, the earth and the sun in their annual revolutions (25)

Parrish was not appointed to assist Smith until October 29, 1835. Cowdery had left Kirtland and returned on November 20, being gone about two weeks, and brought with him some Hebrew, Greek, and English books. There is no record that Smith did any additional work on the Alphabet from October 8 to October 31. A revelation to Smith given on November 14, 1835, mentions Parrish's calling as a scribe, and states, in part:

> behold it shall come to pass in his day that he shall see much of my ancient records, and shall know of hid[d]en things, and shall be endowed with a knowledge of hid[d]en languages, and if he desires and shall seek it at my hand, he shall be privileged with writing much of my word, as a scribe unto me for the benefit of my people, therefore this shall be his calling until I shall order it otherwise, in my wisdom and it shall be said of him in a time to come, behold Warren the Lord[']s Scribe, for the Lord[']s Seer whom he hath appointed in Israel[34]

According to this revelation, Parrish should see "my ancient records." The revelation documents Parrish's call in connection with the Egyptian records. Later, Parrish records on the topic of astronomy, for example, adding the word "Kolob" to Ms. 3. His handwriting also appears on the final pages in the second part of the each of the five degrees in Ms. 1, bringing to a close the written explanations in the bound book.

As an additional scribe to Smith, Parrish also recorded entries in Smith's journal. Parrish wrote entries for part of October 1835, for all of November 1835 (except for part of a letter copied in the journal by Frederick Williams under the entry of November 16), and for all of December 1–18, 1835. Smith attended the School of the Prophets (a kind of adult education for male LDS Church members) from November 2 to November 13, 1835. A revelation given on November 8 states that Phelps and John Whitmer,

[34] Marquardt 1999, p. 276; Jessee 1992, p. 79; *Joseph Smith Papers: Journals*, 99–100.

editor of the *Messenger and Advocate,* were "under condemnation before the Lord"[35] (the condemnation lasted only a short time). On November 17, Smith "ex[h]ibited <the Alphabet> of the ancient records to Mr. [Erastus] Holmes and some others."[36] All indications are that Smith's scribes—Phelps, Cowdery, Williams, and Parrish—took dictation as they worked closely with him on the Egyptian papers project.

THE "BOOK OF ABRAHAM"

The next entries in Smith's personal journal record the work done on translating the text of the Abraham papyrus, or "Book of Abraham," during four days in the second half of November 1835.

> [November 19:] I returned home and spent the day in translating the Egyptian records
> [November 20:] we spent the day in translating, and made rapid progress
> [November 24:] in the after-noon, we translated some of the Egyptian records
> [November 25:] Spent the day in Translating[37]

The story, according to Smith, concerns Abram (or Abraham). Abram's father is an idolater. A priest binds Abram and attempts to have him serve as a human sacrifice. Abram is rescued by an angel. The King (Pharaoh) of Egypt is descended from Ham and has Canaanite blood. All Egyptians come from this Canaanite lineage. The story of the discovery of Egypt by Zeptah (or Egyptus) is told, and a brief explanation of the government of Egypt is provided. The rights of the priesthood—the patriarchal lineage—are explained as coming from Noah. These same elements figure prominently in Smith's "Book of Abraham" translation (Abr. 1:26–27).

In either October or November 1835, Smith dictated to Phelps the opening sentences of what Smith would publish less than seven years later as the "Book of Abraham":

[35] Marquardt 1999, p. 275; Jessee 1992, p. 68; *Joseph Smith Papers: Journals,* 86.

[36] Joseph Smith, Journal, 45; Jessee 1992, p. 85; *Joseph Smith Papers: Journals,* 105.

[37] Joseph Smith, Journal, 47, 49–50, written by Warren Parrish; Jessee 1992, pp. 87–88, 90; *Joseph Smith Papers: Journals,* 107, 109–10.

> Translation of the Book of Abraham written by his own hand upon papyrus and found in the Catacombs of Egypt
>
> In the land of the Chaldeans, at the residence of my fathers, I, Abraham, saw, that it was needful for me to obtain another place of residence, and seeing there was greater happiness and peace and rest, for me, I sought for [the] blessings of the fathers, and the right whereunto I should be ordained to administer the same: Having been a follower of righteousness; desiring to be one who possessed great Knowledge; a greater follower of righteousness; <a possessor of greater knowledge;> a father of many nations; a prince of peace; one who keeps the commandments of God; a rightful heir; a high priest, holding the right belonging to the fathers, from the beginning of time; even from the beginning, or before the foundation of the earth, down to the present time; even the right of the first born, or the first man, who is Adam, or first father, through <the> fathers, unto me.[38]

Smith's dictation is found in the three Translation Manuscripts of the "Book of Abraham" (Translation Mss. 1–3, below). The scribes for Smith were Phelps, Parrish, and Williams. A point of interest is that by comparing the three manuscripts, one concludes that Parrish and Williams wrote simultaneously as Smith dictated. At the top of two translation manuscripts are the words "Sign of the fifth degree of the second part," clearly indicating a connection to the "Egyptian Alphabet." After taking dictation from Smith, Parrish transferred his text from Translation Ms. 3 to Translation Ms. 1 beginning on page 1 (below some text recorded by Phelps) and continuing to page 7. After this text was transferred, Smith continued to dictate to Parrish the remainder of pages 7 to 10 (of Translation Ms. 1). These pages have words crossed through and occasionally words added above the line, indicating that Parrish was taking dictation again directly from Smith. Smith believed the writings he was "translating" had been written by Abraham (see Abr. 1:1, 12, 14, 28, 31).

To the left of the original of the Egyptian papyrus illustration subsequently published as "Book of Abraham" Facsimile No. 1 (1842)

[38]Translation Ms. 1, 1, LDS Archives. See H. Michael Marquardt, comp., *The Joseph Smith Egyptian Papers* (Cullman, AL: Printing Service, 1981), 147–48.

is writing in two columns (JSP XI, see below). Copies of the Egyptian characters in the first column nearest the illustration appear on all three of Smith's Translation Manuscripts. They come from the first three lines of the Egyptian text. There is an exception, however; where there is a lacuna (gap or break) in the original, there were no characters available to copy. To rectify this, restorations were drawn by Smith or his scribes to fill in the missing area.[39] Smith believed that line 1 of the original Egyptian papyrus was the commencement of the "Book of Abraham" text.

JOSEPH SMITH'S "BOOK OF ABRAHAM" TRANSLATION MANUSCRIPTS, 1835

Translation Ms. 1: "Translation of the Book of Abraham written by his own hand upon papyrus and found in the Catacombs of Egypt"; English text of Abraham 1:1–2:18; in Phelps's and Parrish's handwriting. No date, written October–November 1835. 10 pp. grouped as follows:

1. First half of p. 1 recorded from dictation by Smith to Phelps.
2. Second half of p. 1 copied from Ms. 3 (below) by Parrish.
3. P. 2 to part of p. 7 mostly copied by Parrish from Ms. 3 (below).
4. Part of p. 7 to p. 10 recorded from dictation by Smith to Parrish.

The above pages have Egyptian characters and proposed "restored" symbols in left-hand margins. Source of Egyptian characters for JSP XI, column 1, lines 1, 2, 3, and part of 4. Column 1 immediately adjoins left-hand side of original of Facsimile No. 1 and is part of same papyrus roll.

Translation Ms. 2: English text of Abraham 1:4 to 2:6 (2:3–5 repeated); in Williams's handwriting; 4 pp., lettered J, K, L, and M; recorded from dictation by Smith at the same time as Ms. 3 (below) was recorded. "Sign of the fifth degree of the second part" with Egyptian characters and proposed "restorations" in left-hand margin. No date, written November 1835. Source of Egyptian characters in JSP XI, column 1, lines 1 and 2.

Translation Ms. 3: English text of Abraham 1:4 to 2:2; in Parrish's handwriting; 6 pp., lettered S, R, Q, P, N, and O; recorded from dictation by Smith at the same time as Ms. 2 (above) was recorded; copied into Ms. 1 (above) by Parrish. "Sign of the fifth degree of the second part" with Egyptian characters and proposed "restored" symbols in left-hand margin. No date, written November 1835. Source of Egyptian characters: JSP XI, column 1, lines 1 and 2.

[39] See Baer 1968, pp. 129–32.

PRINTER'S AND OTHER "BOOK OF ABRAHAM" MANUSCRIPTS, 1842

Printer's Ms. 4: Abraham 1:1–9, 12–31; 2:1–18; no date, transcribed ca. February 1842; Abraham 3:18–26; transcribed March 1842; in Willard Richards's handwriting; 16 pp., one of which (i.e., p. 4) is presently missing.

"A Fac-Similee [*sic*] from the Book of Abraham—Explanation of the <above> cut": twelve explanations of Facsimile No. 1 in Richards's handwriting; 1 p.; no date, transcribed February 1842.

"Cut 2": 21 explanations of Facsimile No. 2 of "Book of Abraham" (Fig. 20 skipped); in Richards's handwriting; 3 pp.; no date, transcribed March 1842.

Drawing of damaged original of Facsimile No. 2 (hypocephalus, to be placed under the head of the deceased).

From the entries of November 19–20 and 24–25, 1835, in Smith's personal journal, recorded by Parrish, it appears that Smith on these days dictated the final text of what is now Abraham 1:1 through Abraham 2:18. Parrish was the last scribe to have recorded in "Egyptian Alphabet" Ms. 1 and in Translation Ms. 1, which ends at what is now Abraham 2:18.

On November 26, Parrish recorded in Smith's diary: "we spent the day in transcribing Egyptian characters from the papyrus."[40] This entry only mentions copying characters, not "translating." Smith and Parrish were both battling colds, and no work was done in connection with the "Book of Abraham" translation on November 27. Smith's journal entry for November 28 reads, "I am conciderably [considerably] recovered from my cold, & I think I shall be able in a few days to translate again, with the blessings of God."[41] In fact, Smith did not immediately return to his work on the "Book of Abraham," though he did continue to speak about the project.

A year later, on November 25, 1836, returning to Kirtland from a proselytizing mission, Wilford Woodruff and missionary companion Abram O. Smoot went to the House of the Lord (Kirtland temple), accompanied by Warren Parrish, to view the Egyptian records and mummies. Woodruff, later ordained an LDS Church apostle, subsequently

[40] Joseph Smith, Journal, 50; Jessee 1992, p. 90; *Joseph Smith Papers: Journals,* 110–11.

[41] Joseph Smith, Journal, 51; Jessee 1992, p. 91; *Joseph Smith Papers: Journals,* 112; not included in *History of the Church,* 2:321.

wrote in his journal: "visited the upper rooms & there viewed four Egyptian Mum[m]ies & also the Book of Abram [Abraham] Written by his own hand & not ownly [only] hieroglyphicks [*sic*] but also many figures that this precious treasure Contains are Calculated to make a lasting impression upon the mind which is not to be erased."[42] Smoot recorded in his personal journal for the same day: "we had the privilege of beholding the great wonders of Egypt, the mummies that were taken from the Calicomes [Catacombs] in Egypt; these were the greatest wonders I ever saw. I had also a view of the records that came with them, the Book of Abraham which was written by his own hand in Hyrogliphics [*sic*]."[43]

Non-Mormon William S. West of Braceville, Ohio, came to Kirtland to learn firsthand about the Latter-day Saints. After paying twenty-five cents to see the temple, including the Egyptian mummies and records, he returned to examine the objects again the next day. He later reported:

> They say that the mummies were Egyptian, but the records are those of Abraham and Joseph.... These records were torn by being taken from the roll of embalming salve which contained them, and some parts entirely lost, but Smith is to translate the whole by divine inspiration, and that which is lost, like Nebuchadnezzar's dream, can be interpreted as well as that which is preserved; and a larger volume than the Bible will be required to contain them.... Is it possible that a record written by Abraham, and another by Joseph, containing the most important revelation that God ever gave to man, should be entirely lost by the tenacious Israelites, and preserved by the unbelieving Egyptians, and by them embalmed and deposited in the catacombs with an Egyptian priest[?].... I venture to say no, it is not possible. It is more likely that the records are those of the Egyptians.[44]

Of his experience as a scribe for the "Book of Abraham," Parrish recalled not quite three years later: "I have set [*sic*] by his [Joseph Smith's]

---

[42] Wilford Woodruff, Journal, Nov. 25, 1836, LDS Archives; Scott G. Kenney, ed., *Wilford Woodruff's Journal,* Typescript, 9 Vols. (Midvale, UT/Salt Lake City: Signature Books, 1983–85), 1:107.

[43] Abram O. Smoot, Journal, Nov. 25, 1836, Perry Special Collections.

[44] William S. West, *A Few Interesting Facts Respecting the Rise, Progress and Pretensions of the Mormons* (Warren, Ohio?, 1837), 5–6.

side and penned down the translation of the Egyptian Hieroglyphicks [*sic*] as he claimed to receive it by direct inspiration from Heaven."[45] Parrish's statement indicates that he, and presumably the other scribes, sat alongside Smith as he interpreted and dictated the Egyptian characters.

The following chart chronicles the work done on the "Egyptian Alphabet" and on the "Book of Abraham," as well as Smith's occasional exhibitions of his Egyptian relics and study of biblical Hebrew, during the second half of 1835, into 1836, and finally the publication of Smith's "Book of Abraham" in early 1842 in Nauvoo, Illinois. (A more detailed account of 1842's activities is given farther below.)

A TIME-LINE OF JOSEPH SMITH'S INVOLVEMENT WITH THE EGYPTIAN PAPERS

1835

Jun. 30: Michael H. Chandler arrives in Kirtland, Ohio, with four Egyptian mummies and some papyri. Smith examines the papyri and determines they include the writings of biblical patriarchs Abraham and Joseph.

Jul. 6: Chandler gives Smith a certificate relating to his knowledge of the writings. Shortly afterwards, the mummies and papyri are purchased from Chandler.

Jul. 7–31: Smith, Cowdery, and Phelps work on "Egyptian Alphabet."

Aug.: No known work on the Egyptian papers.

Sep.: No known work on the Egyptian papers.

Oct. 1: Smith, Cowdery, and Phelps work on the astronomy portion of the "Egyptian Alphabet"; "The System of astronomy was unfolded."

Oct. 3, 19, 24, 29: Smith exhibits the Egyptian artifacts, and offers explanations of their meaning.

Oct. 7: Smith, and presumably Phelps, recommences translating the ancient Egyptian records.

Oct. 29: Parrish starts writing for Smith.

Nov. 14: Revelation for Parrish to be a scribe.

---

[45] Parrish, Letter to the Editor, Feb. 5, 1838, *Painesville Republican* 2 (Feb. 15, 1838). Parrish, for a variety of reasons, had left the LDS Church by this time.

Nov. 17, 23, 30: Smith exhibits the Egyptian artifacts, and offers explanations of their meaning.

Nov. 19, 20, 24, 25, 26: Smith spends most of each day "translating," and on the 26 "transcribing" the Egyptian records.

Nov. 20, 21, 23, 27: Cowdery returns from New York with books. Smith studies Hebrew.

Dec. 4–5, 7–8, 14, 26, 30: Smith studies Hebrew.

Dec. 7, 10, 12, 14–16, 20, 23: Smith exhibits the Egyptian artifacts and offers explanations of their meaning.

Dec. 23: Smith studies Greek.

1836

Jan. 12, 30: Smith exhibits the Egyptian artifacts.

Jan. 4–6, 8–9, 14, 18–21: Smith attends Hebrew school. There is no teacher.

Jan. 26: Joshua Seixas of Hudson, Ohio, arrives in Kirtland to teach Hebrew.

Feb. 3, 11, 16: Smith exhibits the Egyptian records.

Mar. 27: Dedication of the Kirtland temple.

Mar. 29: Last day of Hebrew school taught by Seixas.

1842

Feb. 19: The first installment of "Book of Abraham" is typeset for publication in the *Times and Seasons* (Nauvoo, Illinois).

Feb. 23: Smith gives engraver Reuben Hedlock instructions to make a cut (or engraving) "for the altar & Gods in the Records of Abraham" for the *Times and Seasons.*

Feb. 24: Smith explains the records of Abraham.

Mar. 1: This issue of the *Times and Seasons* prints Abraham 1:1–2:18, plus Fascimile No. 1.

Mar. 2: Smith proofs the *Times and Seasons* (issue dated March 1); issue is mailed ca. March 4.

Mar. 4: Smith exhibits the original papyrus to Hedlock for several illustrations, and gives instructions for engraving Facsimile No. 2.

Mar. 8: Smith commences translating for next issue of the *Times and Seasons.*

Mar. 9: Smith continues translating "Book of Abraham."

Mar. 15: This issue of the *Times and Seasons* prints Abraham 2:19–5:21, plus Facsimile No. 2. The issue is mailed ca. March 19.

May 16: This issue of the *Times and Seasons* prints Facsimile No. 3.

In summary, Joseph Smith's Egyptian papers project began about July 7 and ended on November 26, 1835, then resumed again with preparations for publication, and the actual publication, of the text and engraved facsimiles of the "Book of Abraham" from February 19 to May 16, 1842. Smith dictated most of the text from "Book of Abraham" chapter 1 through chapter 2, verse 18, in about three and a half days. W. W. Phelps's work as scribe on Translation Ms. 1 may have extended into November 1835. Frederick G. Williams's work occurred about November 19–20, 1835; and Warren Parrish's on November 19–20 and 24–26, 1835. Six years later, with the help of Wilford Woodruff, another scribe (Willard Richards), and an engraver (Reuben Hedlock), Smith's "Book of Abraham" text and explanations of three facsimiles (of illustrations from the papyri) were published in the *Times and Seasons* (see below).

THE "EGYPTIAN ALPHABET," GENESIS, AND THE "BOOK OF ABRAHAM"

The "Book of Abraham" text contains ideas that clearly depend upon material found in "Egyptian Alphabet" Ms. 1. In the examples below are some of the ideas and wording that were first interpreted in the Alphabet and subsequently incorporated into the text of the "Book of Abraham." This is especially evident where there is new information regarding Abraham. Included in the Alphabet are some Egyptian-like characters nowhere found on the papyri. The English explanations in the "Book of Abraham" are found in their fullest context in the Alphabet's 5th Degree. For example, in Abraham chapter 1, the name "Abraham" comes from a character in the Alphabet having the sound "Ah broam" or "Ah brah-oam" which is interpreted through the Alphabet's five degrees to mean:

1st Degree: "The Father of the faithful. The first right—The elder" (20)
2nd Degree: "a follower of righteousness" (16)
3rd Degree: "one who possesses great knowle[d]ge" (13)
4th Degree: "a follower of righteousness a possessor of greater knowledge" (9)
5th Degree: "a father of many nations a prince of peace, one who keeps the commandments of God. A patriarch a rightful heir, a high priest" (2)[46]

The corresponding "Book of Abraham" text (1:2) reads:

> having been myself a follower of righteousness, desiring also to be one who possessed great knowledge, and to be a greater follower of righteousness, and to possess a greater knowledge, and to be a father of many nations, a prince of peace, and desiring to receive instructions, and to keep the commandments of God, I [Abraham] became a rightful heir, a High Priest, holding the right belonging to the fathers.[47]

According to the "Egyptian Alphabet," another character has the sound "Iota toues-Zip Zi." This character described how the land of Egypt was discovered:

1st Degree: "The land of Egypt" (21)
2nd Degree: "The land which was discovered under water by a woman" (18)
3rd Degree: "The woman sought to settle her sons in that land. She being the daughter of Ham" (14)
4th Degree: "The land of Egypt discovered by a woman who afterwards sett[l]ed her sons in it" (10)
5th Degree: "The land of Egypt which was first discovered by a woman <whter [while?] under water>, and afterwards settled by her sons she being a daughter of Ham" (5)

---

[46] See also the 5th Degree for "Kiah abran oam," in "Egyptian Alphabet" Ms. 1, 3.

[47] The wording differs slightly from that in Translation Manuscript No. 1, 1. In quoting the published version of the "Book of Abraham," I cite the 1981 edition published by the LDS Church which follows the 1902 division into chapters and verses. The versification in the 1981 version differs from the paragraph numbering that was first published in the *Times and Seasons*.

The corresponding "Book of Abraham" text (1:23–24) reads:

> The land of Egypt being first discovered by a woman, who was the daughter of Ham.... When this woman discovered the land it was under water, who afterward settled her sons in it; and thus, from Ham, sprang that race which preserved the curse in the land.[48]

For another character, having the sound "Zub Zool eh," the Alphabet's 5th Degree explains:

> In the days of the first patr[i]archs In the reign of Adam; in the days of the first patriarchs; in the days of Noah; in the blessings of Noah; in the blessings of the children of Noah; in the first blessings of men; in the first blessings of the church. (6)

The corresponding "Book of Abraham" text (1:26) agrees:

> ... in the days of the first patriarchal reign, even in the reign of Adam, and also of Noah, his [Ham's] father, who blessed him with the blessings of the earth, and with the blessings of wisdom, but cursed him as pertaining to the Priesthood.

While the meaning of this passage may not be entirely clear, the theme had already been developed in the "Egyptian Alphabet": Shem obtained the priestly blessings (that is, the right to the patriarchal priesthood) from his father, Noah. Smith's Alphabet interpreted the character with the sound "Ho-e-oop" in the 5th Degree to mean: "A prince of the royal blood, a true des[c]endant from Ham, the son of Noah, and inheritor of the Kingly blessings from under the hand of Noah, but not according to the priestly blessing, because of the tran[s]gressions of Ham, which blessings fell upon Shem from under the hand of Noah (4)."[49]

---

[48] For the use of Noah's curse to support slavery, see Stephen R. Haynes, *Noah's Curse: The Biblical Justification of American Slavery* (New York: Oxford University Press, 2002).

[49] The 1830 manuscript for Smith's revision of Genesis 9:26 reads, "And he [Noah] said blessed be the Lord God of Shem and Canaan shall be his servent [servant] and a vail [veil] of darkness shall cover him that he shall be known among all men" (Old Testament Manuscript 1, 25, Community of Christ Archives). See also *Messenger and Advocate* 2 (Apr. 1836): 290, in *The Essential Joseph Smith* (Salt Lake City: Signature Books, 1995), 87.

From the "Egyptian Alphabet," Smith proceeded to explore other topics also found in the "Book of Abraham" text. Thus, Abraham 1:26 is more understandable when compared to what Smith dictated to Phelps regarding the blessing and cursing of Ham who could not officiate in the patriarchal priesthood.[50]

While dictating "Book of Abraham" chapter 2, Smith used the King James Version of Genesis as a guide. In fact, the actual wording of Smith's "translation" relies heavily on Genesis in forming part of the text. Smith believed that Genesis had been written by Moses after the time of Abraham. (It may be of some interest that the wording from Genesis begins where Smith left off editing Genesis 11:16 in his Bible revision.)[51] The "Book of Abraham" account is represented as being a first-person autobiographical record. The name "Abraham" was spelled "Abram" in a number of places when Smith's "translation" was first published in the *Times and Seasons* (1842), but currently appears as "Abraham" in the 1981 text (published by the LDS Church) below.[52] It seems clear that Smith had the Bible open to Genesis as he dictated this section of the "Book of Abraham." Smith's additions to the Genesis account are shown in bold (except for the name Abraham and some other minor variations).[53]

---

[50] In Smith's day, the patriarchal priesthood was understood to mean the LDS Church priesthood office of presiding Church Patriarch. It was a hereditary office that passed from father to son. See LDS D&C 107:40 and H. Michael Marquardt, comp., *Early Patriarchal Blessings of The Church of Jesus Christ of Latter-day Saints* (Salt Lake City: Smith-Pettit Foundation, 2007), vii–xvi.

[51] Old Testament Manuscript 2, 34, Community of Christ Archives. See Scott H. Faulring, Kent P. Jackson, and Robert J. Matthews, eds. *Joseph Smith's New Translation of the Bible: Original Manuscripts* (Provo, UT: Religious Studies Center, Brigham Young University, 2004), 587, 635.

[52] After Abram returned from Egypt, his name was changed to Abraham in Genesis 17:5. In the "Book of Abraham," as published in *Times and Seasons,* both names appear. For example, using current versification, Abraham 1:1; 2:2, 20–21, 25; 3:1, 6, 11, 15, 22–23; and 5:13 contained the longer name, while 1:16–17; 2:3, 6, 14, and 17 originally had the shorter.

[53] Smith usually added words to biblical texts. See H. Michael Marquardt, *The Four Gospels According to Joseph Smith* (Longwood, FL: Xulon Press, 2007).

ABRAHAM 2:1–2	GENESIS 11:28–29
Now the Lord God caused the famine to wax sore in the land of Ur, insomuch that Haran, **my brother**, died; **but** Terah, **my** father, **yet lived** in the land of Ur, of the Chaldees.	And Haran died before his father Terah in the land of his nativity, in Ur of the Chaldees.
And **it came to pass that I**, Abraham, **took** Sarai **to** wife, and Nahor, **my brother**, **took** Milcah **to wife**, **who was** the daughter of Haran.	And Abram and Nahor took them wives: the name of Abram's wife was Sarai; and the name of Nahor's wife, Milcah, the daughter of Haran, the father of Milcah, and the father of Iscah.
ABRAHAM 2:3	**GENESIS 12:1**
Now the Lord had said unto **me**: Abraham, get thee out of thy country, and from thy kindred, and from thy father's house, unto a land that I will show thee.	Now the Lord had said unto Abram, Get thee out of thy country, and from thy kindred, and from thy father's house, unto a land that I will shew thee:
ABRAHAM 2:9	**GENESIS 12:2**
And I will make of thee a great nation, and I will bless thee **above measure**, and make thy name great **among all nations**, and thou shalt be a blessing **unto thy seed after thee, that in their hands they shall bear this ministry and Priesthood unto all nations**;	And I will make of thee a great nation, and I will bless thee, and make thy name great; and thou shalt be a blessing:
ABRAHAM 2:11	**GENESIS 12:3**
And I will bless them that bless thee, and curse **them** that curse thee; and in thee **(that is, in thy Priesthood) and in thy seed (that is, thy Priesthood), for I give unto thee a promise that this right shall continue in thee, and in thy seed after thee (that is to say,**	And I will bless them that bless thee, and curse him that curseth thee: and in thee shall all families of the earth be blessed.

the literal seed, or the seed of the body) shall all the families of the earth be blessed, **even with the blessings of the Gospel, which are the blessings of salvation, even of life eternal.**

ABRAHAM 2:14–15, 18	**GENESIS 12:4–6**
So **I**, Abraham, departed as the Lord had **said** unto **me**, and Lot with **me**; and **I**, Abraham, was **sixty** and **two** years old when **I** departed out of Haran.	So Abram departed, as the Lord had spoken unto him; and Lot went with him; and Abram was seventy and five years old when he departed out of Haran.
And **I** took Sarai, **whom I took to** wife **when I was in Ur**, **in Chaldea**, and Lot, **my** brother's son, and all **our** substance that **we** had gathered, and the souls that **we** had **won** in Haran, and **came** forth **in the way** to the land of Canaan, and **dwelt in tents as we** came **on our way**	And Abram took Sarai his wife, and Lot his brother's son, and all their substance that they had gathered, and the souls that they had gotten in Haran; and they went forth to go into the land of Canaan; and into the land of Canaan they came.
And **then we** passed **from Jershon** through the land unto the place of Sechem; **it was situated in** the plains of Moreh, and **we had already come into the borders of the** land **of** the Canaanites, **and I offered sacrifice there in the plains of Moreh, and called on the Lord devoutly, because we had already come into the land of this idolatrous nation.**	And Abram passed through the land unto the place of Sichem, unto the plain of Moreh. And the Canaanite was then in the land.

The "Book of Abraham" next includes what was dictated by Smith in March 1842 and continues its narration of what took place prior to Abraham's going to Egypt. This explains why the corresponding text from Genesis stops before the first mention of Pharaoh (Gen. 12:15).

ABRAHAM 2:19–25

And the Lord appeared unto **me in answer to my prayers**, and said **unto me**: Unto thy seed will I give this land.

And **I**, Abraham, **arose from the place of the** altar **which I had** built unto the Lord, and removed from thence unto a mountain on the east of Bethel, and pitched **my** tent **there**, Bethel on the west, and Hai on the east; and there **I** built **another** altar unto the Lord, and called **again** upon the name of the Lord.

And **I**, Abraham, journeyed, going on still towards the south; and there was a **continuation of a** famine in the land; and **I**, Abraham, **concluded to go** down into Egypt, to sojourn there, for the famine **became very** grievious.

And it came to pass when **I** was come near to enter into Egypt, the **Lord** said unto **me**: Behold, Sarai, **thy** wife, **is** a **very** fair woman to look upon;

Therefore it shall come to pass, when the Egyptians shall see **her**, they **will** say—**She** is his wife; and they will kill **you**, but they will save her alive; **therefore see that ye do on this wise**:

Let her say **unto the Egyptians, she is thy** sister, and **thy** soul shall live.

And it came to pass that I, Abraham, **told Sarai, my wife, all**

GENESIS 12:7–13

And the Lord appeared unto Abram, and said, Unto thy seed will I give this land: and there builded he an altar unto the Lord, who appeared unto him.

And he removed from thence unto a mountain on the east of Bethel, and pitched his tent, having Bethel on the west, and Hai on the east: and there he builded an altar unto the Lord, and called upon the name of the Lord.

And Abram journeyed, going on still toward the south.

And there was a famine in the land: and Abram went down into Egypt to sojourn there; for the famine was greivous in the land.

And it came to pass, when he was come near to enter into Egypt, that he said unto Sarai his wife, Behold now, I know that thou art a fair woman to look upon;

Therefore it shall come to pass, when the Egyptians shall see thee, that they shall say, This is his wife: and they will kill me, but they will save thee alive.

that the Lord had said unto me— **Therefore** say **unto them**, I pray thee, thou art my sister, that it may be well with **me** for thy sake, and my soul shall live because of thee.	Say, I pray thee, thou art my sister: that it may be well with me for thy sake; and my soul shall live because of thee.

Abraham next mentions the stars, the moon (lesser light), and the sun (greater light). He also describes spirits that are intelligent, have no beginning and no end, and were organized before the formation of the Earth, which was created from already existing materials. He explains that a great star named Kolob is nearest the throne of God. According to Abraham, a day to the Lord is a thousand years (3:4; compare Ps. 90:4 and 2 Pet. 3:8), while the time of the moon is longer than that of the Earth (Abr. 3:7).

In the text of the "Book of Abraham" dictated in Nauvoo, Smith followed very closely the transliteration pattern given on page 6 of a Hebrew grammar book used in Kirtland in 1836. The following are the Hebrew words Smith used: *kokob* for a star (Abr 3:13), *kokaubeam* for stars (Abr. 3:13, 16), and *gnolaum* for eternal (3:18). When Smith worked on the explanations of Facsimiles 1 and 2, he used some additional Hebrew words: *raukeeyang* for expanse or firmament (Fac. 1, Fig. 12; Fac. 2, Fig. 4), *shaumahyeem* for heavens (Fac. 1, Fig. 12), and *hah-ko-kau-beam* for the stars (Fac. 2, Fig. 5).[54] This indicates that Abraham chapter 3 and Smith's explanations were written after Translations Mss. 1–3.

In addition, the basic narrative in Abraham chapters 4–5 concerning the creation of the Earth draws upon Genesis chapters 1–2. Note in the Abraham text the use of the plural form of God. The author of the Kirtland Hebrew grammar would probably not have agreed with Smith's interpretation of Genesis as including a plurality of gods.

While incarcerated in Liberty Jail, Clay County, Missouri, in 1838–39, Smith gave instructions to the Church that included a shift from a belief in monotheism (one god) to polytheism (many gods). God, explained Smith, would reveal knowledge not previously revealed. There would be "a time to

[54] Louis C. Zucker, "Joseph Smith as a Student of Hebrew," *Dialogue: A Journal of Mormon Thought* 3 (Summer 1968): 51; J[oshua]. Seixas, *A Manual Hebrew Grammar for the Use of Beginners* (2nd ed., Gould and Newman, 1834), 12, for *raukeeyang*, and 78, for the Hebrew form of *raukeeyang* with the definition "an expanse."

come in the which nothing shall be with held whither [whether] there be one god or many gods they shall be manifest all thrones and dominions, principalities and powers shall be revealed and set forth upon all who have indured [endured] valiently [valiantly] for the gospel of Jesus Christ." Smith told the Church in 1839:

> if there be bounds set to the heavens or to the seas or to the dry land or to the sun, moon or starrs [stars] all the times of their revolutions all their appointed days, month[s] and years and all the Days of their days, months and years, and all their glories, laws and set times shall be reveal[e]d in the days of the dispensation of the fullness of times according to that which was ordained in the midst of the councyl [council] of the eternal God of all other Gods before this world was.[55]

Later, a year prior to recommencing his work on the "Book of Abraham," Smith made use of his study of Hebrew in sermons he delivered in Nauvoo. On March 9, 1841, he said:

> This earth was organized or formed out of other planets which were broke up and remodelled [remodeled] and made into the one on which we live.... The sun has no beginning or end, the rays which proceed from himself have no bounds, consequently are eternal.... In the translation, "without form and void" it should read "empty and desolate." The word "created" should be formed or organized.[56]

In revising the text of Genesis in 1830, Smith had retained the wording: "the earth was without form and void" (Moses 2:2). But in 1842, his new teaching about the formation of the Earth was incorporated in the "Book of Abraham." What Smith brought to Abraham was a developed understanding of Genesis based on his study of Hebrew in 1836.

---

[55] Marquardt 1999, p. 297, epistle of Joseph Smith Jr. et al. "To the church of Latter-day Saints at Quincy[,] Illinois and scattered abroad and to Bishop Partridge in particular," March 20, 1839; LDS D&C 121:28–32. When the letter was printed, the edited version omitted the words "of all other Gods" (*Times and Seasons* 1 [May 1840]: 103).

[56] "Extracts from William Clayton's Private Book," as cited in Andrew F. Ehat and Lyndon W. Cook, comps. and eds., *The Words of Joseph Smith: The Contemporary Accounts of the Nauvoo Discourses of the Prophet Joseph* (Provo, UT: Religious Studies Center, Brigham Young University, 1980), 60. See Seixas 1834, p. 85.

On May 4–5, 1842, Smith introduced the temple endowment ceremony to the founding members of his Quorum of the Anointed. Smith's new ceremony included an account of the council of the creation gods. The next month, June 1842, Smith told Rev. George Moore: "We believe in three Gods, equal in power and glory. There are three persons in heaven, but those three are not one."[57] When the endowment was later fully administered in the Nauvoo temple, the names of the three gods involved in the planning and organization of the Earth were identified as Eloheem [Elohim], Jehovah, and Michael.[58]

When revising the Bible in June 1830, Smith had reported that God (singular) was the Creator.[59] While the teaching of one god is found in the Book of Mormon (1829–30), by the time Smith worked on the last chapters of the "Book of Abraham" twelve years later in early March 1842, he had come to accept polytheism.[60] There are forty-eight references to the plurality of gods in Abraham chapters 4–5. (Again, bold type signals Smith's additions to the Genesis account.)

ABRAHAM 4:1–31	GENESIS 1:1–31
And then the Lord said: Let us go down. And they went down at the beginning, **and they, that is the Gods, organized and formed** the heavens and the earth.	In the beginning God created the heaven and the earth.
And the earth, **after it was formed**, was **empty** and **desolate, because they had not formed anything but the earth**; and darkness **reigned** upon the face of the deep, and the Spirit of the	And the earth was without form, and void; and darkness was upon the face of the deep. And the Spirit of God moved upon the face of the waters.

[57] George Moore, Journal, entry for June 3, 1842, American Antiquarian Society, Worcester, Massachusetts. See also "A Visit to Joe Smith," *Times and Seasons* 3 (Sept. 15, 1842): 926.

[58] Jessee 1992, p. 380. See Devery S. Anderson and Gary James Bergera, eds., *The Nauvoo Endowment Companies, 1845–1846: A Documentary History* (Salt Lake City: Signature Books, 2005), 5, 21, 23n20.

[59] Old Testament Manuscript 1, 3, Community of Christ Archives; Moses 2:1.

[60] For essays on the LDS concept of God, see Gary James Bergera, ed., *Line Upon Line: Essays on Mormon Doctrine* (Salt Lake City: Signature Books, 1990).

Gods was brooding upon the face of the waters.	
And **they (the Gods)** said: Let there be light; and there was light.	And God said, Let there be light: and there was light.
And **they (the Gods) comprehended** the light, **for** it was **bright**; and **they** divided the light, **or caused it to be divided**, from the darkness.	And God saw the light, that it was good: and God divided the light from the darkness.
And **the Gods** called the light Day, and the darkness **they** called Night. And **it came to pass that from** the evening **until** morning **they called night; and from the morning until the evening they called day; and this was** the first, **or the beginning, of that which they called** day **and** night.	And God called the light Day, and the darkness he called Night. And the evening and the morning were the first day.
And **the Gods also** said: Let there be an **expanse** in the midst of the waters, and it **shall** divide the waters from the waters.	And God said, Let there be a firmament in the midst of the waters, and let it divide the waters from the waters.
And **the Gods ordered** the **expanse, so that it** divided the waters which were under the **expanse** from the waters which were above the **expanse**; and it was so, **even as they ordered.**	And God made the firmament, and divided the waters which were under the firmament from the waters which were above the firmament: and it was so.
And **the Gods** called the **expanse**, Heaven. And **it came to pass that it was from** evening **until** morning **that they called night; and it came to pass that it was from morning until evening that they called** day; **and this was** the second **time that they called night and day.**	And God called the firmament Heaven. And the evening and the morning were the second day.

And **the Gods ordered**, saying: Let the waters under the heaven be gathered together unto one place, and let the **earth come up** dry; and it was so **as they ordered**;

And God said, Let the waters under the heaven be gathered together unto one place, and let the dry land appear: and it was so.

And **the Gods pronounced** the dry land, Earth; and the gathering together of the waters, **pronounced they, Great Waters**; and **the Gods** saw that **they were obeyed**.

And God called the dry land Earth; and the gathering together of the waters called he Seas: and God saw that it was good.

And **the Gods** said: Let **us prepare** the earth **to** bring forth grass; the herb yielding seed; the fruit tree yielding fruit, after his kind, whose seed in itself **yieldeth its own likeness** upon the earth; and it was so, **even as they ordered**.

And God said, Let the earth bring forth grass, the herb yielding seed, and the fruit tree yielding fruit after his kind, whose seed is in itself, upon the earth: and it was so.

And **the Gods organized** the earth **to bring** forth grass **from its own seed**, and **the** herb **to bring forth herb from its own seed**, yielding seed after his kind; **and the earth to bring forth** the tree **from its own seed**, yielding fruit, whose seed **could only bring forth the same** in itself, after his kind; and **the Gods** saw that **they were obeyed**.

And the earth brought forth grass, and herb yielding seed after his kind, and the tree yielding fruit, whose seed was in itself, after his kind: and God saw that it was good.

And **it came to pass that they numbered the days**; **from** the evening **until** the morning **they called night; and it came to pass, from the morning until the evening they called** day; and **it was the** third **time**.

And the evening and the morning were the third day.

And **the Gods organized the** lights in the **expanse** of the heaven, **and caused them** to divide the

And God said, Let there be lights in the firmament of the heaven to divide the day from the

day from the night; and **organized them to** be for signs and for seasons, and for days and **for** years;	night; and let them be for signs, and for seasons, and for days, and years:
And **organized them to** be for lights in the **expanse** of the heaven to give light upon the earth; and it was so.	And let them be for lights in the firmament of the heaven to give light upon the earth: and it was so.
And **the Gods organized** the two great lights, the greater light to rule the day, and the lesser light to rule the night; **with the lesser light they set** the stars also;	And God made two great lights; the greater light to rule the day, and the lesser light to rule the night: he made the stars also.
And **the Gods** set them in the **expanse** of the heavens, to give light upon the earth, and to rule over the day and over the night, and to **cause to** divide the light from the darkness.	And God set them in the firmament of the heaven to give light upon the earth, And to rule over the day and over the night, and to divide the light from the darkness: and God saw that it was good.
And **the Gods watched those things which they had ordered until they obeyed.**	
And **it came to pass that it was from** evening **until** morning **that it was night; and it came to pass that it was from morning until evening that it was day; and it was** the fourth **time.**	And the evening and the morning were the fourth day.
And **the Gods** said: Let **us prepare** the waters **to** bring forth abundantly the moving creatures that have life; and **the** fowl, that **they** may fly above the earth in the open **expanse** of heaven.	And God said, Let the waters bring forth abundantly the moving creature that hath life, and fowl that may fly above the earth in the open firmament of heaven.
And **the Gods prepared the waters that they might bring forth** great whales, and every living creature that moveth, which the waters **were to bring** forth	And God created great whales, and every living creature that moveth, which the waters brought forth abundantly, after their kind, and every winged fowl after his

abundantly after their kind; and every winged fowl after **their** kind. And **the Gods** saw **that they would be obeyed, and** that **their plan** was good.

And **the Gods** said: **We will** bless them, **and cause them to** be fruitful and multiply, and fill the waters in the seas **or great waters**; and **cause the** fowl to multiply in the earth.

And **it came to pass that it was from** evening **until** morning **that they called night; and it came to pass that it was from morning until evening that they called** day; **and it was the** fifth **time**.

And **the Gods prepared** the earth to bring forth the living creature after his kind, cattle and creeping things, and beasts of the earth after **their** kind; and it was so, **as they had said**.

And **the Gods organized** the earth **to bring forth** the beasts after **their** kind, and cattle after their kind, and every thing that creepeth upon the earth after **its** kind; and **the Gods** saw **they would obey**.

And **the Gods took counsel among themselves and** said: Let us **go down and form** man in our image, after our likeness; **and we will give** them dominion over the fish of the sea, and over the fowl of the air, and over the cattle, and over all the earth, and over every

kind: and God saw that it was good.

And God blessed them, saying, Be fruitful, and multiply, and fill the waters in the seas, and let fowl multiply in the earth.

And the evening and the morning were the fifth day.

And God said, Let the earth bring forth the living creature after his kind, cattle, and creeping thing, and beast of the earth after his kind: and it was so.

And God made the beast of the earth after his kind, and cattle after their kind, and every thing that creepeth upon the earth after his kind: and God saw that it was good.

And God said, Let us make man in our image, after our likeness: and let them have dominion over the fish of the sea, and over the fowl of the air, and over the cattle, and over all the earth, and over every creeping thing that creepeth upon the earth.

creeping thing that creepeth upon the earth.	
So **the Gods went down to organize** man in **their** own image, in the image of **the Gods to form they** him, male and female **to form they** them.	So God created man in his own image, in the image of God created he him; male and female created he them.
And **the Gods said: We will** bless them. And **the Gods** said: **We will cause them to** be fruitful and multiply, and replenish the earth, and subdue it, and **to** have dominion over the fish of the sea, and over the fowl of the air, and over every living thing that moveth upon the earth.	And God blessed them, and God said unto them, Be fruitful, and multiply, and replenish the earth, and subdue it: and have dominion over the fish of the sea, and over the fowl of the air, and over every living thing that moveth upon the earth.
And **the Gods** said: Behold, **we will give them** every herb bearing seed **that shall come** upon the face of all the earth, and every tree which **shall have fruit upon it; yea**, the fruit of **the** tree yielding seed to **them we will give it**; it shall be for **their** meat.	And God said, Behold, I have given you every herb bearing seed, which is upon the face of all the earth, and every tree, in the which is the fruit of a tree yielding seed; to you it shall be for meat.
And to every beast of the earth, and to every fowl of the air, and to every thing that creepeth upon the earth, **behold, we will give them** life, **and also we will** give **to them** every green herb for meat, and **all these things shall be thus organized**.	And to every beast of the earth, and to every fowl of the air, and to every thing that creepeth upon the earth, wherein there is life, I have given every green herb for meat: and it was so.
And **the Gods said: We will do** every-thing that **we have said**, and **organize them**; and behold, **they shall be very obedient**. And **it came to pass that it was from** evening **until** morning **they called**	And God saw every thing that he had made, and, behold, it was very good. And the evening and the morning were the sixth day.

night; and it came to pass that it was from morning until evening that they called day; **and they numbered** the sixth **time**.

ABRAHAM 5:1–7

And thus **we will** finish the heavens and the earth, and all the hosts of them.

And **the Gods said among themselves**: On the seventh **time we will** end **our** work, which **we have counseled**; and **we will** rest on the seventh **time** from all **our** work which **we have counseled**.

And **the Gods concluded upon** the seventh **time**, because that **on the seventh time they would rest from all their works which they (the Gods) counseled among themselves to form**; and sanctified it. **And thus were their decisions at the time that they counseled among themselves to form the heavens and the earth.**

And the Gods came down and formed these the generations of the heavens and of the earth, when they were **formed** in the day that the **Gods formed** the earth and the heavens,

According to all that which they had said concerning every plant of the field before it was in the earth, and every herb of the field before it grew; for the **Gods** had not caused it to rain upon the earth **when they counseled to do**

GENESIS 2:1–7

Thus the heavens and the earth were finished, and all the host of them.

And on the seventh day God ended his work which he had made; and he rested on the seventh day from all his work which he had made.

And God blessed the seventh day, and sanctified it: because that in it he had rested from all his work which God created and made.

These are the generations of the heavens and of the earth when they were created, in the day that the Lord God made the earth and the heavens,

And every plant of the field before it was in the earth, and every herb of the field before it grew: for the Lord God had not caused it to rain upon the earth, and there was not a man to till the ground.

them, and **had** not **formed** a man to till the ground.	
But there went up a mist from the earth, and watered the whole face of the ground.	But there went up a mist from the earth, and watered the whole face of the ground.
And the **Gods** formed man **from** the dust of the ground, **and took his spirit (that is, the man's spirit), and put it into him**; and breathed into his nostrils the breath of life, and man became a living soul.	And the Lord God formed man of the dust of the ground, and breathed into his nostrils the breath of life; and man became a living soul.
ABRAHAM 5:8–10	**GENESIS 2:8–14**
And the **Gods** planted a garden, eastward in Eden, and there **they** put the man, **whose spirit they** had put **into** the **body which they** had formed.	And the Lord God planted a garden eastward in Eden; and there he put the man whom he had formed.
And out of the ground made the **Gods** to grow every tree that is pleasant to the sight and good for food; the tree of life, also, in the midst of the garden, and the tree of knowledge of good and evil.	And out of the ground made the Lord God to grow every tree that is pleasant to the sight, and good for food; the tree of life also in the midst of the garden, and the tree of knowledge of good and evil.
There was a river **running** out of Eden, to water the garden, and from thence it was parted and became into four heads.	And a river went out of Eden to water the garden; and from thence it was parted, and became into four heads.
	The name of the first is Pison: that is it which compasseth the whole land of Havilah, where there is gold;
	And the gold of that land is good: there is bdellium and the onyx stone.
	And the name of the second river is Gihon: the same is it that

compasseth the whole land of Ethiopia.

And the name of the third river is Hiddekel: that is it which goeth toward the east of Assyria. And the fourth river is Euphrates.

Smith probably decided not to include Genesis 2:11–14, which named the four rivers flowing out of Eden (and which he retained in his 1830 revision of Genesis),[61] in the "Book of Abraham" because he now believed that Adam had lived in what is now the state of Missouri.[62] On July 8, 1838, Smith received a revelation that contained the following question: "Is there not room enough upon the mountains of Adam Ondi Awmen [Ahman], and upon the plains of Olah[a] Shinehah, or in the land where Adam dwelt."[63]

In a new settlement named Adam-ondi-Ahman (shortened to Diahman), LDS Church members later recalled, Smith discovered what was believed to be the remains of an altar on which Adam offered sacrifices.[64] The name Adam-ondi-Ahman was used prior to 1838 as the place of Adam's residence. It was used in Kirtland; and a hymn composed by W. W. Phelps bore the same title. This may explain why the names of the rivers were omitted in preference to the new location revealed in 1838.

ABRAHAM 5:11–14	**GENESIS 2:15–18**
And the **Gods** took the man and put him in the Garden of	And the Lord God took the man, and put him into the garden

[61] Old Testament Manuscript 1, 5, Community of Christ Archives. See Faulring 2004, p. 89; Moses 3:11–14.

[62] Brigham Young, second LDS Church president, said he heard about the location of the biblical Garden of Eden from Joseph Smith. Wilford Woodruff reported Young saying, "Now Jackson County is the garden of Eden Joseph has declaired [declared] this & I am as much bound to believe it as much as I am to believe Joseph is a prophet of God" (*Wilford Woodruff's Journal,* 5:33, entry for Mar. 15, 1857; see also 7:129).

[63] Marquardt 1999, p. 294; LDS D&C 117:8.

[64] For example, see Benjamin Franklin Johnson, "A Life Review," 30, LDS Archives; Benjamin F. Johnson, *My Life's Review* (Independence, MO: Zion's Printing and Publishing Co., 1947), 36.

Eden, to dress it and to keep it.

And the **Gods** commanded the man, saying: Of every tree of the garden thou mayest freely eat,

But of the tree of knowledge of good and evil, thou shalt not eat of it; for in the **time** that thou eatest thereof, thou shalt surely die. **Now I, Abraham, saw that it was after the Lord's time, which was after the time of Kolob; for as yet the Gods had not appointed unto Adam his reckoning.**

And the **Gods** said: **Let us** make an help meet for the man, **for** it is not good that the man should be alone, **therefore we** will **form** an help meet for him.

of Eden to dress it and to keep it.

And the Lord God commanded the man, saying, Of every tree of the garden thou mayest freely eat:

But of the tree of the knowledge of good and evil, thou shalt not eat of it: for in the day that thou eatest thereof thou shalt surely die.

And the Lord God said, It is not good that the man should be alone; I will make him an help meet for him.

The text of Abraham now follows Genesis in wording except for the substitution of "Gods" instead of "Lord God." Besides two verses from Genesis 2 being rearranged (verses 19–20), the text of the "Book of Abraham" follows Genesis closely.

ABRAHAM 5:15–21

And the **Gods** caused a deep sleep to fall upon Adam; and he slept, and **they** took one of his ribs, and closed up the flesh in **the** stead thereof;

And **of** the rib which the **Gods** had taken from man, **formed they** a woman, and brought her unto the man.

And Adam said: This **was** bone of my bones, and flesh of my flesh; **now** she shall be called Woman, because she was taken out of man;

GENESIS 2:21–25, 19–20

And the Lord God caused a deep sleep to fall upon Adam, and he slept: and he took one of his ribs, and closed up the flesh instead thereof;

And the rib, which the Lord God had taken from man, made he a woman, and brought her unto the man.

And Adam said, This is now bone of my bones, and flesh of my flesh: she shall be called Woman, because she was taken out of Man.

Therefore shall a man leave his father and his mother, and shall cleave unto his wife, and they shall be one flesh.	Therefore shall a man leave his father and his mother, and shall cleave unto his wife: and they shall be one flesh.
And they were both naked, the man and his wife, and were not ashamed.	And they were both naked, the man and his wife, and were not ashamed.
And out of the ground the **Gods** formed every beast of the field, and every fowl of the air, and brought them unto Adam to see what he would call them; and whatsoever Adam called every living creature, that **should be** the name thereof.	And out of the ground the Lord God formed every beast of the field, and every fowl of the air; and brought them unto Adam to see what he would call them: and whatsoever Adam called every living creature, that was the name thereof.
And Adam gave names to all cattle, to the fowl of the air, to every beast of the field; **and** for Adam, there was found an help meet for him.	And Adam gave names to all cattle, and to the fowl of the air, and to every beast of the field; but for Adam there was not found an help meet for him.

The Abraham revision of Genesis 2 concludes at the last verse of chapter 5. In all, nearly half of the "Book of Abraham" clearly reflects a dependency upon the King James Version of Genesis. As David P. Wright, a professor of the Bible and Ancient Near East at Brandeis University, observed of Smith's "translations": "in all his work there is a consistency in approach and method: he is not working in any of them with ancient languages (except for the bit of Hebrew in Abraham) and in all of them there is attention (to a greater or lesser degree) to revising or responding to the KJV."[65]

[65] David P. Wright, "'In Plain Terms that We May Understand': Joseph Smith's Transformation of Hebrews in Alma 12–13," in Brent Lee Metcalfe, ed., *New Approaches to the Book of Mormon: Explorations in Critical Methodology* (Salt Lake City: Signature Books, 1993), 211. See also Wright, "Isaiah in the Book of Mormon: Or Joseph Smith in Isaiah," in Dan Vogel and Brent Lee Metcalfe, eds., *American Apocrypha: Essays on the Book of Mormon* (Salt Lake City: Signature Books, 2002), 157–234.

AN EARLIER ATTEMPT AT AN ALPHABET

When dictating the text of the Book of Mormon (1828–29), Joseph Smith reportedly transcribed an alphabet he said was found on one of the Book of Mormon golden plates. The characters were to be shown to those who professed knowledge in languages other than English. Lucy Mack Smith (1775–1856), Smith's mother, recalled in her history (dictated in 1844–45) the following concerning the year 1827:

> It soon became necessary to take some measures to accomplish the translation of the record [the Book of Mormon] into English but he [Joseph Smith] was instructed to take off a fac simile of the ~~alphabet Egyptian~~ characters <composing the alphabet which were called reformed egyptian> Alphabetically and send them to all the learned men that he could find and ask them for the translation of the same.[66]

Lucy continued her narrative concerning the Book of Mormon's "reformed Egyptian" alphabet:

> Joseph started [in] Dec[ember]. [1827] for Penn[sylvania] it was agreed that Martin Har[r]is [another early scribe] should follow him as soon as ~~he~~ <Joseph> should have sufficient time to transcribe the Egyptian alphabet which Mr. Harris was to take to the east and through the country in every direction to all who professed linguists to give them an opertunity [opportunity] of showing their talents.[67]

Lucy added in comments to LDS Church members in October 1845 that she had been called "upon by Joseph to go & tell Martin Harris & family that he [Joseph Smith] had got the Plates & he wanted him [Martin] to take an a[l]phabet of the Characters & carry them to the learned men to decypher [decipher]."[68]

Smith's father understood that the last engraved golden plate of the Book of Mormon contained an alphabet. As he explained to Fayette

---

[66] Lavina Fielding Anderson, ed., *Lucy's Book: A Critical Edition of Lucy Mack Smith's Family Memoir* (Salt Lake City: Signature Books, 2001), 393.

[67] Lucy Mack Smith, Manuscript Draft, LDS Archives; see Anderson 2001, p. 402.

[68] Norton Jacob, Journal, Oct. 8, 1845, LDS Archives. See Ronald O. Barney, *The Mormon Vanguard Brigade of 1847: Norton Jacob's Record* (Logan: Utah State University Press, 2005), 53.

Lapham about 1830: "The remaining pages [of the golden plates] were closely written over in characters of some unknown tongue, the last containing the alphabet of this unknown language."[69]

One of the learned persons whom Martin Harris visited in 1828 with the transcribed characters was Professor Charles Anthon (1797–1867) of Columbia College in New York City. In two letters, Anthon wrote that the sheet of paper looked to him as though the characters came from various alphabets. The first extract is from an 1834 letter, the second from an 1841 letter:

> This paper ... consisted of all kinds of crooked characters disposed in columns, and had evidently been prepared by some person who had before him at the time a book containing various alphabets.[70]
>
> ... the marks in the paper appeared to be merely an imitation of various alphabetic characters, and had in my opinion no meaning at all connected with them.[71]

The above references indicate that one of the first things Smith did was to prepare an alphabet to the Book of Mormon. This consultation with Anthon was used to explain that the learned could not read the writing or book but the unlearned man, Smith, could.

In April 1829, Smith received a revelation for Oliver Cowdery. Cowdery evidently tried to translate some words of the Book of Mormon text but had failed. The revelation explained:

> But, behold, I say unto you [Cowdery], that you must study it [the meaning] out in your mind; then you must ask me if it [the meaning] be right, and if it is right I will cause that your bosom shall burn within you; therefore, you shall feel that it is right. But if it be not right you shall have no such feelings, but you shall have a stupor of thought that shall cause you to forget the thing which is

[69] "The Mormons," *Historical Magazine* 7 (May 1870): 307. See Dan Vogel, ed., *Early Mormon Documents,* 5 vols. (Salt Lake City: Signature Books, 1996–2003), 1:462–63.

[70] Charles Anthon, Letter to Eber D. Howe, Feb. 17, 1834, in Eber D. Howe, *Mormonism Unvailed* (Painesville, OH: Printed and Published by the Author, 1834), 271; Vogel 1996–2003, 4:380.

[71] Anthon, Letter to Rev. T. W. Coit, Apr. 3, 1841, *The Church Record* 1 (1841): 231; Vogel 1996–2003, 4:384–85.

> wrong; therefore, you cannot write that which is sacred save it be given you from me.[72]

If this is also a description of how Smith approached the "translation" of the Book of Mormon, then it may offer some insight into the production of Smith's revelations, restoration of biblical texts, "Egyptian Alphabet," and "Book of Abraham." Whatever interpretation entered Smith's bosom (mind and heart) and was then dictated was considered to be revelatory.

As he would later do in producing the "Book of Abraham," Smith also used the Bible in dictating the Book of Mormon. In 1829, when he "translated" portions of the Book of Mormon, he read directly from the common Bible of the day, the King James Version. Passages in the Book of Mormon, when compared to passages in the King James Version, show that the Bible was used when certain portions of the Book of Mormon were being dictated and recorded.[73]

THE "BOOK OF ABRAHAM" PUBLISHED

That portion of the "Book of Abraham" produced in November 1835 was finally published in early March 1842 in the Church's new headquarters, Nauvoo, Illinois.[74] Smith also published some additional "Book of Abraham" text, which he had recently dictated to scribe Willard Richards (1804–54). This included "explanations" based on the three illustrations—or facsimiles—from the Egyptian papyri Smith said contained the "Book of Abraham," and which accompanied the 1842 publication of the same.

In early 1842, Smith and an engraver, Reuben Hedlock (1809–69), worked on re-rendering the three original illustrations for publication. Accompanying the "Book of Abraham" text, they are known today as Facsimiles Nos. 1, 2, and 3. From the "Egyptian Alphabet" and Smith's published explanations, we know that Smith believed the illustrations represented teachings regarding ancient Egyptian astronomy. As Facsimile No. 1 was being prepared for publication, the hieroglyphs in the columns on the original papyrus were omitted and the damaged papyrus was "restored." The original illustration of Facsimile No. 3 was evidently

[72] Marquardt 1999, p. 37; LDS D&C 9:8–9.

[73] See H. Michael Marquardt, *Literary Dependence in the Book of Mormon: Two Studies* (Grand Rapids, Michigan: Institute for Religious Research, 2000).

[74] See *Times and Seasons* 3 (Mar. 1, 1842): 704–706, Joseph Smith, editor.

on the inside of the papyrus roll, and thus was better preserved. The head of Figure 6 (in Fac. 3)—"a slave belonging to the prince"—was altered by Smith or Hedlock (with Smith's approval) and included the original Egyptian characters that accompanied the illustration. Facsimile No. 2—the hypocephalus (which would have been placed under the head of the mummy)—was re-drawn as a complete circle with "restored" portions inserted from a number of places. Characters from the Egyptian papyrus used in preparing the three Translation Manuscripts were also added to an area of the damaged document. To a casual reader, Facsimile No. 2 probably does not appear to have been once damaged. However, persons comparing it with the sketch of the original easily see it as fragmented. These three "restored" and "reconstructed" illustrations have since appeared in almost all subsequent printings of the "Book of Abraham."[75]

Smith spent some additional time in early 1842 working on the "Book of Abraham" text and preparing his explanations of the three "restored" facsimiles. They first appeared in the LDS Church periodical the *Times and Seasons,* published semi-monthly in Nauvoo. Apostle Wilford Woodruff helped set some of the type for the "Book of Abraham." Woodruff wrote a summary statement in his journal:

> Joseph [Smith] the Seer has presented us some of the Book of Abraham which was written by his [Abraham's] own hand but hid from the knowledge of man for the last four thousand years but has now come to light through the mercy of God. Joseph has had these records in his possession for several years but has never presented them before the world in the English language untill now. But he is now about to publish it to the world or parts of it by publishing it in the Times & Seasons, for Joseph the Seer is now the Editor of that paper & Elder [John] Taylor assists him in writing while it has fallen to my lot to take charge of the Business part of the esstablishment [establishment]. I have had the privilege this day of assisting in setting the TIPE for printing the first peace [piece] of the BOOK OF ABRAHAM that is to be presented to the inhabitants of the EARTH in the LAST DAYS.[76]

[75] For more, see Edward H. Ashment, "The Facsimiles of the Book of Abraham: A Reappraisal," *Sunstone* 4 (Dec. 1979): 33–48.

[76] Kenney 1983–85, 2:155, entry for Feb. 19, 1842. The text of the "Book of Abraham"

The Council of the Twelve Apostles—a presiding quorum second only in authority to Smith's First Presidency—issued a notice asking the Church's local congregations to send their tithes to the Trustee in Trust (Smith) to support various works, including the "new translation of the bible, and the record of Father Abraham [to be] published to the world."[77] The March 1, 1842, issue of the *Times and Seasons* states, "This paper commences my [Joseph Smith's] editorial career, I alone stand responsible for it." The original version of Smith's editorial, as written by Willard Richards, contained the following:

> In the present no. [number] will be found the commencement of the Records discovered in Egypt, some time since, as penned by the hand of Father Abraham, which I shall continue to translate & publish as fast as possible till the whole is completed.—and as the saints have long been anxious to obtain a copy of these records, those [who] are now taking the Times & Seasons, will confer a special favor on their brethren, who do not take the paper.[78]

A volume entitled "The Book of the Law of the Lord" kept by Richards recorded Smith's activities in the latter half of February and early March 1842. Under the date of February 23, Richards writes that Smith "gave R. Hadlock [Reuben Hedlock] instructions concerning the cut for the altar & Gods in the Records of Abraham. As designed for the Times and Seasons." The next day, Smith "was explaining the Records of Abraham To the Recorder [Willard Richards]." On March 4, Smith exhibited the "Book of Abraham" "in the original, To Bro[ther] Reuben Hadlock [Hedlock]. so that he might take the size of the several plates or cuts. & prepare the blocks for the Times & Seasons. & also gave instruction concerning the

---

was published in *Times and Seasons* 3 (Mar. 1, 1842): 704–706, paragraphs 1–13 (Abr. 1:1–2:18, written in Oct.–Nov. 1835), and ibid. 3 (Mar. 15, 1842): 719–22, paragraphs 14–32 (Abr. 2:19–5:21, written in Mar. 1842).

[77] "Temple Friends," *Times and Seasons* 3 (Mar. 1, 1842): 715; *History of the Church* 4:517. The new translation (revision) of the Bible was not published in Joseph Smith's lifetime.

[78] The draft editorial is in the handwriting of Willard Richards, with spelling of words by Richards completed ("Times & Seasons," Joseph Smith Collection, LDS Archives). Only a portion of the editorial (first paragraph reworded) was published in *Times and Seasons* 3 (Mar. 1, 1842): 710. Richards had been appointed recorder for the Nauvoo temple and scribe for President Joseph Smith on December 13, 1841.

arrangement of the writing on the Large cut. illustrating the principles of Astronomy."[79] The "Large cut" refers to Facsimile No. 2 and was printed in the *Times and Seasons* as a two-page fold-out. Though represented as "A Fac-simile from the Book of Abraham," the illustration was larger in size and not from the same papyrus scroll as Facsimiles Nos. 1 and 3.

The "Book of Abraham" begins with the deaths of three virgins upon an altar because they would not worship gods of wood or stone. As an aid to the reader, the text notes in reference to "this altar" (Abr. 1:12): "that you may have a knowledge of this altar, I will refer you to the representation at the commencement of this record. It was made after the form of a bedstead" (vv. 12–13), meaning Facsimile No. 1. The text also indicates that it was Abraham himself who drew the original of this illustration: "That you may have an understanding of these gods, I have given you the fashion of them in the figures at the beginning" (v. 14).

FACSIMILE NO. 1

Sometime soon after the original papyri were purchased by Smith (and others) in mid-1835, the original of this papyrus vignette was glued to a piece of backing paper, presumably for support. On the backing paper someone filled in the missing pieces of the illustration by drawing a head and a knife for the standing figure (Fig. 3) to hold. In his engraving, Hedlock did not use this sketch. Instead, he had Fig. 3's head (white attached to an apparently black-skinned body) resemble Fig. 2's head. (According to Smith, Fig. 3 is an idolatrous priest, whereas Fig. 2 is Abraham.)

The characters on the side of the original illustration were not included in Hedlock's engraving in order to fit the illustration vertically into the text block of the *Times and Seasons* page without having to turn the page horizontally. Though the original illustration was damaged, the reproduction as engraved by Hedlock was printed as though the original was complete and not damaged.

Various newspapers subsequently reproduced Facsimile 1 according to the *Times and Seasons* engraving. While there was interest in what Smith

[79] "The Book of the Law of the Lord," as cited in Jessee 1992, pp. 360, 366. Regarding Facsimile No. 1, Richards wrote that Smith was at "the printing office correcting the first plate or cut. of the Records of father Abraham. prepared by Reuben Hadlock [Hedlock] for the Times & Seasons" (ibid., 2:363–64, entry for Mar. 1, 1842). The next day, Smith "Read the Proof of the 'Times and Seasons' as Editor for the first time, No. 9-Vol 3d in which is the commencement of the Book of Abraham" (ibid., 2:364).

was doing, virtually none of the newspapers took his translation work seriously. Smith said that Facsimile 1 represented Abraham on an altar about to be sacrificed.

FACSIMILE NO. 2

In publishing Facsimile No. 2, which dealt with Egyptian astronomical beliefs, Smith paid careful attention to filling in the missing areas in and around the hypocephalus. The damaged parts were filled in from other papyri in order to make the hypocephalus appear complete.

Smith spent a total of two days in early March 1842 working on the "Book of Abraham" text, evidently producing the material from Abraham 2:19 through 5:21. Richards recorded for March 8, 1842, that Smith "Commenced Translating from the Book of Abraham, for the 10 No [Number] of the Times and Seasons—and was engaged at his office day & evening." The next afternoon, Smith "continued the Translation of the Book of Abraham ... with the Recorder [Willard Richards]. & continued translating & revising."[80] The same day, March 9, Smith wrote, "I am now very busily engaged in Translating,"[81] and Richards told his brother he was "writing the translation of the Book of Abraham in which I am engaged today."[82]

FACSIMILE NO. 3

Two months later, Smith's explanation of Facsimile 3—the last of the three facsimiles—was printed in the May 16, 1842, issue of the *Times and Seasons*. The original papyrus illustration is not extant. Three of the figures (nos. 2, 4, and 5, see below) on Facsimile 3 point to Egyptian writing above the illustration. Under the various explanations is: "Abraham is reasoning upon the principles of astronomy, in the king[']s Court."

[80] Jessee 1992, p. 367; *History of the Church* 4:548.

[81] Smith, Letter to Edward Hunter, Mar. 9–11, 1842, Joseph Smith Collection, LDS Archives; in Jessee 2002, p. 550. A copy of the letter was recorded in Joseph Smith Letterbook 2:229.

[82] Willard Richards, Letter to Levi Richards, Mar. 7–25, 1842, in Joseph Grant Stevenson, ed., *Richards Family History* (Provo, UT: Stevenson's Genealogical Center, 1991), 3:88. This portion of the letter was written on March 9. Richards's manuscript (Ms. 4) contains Abraham 1:1–9, 12–2:18 and 3:18–26, English text only.

Fig. 2. "King Pharaoh; whose name is given in the characters above his head."
Fig. 4. "Prince of Pharaoh, King of Egypt; as written above the hand."
Fig. 5. "Shulem; one of the king[']s principle waiters; as represented by the characters above his hand."[83]

In giving the above explanations, Smith has his interpretations closely aligned with the original papyrus illustration. This confirms that the Egyptian records Smith purchased in 1835 were associated with Smith's interpretation of the characters and the "restored" symbols.

Though Smith promised "further extracts from the Book of Abraham" to subscribers of the *Times and Seasons,* this did not materialize.[84] In mid-May 1844, a month before Smith's death on June 27, Josiah Quincy Jr. (future mayor of Boston) and his cousin Charles Francis Adams visited Nauvoo, viewed the Egyptian mummies, and talked to Smith about the ancient records. Adams recorded in his diary: "He [Joseph Smith] then took us down into his mother's chamber and showed us four Egyptian mummies stripped and then undertook to explain the contents of a chart or manuscript which he said had been taken from the bosom of one of them.... 'This,['] said he, [']was written by the hand of Abraham and means so and so. If anyone denies it, let him prove the contrary. *I* say it.'"[85]

From Adams and others, it is clear that Smith continued to believe that the "Book of Abraham" had originally been written by Abraham himself. The text of the "Book of Abraham" states that Abraham retained the records, was going to write on them, and that they were in his possession at the time he was writing: "for the records have come into my hands, which I hold unto this present time" (1:28). In fact, these preserved records are the very ones Abraham is now writing on: "But the records of the fathers ... the Lord my God preserved in mine own hands; therefore a knowledge of the beginning of the creation, and also of the planets, and

[83] "Explanation of Cut on First Page," *Times and Seasons* 3 (May 16, 1842): 784.

[84] "Notice," *Times and Seasons* 4 (Feb. 1, 1843): 95.

[85] Charles Francis Adams, Diary, May 15, 1844, emphasis retained, Adams Papers, Massachusetts Historical Society, Boston; "Charles Francis Adams Visits the Mormons in 1844," *Proceedings of the Massachusetts Historical Society* 68 (1952): 285.

of the stars, as they were made known unto the fathers, have I kept even unto this day, and I shall endeavor to write some of these things upon this record, for the benefit of my posterity that shall come after me" (v. 31).

THE "BOOK OF ABRAHAM" AFTER JOSEPH SMITH

After Smith's death on June 27, 1844, his younger brother William (1811–93) and mother, Lucy, continued periodically to display the Egyptian records and mummies to visitors. In August 1851, newly appointed Church Apostle Franklin D. Richards (1821–99) published a small pamphlet in England entitled *The Pearl of Great Price,* which featured the text of Smith's "Book of Abraham" and the three facsimiles, which had been re-engraved. Some five years later, Théodule Devéria (1831–72), a young artist, photographer, and student of Egyptology working in the Louvre Museum (Paris, France), examined the "Book of Abraham" facsimiles. In commenting on Facsimile No. 3, Fig. 5, he wrote: "The deceased led by Ma into the presence of Osiris. His name is Horus, as may be seen in the prayer which is at the bottom of the picture, and which is addressed to the divinities of the four cardinal points."[86] Devéria was thus the first to observe that what Joseph Smith had published as a "Facsimile from the Book of Abraham" was actually an ancient funeral illustration for a deceased Egyptian man named Horus.

Less than two weeks after Lucy Smith's death in May 1856, her son Joseph's Egyptian papyri and mummies were purchased by a man named Abel Combs (1823–92). The bill of sale gave a brief history of the artifacts including: "From translations by Mr. [Joseph] Smith of the records, these [four] mummies were found to be in the family of Pharo [Pharaoh], king of Egypt." The bill was signed by Lewis C. Bidamon, his wife Emma Hale Smith Bidamon (Joseph Smith's widow), and her eldest son Joseph Smith III.[87]

Combs subsequently sold two of Smith's mummies and some of the papyri to Edward Wyman's St. Louis Museum (in Missouri) and kept the

[86] First published in French in Jules Remy, *Voyage au Pays des Mormons,* 2 vols. (Paris: E. Dentu, 1860), and in English in Jules Remy and Julius Brenchley, *A Journey to Great Salt Lake City* (London: W. Jeffs, 1861), 2:546.

[87] The bill of sale is dated May 26, 1856, LDS Archives. See Todd 1969, p. 290; Peterson 1995, p. 203. The bill was printed in "The Mormon Prophet's Mummies," *Daily Missouri Democrat,* June 12, 1857, St. Louis, Missouri.

others. When the museum placed some of the items on display in 1856, Gustaf Seyffarth, a visiting professor at the Concordia Seminary in St. Louis County who had studied Egyptian, also read the name of the person for whom Facsimile No. 3 had been made: "the papyrus roll is not a record, but an invocation to the Deity Osirus, in which occurs the name of the person, (Horus,) and a picture of the attendant spirits, introducing the dead to the Judge, Osiris."[88]

The mummies and papyri were eventually resold to Joseph H. Wood, owner of the popular Col. Wood's Museum in Chicago (the museum changed its name a number of times). They were on exhibit and were probably destroyed in the Chicago Fire in October 1871.[89] This is the last known location of the two mummies and artifacts. Also after Lewis Bidamon's death in 1891, his son Charles Edwin Bidamon retained in his possession the ten pages of "Book of Abraham" Translation Manuscript 1. This manuscript, together with other historical items, was later sold by Bidamon to LDS collector Wilford Wood in July 1937. Wood afterwards donated the pages to the LDS Church.[90]

In 1873, T. B. H. Stenhouse, a dissident Mormon, published his book *The Rocky Mountain Saints: A Full and Complete History of the Mormons,* which reprinted Devéria's comments on the "Book of Abraham" facsimiles. Stenhouse's book was republished at least four times by 1905.[91] These republications circulated more widely Devéria's observation that some of the "Book of Abraham" material was funerary in nature and that Facsimile No. 3, in particular, had originally been made for an Egyptian named Horus.

The second edition of the *Pearl of Great Price,* as edited by LDS Apostle Orson Pratt (1811–81), was issued in 1878. It was here that the words "purporting to be" were removed from the heading description of the "Book of Abraham," thereby cementing the assertion that Abraham

[88] As cited in *Catalogue of the St. Louis Museum* (1859), 45, in Todd 1969, p. 298. See also Stanley B. Kimball, "New Light on Old Egyptiana: Mormon Mummies, 1848–71," *Dialogue: A Journal of Mormon Thought* 16 (Winter 1983): 73–74.

[89] See Kimball 1983, pp. 77–82; Webb 2005, p. 4–5.

[90] Todd 1969, p. 326–31.

[91] T. B. H. Stenhouse, *The Rocky Mountain Saints: A Full and Complete History of the Mormons* (New York: D. Apppleton and Co., 1873), 513–19. Republished in 1874 (London), 1878 (London), 1900 (New York), and 1904 (Salt Lake City).

himself wrote the "Book of Abraham." George Reynolds, another LDS Church official, the next year published a defense of the "Book of Abraham" as a divine and ancient record.[92] Then, on October 10, 1880, the *Pearl of Great Price,* including the text of the "Book of Abraham," was publicly canonized by LDS Church members as official scripture together with the Holy Bible, Book of Mormon, and Doctrine and Covenants.[93] Later, in a new edition, the *Pearl of Great Price* was again publicly voted upon as official scripture on October 6, 1902.[94] (Until 1981, the LDS Church printed the text of the 1902 edition of the "Book of Abraham," which relied on re-engraved copies of the facsimiles first published by Franklin Richards in 1851. Beginning in 1981, the Church returned to printing all three facsimiles as originally engraved by Reuben Hedlock in 1842.)

In 1912, the Rev. Franklin S. Spalding (1865–1914), Episcopalian Bishop to Utah, released his own independent study of the "Book of Abraham." Spalding's work printed letters from eight prominent Egyptologists, Orientalists, linguists, and historians who had responded to his inquiry regarding Joseph Smith's interpretations of the three facsimiles.[95] (The published facsimiles provided at the time the only means for evaluating the accuracy of Smith's "translations.") All eight scholars independently reported that the facsimiles were ancient Egyptian funerary illustrations and bore no relationship to the English text of Smith's "translation."

In the intervening years, a few rebuttal articles appeared in LDS Church periodicals dealing with Spalding's book, and attempting to establish an

---

[92] See George Reynolds, *The Book of Abraham. Its Authencity Established as a Divine and Ancient Record* (Salt Lake City: Deseret News and Publishing Establishment, 1879). This forty-nine-page booklet had previously appeared serially in the *Deseret Evening News,* Dec. 1878–Mar. 1879.

[93] See *Latter-day Saints' Millennial Star* 42 (Nov. 15, 1880): 724. Six years later, Devéria's examination was published in W. Wyl [pseud. Wilhelm Ritter von Wymetal], *Mormon Portraits or the Truth about Mormon Leaders from 1830 to 1886* (Salt Lake City: Tribune Printing and Publishing Co., 1886), 221–23.

[94] This edition was prepared by James E. Talmage and contains chapters and verses to the text of the "Book of Abraham."

[95] Franklin S. Spalding, *Joseph Smith, Jr., As a Translator* (Salt Lake City: Arrow Press, 1912); Roger R. Keller, "Episcopalian Bishop Franklin S. Spalding and the Mormons," *Utah Historical Quarterly* 69 (Summer 2001): 244–45. While Spalding was aware of *The Rocky Mountain Saints* and *Journey to Great Salt Lake City,* he solicited his own independent evaluations.

ancient origin for the "Book of Abraham." Except for a handful of articles or books mentioning the controversy, nothing of importance occurred again until the 1960s.

As it turned out, Abel Combs retained in his possession the bill of sale and some of the papyri he had purchased from Lucy Smith's estate in 1856. After his death in 1892, these items passed to his nurse Charlotte Benecke Weaver. The papyri and bill of sale eventually ended up in the possession of Weaver's daughter Alice Combs Weaver Heusser, who approached the Metropolitan Museum of Art in New York City about selling them in 1918. At the time, the museum was not interested in acquiring the materials. Almost three decades later, however, the museum revisited its decision and purchased the papyri artifacts in 1947 from Edward Heusser, Alice's widower.[96] (The fate of the two remaining Chandler mummies is unknown, though Combs probably sold them to another museum or private individual.)[97]

By the mid-1960s, the Metropolitan Museum of Art had decided to raise funds by selling some of its less unique holdings. Coincidently, Aziz S. Atiya, a Coptic studies scholar at the University of Utah in Salt Lake City, was shown the papyri while researching some of the museum's collections in 1966.[98] Though not a member of the LDS Church, Atiya knew of the papyri's importance to Mormons and soon was in touch with N. Eldon Tanner of the Church's First Presidency. Negotiations with the museum began a few weeks later. Eventually, an anonymous patron agreed to make a donation to the museum to cover the cost of the transfer, thereby facilitating the museum's "gift" of the items to the LDS Church on November 27, 1967.[99]

---

[96] Peterson 1995, p. 242–47.

[97] Stanley Kimball concluded in 1983: "If they indeed exist, they are probably in storage, unknown, unidentified, and forgotten. Would the papyri be with them? Probably not" (Kimball 1983, p. 90).

[98] Also in April 1966, Jerald and Sandra Tanner, critics of the LDS Church, published a photographic reproduction (based on a microfilm copy) and a transcription of Joseph Smith's various Egyptian alphabet manuscripts: *Joseph Smith's Egyptian Alphabet and Grammar* (Salt Lake City: Modern Microfilm Co., 1966).

[99] "An Interview with Dr. [Henry G.] Fischer," conducted by Norman Tolk, Lynn Travers, George D. Smith Jr., and F. Charles Graves, *Dialogue: A Journal of Mormon Thought* 2 (Winter 1967): 64.

The museum's transfer included eleven pieces, or fragments, of papyri—including the original of Facsimile No. 1—which once belonged to three separate papyri. These fragments have since been numbered as JSP (Joseph Smith Papyri) I–VIII, X–XI, and may be described as follows:[100]

JOSEPH SMITH'S EGYPTIAN PAPYRI (JSP) TRANSFERRED TO LDS CHURCH IN 1967

JSP Numbers	Text	Document	Date of Composition
I, XI, X, partof IV; Facsimile No. 1 from JSP I	"Book of Breathings Made by Isis"	Papyrus of Horus (also Horos, Hor)	ca. 150 B.C.E., oldest dated Book of Breathings
VII, VIII, V, VI, IV, II	"Book of the Dead" chapters 3–6, 53–54, 57, 63, 65, 67, 70, 72, 74–77, 83, 86–89, 91, 100–101, 103–106, 110, 125	Papyrus of Ta-sherit-Min (also Tshemmin, Semminis)	after 500 B.C.E.
III a–b	"Book of the Dead" Chapter 125	Papyrus of Nefer-ir-nebu (also Neferirtnub, Noufianoub)	after 500 B.C.E.

These eleven fragments joined a twelfth fragment of pieced-together papyri long-held by the LDS Church and known as the "Church Historian's Fragment" (now JSP IX, originally part of Ta-sherit-Min's "Book of the

[100] Hugh W. Nibley numbered the papyri in *Improvement Era* 71 (Feb. 1968): 40, 40-A to 40-I; see also Gee 2000b, pp. 188–89; and John Gee, *A Guide to the Joseph Smith Papyri* (Provo, UT: FARMS, 2000), pp. 10–11. For the dating of JSP I, X, and XI, see Marc Coenen, "The Dating of the Papyri Joseph Smith I, X and XI and Min Who Massacres His Enemies," *Egyptian Religion: The Last Thousand Years, Part II, Studies Dedicated to the Memory of Jan Quaegebeur* (*Orientalia Lovaniensia Analecta,* vol. 85), eds. Willy Clarysee, Antoon Schoors, and Harco Willems (Leuven: Uitgeverij Peeters en Departement Oosterse Studies, 1998), 1103–15. For the dating of JSP II, IV, V, VI, VII, and VIII, see John A. Wilson, "A Summary Report," *Dialogue: A Journal of Mormon Thought* 3 (Summer 1968): 70.

Dead"). The LDS Church subsequently published photographs of all of these papyri in the February 1968 issue of its official *Improvement Era* magazine. Scholarly translations by Egyptologists John A. Wilson and Klaus Baer of some of the papyri followed in the independent LDS periodical *Dialogue: A Journal of Mormon Thought* in its summer and autumn 1968 issues.[101] Their translations again confirmed the status of the papyri as Egyptian funerary materials.

In addition to the fragments listed above, there are other Egyptian documents known to have once been in Joseph Smith's possession, the present location of which, if any, is not known.

OTHER EGYPTIAN DOCUMENTS KNOWN TO HAVE BEEN IN JOSEPH SMITH'S POSSESSION

Document	Contents	Presumed Status	Prepared for
Papyrus of Amenhotep	"Book of the Dead" Chapter 45 and other texts	Destroyed in Chicago fire of 1871?	Amenhotep (also Amen-ophis)
Original of Facsimile No. 2	Hypocephalus of Sheshonq	Destroyed in Chicago fire of 1871?	Sheshonq (also Shashaq, Sesonchis)
Original of Facsimile No. 3	Vignette from Horus "Book of Breathings Made by Isis"	Destroyed in Chicago fire of 1871?	Horus (also Horos, Hor)

THE "BOOK OF ABRAHAM" TODAY

The conclusion of all scholarly studies of the Joseph Smith Egyptian Papers—beginning in 1859–60 and continuing to the present—is that

[101] For later translations, see Robert K. Ritner, "The 'Breathing Permit of Hôr' Thirty-four Years Later," *Dialogue: A Journal of Mormon Thought* 33 (Winter 2000): 97–119; Ritner, "The 'Breathing Permit of Hôr' among the Joseph Smith Papyri," *Journal of Near Eastern Studies* 62 (2003): 161–80; and Michael D. Rhodes, *The Hor Book of Breathings: A Translation and Commentary* (Provo, UT: FARMS, Brigham Young University, 2002). Ritner's publication in *Dialogue* is dated 2000, but was actually completed in 2001 and was printed in March 2002. Rhodes's work was published several months later in 2002.

Smith, like other Americans of his time, had no knowledge or understanding of ancient Egyptian language(s). Before the Egyptian papyri were relocated to the Metropolitan Museum of Art, most Latter-day Saints believed that Smith could accurately translate Egyptian. Since 1967, most analyses of the "Book of Abraham" by LDS Church members no longer argue for the work as a literal translation of an ancient text. The papyrus that contains the Egyptian characters appearing on the three Translation Manuscripts is today preserved in the LDS Archives.

There has been a variety of Church-related responses to the "Book of Abraham." The *Encyclopedia of Mormonism,* published in 1992, proposed: "Since it is not known just how Joseph Smith translated, it is reasonable to postulate that, when studying the Egyptian papyri purchased from Michael Chandler, Joseph Smith sought revelation from the Lord concerning them [the papyri] and received in that process the book of Abraham."[102] Eight years later, a study guide published by the LDS Church recommended: "The greatest evidence of the truthfulness of the book of Abraham is not found in an analysis of physical evidence nor historical background, but in prayerful consideration of its content and power."[103]

LDS historian Glen M. Leonard, in his history of the LDS Church in Nauvoo (published in 2002), referred explicitly to the "Book of Abraham" as a "revelation," explaining: "Joseph Smith's biblical studies relied more upon supernatural knowledge than earthbound book learning."[104] Some other faith communities originating with Smith, such as the Community of Christ (formerly the Reorganized Church of Jesus Christ of Latter

[102] Michael D. Rhodes, "Facsimiles from the Book of Abraham," in *Encyclopedia of Mormonism: The History, Scripture, Doctrine and Procedure of the Church of Jesus Christ of Latter-day Saints,* 4 vols., ed. Daniel H. Ludlow (New York: Macmillan Publishing Co., 1992), 1:136. Smith himself said that it was by revelation that he concluded that the two papyri scrolls contained the writings of Abraham and Joseph. That the Egyptian records that illustrate the "Book of Abraham" were copies and not written by Abraham and other arguments concerning the revelation worked out by Joseph Smith are interesting topics for future research.

[103] Church Educational System, *The Pearl of Great Price: Student Manual Religion 327* (Salt Lake City: Church of Jesus Christ of Latter-day Saints, 2000), 28.

[104] Glen M. Leonard, *Nauvoo: A Place of Peace, a People of Promise* (Salt Lake City: Deseret Book Co./Provo, UT: Brigham Young University Press, 2002), 210–11.

Day Saints), approach the "Book of Abraham" as a work of theological speculation and do not include it in their own scriptural canon.[105]

While Joseph Smith may be "the first native-born American who is known to have made an effort to translate writings and to interpret vignettes found on ancient Egyptian funerary papyri," his translations, according to John A. Larson of the Oriental Institute at the University of Chicago in 1994, "can, at best, be described as unorthodox." Nevertheless, Larson continues, "the position of the Mormon prophet is secure within the early history of American speculation about ancient Egypt. As a manifestation of American interest in the culture of ancient Egypt, the story of Joseph Smith and his ancient Egyptian mummies and papyri is one of the more curious chapters in the early history of American Egyptology."[106] Egyptologist Lanny Bell, formerly of the University of Chicago and more recently of Brown University, adds:

> Smith's approach to the translation of ancient Egyptian documents ranks him squarely in the tradition of the esoteric interpretation of hieroglyphics ... [Given the] disagreement[s], even rancor, over the decipherment of hieroglyphics persisting among Egyptologists until well after his death in 1844, we should hardly expect Joseph Smith to have been able to familiarize himself with Champollion's work, properly assess its validity, and possibly incorporate it into his own translation of the papyrus he had before him.[107]

[105] See Richard P. Howard, *Restoration Scriptures: A Study of Their Textual Development,* 2nd ed., rev. and enl. (Independence, MO: Herald Publishing House, 1995), 192–210.

[106] John A. Larson, "Joseph Smith and Egyptology: An Early Episode in the History of American Speculation about Ancient Egypt, 1835–1844," in David P. Silverman, ed., *For His Ka: Essays Offered in Memory of Klaus Baer* (Chicago: Oriental Institute of the University of Chicago, 1994), 160.

[107] Lanny Bell, "The Ancient Egyptian 'Books of Breathing,' the Mormon 'Book of Abraham,' and the Development of Egyptology in America," in Stephen E. Thompson and Peter Der Manuelian, eds., *Egypt and Beyond: Essays Presented to Leonard H. Lesko upon His Retirement from the Wilbour Chair of Egyptology at Brown University, June 2005* (Providence, RI: Brown University, Department of Egyptology and Ancient Western Asian Studies, 2008), 30, 33.

Marc Coenen

THE OWNERSHIP AND DATING OF CERTAIN JOSEPH SMITH PAPYRI

After the rediscovery in 1966 of the Joseph Smith Egyptian papyri in the Metropolitan Museum of Art in New York City, it became clear that the documents now classified as Papyri Joseph Smith (PJS hereafter) I, X, XI, as well as four fragments from the manuscript glued onto PJS IV, were parts of the same Egyptian papyrus scroll Smith had "translated" and published in early 1842 as the "Book of Abraham." In fact, these papyrus fragments contain not a narrative of the legendary ancient Hebrew patriarch but a copy of the Document (or Book) of Breathing Made by Isis, a relatively common funerary composition that gradually replaced the Book of the Dead in Thebes, Egypt, and surrounding areas during the Greco-Roman Period (332 B.C.E. to 284 C.E.).[1]

According to ancient Egyptian belief, a human being is composed of five parts, the best known being the body, the *ba,* and the *ka* (also ba-spirit and ka-spirit). The *ba* is a person's "soul" or individual personality,

---

Marc Coenen holds M.A. and PhD degrees in Oriental Studies: Ancient Near East from Katholieke Universiteit in Leuven, Belgium. He is the author of *The Lamentations of Isis and Nephthys* (with A. Kucharek, forthcoming) and *De Papyrus Denon of het Boek van het Ademen van Isis* (with Jan Quaegebeur, 1995), as well as several studies of Books of the Dead, Documents of Breathing, and other ancient Egyptian funerary papyri. He currently lives in Rotselaar, Belgium, and works as procurement officer at KBC Global Services Company in Brussels. He is also an officer of the fire department of the city of Aarschot.

[1] This funerary composition was formerly known as the "First Book of Breathings." For current terminology, see Marc Coenen, "Books of Breathings: More than a Terminological Question?" *Orientalia Lovaniensia Periodica* 26 (1995): 29–38. An outline of this composition is provided in Marc Coenen, "An Introduction to the Document of Breathing Made by Isis," *Revue d'Egyptologie* 49 (1998): 39–47.

and survives the death of the body. The *ka* is the individual's life force. At death, the *ka* departs the body. The purpose of Egyptian burial practice was to reunite the *ba* and the *ka* with the body in the hereafter, resulting in the creation of an *akh* ("glorified one"). These practices included the preparation of the corpse and its mummification, the performance of certain magical spells and rituals (such as the "opening of the mouth"), and the placing with the deceased certain goods—statues, jewelry, food (to nourish the *ka*). Also included was the deceased's own copy of the Book of the Dead (also Book of the Coming/Going Forth by Day; later Document of Breathing or Breathing Permit), as well as a hypocephalus, a small round piece of papyrus, linen, metal, wood, or clay placed under the mummy's head. The Book of the Dead was usually written on a papyrus scroll and divided into spells containing hymns, lamentations, incantations, and instructions for surviving the next life. Chapter or Spell 125, perhaps the best known, addresses the deceased's judgment by the god Osiris. While all extant copies of the Book of the Dead and Document of Breathing are very similar, no two are exactly identical.

PAPYRUS JOSEPH SMITH I

PJS I features a portrayal of the resurrection of the god Osiris and the conception of his son Horus, a well-known scene in the Osiris mysteries depicted on Egyptian temple walls but for which no other parallels on papyrus are presently known to exist.[2] As a part of this vignette, the three columns with hieroglyphs on the right contain the names of the original owner of the papyrus and his parents, and list the priestly function(s) held by them during their lifetime(s). Although a small portion of the upper and lower ends of these columns is missing, the hieroglyphic text can be deduced based on a good parallel in another papyrus copy (housed in the Louvre Museum) of this written text.[3] Here follows the complete text

[2] Compare the scene depicted on the papyrus with, for example, the reliefs carved in the Osiris chapels on the roof of the Hathor temple in Dendera. See S. Cauville, *Le temple de Dendara: Les chapelles osiriennes,* Dendara 10 (Cairo: Institut Français d'Archéologie Orientale, 1997): 2, plates 236–39.

[3] The damaged titles are restored on the basis of Papyrus Louvre N 3207, N 3208, and N 3209. This Book of the Dead was commissioned for the owner of the Joseph Smith papyri; see below.

translated into English. Broken sections are indicated by brackets []; all proper names are italicized.[4]

> (Column 1:) [...] the god's [father] and prophet of Amon-Re, king of the gods, prophet of Min who massacres his enemies, [prophet] of Khonsu who governs [in Thebes]
>
> (Column 2:) [...] *Horos,* true of voice, son of the priest of the same rank, the keeper of secrets and purifier of the god *Osoroeris,* true of voice, born to [the mistress of the house, the sistrum-player of]
>
> (Column 3:) [Amon-Re] *Chibois,* may she live.

Thus the Joseph Smith papyri were originally written for a certain individual named Horos, who was the son of Osoroeris and Chibois. According to his titles, Horos held the office of "prophet" or "god's servant" in the cults of the Egyptian deities Amon-Re, Min, and Khonsu in Thebes, the religious capital of ancient Egypt some 600 kilometers (370 miles) south of modern Cairo. In the cult of Amon-Re, the latter priestly function is usually combined with the office of "god's father." Horos's father, Osoroeris, is introduced as a "priest of the same rank." This implies that Osoroeris held all of his son Horos's offices in addition to the functions of "keeper of secrets and purifier of the god," which are listed separately.[5] Chibois, Horos's mother, also served in the cult of Amon-Re. She provided musical accompaniment in the cult setting by shaking a sistrum, or musical rattle.

Research into the family of the original owner of this Document of Breathing in other—preferably dated or datable—sources is the only way to date this papyrus precisely. For a long time, a misreading of one of Horos's priestly functions prevented his identification as a member of a Theban family. In his own reading of the Smith papyri, Egyptologist Klaus Baer misread one of the owner's titles as "prophet of Min, Bull-of-his-Mother," whereas the writing on the papyrus clearly shows that the divine name is "Min who massacres his enemies."[6] Because of this corrected reading,

[4] Throughout this essay, I use the Greek form of Egyptian proper names, if known, as it reflects the pronunciation better than the conventional Egyptological format.

[5] Robert K. Ritner, "'The Breathing Permit of Hôr' among the Joseph Smith Papyri," *Journal of Near Eastern Studies* 62 (2003): 168n45.

[6] Klaus Baer, "The Breathing Permit of Hôr: A Translation of the Apparent Source of

Horos is now identified as a member of an important Theban priestly family that flourished during the second and first centuries B.C.E., as will be shown later in this essay.[7]

ANOTHER FUNERARY PAPYRUS BELONGING TO HOROS

In Ptolemaic Thebes, a well-to-do Egyptian could be buried with various funerary papyri in order to ensure a life in the hereafter free of care. Horos, the original owner of the Joseph Smith papyri, had at least one other funerary composition at his disposal in the underworld, for in 1998 his abbreviated copy of the Book of the Dead surfaced in Paris, France.[8]

Several parts of Horos's badly damaged copy of the Book of the Dead are kept in the Louvre Museum under the inventory numbers N 3207, N 3208, and N 3209. The papyrus is inscribed with the spells (or chapters) 5–8, 13, 15, 17–19, 28, 30, 77, 83, 89, 125, and (possibly) 164 from the Book of the Dead in hieratic and decorated with vignettes painted black and red. The manuscript as a whole is about 148 centimeters (58 inches) long; the height varies between 31.5 and 33.5 centimeters (12½ and 13 inches).

Of the three major sections of this Book of the Dead, only N 3207 is included in Théodule Devéria's important catalogue of the Louvre papyri,

---

the Book of Abraham," *Dialogue: A Journal of Mormon Thought* 3 (1968), 3:126. The correct reading was first published by Marc Coenen and Jan Quaegebeur, *De papyrus Denon of het Boek van het Ademen van Isis,* Monografieën van het Museum van het Boek 5 (Leuven: Uitgeverij Peeters, 1995), 62; and extensively discussed in Marc Coenen, "The Dating of the Papyri Joseph Smith I, X and XI and Min who Massacres his Enemies," *Egyptian Religion: The Last Thousand Years. Studies Dedicated to the Memory of J. Quaegebeur, Part II, Orientalia Lovaniensia Analecta* 85, ed. W. Clarysse e.a. (Leuven: Uitgeverij Peeters en Departement Oosterse Studies, 1998), 1103–14.

[7] The findings regarding this priestly family were first presented in the following publications: Coenen, "Dating of the Papyri Joseph Smith," 1103–14; Marc Coenen, "Horos, Prophet of Min who Massacres His Enemies," *Chronique d'Egypte* 74 (1999): 257–60; Marc Coenen, "The Funerary Papyri of the Bodleian Library at Oxford," *Journal of Egyptian Archaeology* 86 (2000): 87–94; Marc Coenen, "On the Demise of the Book of the Dead in Ptolemaic Thebes," *Revue d'Egyptologie* 52 (2001): 69–84; and Marc Coenen, "The Funerary Papyri of Horos Son of Estneteretten in the Kunsthistorisches Museum in Vienna," *Zeitschrift für ägyptische Sprache und Altertumskunde* 130 (2003): 160–69. The survey presented here draws on these earlier studies. These publications also contain additional bibliographical references on the various items highlighted here.

[8] See Coenen, "Horos, Prophet of Min," 257–60.

published posthumously in 1881.[9] The facsimile accompanying Devéria's description identifies the owner as Horos son of Osoroeris and Chibois. The father bears no title, but the name of the mother is preceded by the titles "mistress of the house and sistrum-player of Amon-Re."

The biographical information for the owner in Devéria's catalogue can be extended considerably, as more titles are ascribed to Horos in N 3209 than in N 3207, the section consulted by Devéria. On the right end of N 3209, an incomplete hieroglyphic column of text running the complete height of the manuscript is preserved. The text here ascribes the titles "god's father and prophet of Amon-Re, king of the gods, prophet of Min who massacres his enemies, prophet of Khonsu [who governs in Thebes]" to the owner of the papyrus.

On the basis of the exceptional title "prophet of Min who massacres his enemies" and the identical descent, the owner of the Book of the Dead Papyrus Louvre N 3207, N 3208, and N 3209 can now be identified with certainty as the same priest for whom the Joseph Smith papyri were originally made. As a result of the identification established here, a Book of the Dead and a Document of Breathing Made by Isis can be ascribed to the same Theban priest, Horos.

A PRIESTLY FAMILY OF PROPHETS

Now we will focus on the extended family of Horos, the original owner of PJS I, X, and XI and the above-mentioned Louvre Book of the Dead. Genealogical research in Theban funerary papyri brings to light a priestly family whose ancestors served for several generations as prophet(s) in the cult of "Min who massacres his enemies."

The family tree in Figure 1 is based on the thirteen sources listed below, which provide a considerable amount of genealogical data on the priestly family in question. In order to allow readers to verify the validity of the reconstructed family tree and the identifications, all relevant genealogical data contained in these sources are given in translation in the appendix to this essay. In both the family tree and appendix, the letters represent the following sources:

[9] Théodule Devéria, *Catalogue des manuscrits égyptiens écrits sur papyrus, toile, tablettes et ostraca en caractères hiéroglyphiques, hiératiques, démotique, grecs, coptes, arabes et latins, qui sont conservés au Musée égyptien du Louvre* (Paris: Charles de Mourgues Frères, 1881), 70–71 (III, 23). Devéria also commented on Joseph Smith's facsimiles. See Marquardt's essay in this volume.

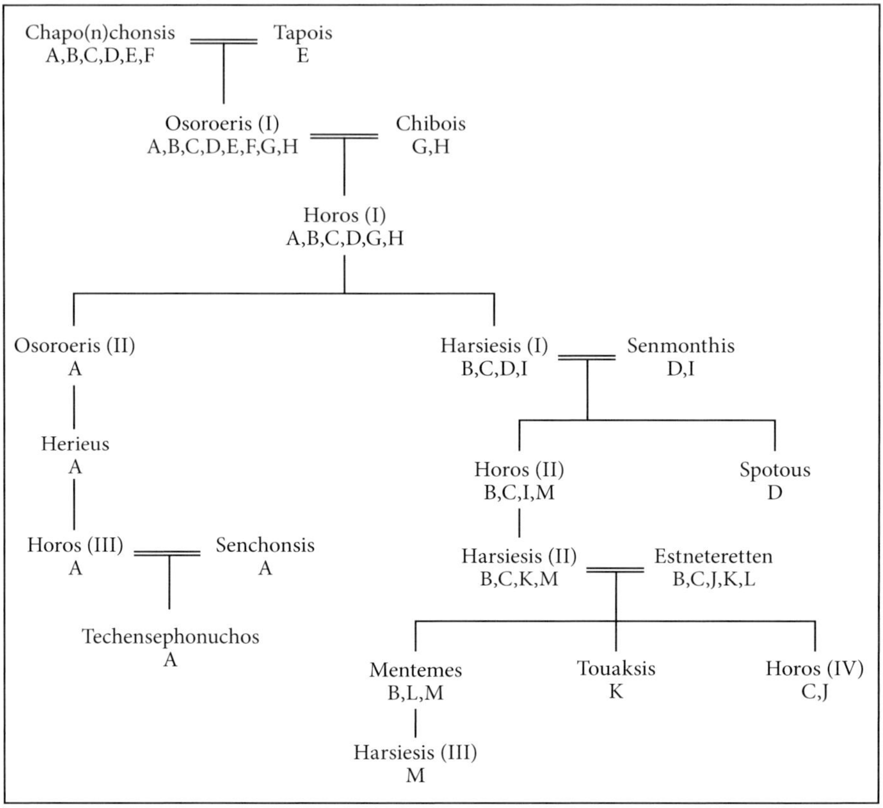

Figure 1. A Family Tree of Prophets of Min Who Massacres His Enemies

A. Papyrus Tübingen 2016 ("Document of Breathing Made by Isis")
B. Papyrus Tübingen 2012 ("Book of the Dead")
C. Papyrus Vienna 3861 ("Book of the Dead")
D. Bodleian Library Ms. Egypt.c.2 ("Document of Breathing Made by Isis")
E. Papyrus Bibliotheca Bodmeriana 104 ("Book of the Dead")
F. Statue Baltimore Walters Art Museum 227
G. Papyri Joseph Smith I, X, and XI ("Document of Breathing Made by Isis")
H. Papyrus Louvre N 3207, N 3208, and N 3209 ("Book of the Dead")
I. Papyrus Vienna 3863 ("Document of Breathing Made by Isis")
J. Papyrus Vienna 10158 ("Document of Breathing Made by Isis")
K. Papyrus Louvre N 3167 and N 3222 ("Document of Breathing Made by Isis")
L. Mummy wrapping Turin 1873
M. Graffito Medinat Habu 229

After all the genealogical information provided by these sources has been assembled, it becomes clear that the persons whom they mention all descend from the same ancestor. Thus we are dealing with one family who from the fourth generation onward began to separate into different branches. Their family tree is set out above in figure 1.

Little doubt may be cast on the historical accuracy of the family tree outlined above, for Osoroeris (I) son of Chapo(n)chonsis of Papyrus Tübingen 2016 shares in common several titles with his namesake in Papyrus Tübingen 2012, Papyrus Vienna 3861, Bodleian Library Ms. Egypt.c.2, and Papyrus Bibliotheca Bodmeriana 104. Conspicuously, most of them include the rare priestly title "prophet of Min who massacres his enemies." Only in Papyrus Vienna 3861 this function is not ascribed to Osoroeris (I). The various other titles which this Vienna Osoroeris shares with his namesake in the other sources (for example, the office of "most unique one who is together with the king of the gods in his dwelling place"), as well as the identical descent and/or offspring, remove all doubt. All of these sources refer to the same priest, who on the basis of the number of titles assigned to him, is easily identified as the most important member of this family. It is clearly their family link to Osoroeris (I) that his descendants of the third and fifth generations stress in their own respective funerary papyri.

Although Horos and Osoroeris are relatively common proper names in Greco-Roman Thebes, the original owner of the Joseph Smith papyri and the Louvre Book of the Dead N 3207, N 3208, and N 3209 is, in my opinion, a member of the above priestly family. The Osoroeris of the Smith papyri is the similarly named son of Chapo(n)chonsis in Papyri Tübingen 2012 and 2016, Papyrus Vienna 3861, Bodleian Library Ms. Egypt.c.2, and Papyrus Bibliotheca Bodmeriana 104 based on the priestly titles ascribed to him in these documents. According to PJS I, this Osoroeris bore the following five titles: "god's father and prophet of Amon-Re, king of the gods, prophet of Min who massacres his enemies, prophet of Khonsu who governs in Thebes, keeper of secrets and purifier of the god," as he has the same rank as his son Horos. These same titles are ascribed to Osoroeris (I) son of Chapo(n)chonsis in Bodleian Library Ms. Egypt.c.2 and in Papyrus Bibliotheca Bodmeriana 104. In Papyrus Tübingen 2016, Osoroeris (I) has also been allotted these five priestly functions albeit indirectly, for he is said to have the same rank as the owner, Techensephonuchos. Only in Papyrus Tübingen 2012 is the office "prophet of Khonsu who governs in Thebes" not assigned to Osoroeris (I). And in Papyrus Vienna 3861, finally, only "prophet of Amon-Re, king of the gods" and "prophet of Khonsu who governs in Thebes" are indirectly attributed to Osoroeris (I), because he has the same rank as the owner (of Papyrus Vienna 3861), Horos (IV).

Let us now focus on Horos (I), owner of the Joseph Smith papyri and Louvre Book of the Dead N 3207, N 3208, and N 3209. He clearly occupied positions of less importance than his father, Osoroeris (I). He served as "prophet" in the Theban cults of Amon-Re and Khonsu who governs in Thebes. Only in his own funerary papyri[10] does he bear the conspicuous title "prophet of Min who massacres his enemies," while most of the other papyri[11] ascribe that function to his father, Osoroeris (I). And in none of the six papyri in which Horos is mentioned are the functions "keeper of secrets" and "purifier of the god"—also held by his father, Osoroeris—allotted to him. On the other hand, Bodleian Library Ms. Egypt.c.2 and Papyrus Tübingen 2016 assign to Horos (I) the office of "the two feet of the fore of Amun," which is absent in his own funerary papyri. However, these minor problems do not adversely impact the proposed identifications.

DATING THE JOSEPH SMITH PAPYRI

Now that we have reconstructed a portion of the extended family to which belonged the original owner of the Joseph Smith papyri and the Louvre Book of the Dead N 3207, N 3208, and N 3209, we can focus on dating the papyri themselves. The extended family tree above shows three generations separating Techensephonuchos, Mentemes, Touaksis, and Horos (IV) on the one side and Horos (I) of the Smith papyri and Louvre Book of the Dead on the other. If we count twenty to twenty-five years for one generation, some seventy years separate Horos (I) from his great grandchildren's children. Mentemes and Horos (IV) both relied upon a copy of the the Book of the Dead for their afterlife. Currently, no examples of the Book of the Dead can be dated with certainty to the Roman period. The most recent copies seem to be late Ptolemaic. Thus the latest possible dating for Mentemes's and Horos's (IV) Book of the Dead[12] is circa 50 B.C.E. Given the fact that the Smith papyri and Louvre Book of the Dead papyri are at least a century older, these papyri must have been written during the first half of the Ptolemaic Period. The latest possible dating for the Papyri

[10] These are the Joseph Smith papyri and Papyrus Louvre N 3207, N 3208, and N 3209.

[11] That is, Papyri Tübingen 2012 and 2016, Bodleian Library Ms. Egypt.c.2, and Papyrus Bibliotheca Bodmeriana 104.

[12] That is, Papyrus Tübingen 2012 and Papyrus Vienna 3861, respectively.

Smith I, X, and XI is, in my opinion, the first half of the second century B.C.E., but the text itself may be slightly older. Thus, the Smith papyri are currently the oldest known datable copy of the Document of Breathing Made by Isis.

A more definitive dating of precisely when this priestly family serving in the cult of Min who massacres his enemies flourished is still lacking. Nevertheless, several observations may be made to corroborate the dating asserted here. In the demotic graffito Medinat Habu 229, a priest is mentioned who is probably a member of this same priestly family. The graffito is written on the eastern wall of room S of the small temple of Medinat Habu, located at the foot of the western cliffs at the southern end of the Theban necropolis. Line 3 commemorates the entry into service of the "god's father and prophet of Amon-Re, king of the gods, Harsiesis, son of Mentemes, son of Har[siesis], son of Horos" (see Appendix, Source M).[13] The antecedents of this Harsiesis coincide with those of the owner of Papyrus Tübingen 2012. As the proper name Mentemes was not very common in Ptolemaic Thebes, his son Harsiesis can now be added to the same priestly family under study.

We would be able to date absolutely the entire family if line 1 with the date of the graffito were still legible. Luckily, there is another way of dating the inscription. The graffito is located in room S of the small temple of Medinat Habu. Excavations conducted by the Oriental Institute of the University of Chicago in the years 1924–33 reveal that the temple had been restored and expanded well into the Roman Period. The northern and southern wings—rooms R and S, respectively—were added in the time of Ptolemy X Alexander I (101–88 B.C.E.).[14] As a graffito cannot appear on a wall before the wall has been constructed, the beginning of the first century B.C.E. is necessarily a *terminus post quem* for the graffito. Seven graffiti are inscribed on the eastern wall of room S, but none can be dated. In order to find a reasonable date for our graffito, we turn to room R, where there is a cluster of eight dated graffiti. All these graffiti were written during the first century B.C.E.—more precisely, between the years

[13] H. J. Thissen, "Die demotischen Graffiti von Medinet Habu," *Demotische Studien* 10 (Sommerhausen: Gisela Zauzich Verlag, 1989), 138–39.

[14] U. Hölscher, *The Temples of the Eighteenth Dynasty,* The Excavation of Medinet Habu II, Oriental Institute Publications 41 (Chicago: University of Chicago Press, 1939), 214.

77 and 37 B.C.E.[15] Room R was constructed at the same time as room S, in which graffito 229 is located. Assuming that graffiti began to appear at around the same time in both rooms, graffito Medinat Habu 229 most probably dates to the early second half of the first century B.C.E. This dating falls well within the range of what we expect on the basis of the genealogical research conducted on the family of which Harsiesis son of Mentemes was a member. From the family tree set out above, we deduce that this son of Mentemes belonged to the generation that flourished between 50 and 25 B.C.E.

Statue Baltimore Walters Art Museum 227 also argues in favor of dating the Joseph Smith papyri to the first half of the second century B.C.E. Only the upper part of this male figure in black granite has been preserved.[16] Notwithstanding the broken-off arms, an inscription in two vertical columns on the back pillar contains several titles and interesting genealogical information (see Appendix, Source F). The statue appears to depict Osoroeris (I) son of Chapo(n)chonsis, the ancestor of the priestly family in question. As in Papyrus Bibliotheca Bodmeriana 104, Osoroeris (I) here has been allotted the rare priestly function of "prophet of Min who massacres his enemies." B. V. Bothmer and H. De Meulenaere, both of whom specialized in Late Period sculpture, date this statue on stylistic grounds to about 200 B.C.E., and in De Meulenaere's opinion, it cannot be reasonably dated much later or much earlier.[17] This dating accords well with our own dating of the Smith papyri.

The information currently available on Min who massacres his enemies comprises the final argument in support of our dating of the Joseph Smith papyri. This belligerent form of the fertility deity Min is mentioned in combination with the Canaanite war god "Reshef who dwells in the house of Montu" on the Bab el-Abd in a listing of gods who love Ptolemy III. The Bab el-Abd is the propylon (i.e., gateway) in the north section of the precinct of the Theban war god Montu in Karnak, Egypt. Construction on this monumental gate started under Ptolemy III Euergetes I (246–221 B.C.E.) and was completed under his successor, Ptolemy IV Philopator (221–205 B.C.E.). This propylon contains the only known reliefs of this particular form of Min. The scenes in which he features are situated on

---

[15] Thissen, 57.

[16] A photograph is published in G. Steindorff, *Catalogue of the Egyptian Sculpture in the Walters Art Gallery* (Baltimore: Walters Art Gallery, 1946), 70, plates 39 and 118.

[17] Information provided by H. De Meulenaere (letter dated August 19, 1996).

the highest portion of the gate doorway, opposite to each other.[18] In the relief on the outside of the western wall, Ptolemy III is shown binding the arm of a prostrate captive behind his back in front of "Min who massacres his enemies, Reshef who dwells in the house of Montu." In this scene, Min is not depicted in his usual ithyphallic form (that is, with an erect penis) but appears in the striding pose typical of the war god Reshef. In the corresponding scene on the outside of the eastern wall, the pharaoh stabs two prisoners kneeling in a metal kettle with their arms tied behind their backs in front of "Min who massacres his enemies." Here Min is portrayed in usual ithyphallic form. Note how the period when these reliefs were carved coincides with the floruit of Chapo(n)chonsis, the founding father of a dynasty of priests who over three generations held the office of "prophet" in the cult of Min who massacres his enemies.

AN UNIDENTIFIED FAMILY VAULT?

In the present discussion, ten funerary papyri—including six copies of the Document of Breathing Made by Isis and four of the Book of the Dead—and one mummy wrapping have been ascribed to the priestly family in question. Funerary papyri and mummy wrappings are part of the standard burial equipment belonging to the better-off Egyptian in Greco-Roman Thebes. Given the impressive number of papyri preserved for this priestly family, one wonders if they might have a common provenance and originate from a family vault, which at some time during the early nineteenth century was discovered only to have its contents plundered and scattered all over the world. In this final section, the provenance and modern history of the various papyri listed above (and in the appendix) are surveyed to discover if they share a common origin.

The provenance for Ms. Egypt.c.2 in the Bodleian Library in Oxford, England (Source D), is unfortunately not recorded in the library files. Neither is there much information on the origin of the papyri housed in the Louvre Museum in Paris, but the letter N in the inventory numbering system indicates that our Sources H and K were catalogued some time between 1852 and 1857.[19]

---

[18] S. H. Aufrère, "Le propylône d'Amon-Rê-Montou à Karnak-Nord," *Mémoires publiés par les Membres de l'Institut Français d'Archéologie Orientale du Caire* 117 (Cairo: Institut Français d'Archéologie Orientale, 2000), 293–98, §210 (10th register), plate 16a, and 271–83, § 203, plate 15a, respectively.

[19] P. Kriéger, "Note concernant les numéros d'inventaire des objets conservés au

For the Tübingen papyri, the information is also meager. Sources A and B were once kept in the Lindenmuseum in Stuttgart, whose collection was acquired by the University of Tübingen in 1964. Most antiquities in the Lindenmuseum came from private collectors living in the Württemberg area who acquired their objects during stays in Egypt between 1900 and the outbreak of World War I.[20]

Little is also known of the origin of the Papyri Vienna 3861, 3863, and 10158. Like most papyri in the Kunsthistorisches Museum, they may have been among the numerous Egyptian antiquities which Dr. E. A. Burghart bought in Egypt in 1821 in behalf of the Austrian Emperor Francis I. Burghart neither excavated nor collected antiquities himself during his stay in Egypt, but obtained the objects from G. di Nizzoli, Chancellor of the Austrian Consulate in Egypt. Like others of his diplomatic colleagues, di Nizzoli built up impressive collections of antiquities only to sell them later to the highest bidder.[21] On several occasions, di Nizzoli acquired antiquities from various excavators, including, notably, Giovanni Pietro Antonio Lebolo,[22] an Italian excavator and adventurer from Piedmont who had been employed in Egypt by the French Consul General Bernardino Drovetti.

The first modern owner of Papyrus Bibliotheca Bodmeriana 104, which subsequently passed through the hands of a considerable number of private collectors, was M. le Chevalier M.[23] This was probably the pseudonym of V. Maunier, a French dealer in antiquities who from 1840 until 1875 acted as consular agent for France in Luxor, Egypt.

Départment des antiquités égyptiennes du Musée du Louvre," *Revue d'Egyptologie* 12 (1960): 94–96.

[20] E. Brunner-Traut and H. Brunner, *Die ägyptische Sammlung der Universität Tübingen* (Mainz am Rhein: Verlag Philipp von Zabern, 1981), 4–5.

[21] H. Satzinger, "Das Kunsthistorische Museum in Wien, Die Ägyptisch-Orientalische Sammlung," *Zaberns Bildbände zur Archaölogie* 14 (Mainz am Rhein: Verlag Philipp von Zabern, 1994): 18 and 26.

[22] W. R. Dawson, E. P. Uphill, and M. L. Bierbrier, *Who Was Who in Egyptology,* 3rd ed. (London: Egypt Exploration Society, 1995), 241.

[23] M. Valloggia, "Les manuscrits hiératiques et hiéroglyphiques de la Bibliotheca Bodmeriana," *Sortir au jour. Art égyptien de la Fondation Martin Bodmer,* Cahiers de la Société d'Egyptologie, Genève 7, eds. J. L. Chappaz and S. Vuilleumier (Geneva: Société d'Egyptologie; Genève: Musées d'art et d'histoire de la Ville de Genève; et Munich: K. G. Saur Verlag, 2001), 139–40.

Fortunately, more information is available on the origins of the Joseph Smith papyri. Prior to their acquisition by Smith in July 1835, a description of the mummies with which the papyri were associated was published in a Painesville, Ohio, newspaper on March 27, 1835. It contains the following information on the tomb in which the mummies were discovered:

> They [i.e., the mummies] were found in June, 1832 [*sic*, actually 1817–22]—three miles from Thebes, 236 feet deep in a catecomb [*sic*] or vault 94 by 18 feet in the clear ... Some of the bodies stood in nitches [*sic*] of the wall; a row of bodies, however, laid on the bottom 8 feet deep (reversed,) more or less decayed.[24]

In July 1835, Michael Chandler exhibited four of these mummies in Kirtland, Ohio, home to Smith and the church he had founded five years earlier. With the financial assistance of some of his followers, Smith acquired Chandler's antiquities. The official history of Smith's church contains the following account of the origin of the mummies and papyri (historical errors are signaled by "[*sic*]"):

> The records [i.e., papyri] were obtained from one of the catacombs in Egypt, near the place where once stood the renowned city of Thebes, by the celebrated French traveler, Antonio Sebolo [*sic*, Lebolo], in the year 1831 [*sic*, 1817–22]. He procured license from Mehemet Ali, then Viceroy of Egypt, under the protection of chevalier Drovetti, the French Consul, in the year 1828 [*sic*], ... He entered the catacomb June 7, 1831 [*sic*], and obtained eleven mummies. There were several hundred mummies in the same catacomb; about one hundred embalmed after the first order, and placed in niches, and two or there hundred after the second and third orders, and laid upon the floor or bottom of the grand cavity. The two last orders of embalmed were so decayed, that they could not be removed, and only eleven of the first, found in niches. On his way from Alexandria to Paris, he put in at Trieste, and, after ten day's illness, expired. This was in the year 1832 [*sic*, 1830]. Previous to his decease, he made a will of the whole, to Mr. Michael H. Chandler, (then in Philadelphia, Pa.,) his nephew [*sic*, no known relation], whom he supposed to be

[24] Quoted in John A. Larson, "Joseph Smith and Egyptology: An Early Episode in the History of American Speculation about Ancient Egypt, 1835–1844," in David P. Silverman, ed., *For His Ka: Essays Offered in Memory of Klaus Baer* (Chicago: Oriental Institute of the University of Chicago, 1994), 161–62.

> in Ireland. Accordingly, the whole were sent to Dublin [*sic*], and Mr. Chandler's friends ordered them to New York, where they were received at the Custom House, in the winter or spring of 1833. In April, of the same year, Mr. Chandler paid the duties and took possession of his mummies.[25]

The different orders of mummification are the three methods of embalming described by Classical writers Herodotus and Diodorus Siculus. Note that both of the above accounts make no mention whatsoever of coffins. This seems to date the burials to the Greco-Roman Period when many mummies were buried without coffins. The absence of other burial equipment is also noticeable.

IMPLICATIONS FOR THE "BOOK OF ABRAHAM"

The rediscovery in 1966 of the Smith papyri sparked an important discussion regarding this damaged scroll and its relationship to Smith's "Book of Abraham." Egyptologists have long concluded that Smith's "translation" does not correspond to the actual words on the papyri. As this essay has shown, the original owner of the Smith papyri, who like several of his relatives held position(s) of some importance in the cult of certain Egyptian deities, was buried with copies of the Book of the Dead and the Document of Breathing Made by Isis. Sometime during the years 1817–22, Antonio Lebolo set foot in this priest's tomb in Thebes. Subsequently, this priest's copy of the Book of the Dead made its way into the Louvre Museum, while his Document of Breathing ended up in the hands of Joseph Smith. Like the Book of the Dead, the Smith papyri are firmly rooted in the funerary customs of Ptolemaic Egypt.

Some writers have suggested that the actual text of the "Book of Abraham" was not inscribed on the fragments rediscovered in 1966, but on a portion of the papyrus scroll still missing. Unquestionably, PJS I, X, and XI were originally longer. A comparison with Papyrus Louvre N 3158, which contains the most complete version extant of the Document of Breathing Made by Isis, indicates that as many as three to four columns of hieratic text may be missing between the end of PJS X and the segment Smith identified as "Book of Abraham" Facsimile 3. The Louvre parallel shows that the content of the missing columns concerns

---

[25] Quoted in Larson, 167. See also the more accurate account in Marquardt, in this volume.

only the afterlife of the deceased and not the narrative found in Smith's "Book of Abraham." Finally, some writers have rightly pointed out that papyri from Greco-Roman Egypt are sometimes inscribed with more than one text. No one denies that other funerary and/or ritual compositions were sometimes appended to a Book of the Dead or other funerary compositions. However, concluding that a record of Abraham or any other text foreign to Ptolemaic Egyptian funerary and/or liturgical practice was once attached to the Smith papyri is an assertion not based upon widely accepted Egyptological analysis.

APPENDIX: THE SOURCES

In the following, all of the biographical and genealogical information in the sources is translated.[26] In the various genealogies, all proper names are italicized and broken sections are indicated by brackets [].

SOURCE A = PAPYRUS TÜBINGEN 2016[27]

> … the god's father and prophet of Amon-Re, king of the gods, prophet of Khonsu who governs in Thebes *Techensephonuchos,* true of voice, born to *Senchonsis,* true of voice, son of the priest of the same rank, keeper of secrets and purifier of the god *Horos,* true of voice, son of *Herieus,* true of voice, son of the priest of the same rank, keeper of secrets and purifier of the god *Osoroeris,* true of voice, son of the priest of the same rank, the two feet of the fore of Amun *Horos,* true of voice, son of the priest of the same rank, prophet of Min who massacres his enemies, keeper of secrets, purifier of the god, great primate in Thebes, overseer of the prophets in the Eye of Re (= Thebes), he who enters the horizon and sees what is in it, he who sees the great god […] and the most unique one who is together with the king of the gods […] *Osoroeris,* true of voice, son of *Chapochonsis,* true of voice

SOURCE B = PAPYRUS TÜBINGEN 2012[28]

> … the god's father and prophet of Amon-Re, king of the gods, *Mentemes,* son of the priest of the same rank *Harsiesis,* son of the priest of the same rank, keeper of secrets, purifier of the god, stolist[29] of Khonsu and Osiris of Ipet-weret *Horos,* son of the priest of the same rank *Harsiesis,* son of the priest of the same rank *Horos,* son of the priest of the same rank, keeper of secrets, purifier of the god, great primate [in Thebes], he who opens the doors of heaven in Karnak, he who enters the horizon and sees what is in it, he who decorates the great god with his ornaments, prophet of Min who

[26] The various sources translated here are presented in greater detail, and with numerous bibliographical references, in the studies listed in note 7.

[27] Photograph in Brunner-Traut and Brunner, plates 12–13; transliteration and comment in Coenen, "Dating of the Papyri Joseph Smith," 1104–1106.

[28] Photograph in Brunner-Traut and Brunner, plates 151–52; transliteration and comment in Coenen, "Dating of the Papyri Joseph Smith," 1106–1107.

[29] That is, the priest who clothes, cleanses, and anoints the cult statues of the gods.

massacres his enemies *Osoroeris*, son of the priest of the same rank *Chaponchonsis*

According to Papyrus Tübingen 2012, I, 3–4, Mentemes's mother was the "mistress of the house and the sistrum-player of Amon-Re *Estneteretten*."

SOURCE C = PAPYRUS VIENNA 3861[30]

... the god's father and prophet [of Amon]-Re, king of the gods, servant of the gods, prophet of Khon[su who governs in Thebes, the great god] who repels the wanderers, prophet of Mut, mistress of beautiful women, *Horos*, true of voice, son of the priest of the same rank [*Harsiesis*], by [Osiris], son of the priest of the same rank, keeper of secrets, purifier of the god, sto[list of Khonsu-in]-Thebes-Neferhotep, and of Osiris-Onnophris, king of the gods, sovereign in Ipet-weret, scribe of the place [...] *Horos*, lord of [honor], son of the priest of the same rank *Harsiesis*, by the [one greatly praised, son of the priest of the same rank] *Horos*, true of voice, son of the priest of the same rank, great primate, overseer of the prophets in Thebes, the most unique one who is together with the king of the [gods, the one cove]red of belly and secret of throat who does not disclose what he has seen [*Osoroeris*, by those who re]st, son of the priest of the same rank *Chaponchonsis*, and made by the mistress of the house and sistrum-player of Amon-Re *Estneteret*[*ten*, true of voice]

SOURCE D = BODLEIAN LIBRARY MS. EGYPT.C.2[31]

... the god's father and prophet of Amon-Re, king of the gods, great scholar in Thebes, deft of fingers of the domain of Amon-Re, king of the gods, overseer of the priests of Sekhmet in Hermonthis *Spotous*, son of the god's father and prophet of Amon-Re, king of the gods, prophet of Khonsu who governs in Thebes, keeper of secrets, purifier of the god of the domain of Osiris-Onnophris, may he live, *Harsiesis*, true of voice, son of the god's father and prophet of Amon-Re, king of the gods, prophet of Khonsu who governs in Thebes, the two feet of the fore of Amun *Horos*, son of the god's father and prophet

[30] Transliteration, comment, and photograph in Coenen, "Funerary Papyri of Horos Son of Estneteretten," 160–64, and plates 37–38.

[31] Transliteration, comment, and photographs in Coenen, "Funerary Papyri of the Bodleian Library," 87–93 and plates 12–15.

of Amon-Re, king of the gods, prophet of Khonsu who governs in Thebes, prophet of Min who massacres his enemies, keeper of secrets, purifier of the god in Thebes, the victorious, he who opens the doors of heaven in Karnak, the most unique one who is together with the king of the gods in (his) dwelling place *Osoroeris,* son of the priest of the same rank *Chapochonsis*

According to Bodleian Library Ms. Egypt.c.2, V, 10, Spotous's mother was named "*Senmonthis.*"

SOURCE E = PAPYRUS BIBLIOTHECA BODMERIANA 104[32]

… the god's father and [prophet of] Amon-Re, king of the gods, keeper of secrets, purifier of the god, he who enters the horizon and sees what is in it, prophet of Khonsu who governs in Thebes, prophet of Min who massacres his enemies *Osoroeris,* true of voice, son of the god's father and [prophet] of Amon-<Re>, king of the gods, prophet of Min who massacres his enemies *Chaponchonsis,* true of voice, and made by the mistress of the house and sistrum-player of Amon-Re *Tapois,* true of voice

SOURCE F = STATUE BALTIMORE WALTERS ART MUSEUM 227[33]

… the god's father and prophet of Amon-Re, king of the gods, prophet of Min who massacres his enemies, prophet of Khonsu who governs in [Thebes …] *Osoroeris* son of *Chapochonsis*

SOURCE G = PJS I, X, AND XI[34]

… the god's [father] and prophet of Amon-Re, king of the gods, prophet of Min who massacres his enemies, [prophet] of Khonsu who governs [in Thebes …] *Horos,* true of voice, son of the priest of the same rank, the keeper of secrets and purifier of the god *Osoroeris,* true of voice, born to [the mistress of the house and the sistrum-player of Amon-Re] *Chibois,* may she live

[32] Transliteration and comment in Coenen, "On the Demise," 72–77.

[33] Transliteration and comment in Coenen, "Dating of the Papyri Joseph Smith," 1111.

[34] See the references in notes 5 and 6.

SOURCE H = PAPYRUS LOUVRE N 3207, N 3208, AND N 3209[35]

> ... the god's father and prophet of Amon-Re, king of the gods, prophet of Min who massacres his enemies, prophet of Khonsu [who governs in Thebes ... *Horos*]

Elsewhere in the papyrus the parents of Horos are identified as "*Osoroeris*" and the "mistress of the house and the sistrum-player of Amon-Re *Chibois.*"

SOURCE I = PAPYRUS VIENNA 3863[36]

> ... the god's father and prophet of Amon-Re, king of the gods, keeper of secrets, purifier of the god and prophet of Khonsu who governs in Thebes *Horos,* son of the priest of the same rank *Harsiesis,* and the name of his mother is *Senmonthis*

SOURCE J = PAPYRUS VIENNA 10158[37]

> ... *Horos,* born to *Estneteretten,* true of voice

SOURCE K = PAPYRUS LOUVRE N 3167 AND N 3222[38]

> ... the sistrum-player of Amon-Re *Touaksis,* true of voice, daughter of the god's father and prophet of Amon-Re, king of the gods, *Harsiesis,* true of voice, and born to *Estneteretten,* may she live

SOURCE L = MUMMY WRAPPING TURIN 1873[39]

> ... *Mentemes,* true of voice, born to *Estneteretten,* true of voice

SOURCE M = GRAFFITO MEDINAT HABU 229,3[40]

> ... the god's father and prophet of Amon-Re, king of the gods, *Harsiesis,* son of *Mentemes,* son of *Har*[*siesis*], son of *Horos*

---

[35] Transliteration and comment in Coenen, "Horos, Prophet of Min," 257–60.

[36] Transliteration and comment in Coenen, "Funerary Papyri of the Bodleian Library," 91–92.

[37] Transliteration and comment in Coenen, "Funerary Papyri of Horos Son of Estneteretten," 164–65.

[38] Comment in Coenen, "Dating of the Papyri Joseph Smith," 1107.

[39] See A. Fabretti, F. Rossi, and R. V. Lanzone, *Regio Museo di Turino, Antichità egizie* (Turin: Paravia, 1882), 238. Comment in Coenen, "Dating of the Papyri Joseph Smith," 1107.

[40] See note 13.

Christopher Woods

THE PRACTICE OF EGYPTIAN RELIGION AT "UR OF THE CHALDEES"?

One of the more remarkable claims encountered in the Book of Abraham is the attestation of Egyptian religious and cultic practices at Ur. The location of "Ur of the Chaldees"—biblical *Ur Kaśdim* (Genesis 11:28, 31; 15:7), the birthplace of Abraham—remains open for debate, although the current scholarly *communis opinio* identifies it with the major southern Babylonian city of Ur (Tell el-Muqayyar), which flourished in the third millennium and first centuries of the second millennium BC. Notably, the early second millennium is the likely date of the patriarchal age (McCarter 1999: 6–10). Objections to identifying biblical Ur with Babylonian Ur have been considered elsewhere (see Machinist apud Shanks 2000; Millard 2001), and so we need not belabor the point here. Suffice it to point out that the Hebrew qualification *Kaśdim*—Chaldeans—identifies Ur with southern Mesopotamia. The passages of Genesis that contain the term derive from the Priestly source of the Pentateuch written at a time when the designation was in widespread usage, during the period of the Neo-Babylonian—that is the Chaldean—kings (626–539 BC) (see Milliard 2001, 57 and Machinist apud Shanks 2000, 66). As such, the designation represents a specification contemporaneous with the writing of the text that the Ur in question is Babylonian Ur. The objection that Babylonian Ur is too

Christopher Woods is Associate Professor of Sumerology in the Oriental Institute, Department of Near Eastern Languages and Civilizations, Program on the Ancient Mediterranean World in the Department of Classics, and in the College, University of Chicago. His research interests include Sumerian language and writing, as well as early Mesopotamian religion, literature, and history. He is the author of *The Grammar of Perspective: The Sumerian Conjugation Prefixes as a System of Grammatical Voice* (2008).

far from Haran, entailing a journey approximately one thousand miles, is countered by the fact that cuneiform documents of Old Babylonian date (c. 2000–1600 BC) detailing merchant activities describe journeys of precisely this route and length. Further, it should not be overlooked that Ur and Haran share important religious, cultural, and historical bonds as major centers for the worship of the Mesopotamian moon god Sin, a fact conspicuously evident for the reign of Nabonidus (556–539 BC).

If we are correct in identifying Abraham's Ur with Babylonian Ur, this poses grave difficulties for the account given in the Book of Abraham, as there is no evidence whatsoever for the cults of the purported Egyptian gods described in the narrative or for established Egyptian religious practices more generally in the city. Of this we can be sure based on the thousands of cuneiform records that concern Ur and excavations of the city conducted by Sir Leonard Woolley between 1922–1934 and, moreover, on everything we know of the history, culture, and religions of the ancient Near East. If we assume a northern location for Abraham's Ur—as was assumed by scholars prior to Rawlinson's identification of Tell el-Muqayyar in 1855 (and so thirteen years after the appearance of the Book of Abraham in print) and as more recently advocated by Cyrus Gordon (Gordon 1958, 1963, 1977; Gordon as cited in Shanks 2000)—the prospects hardly improve. Cuneiform sources attest a number of settlements bearing the name Ur (or a name phonetically similar) in northern Syria, southeastern Turkey, and northern Mesopotamia, mostly small villages, and so making for unlikely candidates for biblical Ur (see Millard 2000, 52–53). Several of these—Ura, Uraʾu, Uram, Uriʾum, Urru, and Uru (Bonechi 1993, 310–14)—are encountered in the Ebla archives dating from the mid-third millennium. And while fragments of Egyptian vessels and other items found at Ebla attest to commercial and trade contacts (note that Ebla lay on the trade route that brought lapis lazuli from Afghanistan to Egypt—see Matthews and Roemer 2003, 7–8), these artifacts cannot be marshaled as evidence for the presence of established Egyptian cults in the Syrian city or its environs. Eblaite administrative, literary, lexical, legal, and religious texts (totaling roughly 20,000 tablets), as well as personal names and toponyms, provide ample evidence for the worship of familiar northern Syrian gods, and some Sumero-Babylonian and regional gods, but, to my knowledge, of no Egyptian gods (see Pomponio and Xella 1997). Similarly, at Haran—which figures prominently in Abraham's journey and in the vicinity of which Ur has been sought—virtually all of the evidence for the practice of religion prior to the Persian conquest involves the worship of the moon god Sin

(Tamara Green 1992, 22). There is no evidence for the regular worship of Egyptian gods at Haran or, for that matter, at any other location in northern Mesopotamia. An Old Babylonian copy of an inscription of the Sargonic ruler Naram-Sin (c. 2190–2154 BC) mentions a place named Ulishem (*U_2-li-śi-im*^{ki} [Ur Excavation Texts 1, 275 ii 13; see Frayne 1993, 133]), which must have been roughly in the area of Ebla, west of the Euphrates and far west of Haran (see Edzard et al. 1977, 164). Certainly, Ulishim could be superficially linked on phonetic grounds to the Olishem mentioned in the Book of Abraham in connection with the location of "Ur of Chaldea," where Abraham's kin are said to have turned to the worship of Egyptian gods and Egyptian sacrificial rites. But a convincing identification would have to be based on much more substantial evidence. As stressed above, everything we know about the region during the period in question—not to mention the likely location of Biblical Ur in southern Mesopotamia—speaks strongly against it. That the phonetic similarity is accidental (and here it should be pointed out that cuneiform sources attest thousands of place names) is again suggested by its coupling to the place "Potiphar's Hill," which likewise is said to be in the land of Ur. Potiphar, of course, is the Egyptian official to whom Joseph is sold in Genesis (37:36; 39:1)—the name Potiphar is Egyptian in derivation ("He-whom-[the sun god]-Re-has-given") and has no place linguistically or culturally in the toponymy of southern or northern Mesopotamia. Finally, it must be observed that the identification of Ulishim with an Olishem alleged to be in the area of Ur makes little geographic sense within the context of Abraham's travels from Ur to Haran and subsequently to Canaan as described in Genesis and the Book of Abraham itself—for Ulishim no doubt lay west of Haran and so the latter could in no conceivable way be considered to be *en route* from Ulishim to Canaan, Haran being diametrically in the wrong direction.

THE JOSEPH SMITH EGYPTIAN PAPYRI:

PHOTOGRAPHS, TRANSLITERATIONS, TRANSLATIONS AND COMPARISONS

The following contribution represents the first complete textual edition of all the known Joseph Smith Egyptian papyri,[1] including the surviving ancient manuscripts themselves (Fragments I–XI), Joseph Smith's problematic nineteenth-century hand copies, and the yet more inexact woodcuts produced for the Book of Abraham and first published in the Mormon newspaper *Times and Seasons* (March 1842). Each of these sources presents its own special set of problems.

The surviving papyri are fragmentary and now glued to card backings that prevent examination of the verso and its fibers. Their deterioration almost certainly was hastened during their repeated handling by Joseph Smith and his associates,[2] but the disorder of the original materials is compounded by early attempts to "improve" the look of the broken sheets

---

In these editions I have followed the practice of T. G. Allen (1960) in providing transliteration and photographs of the texts, but not transcription from hieratic into hieroglyphs. For Egyptologists, transcription of hieratic should be unnecessary; for non-specialists, it is of little value.

[1] This edition does not include the hand copy of an Arabic text labeled as "Document H" by John Wilson (1968, pp. 68–69).

[2] See the introductory remarks on P. Joseph Smith 2. It is probable that the papyri were already in somewhat damaged condition prior to their purchase by Smith in July 1835; see Baer 1968, pp. 132–33. Wilson's statement (1968, p. 68) that the slicing and mounting of the papyri occurred prior to Smith's purchase is contradicted by the admissions of Nibley (1968, pp. 101–02) that the papyri were in "beautiful condition" when purchased and unrolled through two rooms of the Mansion House, and by the fact that they are now mounted on maps of former Mormon property in the Kirtland, Ohio, area, indicating "that the mounting took place only after the Kirtland period" (p. 101) under Mormon authority. Rhodes 2002, p. 3, also noted that P. Joseph Smith 1

by pasting detached fragments over holes in the text. Done haphazardly and with no competence in reading the ancient script, or in recognizing the handwriting of distinct manuscripts, lacunae spacings or even the direction of writing, this amateurish cosmetic makeover has mingled sections of Papyrus Joseph Smith 1 and 2, garbled much of the latter papyrus and even produced an artificial "sheet" composed only of randomly pasted patches and hand copies (Fragment IX). Baer's edition of Papyrus Joseph Smith 1 (followed by my own) noted these patches and employed a simple alphabetic system (P. JS IV a–d) to indicate those few that were originally part of that one text.[3] As the current edition includes as well the far more patchwork Papyrus Joseph Smith 2, this alphabetic system is inadequate, and a new, more inclusive numbering system has been devised. The numbered patches are indicated on five attached plates (nos. XXIV–XXVIII) in this volume. Baer named the patches as he discovered them, but the current system numbers them by their proper place of insertion, not their present, incorrect position.[4]

Identification of these misplaced patches has long been hindered by the LDS policy of denying scholarly access to the original papyri—in favor of apologists for church teachings.[5] As noted by Wilson following their peculiar removal from the legal stewardship of the Metropolitan Museum in 1968, "No Egyptologist is happy at studying either photographs or copies made by someone else. He wants to see the original. The present photographs are not particularly good: they are small scale and blurred around the margin. Further, although they pick up the black ink, they often fail completely on the red ink (the "rubrics")."[6] The first true, four-color separation images of most of the papyri appeared only in 1992,[7] and these facilitated my previous re-editions of P. Joseph Smith 1.

"was glued onto three sheets of paper between 1835 and 1837." See further Nibley 1975, pp. 2–3.

[3] Baer 1968, pp. 109–34, esp. 112–16.

[4] Unplaced patches are given numbers at the end of the list.

[5] See the introductory note in Ritner 2003a, p. 161. Though Baer was ultimately able to examine P. Smith 1 personally due to his friendship with Hugh Nibley (after completion of his translation, see Baer 1968, pp. 133–34), his published study was conducted primarily from *The Improvement Era* photos and was considered by himself to be nothing more than a "preliminary study" (Baer 1968, p. 111).

[6] Wilson 1968, p. 69.

[7] Charles M. Larson 1992, folded color plate = pp. 33–34. The complex history of the

The current volume now includes digital images of these primary papyri (with corrected alignment for P. Joseph Smith 2) and adds the first true color digital photographs of materials long retained, but restricted, by the LDS Church Historian's Office. These include the patchwork "Fragment IX," commonly designated the "Church Historian's Fragment," whose existence was first revealed in 1968.[8] Associated with this fragment in the Historian's Office Vault is the document now published as *Joseph Smith's Egyptian Alphabet and Grammar,* which comprises manuscripts of Smith's "Grammar and Alphabet of the Egyptian Language" and his "Valuable Discovery of hiden [*sic*] reccords [*sic*] that have been obtained from ancient buring [*sic*] place of the Egyptitiens [*sic*]," previously available only in black and white reproductions from Modern Microfilm Co.[9] These manuscripts are of particular importance for any modern restoration of the damaged and lost papyri, and color digital images are included from these sources as well. Subsequently re-designated the "Kirtland Egyptian Papers" by Nibley,[10] these sources are critical as well for understanding Smith's translation process, and they are discussed at length by H.

release of color images is clearly detailed in Jerald and Sandra Tanner 1992, pp. 1–2, *contra* the assertion of Gee 1992, pp. 93–94, who confused the sepia-toned 1968 photos disparaged by Wilson with true color photography.

[8] Green 1968 and, for its history, see Todd 1968, with sepia-toned photograph p. 40·H. As Todd notes (p. 40·A) in this formal LDS publication, assistant Church historians A. William Lund and Earl E. Olson "believe that the fragment has been a part of the manuscript of the Egyptian Alphabet and Grammar prepared by Joseph Smith preparatory to the translation of the Book of Abraham and that it has always been in the Church's hands."

[9] Tanner 1966. For Joseph Smith's authorship of these works, see the previous note and Ashment 2000, pp. 121–26. See further Wilson 1968, pp. 68 and 72, and note his reluctance to incorporate the hand copies "because I always want to see with my own eyes" (p. 73). For reasons of consistent reference, the current volume adopts the pagination of Tanner 1966 and Wilson 1968 in numbering the title page of "Valuable Discovery" as p. 1. It must be noted that in the Tanner publication, the "Valuable Discovery" appears twice and with differing pagination, with the 2 columns of Arabic material (not included in the current volume) grouped together as p. 10 (first example) or, copied separately, as pp. 10–11. Again, the current volume adopts the published pagination: "The tenth page contains two sheets reduced down. The writing has been identified as Arabic" (Tanner, unnumbered page). Cf. Wilson 1968, pp. 68–69 (Document H) in numbering the Arabic papyrus as p. 10 only. Page 11 is a hand copy of the hieroglyphic text and two hieratic signs from the "Breathing Permit of Hôr" (Papyrus Joseph Smith 1). Page 13 is the hypocephalus of Sheshonq.

[10] Nibley 1971.

Michael Marquardt in this volume.[11] Digital photographs were kindly provided by Gary James Bergera of the Smith-Pettit Foundation and Luke P. Wilson, the executive director of the Institute for Religious Research (IRR), and appear with their permission.[12] Although it would still be best to examine the original materials personally, the advent of digitized color photographs and photo-enhancing computer software has made it possible to examine the papyri (and hand copies) in remarkable detail, and the current publication includes many identifications previously unrecognized or wrongly explained. Moreover, this edition is the first to determine the proper alignment of all the surviving papyrus Fragments.

Further hindering clarity, the designations of the "papyri" themselves have been inconsistent. Although it has been recognized since their rediscovery in 1968 that six distinct "documents" could be distinguished among the original Smith Egyptian collection,[13] the publication of surviving papyrus "Fragments" in the official Mormon magazine *The Improvement Era* (February 1968, pp. 40A–I), led to the characterization of each numbered "Fragment" as an individual "papyrus." Thus in his treatment of "The Breathing Permit of Hôr" (here Papyrus Joseph Smith 1), K. Baer acknowledged that the "eleven fragments (as now mounted) are the surviving parts of three ancient papyri," but he then designated each of these fragments as "P." for "Papyrus."[14] As these fragment/papyrus designations are arbitrary and correspond only to the order in which they were initially published in *The Improvement Era,* the single papyrus document in Baer's publication consists of "papyri " ("P.") JS I, XI and X in that order (plus patches from "papyrus" JS IV). The renaming of the "Fragments" as "P." ("papyri") has now become conventional and was used by Nibley in 1975,[15] myself in 2002 and 2003,[16] by Rhodes late in 2002,[17] and by Gee and Rhodes in their reworking of Nibley's publication

[11] A brief overview of the history appears in Charles M. Larson 1992, pp. 41–52.

[12] Luke Wilson passed away on November 19, 2007, and I regret that he has not lived to see the completion of this project.

[13] Wilson 1968, pp. 67–68.

[14] Baer 1968, p. 111.

[15] Nibley 1975, p. 19, "the Joseph Smith Papyri XI & X" and *passim.*

[16] Ritner 2002 and 2003a (with the addition of a preface and photographs).

[17] Rhodes 2002. The Rhodes volume appeared well after my own *Dialogue* article. FARMS-sponsored reviews of the Ritner and Rhodes editions appeared in Morris

in 2005.[18] Any scholarly—or even "popular"—edition of the papyri must employ references to designate the now-separated papyrus components of the original papyri. Although it was convenient to maintain Baer's "P." in the re-publication of a single text, that usage is less desirable when publishing six original "papyri," some of which do not survive as a fragmentary "P." For the sake of clarity, I have revived the original designation "Fragment" for the surviving *portions* of those papyri. Thus in this edition P. Joseph Smith 1 is the "Breathing Permit of Hôr," which consists of Fragments I, XI and X (with patches from Fragment IV). As the numbering of these fragments remains unchanged, and in Roman numerals, there should be little confusion.[19] A variant of the Papyrus ("P.") system adopted here was also employed in Ashment 2001 (pp. 4–5), adding decimal notations for the surviving segments (Fragments) in the order of their original position within the reconstituted papyri. For ease of reference, a concordance to that system follows:

P. JS 1 (THE BREATHING PERMIT OF HÔR)

Fragment I = P JS 1.1 (formerly MMA. 47.102.11)[20]
Fragment XI = P. JS 1.2 (formerly MMA. 47.102.9)[21]
Fragment X = P. JS 1.3 (formerly MMA. 47.102.8)
Patches in Fragment IV = P. JS 2.6 (formerly MMA. 47.102.1)

2004 and Muhlestein 2005. Morris has no Egyptological training, but Muhlestein of BYU-Hawaii was trained in general Egyptology at UCLA. Regarding the latter's accuracy on less-studied Ptolemaic scripts, see the detailed comments in the following analysis of P. Joseph Smith 1.

[18] Gee, Rhodes and Nibley 2005.

[19] A concordance of the earlier numbering systems is found in Rhodes 2002, Appendix C (p. 49), but with Metropolitan Museum numbers reversed for Fragments I and XI. In his review of Rhodes' edition, Muhlestein 2005, p. 474, inexplicably praised Rhodes' retention of the "now standard system" of numbered Fragments assigned "in their initial publication in *The Improvement Era*" so as to avoid greater confusion. In fact, Rhodes *did not* use the traditional Fragment numbers in his edition but substituted consecutive column numbers.

[20] Misidentified as MMA 47.102.9 by Rhodes 2002, Appendix C (p. 49); correct in Herbin 2008, p. 203, n. 19. Confirmed by Marsha Hill, Metropolitan Museum of Art, email and scanned file image, September 13, 2010.

[21] Misidentified as MMA 47.102.11 by Rhodes 2002, Appendix C (p. 49); correct in Herbin 2008, p. 203, n. 19. Confirmed by Marsha Hill, Metropolitan Museum of Art, email September 13, 2010.

P. JS 2 (BOOK OF THE DEAD OF TA-SHERIT-MIN)

Fragment IX = P. JS 2.1
Fragment VII = P. JS 2.2 (formerly MMA. 47.102.5)
Fragment VIII = P. JS 2.3 (formerly MMA. 47.102.6)
Fragment V = P. JS 2.4 (formerly MMA. 47.102.4)
Fragment VI = P. JS 2.5 (formerly MMA. 47.102.7)
Fragment IV = P. JS 2.6 (formerly MMA. 47.102.1)
Fragment II = P. JS 2.7 (formerly MMA. 47.102.10)

P. JS 3 (BOOK OF THE DEAD CHAPTER 125 VIGNETTE OF NEFER-IR-NEBU)

Fragment III = P. JS 3 (formerly MMA. 47.102.2–3)

It is well-recognized that hand copies in *Joseph Smith's Egyptian Alphabet and Grammar* and "Valuable Discovery" clearly link P. Joseph Smith 1 to his Book of Abraham. Not only do these manuscripts indicate the process of Smith's "translation," but the earlier hand copy of the Sheshonq hypocephalus served as the basis of the later woodcut of "Facsimile No. 2" published in *The Pearl of Great Price.*[22] Differences between those two versions reveal a fraudulent attempt to "improve" a damaged original, an editorial counterpart to the physical "patching" performed on P. Joseph Smith 2. Employing the earlier hand copy, it has been possible to provide a (necessarily tentative) full translation of this now lost amuletic text.

It is, however, P. Joseph Smith 2, the Book of the Dead of Ta-sherit-Min, that benefits most from a close examination of the nineteenth-century hand copies by Smith and his "scribes" (for whom, see H. Michael Marquardt, above). Extended sections now missing from that Book of the Dead were copied—sometimes in multiple versions in the Smith manuscripts. Although Wilson recognized the connection between these texts, he failed to edit or translate the hand copies, which are here fully edited for the first time.

The attempt by Nibley et al. to minimize Smith's role in these "Kirtland Egyptian Papers" derives from the harsh verdict of Egyptological scholarship. As noted by I. E. S. Edwards, late Keeper of the Department of Egyptian Antiquities at the British Museum, Smith's *Egyptian Alphabet and Grammar* was "largely a piece of imagination and lacking in any kind of scientific value" and reminded him of "the writings of psychic

[22] Heward and Tanner 1968, pp. 92–98. Nibley (1968, p. 100) explained these links as evidence of Smith's "independent thinking and speculation."

practitioners which are sometimes sent to me."[23] Smith clearly could not read, understand or faithfully reproduce Egyptian hieroglyphic or hieratic texts, so the copies are often inexact, truncated or badly garbled, faults probably exacerbated by damage to the papyrus. Nevertheless, sufficient clarity is found in enough passages to identify contexts and to reconstruct most of the original text of the Sheshonq Hypocephalus and the Papyrus of Ta-sherit-Min even through the distorted prism of the copies by Smith and his assistants.

[23] Larson 1992, pp. 43 and 230, letter dated June 9, 1966.

"There was found deposited in the arms of the old man … a book of ancient form and construction, which, to us, was by far the most interesting part of the exhibition. … The characters are the Egyptian hyeroglyphics [*sic*]; but of what it discourses none can tell. That probably … will never be unfolded."

Cleveland Whig,
27 March 1835
(Wolfe and Singerman 2009, p. 108)

PAPYRUS JOSEPH SMITH 1: THE BREATHING PERMIT OF HÔR

(Fragments I, XI and X with patches in Fragment IV)

PART ONE: COMPARATIVE TRANSLITERATIONS AND TRANSLATIONS

THE PUBLISHED TRANSLITERATIONS AND TRANSLATIONS

By virtue of its link to the Book of Abraham, P. Joseph Smith 1 has received the greatest attention of the three surviving Smith papyri. The following presentation generally follows my own first edition with full transliteration and translation, published initially in *Dialogue: A Journal of Mormon Thought* (April 2002) and reprinted with an expanded preface for an Egyptological audience in *Journal of Near Eastern Studies.*[1] This primary edition was by no means the first article to examine the text of P. Joseph Smith 1 and is deeply indebted to the work of earlier scholarship.

In the summer 1968 issue of *Dialogue,* Egyptologists John A. Wilson and Richard A. Parker identified fragments within the Smith collection as sections of a late mortuary text known as a "Book of Breathings," copied for a Theban priest named Hôr.[2] Parker further contributed a provisional

[1] R. K. Ritner, "The 'Breathing Permit of Hôr' Thirty-four Years Later," *Dialogue* 33/4 [Winter 2000] (2002): 97–119; and *idem,* "The 'Breathing Permit of Hôr' among the Joseph Smith Papyri," *Journal of Near Eastern Studies* 62 (2003a): 161–80. I was invited to undertake the earlier translation and commentary on May 11, 2001, and my edition was complete by August 21 of the same year. Minor changes in the current publication include the correction of a typographical error in the bibliography of both earlier editions, in which *Dialogue* (1968) V. III became *Dialogue* 8. Other changes are found in the notes, below.

[2] John A. Wilson, "The Joseph Smith Egyptian Papyri, Translations and Interpretations: A Summary Report," *Dialogue* 3/2 (1968): 67–85, especially 68–69 (document D); and Richard A. Parker, "The Joseph Smith Papyri: A Preliminary Report," *Dialogue* 3/2 (1968): 86–88, especially 86, and "The Book of Breathings (Fragment 1, the 'sensen' Text, with Restorations from Louvre Papyrus 3284)," *Dialogue* 3/2 (1968): 98–99

translation of the beginning of this text, and that is included as Parker 1968b in the comparisons below.

The first extensive translation of this document appeared in the autumn 1968 issue of the same journal, in a study authored by Klaus Baer.[3] Baer provided a translation annotated for a popular audience, with phrases restored from parallel texts indicated by italic script.[4] Although intended to be merely a "preliminary study,"[5] Baer's analysis and translation of "The Breathing Permit of Hôr" has served as the basis of all further editions of the text. His translation appears below as Baer 1968.

In 1975, Hugh Nibley attempted both a transliteration and a literal, interlinear translation of only the unrestored portions of Fragments XI and X (with the "patches"in Fragment IV).[6] Designed strictly for an audience of believers, Nibley's volume was expressly composed to provide a Mormon rebuttal to the interpretive analysis of Egyptologists, including Baer, with whom he had studied briefly and informally.[7] These word for word, incomplete translations produced such results as "(avenger of) father his Horus (of) Edfu has enfolded body being about to deify spirit thine as do gods all," and were recognized by Nibley as "nonsense."[8] Moreover, his transliterations defy both conventional and internal systems, with inconsistency and conflation of alphabetic signs (iw vs. yw, sh vs. š̱h, ʿa vs. ʿ vs. aʿ, h for ḥ), punctuation, etc.[9] While intended to highlight his

(partial translation). Prior to the rediscovery of the papyri, Wilson had provided a brief synopsis of the Book of Abraham episode; see John A. Wilson 1964, pp. 37–38. In his autobiography (1972, pp. 173–77), Wilson recounted the further involvement by Baer and himself with the translations published in *Dialogue*.

[3] Klaus Baer, "The Breathing Permit of Hôr. A Translation of the Apparent Source of the Book of Abraham," *Dialogue* 3/3 (1968): 109–34.

[4] Ibid., p. 119.

[5] Ibid., p. 111.

[6] Hugh Nibley, *The Message of the Joseph Smith Papyri: An Egyptian Endowment,* Salt Lake City: Deseret Book Company, 1975, pp. 19–45.

[7] For Nibley's intentions, see the remarks in Nibley 1968, p. 105; and 1975, p. 1, opposing "people innocent of any bias in favor of Joseph Smith … So now it is time to hear the other side of the story." See also the response in Ritner 2003a, p. 163, n. 13.

[8] Nibley 1975, pp. 37 (translation) and 47: "Though as correct and literal as we can make it, the translation in the preceding chapter is not a translation. It is nonsense."

[9] Cf. ibid., pp. 20 (iw) and 21 (yw); pp. 19 (sh) and 26 (š̱h); p. 20 (both ʿa.wy and ʿ.wy);

quibbles over the nature of translations (to defend Joseph Smith's use of the term), Nibley's interlinear method of literal translation would necessarily produce gibberish from any language.[10]

Tacitly acknowledging this source of embarrassment, John Gee and Michael D. Rhodes have attempted to justify Nibley's methods—while promptly dropping them—in their heavily reworked "re-edition" of the 1975 volume.[11] As noted by Gee,

> "we need to explain the numerous changes we have made in this new edition of Nibley's 1975 *Message of the Joseph Smith Papyri*. First, we have returned the Egyptian transliterations to the standard transliteration system...[12]
>
> Fifth, the greatest changes occur in the second chapter, where typesetting considerations have led us to abandon Nibley's original interlinear presentation. Originally, Nibley presented the papyrus in interlinear translation in part because of accusations that he could not read Egyptian. ... The new presentation should be both easier to follow and clearer than the old."[13]

The relevant second chapter of this 2005 edition is hardly a representation of Nibley's individual work, and the volume is more appropriately cited throughout this chapter as the combined efforts of Gee, Rhodes and Nibley 2005. Even in the "clearer" reworking, the translation by Nibley—with or without the input of Gee and Rhodes—remains problematic:

> "after clasp-ed (two)arms his upon breast his ..." (1975, p. 20)
> "after clasped his (two) arms upon his breast ..." (2005, p. 35)

---

and p. 26 (waʿb) vs. p. 27 (wʿb). Cf. also the inconsistent use of dashes and dots: (snsn f) p. 23, (imi.k) p. 25, (t-wr-t) p. 26, (wnw.t) p. 27.

[10] Cf. French "Qu'il me donne cette pomme rouge" ("Let him give me this red apple") rendered literally as "That he to me give this apple red."

[11] John Gee and Michael D. Rhodes, eds., The Collected Works of Hugh Nibley, vol. 16: Hugh Nibley, *The Message of the Joseph Smith Papyri: An Egyptian Endowment,* second edition (Salt Lake City: Deseret Book Company, 2005).

[12] Ibid., p. xx.

[13] Ibid. p. xxi. In the skipped section of the quotation, Gee included a testimonial that he watched Nibley read Egyptian.

Nibley's skill with Egyptian texts may be judged by the reader below. Although Gee in particular has not hesitated to criticize all those who have taken exception to his writings in support of the fundamentalist Foundation for Ancient Research and Mormon Studies (FARMS, now within the Neal A. Maxwell Institute for Religious Scholarship), his otherwise updated 2005 edition consciously ignores my own editions of this Book of Breathing (while acknowledging the later effort of Rhodes on pp. xxi and 558). Nibley's original contribution is included below as Nibley 1975, with the re-edition as Gee, Rhodes and Nibley 2005.

Between the appearance of my first edition and the re-edition of Nibley, Michael D. Rhodes published *The Hor Book of Breathings: A Translation and Commentary* (July 2002). The volume includes color plates with misplaced patches (identified by Baer) now scanned into position (but not without problems).[14] Though never acknowledging the prior appearance of my own study, the transliterations and translations bear striking resemblance to them. Evidence of incomplete reworking of Rhodes' text shows obvious changes from readings by Nibley to readings by myself (incorporating arcane Demotic).[15] As my earlier *Dialogue* edition was widely distributed and advance copies were sent to FARMS by the editors of *Dialogue* in March 2002,[16] one can legitimately raise the

[14] See the issue of misalignment of patches in col. IV/1, discussed below.

[15] Since Rhodes made critical errors in the reading of simple hieroglyphs (see col. I/2, 3 and 5), his expertise in Demotic is unbelievable (see the comments on col. IV/9 nhs⸗k tw). Contrast the basic transcription in Rhodes 2002, p. 35, line 3 (ḥr) with his comments on pp. 11 and 27 (now suddenly Demotic 2). Note that in his paleographic comments, p. 6, the Demotic 2 is unmentioned. *Contra* Rhodes (following Nibley), an initial writing of ḥr was not reworked in this passage. Given these errors and inconsistencies, praise for Rhodes' "discussion of the use of a Demotic sign instead of its hieratic equivalent"(!) is without merit in the partisan review by Muhlestein 2005, p. 475. This same uncredited borrowing appears in Gee, Rhodes and Nibley 2005, p. 35, n. 7. For further "borrowings" in Rhodes 2002, see the incompletely incorporated "n" in col. II/1; the incompletely incorporated reading of p(ꜣy)⸗s (for Nibley's gs) in col. II/7 (read both gs and ps on p. 80!); the incomplete substitution of qd⸗k for tꞽ.t⸗k in col. V/7; the incomplete revision of grg into sḏr in the same line; and the hasty, but poorly executed, insertion of my reading ꞽr sꜣ in the final vignette, noted below. These obvious "smoking gun" examples leave unanswered the question of how many other (better incorporated) borrowings might exist. Note, however, that I have given him credit for his contribution in col. III/3.

[16] Personal communication by Neal Chandler, editor of *Dialogue,* Mar. 2, 2002: "We

question of plagiarism, but far more important is the general agreement of our versions, a factor significant in reaffirming the proper nature of the text.[17] One major distinction in our editions is that Rhodes fails to make use of the "Valuable Discovery" manuscript (perhaps for ideological reasons[18]) so that his analysis lacks critical information. While a marked improvement over the work by Nibley, his edition contains numerous misreadings of hieroglyphic and hieratic text (noted below).[19] Multiple inconsistencies in the Rhodes edition suggest that it was hastily edited, probably with the intent of ensuring that the volume appeared in the same calendar year as my initial edition.

Following my prior editions of this text in *Dialogue* and *Journal of Near Eastern Studies,* the column numbers in this edition have been increased by one over Baer's traditional numbering, with the final word on Fragment I now considered to constitute column I. The placement of this initial word at the end of Fragment I is based on its consistent placement in three nineteenth-century handcopies ("Egyptian Alphabet and Grammar," pp. F, V, and 11 of "Valuable Discovery"; see Figure 1 for the last example).

---

plan to send an advance copy of the article to John Gee this week." Gee (and Rhodes) had approximately four months (early March to early July) to examine my 2002 edition prior to the appearance of Rhodes' volume. The July publication date for the Rhodes volume is stated in Morris 2004, p. 357, n. 7; the new book announcement reached me by email on August 15. My *JNES* article had been sent to press on June 28, 2002. For reasons given above and throughout this study, I strongly doubt the assertion of Morris 2004, p. 357, that our editions were entirely made "independently of each other." Mr. Morris, it should be noted, performed editorial duties for Gee, Rhodes and Nibley 2005; see that volume, p. xxiii. Since my "2003a" article was in press before the appearance of Rhodes 2002, one must disregard the criticism of Muhlestein 2005, p. 473, regarding my failure to cite it. Notably, Muhlestein had no objections to Rhodes' failure to cite my prior work.

[17] Our works (mine available, his in press) were discussed publicly in 2002 at the fifty-third convention of the American Research Center in Egypt, where Rhodes perhaps slipped in describing the lion couch of Fragment I as an "altar," eliciting either alarm or confusion among attendees (depending upon their knowledge of the Book of Abraham). The term "altar" is now absent from his 2002 publication (pp. 18–20).

[18] See the Mormon discomfort with the materials ("the Kirtland Egyptian Papers") as summarized in Morris 2004, pp. 364–66 and 374–75: "These difficulties associated with the Book of Abraham have been the catalyst for some Saints losing their faith."

[19] The retention of many of Nibley's errors shows clearly that the work of Nibley, rather than that of Baer, was the immediate source from which Rhodes began his work.

Since the Breathing Document seems to have begun at the end of Fragment I, it has been necessary to revise this numbering to avoid beginning the text in column "0."[20]

Given the fragmentary nature of this Smith papyrus, connected sense is only possible by inserting restorations from known parallels. The most important of these, and the text most commonly employed by all translators, is P. Louvre N 3284, first published by Philippe-Jacques de Horrack in 1875.[21] Nibley and Rhodes go so far as to reproduce the text of Louvre N 3284, but over reliance on this text alone can produce errors.[22] P. JS 1 is not a mere duplicate of the Louvre exemplar but shows distinct variations. It is the Smith version that is employed as the base for the translation that follows. For comparative purposes, the recent translation of Louvre N 3284 by Mark Smith (2009) is included *in the footnotes* for each

[20] This text on Fragment I was already recognized by Baer in his notebook and corresponds to the final two signs mentioned in Baer 1968, p. 129 (line 5). For possible complications regarding this renumbering, see discussion of the word ỉw in column I, below.

[21] The initial translation of P. Joseph Smith 1 by Baer specifically listed the Louvre (3284, 3291), British Museum (9995) and Berlin (3135) parallels that he consulted; see Baer 1968, p. 119, n. 38. For additional parallels used by Baer, see Ritner 2003a, p. 164, and 2002, pp. 98–99. The same parallels have been employed in my own editions. In a partisan review for Latter-day Saints, John Gee has deliberately reversed the facts of Baer's edition; see Gee 1996, pp. 46–59. In "quibbling" (Gee's term) with the writing of T. Wilfong, Gee wrote: "more significantly we should note that, as is almost admitted by Wilfong, the papyrus Baer translated was not *P. Joseph Smith* XI–X but *P. Louvre* 3284; where *P. Joseph Smith* XI–X matched *P. Louvre* 3294 the translation of the latter was put in italics. This is not to impugn Baer's work in the least; he was clear about what he was doing, but others, including Wilfong, are less clear about what Baer did." Baer was in fact clear about what he did, and it was the exact opposite of what Gee has claimed: "Fortunately, the manuscripts of the *Breathing Permit* show relatively little variation, so that it is not too difficult to restore the missing passages; restorations are marked by italics in the translation" (Baer 1968, p. 119). Baer translated the Smith version, and where portions were lost (NOT matching), he made use of the Louvre and other parallels. Cf. also Baer's remarks, 1968, p. 124: "The italics will be a reminder that none of what follows comes from the Joseph Smith Papyri." For his citation of variants, see 1968, p. 122, nn. 60, 64 and 65; p. 123, nn. 75 and 76; etc.

[22] See the questionable restoration made by Rhodes in Paragraph VII, below. Rhodes 2002, pp. 51–70, followed Nibley 1975, pp. 57–65, in appending a copy of that text alone to his work. Though he added a few notes on variants in this section, Rhodes does not seem to have employed them in his edition of P. Joseph Smith 1.

paragraph, below. It should be stressed that the corpus of parallel texts has not been published as a group, though lists of such texts have been compiled and collective translations have appeared.[23] The inherent complexity entailed in such a comparative presentation of this, the most discussed of the Joseph Smith Papyri, makes a simple reading of the continuous text difficult. The analysis that follows is for those who wish to contrast the published editions in detail. In contrast, a following section provides a consecutive translation of the Breathing Permit of Hôr with annotations removed.

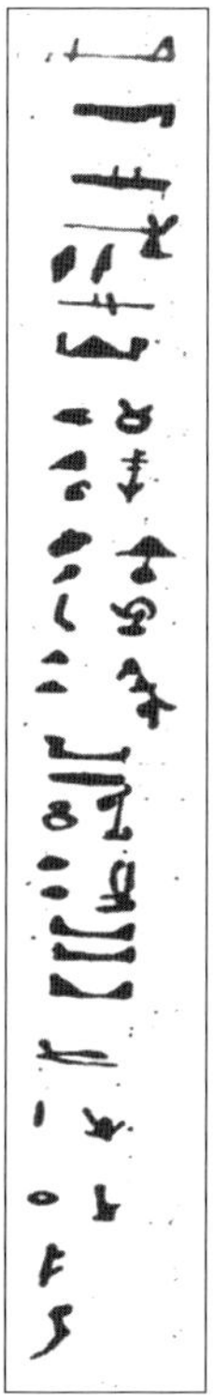

Figure 1. Valuable Discovery, p. 11, with ꜣꞽw at the end of Fragment I, col. I/5.

The comparative editions below are presented with Egyptological treatments first, then LDS publications. All are in reverse chronological order, from the most recent to the oldest. The order is thus Ritner, Baer 1968, Parker 1968b, Gee, Rhodes and Nibley 2005, Rhodes 2002, Nibley 1975, and—for rare translations in the so-called "Kirtland Papers"—Joseph Smith. For most sections the range of editions will be shorter, as several authors have not translated the full papyrus.

THE PAPYRUS

Despite its association with the Book of Abraham, the content of P. JS 1 concerns only the afterlife of the deceased Egyptian priest Hôr. "Books of Breathings" are late funerary compositions derived from the traditional

[23] A full publication of such documents exists only for the British Museum collection; see Herbin 2008. The "Books of Breathing made by Isis for her brother Osiris" include three exemplars; see pp. 11–49. Parallels from P. JS I are included by Herbin (following Baer's column numbering), but with incomplete bibliography (p. 203). A list of Books of Breathings appears in Vallogia 1979, p. 293, with fuller references in Coenen 1995, pp. 29–38. A terse summary is found in Rhodes 2002, pp. 71–72. Translations appear in de Horrack 1907, pp. 109–37 (reprinted from Paris, 1877); 1875, pp. 121–28 (reprinted in 1907, pp. 99–107); and in Goyon 1972, pp. 183–317.

"Book of the Dead." Like their antecedents, the sole purpose of the later texts is to ensure the blessed afterlife of the deceased individual, who is elevated to divine status by judgment at the court of Osiris and is thereby guaranteed powers of rejuvenation. Such powers are summarized in the term snsn, or "breathing," which refers to the Egyptian expression ṯ3w n ꜥnḫ "breath of life," the fundamental characteristic that distinguishes the living. The title šꜥ.t n snsn, literally, "Document of (or 'for') Breathing" employs the term for an official document or letter (šꜥ.t), so that these "books" serve as formal "permits"—or perhaps more accurately "passports"—to the world of the gods. To be effective, they had to accompany the corpse, and the directions for using the texts declare explicitly that the document must be placed below the mummy's crossed arms and wrapped within the bandages. This usage corresponds directly to the condition of Smith's lost mummy "No. 3," which must be identified with the corpse of Hôr. As described by the *Painesville Telegraph* on 27 March 1835 (before its purchase by Smith): "No. 3—Heighth [*sic*] 4 ft 4 1–2, male, very old, say 80; arms crossing on the breast, each hand on its opposite shoulder; had a roll of writing."[24] The *Cleveland Whig* of 27 March 1835 was more specific in its discussion of this mummy of an "old man": "There was found deposited in the arms of the old man referred to above, a book of ancient form and construction, which, to us, was by far the most interesting part of the exhibition. Its leaves were of bark, in length some 10 or 12 inches and 3 or 4 in width. The ends are somewhat decayed, but at the centre the leaves are in a state of perfect preservation. It is the writing of no ordinary penman, probably of the old man near whose heart it was deposited at the embalming."[25]

The modern designation "Books of Breathings" includes a variety of late funerary compositions, but the text found in the Joseph Smith collection represents a specific type termed in antiquity "The Document of Breathings Made by Isis for Her Brother Osiris."[26] P. JS 1 is thus a formal document or

[24] Wolfe and Singerman 2009, p. 110. The mummy is further described phrenologically: "superior head, it will compare in the regions of the sentiments with any in our land; passions mild."

[25] Ibid., p. 108.

[26] Formerly known as the "First Book of Breathings"; for the current terminology, see Coenen 1995, pp. 29–38. Translations and comments regarding the various "Documents/Letters for Breathing" are found in Mark Smith 2009, pp. 462–525,

"permit" created by Isis and copied by Thoth to assure that the deified Hôr regains the ability to breathe and function after death, with full mobility, access to offerings and all other privileges of the immortal gods. This specific form of "permit" was used by (often interrelated) priestly families in Thebes and its vicinity from the middle Ptolemaic to early Roman eras, and the limited distribution probably accounts for their uniform pattern, which displays only minor modifications.

As a result of this uniformity, the original size of the papyrus is not in doubt. With textual restorations and the now lost Facsimile 3, the papyrus will have measured about 150–155 cm.[27] At most, the papyrus might have been expanded by the inclusion of a further, middle vignette, as found in Papyrus Tübingen 2016,[28] but on the basis of the known parallels there is no reasonable expectation of any further text. Gee has repeatedly insisted that the Breathing Permit was "followed by another text, the only portions of which have been preserved are the maddeningly elliptical opening words: 'Beginning of the Book of . . . .'"[29] No such words "have been preserved," and the statement derives from an early error in reading the text by Seyffarth and a guess, recast as a fact, by Gee.[30]

Texts 25–33.

[27] Baer 1968, p. 127, n. 113. See further Ritner 2003a, p. 166. Gee 2000a, pp. 10 and 12–13, has claimed that this papyrus will have measured "320 cm (about 10 feet)," but that is the average length of a blank papyrus roll as manufactured in the Ptolemaic era—not the length of the known Books of Breathing copied on sections cut from such rolls. Rhodes 2002, p. 4, was intentionally ambiguous, noting that "the entire Book of Breathings would have been about 156 cm," and that "the Hor Book of Breathings would have taken up about half the length of one of these rolls." Rhodes did not state that the Book of Breathings *papyrus* would have been about 156 cm, since that would deny the possibility of the Book of Abraham's appearance elsewhere on the same papyrus. There is, however, no such possibility. For mathematical refutation that the scroll could have contained a further text, see Cook and Smith 2010 and the thoroughly convincing defense of that article in Cook 2012.

[28] Brunner-Traut and Brunner 1981, pp. 296–97 and pls. 12–13, 150 (bottom), and 151 (left).

[29] See Gee 2005, p. 96; and 2000a, p. 10.

[30] See Gee 2000b, pp. 187, 189 and 212, n. 57, where Gee discusses an admittedly false reading of Seyffarth (ḥꜣ.t-ꜥ m šꜥy as "Book of Hymns") and suggests—with contorted logic—that in a different context Seyffarth, noting an "invocation," "might have read the beginning lines of another text, one after the Book of Breathings." Gee's declarations rest exclusively on this flimsy evidence.

Seyffarth was an early outcast from Egyptology, notable for being the last holdout against the decipherment of hieroglyphs by Champollion. In any case, his own statements do not support the existence of a second text on the Hôr papyrus.[31]

Once dated to the late Ptolemaic or Roman period, the papyrus is now generally placed in the first half of the Ptolemaic era (first half of the second century B.C.) on the basis of family names and titles. For this dating, see the full discussion of the family by Marc Coenen, above.[32]

THE INDIVIDUALS

The individuals named in the "Breathing Permit" include the priest Hôr, his father Osorwer and his mother Taikhibit.[33] Like his father, Hôr held

[31] Seyffarth 1860; most of the article concerns his quarrels with Champollion and others, and it well reflects his "outsider status" (as acknowledged by Gee 2000b, pp. 209–10, n. 45). The most relevant pages for Gee's statement are on p. 8 of the introductory hand copies (= plate XIX/8 of the 16 pages preceding the title page, indicated as plate XIX only in the article), and pp. 530 and 535–36. Seyffarth did translate the phrase ḥꜣ.t-ꜥ m šꜥy.t n snsn with "The book of praises laudatory for singing the glories of him" on plate XIX/8 § VI. nos. 1–7, and as "Book of Hymns for singing" on pp. 530 and 535–36. Aside from these specific references to the known beginning of the Hôr Book of Breathing, no other ḥꜣ.t-ꜥ m šꜥy.t is found. Seyffarth misunderstood the word "beginning" as "the book" (supposedly equalling Coptic ϫⲱⲱⲙⲉ ⲡⲉ), and *contra* the implication of Gee, the term šꜥy.t (literally, "letter") does not typically designate "books" other than the "Books of Breathing." The term "invocation" attributed to Seyffarth appears in the St. Louis Museum catalogues of 1855 and 1859: "according to Prof. Seyffarth, the papyrus roll is not a record, but an invocation to the Deity Osirus, in which occurs the name of the person, (Horus), and a picture of the attendant spirits, introducing the dead to the Judge, Osirus" (Todd 1969, p. 298). This description matches the now-lost original of Facsimile 3 (admitted in Gee 2000b, p. 187), not an additional lost text. It is certainly not credible evidence for the restoration of a missing "Book of [Abraham]" attached to the papyrus! In fact, an "invocation" does appear at the bottom of Facsimile 3; see below. Seyffarth's conclusions, probably restated in his 1856 lectures at St. Louis' Lutheran Concordia College, were repeated in the St. Louis *Evening Pilot,* September 13, 1856, and the *St. Louis Christian Advocate,* September 10, 1857; see the texts and links in Mormon History, "Joe Smith's Egyptian Mummies—1857."

[32] This discussion supersedes Ritner 2003a, pp. 164–65, and Bell 2008, pp. 22, n. 7 and 23, n. 14. *Contra* Bell, his research notes on the illustrations were forwarded to me only after the completion of my manuscript. See also Mark Smith 2009, pp. 482–83.

[33] The males of the family are cited in *Prosopographia Ptolemaica IX;* see Clarysse 1981, pp. 94 (Osorwer, no. 5672b) and 128 (Hôr, no. 5898a). In both cases, their titles

various titles in the Theban clergy, with roles in the cults of Amon ("god's father, prophet of Amon-Re, King of the Gods"), his associated aspect Min ("prophet of Min who slaughters his enemies") and his son Khonsu ("prophet of Khonsu, the one who exercises authority in Thebes").[34] In addition to these roles, Osorwer was an overseer of secrets, or "stolist" priest, and a purifier of the god, thus having responsibility for the dressing and purification of the cult statue. On the basis of documents now in the Louvre, Taikhibit was both a housewife and a musician (a sistrum player) of Amon-Re. In such additional documents belonging to the family, however, and after the initial mention of these individuals within the Breathing Document itself, titles may be dropped, abbreviated or changed.[35] This variety is typical of Egyptian records from all periods, and reflects not only career changes, but selective mentions within individual contexts.

Regarding the family, one of the more important revisions since the edition by Baer in 1968 has been the reinterpretation of the name of Hôr's mother, Taikhibit. Although discussed by me in detail in 2002 and 2003,[36] the issue is repeated here for the convenience of the reader. Examples of the name had previously been gathered by Hermann de Meulenaere, whose transliteration Tꜣ(y)-ḫy-bi͗ꜣ.t and translation "The one who is joyous" (literally, "high of character"), have been universally adopted in reference works and articles.[37] Writings of the name vary within the Breathing Document, from spellings consistent with de Meulenaere's examples (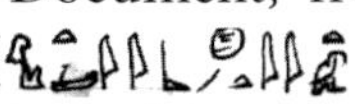 in col. II/2 and  in col. IV/13) to the hieroglyphic spelling in col. I/3 with the "b" shifted before the human

relating to Min follow Baer's incorrect reading (discussed below), as noted by Coenen 1999a, p. 259, n. 9.

[34] For the prominent role of this aspect of Khonsu, especially noted in Ptolemaic propagandistic documents for the cult, see "The Bentresh Stela" in Ritner 2003b. Additional blocks from a large-scale version of this tale, also from Thebes and now dated to the early Ptolemaic period, have been edited by me for a future publication by the Oriental Institute's Epigraphic Survey.

[35] The variety is discussed in Coenen 1999a.

[36] Ritner 2002, p. 100 = 2003a, p. 165.

[37] de Meulenaere 1955, pp. 147–48; Devauchelle 1978, pp. 73–75; Quaegebeur 1982, p. 264; idem 1994, p. 222, n. 56 (disagreeing with Baer); and idem 1995, p. 160; Quack 1996, p. 65; Lüddeckens et al. 1996, vol. 1/14, p. 1081; and Gee 2000a, pp. 11 and 52. The name is rendered into Greek as Chibois; see Coenen 1998a, p. 1104, n. 7, and his chapter on dating P JS I, above.

figure for spatial reasons (see figure 2). While aware of de Meulenaere's reading, Baer rejected it for the mother of Hor because of what he considered a logographic writing in column III/7 (his column II/7) (see figure 3). This he transcribed as  Tꜣy-ḫbỉ.t, translating the human figure as "dancer" (ḫbỉ.t).[38] While the human figure that terminates this spelling of the name is distinct from that employed to spell "high" (ḫy),[39] it does not really match the figure used for dancer either and seems a scribal peculiarity.[40] The figure with upraised arms (ḫy) is used in column IV/13, so the standard interpretation is most likely correct. The spelling in column III/7 is perhaps best understood as an abbreviated form of the name, Tꜣy-ḫy, otherwise common in hieratic and Demotic.[41] In my transliteration, below, the actual spelling of the name will be reflected, not an artificially uniform reading.

Figure 2

Figure 3

THE TRANSLATION

A major difference in the proposed translations derives from the ambiguity of Egyptian grammar as reflected in the script. However odd it may seem to modern readers, the Late Egyptian basic conjugation form (sḏm=f) has various translational equivalents that can be distinguished only by context ("he did" vs. "may he do" vs. "so that he might do"). Where

[38] Baer 1968, p. 111, n. 10: "The dancer," based on Erman and Grapow 1957, vol. III, p. 250/15–16, and the assumption that Tꜣy reflected a phonetic spelling of the definite article, as in Coptic ⲧ/ⲧⲉ; Oriental Institute Baer file 2374 (letter of John Wilson, 2 July 1968) and Baer file 2373 (response of 5 July 1968).

[39] Cf. Möller 1912, p. 1, no. 4 = Verhoeven 2001, pp. 106–07 (A28).

[40] The sign is inconsistent with Möller 1912, p. 1, no. 6 = Verhoeven 2001, p. 108 (A32). Few examples are listed, so the range may be greater. The sign most closely resembles Möller 1912, p. 3, no. 30, a seated child, = Verhoeven 2001, pp. 104–05 (A17).

[41] See Devéria 1881, p. 70, no. III.23 (the same individual as Tꜣy-ḫy-bỉ.t in the Joseph Smith papyri), and Lüddeckens et al. 1999, vol. 1/16, p. 1237.

the context is not definitive, the translator is forced to adopt a personal choice. Previous French translations have attempted to avoid the problem by employing an inaccurate present tense,[42] while Baer rather consistently chose the past tense. Baer's preference cannot be termed incorrect, but I have made other choices where context dictated.[43]

As noted in the earlier chapter on photography of the Joseph Smith Papyri, sepia-toned images of P. JS 1 appeared in *The Improvement Era* in 1968, with true color images first published in 1992. New photographs of the papyrus as mounted in the LDS Church Archives were published in 2005.[44] The inserted line divisions in the transliterations and translations below correspond to reconstructed columns, not the traditional fragment numbers.

I. INTRODUCTORY VIGNETTE WITH 5 HIEROGLYPHIC SUB-COLUMNS (Col. I = Fragment I)

As publicly recognized by Egyptologists since 1861 and re-emphasized in 1912,[45] the central feature of the introductory vignette contains one of the most common illustrations from Egyptian mythology: the jackal-headed Anubis, god of mummification, extending his hand to ensure the resurrection of the mummy of the deceased Osiris, who reclines atop the customary lion-headed funerary bier.[46] Although most of Anubis' head is now missing, the back of his wig still appears above his shoulder and his dark skin is evident (and was used for Anubis again in "Facsimile 3"). Above and to the right of Osiris' head is his winged *ba*-spirit, depicted with a bearded, human head.[47] Below the funerary couch are the four

[42] So de Horrack 1907 and Goyon 1972.

[43] Ritner 2002, p. 101 = 2003a, p. 166. See now the similar discussion by Mark Smith regarding the translation of these grammatical forms for a general audience (2009, pp. 54–55).

[44] See the images attached to Green 1968, p. 40 and Todd 1968, p. 40 I; Charles M. Larson 1992, folded color plate "The Book of Abraham Papyrus Scroll" = p. 33; and Gee, Rhodes and Nibley 2005, plates 1–3.

[45] Spalding 1912.

[46] For the order, rationale, and content of the vignettes, see the comments and bibliography in Ritner 2003a, pp. 167–68.

[47] For the human-headed *ba*-bird sitting atop the burial of Osiris, see Davies 1953, plate 3, register V. The same register has a customary scene of Anubis tending the

"canopic jars" for the embalmed viscera of the mummy: human-headed Imseti, protector of the liver, baboon-headed Hapi, protector of the lungs, jackal-headed Duamutef, protector of the stomach, and falcon-headed Qebehsenuef, protector of the intestines. To the right of the couch is a typical offering stand with a spouted vessel and Nile water lily flowers. On either side of the stand are larger offering vessels. Below this resurrection scene is a reference to a preparatory mythological event; a stream of Nile water (shown by hatched lines) contains the crocodile who aided in the collection of the dismembered limbs of Osiris.[48] Late burial rituals included the presence of a small crocodile alongside the funerary procession across the Nile, so that—as with the upper scene—mythological events prefigure the fate of the deceased.[49] The Nile scene may in fact illustrate "the lake of Khonsu" noted in the accompanying directions for use of the Breathing Document.[50] The baseline of the vignette is composed of a "niched-brick" facade, originally an architectural feature (the external palace walls of Egypt's Predynastic era) that became an artistic convention for the decoration of the dado of sacred wall scenes. Its appearance in this context strongly recalls the framing of scenes on Ptolemaic temple walls.[51]

The posture of the reanimated Osiris also copies images found in contemporary temple settings, a parallel that is hardly surprising given the narrow priestly circle that owned and designed Books of Breathings and had ready access to (and also designed) temple imagery. In such reanimation scenes, whether at Abydos, Kharga, Thebes, Dendera or, now lost, on P. JS 1, Osiris appears with an erect phallus, indicating at once his

---

deceased Osiris with canopic jars below the lion bier.

[48] The crocodile is a fusion of Sobek with Horus; see Brovarski 1984a, cols. 1000 and 1014–1015.

[49] Baer 1968, p. 118, n. 35, with reference to earlier studies by H. Junker and G. Möller.

[50] See Baer 1968, p. 119, implicitly following G. Möller: "Probably a liturgical designation of the portion of the Nile that has to be crossed in order to reach the Theban cemetery on the west bank." The visual link to the directions could be another reason for moving the vignette and directions together from the end of the papyrus. The same interpretation is accepted in Rhodes 2002, p. 20. In contrast, Mark Smith has suggested that this "lake" or "sea" is simply a portion of the embalming area; see below, n. 111. Smith does not consider the PJS I illustration in his suggestion.

[51] Rhodes 2002, p. 20, considered the facade "unique" in the sources, which is true for the *papyrus* sources.

return to potent life, the engendering of his son Horus after death and the annual revival of vegetation, which Osiris symbolizes.[52] His moment of waking is further signaled by having a single hand held to his face.[53] Above Osiris, Isis often hovers in bird form as a black kite (*milvus migrans*).[54] In the vignette for P. JS 1, the dappled tip of her wing is probably visible above the hand of Osiris.[55] A particularly close parallel to the Smith vignette appears in the West Osiris Chapel above Dendera, where Anubis stands at the left, beside the foot of the lion couch, Osiris lies with his legs separated and one hand to his face, and Isis hovers as a kite above his erect phallus (see Figure 4).[56]

A vignette of the corpse in the process of reanimation is common in Books of Breathings, where it serves as a pendant to a scene of the deceased at the court of Osiris. P. JS 1 has inverted the typical order of these vignettes, with the resurrection scene placed first (Fragment I) and the court scene moved to the end (now preserved only as the woodcut "Facsimile 3").[57] Correspondingly, the directions for use of the text have been shifted by the ancient copyist from the end of the papyrus to its beginning.

With false restorations and interpretative distortions, Joseph Smith reworked vignette 1 as "A Facsimile from the Book of Abraham No. 1." The explicit statement that the facsimile is *from* the Book of Abraham refutes any *reasonable* (as opposed to apologetic) skepticism that P. JS 1

---

[52] For the Abydos resurrection scenes, see Otto 1967, plates 16–17. For Dendera, see ibid, p. 60 and plate 20; and Mariette 1873, plates 68–70, and 88–90. For the temple of Hibis at Kharga, see Davies 1953, plates 3 (registers III and IX) and 4 (registers IV and VI). For the temple of Opet at Thebes, see de Wit 1958 and 1962, pp. 120–21 and plate 4 (top, phallus not copied); and Rochemonteix 1894, plate 11 (phallus not copied). For the explicit association of the erect phallus with sprouting grain, see Jacques Vandier 1961, plate 3, and the common "grain Osiris" figures.

[53] See Otto 1967, plate 16; and Mariette 1873, plates 68, 70, 72 and 90.

[54] See Houlihan 1986, pp. 36–38. See further Otto 1967, p. 60 and plates 17–20; Mariette 1873, plates 68–71 and 88–90; and Davies 1953, plate 4, register IV.

[55] As already noted by Parker 1968, p. 86, and accepted by Baer 1968, p. 119. The traces are not those of a second hand, but might be the tip of a winged sun disk also depicted over the mummy; see Ritner 2003a, p. 167, n. 39.

[56] Mariette 1873, plate 90, upper left. The image corresponds to Porter and Moss 1939, p. 96 §§ 37–41.

[57] For the court scene first and corpse scene last, see Coenen and Quaegebeur 1995, pp. 25, 27, and 31–32; and Brunner-Traut and Brunner 1981, plates 12–13 and 151.

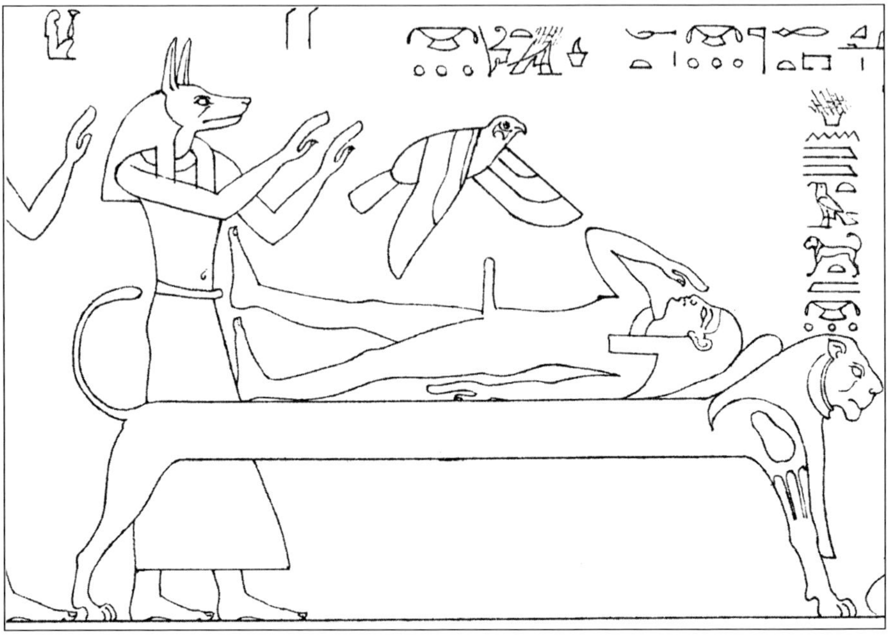

Figure 4. Anubis tending the reawakening Osiris (after Mariette 1973, plate XC).

was the source of the narrative entitled "The Book of Abraham. Translated from the Papyrus, by Joseph Smith."[58] In addition, the iconography of Facsimile 1 is repeatedly cited within the narrative itself: "that you may have a knowledge of this altar, I will refer you to the representation at the commencement of this record" (Abraham 1: 12). After introducing a series of "idolatrous gods" (Abraham 1:13), Abraham is made to say: "That you may have an understanding of these gods, I have given you the fashion of them in the figures at the beginning, which manner of figures is called by the Chaldeans Rahleenos, which signifies hieroglyphics" (Abraham 1:14). In these citations, the imagery of P. JS 1 is said to stand just before ("at the commencement/beginning" of) the text of Abraham, so that the adjacent Book of Breathings of Hôr was Smith's obvious source, not a separate and now lost addition at the end of the roll.

Interconnections between the Abraham tale and P. JS 1 are further demonstrated by Smith's "Explanation" of twelve figures in Facsimile 1 that illustrate supposed events in the text of the narrative. "Fig. 1" corresponds to the *ba*-spirit of Osiris, miscopied with the head of a bird,

[58] See Ritner 2003a, p. 163, n. 13.

rather than that of a human.[59] The *ba*-spirit of Osiris is labeled "The Angel of the Lord." While this is arguably an anachronistic interpretation (using "angel") *if* one accepts Osiris as "the Lord," Smith surely conflated the figure with Christian imagery of "The Holy Spirit" in the form of a dove.

"Fig. 2" corresponds to the prone image of Osiris and is said to represent "Abraham fastened upon an altar." The image inspired Smith's tale of human sacrifice "in the land of Chaldea" (Abraham 1:8) "after the manner of the Egyptians" (Abraham 1:9 and 11) upon an altar "made after the form of a bedstead" (Abraham 1: 13). Osiris has been wrongly provided with a second, upraised hand gesturing against the supposed attack of "Fig. 3," the jackal-headed Anubis, deformed in Smith's illustration into a human-headed figure with a knife.[60] Perverted not only in form but in protective function, Anubis in Smith's explanation became "the idolatrous priest of Elkenah attempting to offer up Abraham as a sacrifice." The restored "hand" of Osiris and the false "head" of Anubis (and the unresolved back line of his wig!) are copied in pencil on the backing of Fragment I.

The lion-couch is designated as "Fig. 4": "The altar for sacrifice by the idolatrous priests, standing before the gods of Elkenah, Libnah, Mahmackrah, Korash, and Pharaoh." As noted above, the drawing of this "altar" is cited in Abraham 1:12 and the associated gods in Abraham 1:13–14. Accordingly, the canopic deities are identified (in inverted, right to left order) with these supposed deities. Qebehsenuef is mislabeled as "Fig. 5. The idolatrous god of Elkenah," Duamutef is mislabeled as "Fig. 6. The idolatrous god of Libnah," Hapi is mislabeled as "Fig. 7. The idolatrous god of Mahmackrah," and Imseti is mislabeled as "Fig. 8. The idolatrous god of Korash." The crocodile, who belongs to a separate register and

[59] See Baer 1968, p. 118, n. 34*.

[60] Since this vignette was probably damaged when acquired by Smith (see Baer 1968, pp. 132–33), little credence can be given to "eyewitness accounts from Joseph's time period which describe the figure in the papyrus as holding the knife" (*contra* Scott Gordon, "Anti-Mormon Video Reaches National Television Audience," http://www.meridianmagazine.com/ideas/030528anti.html). As noted below, Smith's circle could misidentify male and female figures and human and animal forms, so such eyewitness accounts are inherently untrustworthy. *Contra* Nibley, a portrait of Smith's mother, Lucy Mack Smith, in Nauvoo, Illinois, depicts her seated in a rocking chair beneath the framed (and inaccurate) woodcut of Facsimile 1—not the papyrus; see Brodie 1945, facing p. 292 (1971 edition, following p. 298), and for discussion, Todd 1969, pp. 213–16.

mythological event, is joined to the canopic deities as "Fig. 9. The idolatrous god of Pharaoh." Horus-Sobek was a god of Pharaoh, so one out of five is correct.

The dado image of niched brick is styled "Fig. 11. Designed to represent the pillars of heaven, as understood by the Egyptians." The simple offering stand is "Fig. 10. Abraham in Egypt."[61] The Nile water is explained as "Fig. 12. Raukeeyang, signifying expanse, or the firmament over our heads; but in this case, in relation to this subject, the Egyptians meant it to signify Shaumau, to be high, or the heavens, answering to the Hebrew word, Shaumahyeem." On the contrary, the Egyptian representation for the four supports of heaven is 𓊋𓊋𓊋𓊋 (sḫn.wt),[62] not the palace facade, the traditional offering stand is unrelated to Abraham, and there is no Egyptian word "Shaumau" meaning high or heavens.[63] Since 1861, professional Egyptologists have been justifiably dismissive of Smith's uninformed explanations,[64] and now even the FARMS-sponsored publication by Rhodes (2002) has failed to defend or even cite them.[65]

Here, at least, there is agreement that the Smith explanations are untenable, and as the images are *directly cited* in the narrative itself, the underlying text of the Book of Abraham has been found and Smith's interpretation disproved. There can be no question of any "lost" section of the papyrus that contained an ancient text composed by Abraham, since the author of the *supposedly pre-existent* Book of Abraham both claims and depicts the *Ptolemaic* vignette as his own addition (Facsimile 1) to the tale.[66] Abraham cannot have lived as late as the Ptolemaic era, the papyrus illustration of Hôr cannot be dated earlier than the Ptolemaic era, and no

[61] Smith made the same interpretation for such a stand in Facsimile 3, "Fig. 3." See the commentary on this vignette, below.

[62] Erman and Grapow 1957, vol. III, p. 472.

[63] See instead ibid., vol. I, p. 492/1: p.wt.

[64] See Spalding 1912.

[65] Rhodes 2002, pp. 18–20, accepted most of the interpretations offered here, disputing only the wing of Isis as a raised, "second hand" and the issue of Osiris' ithyphallic state (p. 19). As ithyphallic Osiris (or Min) may be shown swathed in mummy wrappings, the kilt on the Smith vignette poses no problem.

[66] On Smith's explicit claim that Abraham himself wrote the now recovered papyrus, see Luke P. Wilson 2006.

rational defense of the narrative is possible.[67] Except for those willfully blind, the case is closed. As an episode in American religious history and early "Egyptomania," the text is still of interest; no investigator seeking ancient evidence should waste his time.[68]

What follows in this and subsequent chapters are my original, annotated transliterations and translations of all the Joseph Smith papyrus sources, followed, for comparison purposes, by excerpts from editions or translations published by others of a portion of this same material. Textual restorations supplied by the translators appear in square brackets. Numbers are inserted to alert readers to the corresponding columns/lines, etc., on the original papyrus documents. Photographs of all the original Smith papyri and related documents are reproduced, courtesy of the Smith-Pettit Foundation and the Institute for Religious Research, as plates at the end of this volume.

[67] Numerous anachronisms also invalidate the text; for a few of these, see Ritner 2003a, pp. 161–62.

[68] This verdict corresponds to archaeological scholarship on Smith as well, see Williams 1991, pp. 156–88.

ADDRESS TO HÔR:

(I/1) [Wsỉr ỉt nṯr[69]] ḥm-nṯr ʾImn-Rʿ ny-sw.t nṯr.w ḥm[70] Mnw smꜣ ḫrwy.w=f[71] ḥ[m] Ḫnsw pꜣ [ỉr][72] sḫr m W[ꜣs.t] (I/2) [...] ... Ḥr mꜣʿ-ḫrw sꜣ mỉ-nn ḥry-sštꜣ ʿb[73] nṯr Wsỉr-wr mꜣʿ-ḫrw ỉr.n n[b.t-pr ỉḥy.(t)

[69] Restored from Hôr's titles in P. Louvre N 3209; see Coenen 1999a, p. 258. For this typical title combination of god's father and prophet, cf. Devéria 1881, pp. 71 (III. 24), 104 (III. 73), 106 (III. 75), 110 (III. 80); and among the owners of Books of Breathing, see pp. 131–37, (IV. 1, 2, 3, 4, 6, and 9).

[70] For the use of ḥm for ḥm-nṯr "prophet," see Coenen 1998a, p. 1106.

[71] Ultimately read by Baer as kꜣ mw.t=f "Bull of His Mother" (1968, p. 116 and n. 21) but marked as uncertain in his own working notes. The correct reading was first published by Quaegebeur 1997, p. 74, and discussed by Coenen 1998a, pp. 1103–15. Herbin 2008, p. 203, has suggested smꜣ rkyw.f(?) "who destroys his enemy." The published photos used by Baer were ambiguous, but improved digital photography now available establishes the writing of smꜣ ḫrwy.w=f with s over the biliteral mꜣ-sickle (rather than a "knife" as seemed visible in the Charles M. Larson 1992, p. 33), oar, plural strokes, enemy determinative, and flesh-sign (for =f). Ritner 2003a, p. 168, n. 44, should be corrected regarding the initial sign. Rhodes 2002, p. 21, wrongly transcribed the oar as a windpipe (smꜣ). For writings of ḫrwy "enemy" with the oar, see Erman and Grapow 1957, vol. III, p. 325. Muhlestein 2005, p. 483, n. 27, has repeated and even expanded upon Rhodes' error. As the basic verb smꜣ "to kill" is commonly used regarding human enemies and sacrificial animals, the negative term "massacre" (employed by Coenen) is here replaced by the more commonplace "slaughter." In addition to the precise parallels noted by Coenen, the martial nature of Min is well attested; see Rochmonteix and Chassinat 1897, pp. 395 (Min "who makes massacres of her (= Isis') enemies" ỉr ʿḏ.w n ḫfty.w=s), 403, line 17 ("who smites his enemies" ḥwỉ ḫfty.w=f), and 404 ("who brings an end to his enemies" ỉn pḥ.wy r ḫfty.w=f); Junker 1917, p. 36a ("who tramples the execration figures" ptpt rsy.w); and Bonnet 1952, p. 465a ("who overthrows his enemies" sḫr ḫfty.w=f).

[72] The missing verb is falsely copied as if it were preserved in Rhodes 2002, p. 21.

[73] The suggestion that this traditional phrase means only "priest of the same rank" among the clergy at Karnak must be discarded, *contra* Quaegebeur 1994, pp. 214 and 219. As long recognized, the expression was used throughout Egypt to indicate a repetition of specific titles, occasionally supplemented—as here—with additions. Examples (from the Third Intermediate Period onward) are gathered in Erman and Grapow 1957, vol. II, p. 37/10–11, and they recur throughout Ritner 1994, pp. 205–26, and the texts collected in Ritner 2009, pp. 19–20 (n. 11) and *passim*. Osorwer will have held all of Hôr's offices in addition to "overseer of secrets" and "purifier of the god." Gee (2004) has perversely insisted that—with regard to this phrase—users of standard references, rather than proponents of new interpretations, must provide initial support for translations. His critique of Ritner vs. Rhodes on this minor point is curious as both Rhodes and I translate "with similar/like titles," *not* "of equal rank";

n] (I/3) [ʾImn]-Rʿ[74] Tꜣy-ḫy-b(y).t[75] mꜣʿ.(t)- ḫrw[76]
ʿnḫ bꜣ=k m-ẖnw=w q(r)ys.t(w)=k[77] ḥr[78] ʾImnt.t [Wꜣs.t][79]
(I/4) [...] ... mꜣʿ(?) (I/5) [... dỉ=k n=f q(r)y]s.t[80] nfr.t mnḫ.t[81] ḥr

---

see Rhodes 2002, p. 23, and cf. Gee 1996 at n. 5 (Ritner 1994 cited with approval). Seemingly unknown to Gee, Egyptian documents are not consistent in listing all titles of an individual, and variations may occur in different or even adjoining inscriptions. Gee has misrepresented the comments of Coenen 1998, pp. 1109–10, who noted the variation of titles given to Chapo(n)chonsis and Horos in different texts and claimed no more than: "It cannot be ruled out that the expression mi nn only applies to the general rank title 'god's father and prophet of Amonrasonther'" (p. 1109, n. 24). Coenen has subsequently abandoned this suggestion; see his commentary in this volume. For the title ʿb "purifier," see Erman and Grapow 1957, vol. I, p. 175 (= Gardiner Sign-List F17: water flowing from a pot over a horn).

[74] The lost titles of Taikhibit are restored from P. Louvre 3207, a Book of the Dead belonging to "the Osiris Hôr, the justified, son of Osorwer, the justified, and born by the housewife and sistrum-player of Amon-Re, Taikhibit, the justified." This surely is the same Hôr as the original owner of the Joseph Smith Book of Breathing. The extract in Devéria 1881, p. 70, no. III. 23, misread the parents' names as Osor-aàou and Taï-xi or Taï-x ..., hindering previous identification. This identification has now been made independently and published by Coenen 1999a, pp. 257–60. Although Coenen was hesitant (p. 258), the title ỉḥy.(t) (n) ʾImn-Rʿ is certain from Devéria's transcription of the Louvre papyrus.

[75] For the varying writings of the mother's name "She who is joyous" (literally, "high of character"), see the discussion of "The Individuals," above.

[76] The signs for mꜣʿ.(t)-ḫrw are influenced by hieratic writing; cf. the identical hieratic writing following the name of Taikhibit in col. II/2.

[77] For the writing of q(r)ys.t with the looped cloth determinative (), see Erman and Grapow 1957, vol. V, p. 63 and below, col. I/5.

[78] For the shape of this sign with extended ears, see col. I/5 (in the same phrase "on the west of Thebes").

[79] Restored from line 5.

[80] Text restored from Joseph Smith copies; see Figure 1 from p. 11 of "Valuable Discovery" and pp. F and V of "Joseph Smith's Egyptian Alphabet and Grammar" (both published in Tanner 1966); and Baer 1968, pp. 117 and 129.

[81] The word mnḫ.t is written in abbreviated form with the customary chisel (); see Erman and Grapow 1957, vol. II, pp. 84ff.

ỉmnt.t n W3s[.t] mỉ.[tt][82] ḏw.w M3[nw][83]

(I/1) ["Osiris, the god's father], prophet of Amon-Re, King of the Gods, prophet of Min who slaughters his enemies, prophet of Khonsu, the [one who exercises] authority in Thebes, (I/2) [...] ... Hôr, the justified, son of the similarly titled overseer of secrets and purifier of the god, Osorwer, the justified, born by the [housewife and sistrum-player of] (I/3) [Amon]-Re, Taikhibit, the justified!

May your *ba*-spirit live among them, and may you be buried on the west [of Thebes]."

(I/4) ["O Anubis(?),[84] ...] justification(?). (I/5) [... May you give

[82] The words n W3s.t mỉ.tt are fully preserved in "Joseph Smith's Egyptian Alphabet and Grammar," pp. F and V (mỉ.tt garbled). The word mỉ.tt is more clearly copied in Smith's "Valuable Discovery," p. 11.

[83] Baer 1968, p. 117, read only "on the west of Thebes just like ..." For Manu, cf. Devéria 1881, pp. 68 and 105. Traces of ink to the left of these final words are probably only remnants of the parallel vertical lines of the column border, which is inconsistently drawn with split lines and varying width (cf. the border lines on either side of the word ḥr in this column).

[84] A divine name (Anubis?) must be lost here, since the following address shifts from Hôr to a deity on his behalf, expressed in the second person. Baer 1968, p. 117, n. 29, suggested Osiris. This passage rebuts Gee 1992, pp. 100 and 104–5: "Where, we may ask, in all of Papyrus Joseph Smith XI–X is there any prayer to any Egyptian God?" A further example occurs in the invocation (col. VIII/11) of Facsimile 3. Actually, since Hôr is repeatedly and explicitly stated to be deified, a member of the company of the gods, and a form of Osiris, the entire Breathing Document is itself an extended "prayer to an Egyptian God." Rhodes 2002, p. 23, also noted the change of person from Hôr to a deity in col. I/5, since "you" are now asked to give "him" (Hôr) benefactions. The implications of this pronoun agreement were consciously ignored in the critical FARMS reviews of my 2003a study by Morris 2004, pp. 358 and 361, and by Muhlestein 2005, p. 484, n. 30. *Contra* Morris, p. 361, Rhodes did far more than offer "simply an ellipsis indicating missing text," and my supposed infraction in failing "to inform the reader of Baer's comment on the matter" would merely have suggested Osiris instead of Anubis, with the same implications for Gee's statement. Had Morris or Muhlestein actually read Baer 1968, p. 117, n. 29, they should have seen that Baer recognized the change of person and indicated an address to "Osiris?" Muhlestein has misrepresented Baer's comments and ignored the same change to an unnamed deity in Rhodes 2002, p. 23. The further assertion by Morris, p. 361, n. 13, that my disassociation (Ritner 2003a, p. 167) from Gee's "apologetic writings" represents a "personal dispute" or a "private matter" is misdirected. This has nothing to do with a secret interpersonal history. Since Gee has *publicly* claimed that his Yale degree justifies his apologetic interpretations, I was constrained to deny that I (as his former

to him] a good and splendid burial[85] on the west of Thebes as on the mountains of Ma[nu]."

Baer 1968 Translation (pp. 116–17):

"... the prophet of Amonrasontêr, prophet [?] of Min Bull-of-his-Mother, prophet [?] of Khons the Governor ... Hôr, justified, son of the holder of the same titles, master of secrets, and purifier of the gods Osorwêr, justified [?] ... Tikhebyt, justified. May your ba live among them, and may you be buried in the West ... May you give him a good, splendid burial on the West of Thebes just like ..."

Rhodes 2002 Transliteration and Translation (pp. 21–22):

(1) [Wsi͗r, i͗t nṯr,] ḥm-nṯr ʾImn-Rꜥ, nsw nṯr.w, ḥm Mnw, smꜣ ḫrwy.w=f,[86] ḥm Ḫnsw, pꜣ i͗r sḫr m Wꜣs.t. (2) ... Ḥr, mꜣꜥ ḫrw, sꜣ mi͗ nn, ḥry sštꜣ, wꜣb[87] nṯr, Wsi͗r-wr, mꜣꜥ ḫrw i͗r n nb[.t pr, i͗hy.t n

advisor) had any involvement in these writings. See the sarcastic claim by Gee 1998, p. 176: "Since I have a Ph.D. in Egyptology, I am an expert. All anti-Mormons should therefore unquestioningly accept my opinion." Gee's apologetic assertions, I stress again, would not have been acceptable in his coursework. I gained no personal pleasure—and remain deeply saddened—by the need to disavow my former student.

[85] For writings of q(r)ys.t "burial" (literally, "embalming/wrapping") with the coffin and looped cloth determinative, see Erman and Grapow 1957, vol. V, p. 64.

[86] Rhodes 2002, p. 21, wrongly transcribed the oar  as a windpipe  (smꜣ). For writings of ḫrwy "enemy" with the oar, see Erman and Grapow 1957, vol. III, p. 325. Muhlestein 2005, p. 483, n. 27, has repeated and expanded upon Rhodes' error.

[87] Rhodes 2002, pp. 21–22, misread the hieroglyphic text as wꜣb (presumably for wꜥb Erman and Grapow 1957, vol. I, p. 280). He has misread the word ꜥb throughout the text, conflating Gardiner Sign-List F 17 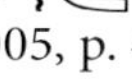 and D 60 . The same mistake is repeated and defended by Muhlestein 2005, p. 483, who revised Rhodes' copy to include a "leg, surmounted by a water pot pouring water over a horn." Muhlestein's supposed "leg" is the flowing water. Muhlestein does not discuss Rhodes' copy of the related noun ꜥb "purity" (without the leg and misread as wꜥb) in the 2002 glossary on p. 79.

(3) ʾImn-rʿ,][88] Tꜣ-ḫy-by.t.s[89] ʿnḫ bꜣ=k m ẖnw=w. kys.tw=k[90] ḫnt[91] ỉmnt.t … (4) … (5) […] dỉ=k n=f ḫ.t[92] nfr.t ꜣḫ.t[93] ḥr ỉmnt.t Wꜣs.t mỉ ḏw.w. mꜣ[nw.][94] …

"(1) [The Osiris, God's father] priest of Amon-Re, king of the gods, priest of Min, who massacres his enemies, priest of Khonsu, who is powerful in Thebes. (2) … Hor, justified, the son of one of like titles, master of the secrets, god's priest, Usirwer, justified, born of [the house wife, the musician (3) of Amon-Re,] Taykhebyt. May your soul live in their midst. May you be buried at the head of the West. … (4) … (5) […] May you give to him[95] beautiful and useful things on the west [of Thebes] like the mountains of Manu."

---

[88] For this restoration, see n. 74, above. The restoration in Rhodes 2002, p. 21, n. 34, follows Coenen 1999a, p. 258, but without mention of the author's hesitation.

[89] The hieratic-influenced signs for mꜣʿ.(t)-ḫrw were rendered as an "s" and a seated woman by Rhodes 2002, p. 21, with the unlikely suggestion that the "s" is the Greek nominative ending. For the similarity of "s" and "mꜣʿ," see Möller 1912, pp. 22 (no. 236) and 41 (no. 432) = Verhoeven 2001, pp. 146–47 and 180–81. Muhlestein 2005, p. 483, n. 29, has failed to recognize the signs and simply repeated the error of Rhodes.

[90] Rhodes 2002, p. 21, wrongly read the looped cloth determinative () of q(r)ys as the letter t () which actually follows  and was misread by Rhodes as w (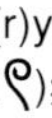); for the cloth determinative in this word, see Erman and Grapow 1957, vol. V, p. 63 and below, col. I/5. The mistake was not noted by Muhlestein 2005.

[91] Rhodes 2002, pp. 21–22, wrongly read ḫnty () "at the head of" for ḥr () "on." Cf. col. I/5 (also in ḥr ỉmnt.t "on the west"). The mistake was not noted by Muhlestein 2005.

[92] The hand copy in Rhodes 2002, p. 21, bears little resemblance to the original and is too short for the space. He has miscopied portions of q(r)ys.t as dỉ=k n=f ḫ.t, with the coffin determinative of q(r)ys.t (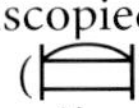) misunderstood as the pronoun f () and the looped cloth determinative () as ḫ (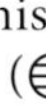). The mistake was not noted by Muhlestein 2005.

[93] The sign for ꜣḫ.t () copied by Rhodes 2002, p. 21, is misread from mnḫ.t (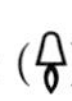) "splendid/effective." The mistake was not noted by Muhlestein 2005.

[94] Rhodes tacitly adopted my reading, but failed to remove his punctuation (.) after ḏw.w (p. 21), indicating his original dependence on Baer's incomplete translation.

[95] For the change of persons, indicating a prayer to a deity beginning in line 4, see above, n. 84.

II. DIRECTIONS FOR USE (Col. I/5–Col. II/9 = Fragment XI.1)[96]

[ỉw[97]](II/1)[=w[98] sṯꜣ Wsỉr r] ẖnw n[99] p(ꜣ)y š wr (n) Ḫnsw (II/2) [Wsỉr Ḥr mꜣꜥ-ḫrw] ms.n Tꜣy-ḫy-by.t mꜣꜥ.(t)-ḫrw mỉ.ty (II/3) m-ḫ[t ḫf]ꜥ=w[100] ꜥ.wy=f 2 r[101] ḥꜣ.ty=f ỉw=w qr(II/4)ỉs tꜣ šꜥy.t (n) snsn ỉr

---

[96] Restored from the parallel text of P. Louvre N 3284, col. 6, in de Horrack 1907, plate 11 and p. 135. For similar instructions, see the discussion and examples in Mark Smith 2009, p. 467 (and n. 25).

[97] Hieratic text restored from Joseph Smith copies ("Egyptian Alphabet and Grammar," pp. F, V, and 11 of "Valuable Discovery"). See Figure 1.

[98] Most editions ignore the ỉw of the hand copies and begin "column I" of the text with Fragment XI; see Rhodes 2002, pp. 34–35. A papyrus scrap now mounted in the upper right of Fragment XI might be considered to contain the initial signs, but their proper placement and reading are uncertain. The two strokes are clearer in photos that were not available to me for my earlier articles but are still problematic; see the images in this volume and those in Rhodes 2002, p. 34. Rhodes, however, neither noted these traces nor incorporated them in his transliteration (p. 35). Baer, in his notebook, p. 84, transcribed the initial sign as ỉ. If the two traces are correctly placed and do read ỉw, then the column numbering would revert to traditional assumptions, with Fragment XI, line 1 = column 1, line 1. One would thus have to believe that Smith's hand copies ("Egyptian Alphabet and Grammar," pp. F, V, and 11 of "Valuable Discovery") combined more than one line, with ỉw moved from Fragment XI to the bottom of Fragment I/5 in the copy. Baer did not accept this, as is indicated by his comments in 1968, p. 129, regarding "about five" lost signs from the column 5 of Fragment I, an assessment which retains ỉw in Fragment I.

[99] The obvious n is omitted from the transliteration in Rhodes 2002, p. 27, but is copied on p. 35 (cf. Ritner 2002, p. 105 = 2003a, p. 169). This is but one of many inconsistencies in the Rhodes volume that suggest uncredited borrowing. As in the case of another such borrowing (cf. col. II/3), the word is provided with an additional editorial note in Gee, Rhodes and Nibley 2005 (here p. 34, n. 1). My recognition of this genitive was already noted online by Ashment 2001, n. 13 (added 12/26/01).

[100] Literally, "grasped."

[101] The scribe has reinterpreted the standard text found in P. Louvre N 3284, converting a visually similar hieratic shape into a later Demotic (and hieratic) form (ḥr > 2 r). The meaning is unaffected. Nibley 1975, p. 20, misread ḥr and assumed the sign was "heavily retouched." My own Demotic reading was inconsistently adopted in Rhodes 2002, cf. pp. 11, 35, 27 n.2, and 84. *Contra* Rhodes and Nibley, ḥr was not corrected on the papyrus to the numeral 2. This uncredited borrowing reappears incompletely adopted in Gee, Rhodes and Nibley 2005, p. 35, n. 7, with the new addition that the form is also hieratic (as noted in Ritner 2002, p. 105, n. 46) and an incorrect lexical comment (ḫfꜥ is rarely construed with ḥr before its object; here r is used in a separate prepositional phrase indicating *where* the arms are grasped).

n[102] nty (II/5) m sš.wy ẖnw bnr n-ỉm≈s m šs ny-sw.t[103] rdỉ.tw (ẖr) ꜥ≈f[104] (II/6) ỉꜣby n mtr[105] ḥꜣ.ty≈f ỉw ỉr≈w[106] p(ꜣ) sp[107] n tꜣy≈f (II/7)

The transcription of the passage in Gee, Rhodes and Nibley retains the inaccurate ḥr (p. 35). Rhodes 2002, p. 27, failed to note the independent preposition r, though it is noted on pp. 11 and 84 and has been found in Gee, Rhodes and Nibley 2005, p. 35, n. 7. This passage was copied by Smith's scribes in the damaged outer rim of the Hypocephalus of Sheshonq, again with no indication of a "retouched" ḥr; see the hypocephalus chapter, n. 17, below.

[102] Emended by Baer 1968, pp. 119–20, and Nibley 1975, p. 21, the phrase ỉr n means simply "which amounts to/corresponds to/equals" in contemporary Demotic Egyptian; see Erichsen 1954, p. 36. The scribe has here deviated from the standard text, which has nothing between snsn and nty. Perhaps, as suggested by Baer, the scribe conflated this passage with the opening of Paragraph I. As noted by Baer, his is "a rather uncertain emendation since the other MSS do not have the phrase." Rhodes 2002, p. 27 followed Baer and read "which [Isis] made."

[103] Rhodes 2002, p. 27, misread the text as šsrw-nsw, employing the wrong value for the looped cloth in an error no trained scholar would make. Nibley 1975, p. 21, had the proper reading (but in non-standard transliteration). For the well-known reading, see Erman and Grapow 1957, vol. IV, p. 540.

[104] The word is misread rmn in Nibley 1975, p. 21, and Gee, Rhodes and Nibley 2005, p. 36. Rhodes 2002, p. 27, read ꜥ.t (reading the otiose "t" from ꜥ.t "limb"). For the term ꜥ "arm" and ẖr ꜥ "under the arm," see Erman and Grapow 1957, vol. I, pp. 156–57.

[105] Following Nibley 1975, p. 21, Rhodes 2002, p. 27, read the flesh determinative of ỉꜣby as a redundant "f." For the similarity of the signs, see the writing of ḥꜣ.ty≈f in the same line. What I have read as the expected preposition "n" Rhodes took as a "t" of mtr, ignoring in his transcription the following stroke. Nibley 1975, p. 21, copied the stroke as a y (deleted in Gee, Rhodes and Nibley 2005, p. 36). The best interpretation of the signs may be the phallus (mt) above a "t" and a vertical stroke.

[106] The form ỉw ỉr≈w here must mark a second tense stressing "over it," not a circumstantial past. Other versions have only ỉr≈w "Let them make."

[107] The sign has been variously read (rmn, mn or sp) and interpreted. For the sign rmn, see Möller 1912, p. 9, no. 101 = Verhoeven 2001, pp. 120–21 (D41). Baer read mn "remainder," see Möller 1912, p. 52, no. 540 (latest examples) = Verhoeven 2001, pp. 204–205 (Y5); and Erman and Grapow 1957, vol. II, pp. 63–64. The originally distinct hieratic signs appear to have visually merged, but (for reasons still to be determined) the rmn-sign acquires the additional value as sp "remainder," replacing the earlier use of p(ꜣ) mn with the same meaning. For this writing of sp, see Chassinat 1966, pp. 192–93; Kurth 2004, pp. 404–405; Kurth 2007, pp. 174 and 191; Quack 2004, p. 473 and Quack 2009. Translated correctly by Baer 1968, p. 120, the passage was mistranslated by Rhodes 2002, pp. 27, 35 (following Goyon 1972): ỉw ỉr p(ꜣ) rmn tꜣy≈f qrỉs m p(ꜣy)≈s bnr "while the bearer of his coffin works on its outside." Following

qrꜣs.(t) r[108] p(ꜣy)⸗s[109] bnr

ỉr ỉr.tw n⸗f md͟ꜣ.t tn ẖr (II/8) snsn⸗f mỉ bꜣ[.w] ntr.w r nḥḥ ḥnꜥ (II/9) d̠.t

[(II/1) Osiris shall be towed in]to the great lake of Khonsu,[110] (II/2) and likewise [the Osiris Hôr, the justified,] born of Taikhibit, the justified, (II/3) after his two arms have been [placed] at his heart, while (II/4) the Breathing Document, being what (II/5) is written on its interior and exterior, shall be wrapped[111] in royal linen and placed (under) his left arm at the midpoint of his heart. The

---

Parker, Nibley 1975, pp. 21–22, read yw irw pa n tay .f qris "having-been-done this for his wrapping." The translation is adjusted in Gee, Rhodes and Nibley 2005, p. 36, "this having been done for his wrapping." Muhlestein 2005, p. 484, noted the difference of readings but made no comments. For the parallel P. Louvre N 3121 (col. VII, line 13), Herbin 1999, pp. 167 and 209, transcribed rmn but could provide no translation.

[108] Nibley 1975, p. 22, followed by Rhodes 2002, pp. 27 and 35, misread the final determinative of qrꜣs as m. The error is retained in Gee, Rhodes and Nibley 2005, p. 36.

[109] *Contra* Nibley 1975, pp. 21–22, who read gs ("side"); the spelling is an abbreviated alphabetic writing of the possessive adjective, common in Ptolemaic and Roman texts. This section of text, unread by de Horrack and Parker, is confirmed by the following variants: P. Louvre N 3284, lines 7–8: ỉr⸗w p(ꜣ) sp (n) tꜣ qrꜣs.(t) r pꜣy⸗s bnr; P. Louvre N 3121: ỉr⸗w p(ꜣ) sp n tꜣy⸗f qrꜣs.(t) r p(ꜣy)⸗s [bnr]; P. Louvre N 3126: ỉr⸗w pꜣ sp (n) tꜣ[y]⸗f qrꜣs.(t) r p(ꜣy)⸗s bnr. For hand copies, see de Horrack 1907, plate 11. Rhodes 2002 has now incompletely adopted my reading p(ꜣy)⸗s; the form is so transcribed on p. 27, but unrecognized on p. 7, where he notes the preceding possessive adjective tꜣy⸗f. Rhodes' likely "borrowing" of my reading is particularly obvious on p. 80, where p(ꜣy)⸗s has been added as the last entry for "p," but his own reading still remains as gs (under bnr): m gs bnr! The reading gs is retained in Gee, Rhodes and Nibley 2005, p. 36, with bnr substituted for Nibley's ḥrw.

[110] The term "lake/sea" is also used to indicate gardens and "bays" of the Nile river; see Erman and Grapow 1957, vol. IV, pp. 397–98. Based only on its mention within instruction texts in the Books of Breathing, Mark Smith has suggested that the "great sea of Khonsu" designated a specific area within the embalming place and not a geographic area; see Mark Smith 2009, pp. 305, 316, 321–22 and 475, n. 54. It is likely, however, that any symbolic area of the embalming workshop will have corresponded to a real (or mythological) geographical area.

[111] The term means "to embalm/wrap," not primarily "to bury/inter," *contra* the translation of Rhodes 2002, pp. 9 and 27: "the Book of Breathings … shall (also) be buried." Because of his error, Rhodes was forced to supply "wrapped" in parentheses on p. 27. Cf. Nibley's "wrapping" (1975, p. 22 = Gee, Rhodes and Nibley 2005, p. 36).

remainder of his (II/7) wrapping shall be made over it.

As for the one for whom this book is made, (II/8) he thus breathes like the *ba*-spirit[s] of the gods, forever and (II/9) ever.[112]

Baer 1968 Translation (pp. 119–20):
Here and below Baer's italics indicate lost text.

"*Osiris shall be conveyed* into the Great Pool of Khons—and likewise Osiris Hôr, *justified,* born to Tikhebyt, justified—after his arms have been *placed* on his heart and the Breathing Permit (which [Isis] made and has writing on its inside and outside) has been wrapped in royal linen and placed under his left arm near his heart; the rest of his mummy-bandages should be wrapped over it. The man for whom this book has been copied will breathe forever and ever as the bas of the gods do."

Parker 1968b Translation (p. 98):

"Column I.

1. [........] this great pool of Khonsu
2. [Osiris Hor, justified], born of Taykhebyt, a man likewise.
3. After his (two) arms are [fast]ened to his breast, one wraps[113] the Book of Breathings, which is
4. with writing both inside and outside of it, with royal linen, it being placed (at) his left arm
5. near his heart, this having been done at his
6. wrapping and outside it. If this Book be recited for him, then
7. he will breath(e)[114] like the soul[s of the gods] for ever and
8. ever."

---

[112] Compare the translation of the parallel P. Louvre N 3284, 6/1–10, by Mark Smith 2009, pp. 475–76: "They should convey Osiris by dragging into the great sea of Khonsu after he has grasped his heart. They should wrap the letter for breathing which is inscribed both inside and out with byssus and it should be placed under his left arm directly above his heart. The rest of the wrapping should be carried out over it. If this book is made for him, then he will breathe together with the bas of the gods for ever and ever."

[113] Parker's printed translation mistakenly joins lines 3 and 4, so that the line numbers end with 8 rather than 9.

[114] Printed "breath" in error.

Gee, Rhodes and Nibley 2005 Transliteration and Translation (pp. 34–37, col. 1, lines 1–9):

1 [… ẖ]nw n py š wr Ḫnsw
[…] ms.n Tꜣy-ḫy-bỉꜣ.t[115] mꜣꜥ-ḫrw mỉtty
3 […] m-ḫ[t ḫf]ꜥ.wy ꜥ.wy=f ḥr[116] ḥꜣty=f ỉw m[117] qr-
ỉs mỉ mḏꜣ.t tꜣ šꜥy snsn ỉr.n nty
5 m sš.wwy ẖnw bnr[118] n-ỉm=s m sš-nsw rdỉ.tw rmn
ỉꜣby=f mtr ḥꜣty=f ỉw ỉrw pꜣ n tꜣy=f
qrỉs m gs bnr ỉr ỉr.tw n=f mḏꜣ.t tn ḫr
8 snsn=f mỉ bꜣ[.w] nṯr.w r nḥḥ ḥnꜥ
ḏ.t

"1 […] inside (of) the lake great (of) Khonsu
[…] born of Taykhebyt, Justified, likewise
3 after clasped his (two) arms upon his breast being as wrapped
like a book (*or* roll); the Book of Breathings being written
according to what is
5 in (the sacred) writings (books) on both inside and outside in
linen (of) the king.
One places (*or* is placed) his left arm
vicinity of his heart, this having been done for his
wrapping on (the) outer side. If one makes for him this book, then
8 he breathes like souls (of the) […] gods for time and
eternity."

[115] The revised transliteration by Gee and Rhodes (p. 34) ignores the actual writing of the name in favor of an (anachronistic) etymological spelling.

[116] See n. 101, above, for the history of this incorrect reading.

[117] Nibley's misreading of the suffix =w as m is retained in Gee, Rhodes and Nibley 2005, p. 35.

[118] Nibley 1975, p. 21, read hrw (bnr), but this has been corrected to bnr in Gee, Rhodes and Nibley 2005, p. 36 (see the editoral addition p. 35, n. 8).

Rhodes 2002 Transliteration and Translation (pp. 27–28):

1. [ꞽw.w[119] <ḥr> sṯꜣ Wsꞽr r]-ẖnw py[120] š wr <n> Ḫnsw, (2) [Wsꞽr Ḥr mꜣꜥ-ḫrw] ms.n Tꜣy-ḫy-by.t, mꜣꜥ-ḫrw mꞽt.t, (3) m-ḫ(.t)[121] [ḫf]ꜥ.wy ꜥ.wy=f ḥr[122] ḥꜣty=f. ꞽw=w <ḥr> qrꞽs (4) tꜣ šꜥy(.t) snsn ꞽr.n <ꜣs.t[123]>, nty (5) m sš ẖnw bnr n-ꞽm=s m sšrw-nsw[124], rdꞽ.tw <ẖr> ꜥ.t=f (6) ꞽꜣby=f <r> mtr ḥ(ꜣ)ty=f. ꞽw ꞽr p(ꜣ) rmn[125] tꜣy=f (7) qrꞽs m p(ꜣy)=s[126] bnr.

ꞽr ꞽr.tw n=f mḏꜣ.t tn, ḫr (8) snsn=f mꞽ bꜣ[.w] nṯr.w r nḥḥ ḥnꜥ (9) ḏ.t

"1. [Osiris shall be brought in] to the great pool of Khonsu, (2) and likewise [the Osiris Hor, justified] born of Taykhebyt, justified, (3) after his two hands have been clasped to his heart. (4) The Document of Breathing which <Isis> made shall (also) be buried, which (5) is written on both the inside and outside of it, (wrapped)[127] in royal

[119] For discussion of the original placement of these initial signs, see n. 98, above, and Rhodes 2002, p. 34, for traces now placed in the upper right of Fragment XI. These signs were ignored in his hand copy on p. 35.

[120] For the suspicious inconsistency between Rhodes' transliteration (p. 27) and hand copy (p. 35) of this pasage, see above n. 99.

[121] Rhodes 2002, p. 27, wrongly transliterated m-ḫ(.t), as if the final "t" were a feminine ending. The error is corrected in Gee, Rhodes and Nibley 2005, p. 35.

[122] For the proper reading of this group as 2 r, see n. 101, above. In a late addition to his manuscript, Rhodes 2002, p. 27. n. 1, has asserted that "Originally a *ḥr* was written, then the numerical figure 2 was written over the top of it." Rhodes' transliteration (p. 27) and hieroglyphic copy (p. 35) show only ḥr, and the supposed original ḥr at this point derives from Nibley's incorrect 1975 reading, followed by Rhodes before seeing my re-edition. The original writing on the papyrus was not corrected from ḥr to 2 r. See also the Hypocephalus chapter, n. 17, below.

[123] Rhodes is inconsistent in his transliteration of "Isis" (ꜣs.t on pp. 27–28 [corrected in bold-face?] vs. ꜣIs.t on p. 25).

[124] For this misreading, see above, n. 103.

[125] The grammar in Rhodes 2002, p. 27, is impossible for his present tense translation, which would require ꞽw p(ꜣ) *rmn ꞽr. For the proper reading of rmn as sp, see n. 107, above.

[126] For Rhodes' incomplete reworking of Nibley's reading m gs to follow my published edition, see above, n. 109.

[127] For this unnecessary insertion in parentheses, see n. 111, above.

linen, being placed <under> his (6) left arm near his heart, while the bearer of (7) his coffin works on its outside.

If this book is made for him, then he will (8) breathe like the souls of the gods forever and (9) ever."

Nibley 1975 Word-for-Word Transliteration and Translation[128] *of Preserved Sections Only (pp. 19–23):*

(I/1) ẖnw n? pi sh wr Khnsw (2) ms n Ta-y-kh b y-t maʿ-khrw mitty (3) m-kht (kh-f)-ʿa.wy ʿwy.f ḥr ḥaty.f iw m[129] q-r-(4)-ỉs mi mḏa.t ta sʿy(t) sn-sn ir.n nty (5) m s-sh(w-y) ẖnw hrw(bnr) n im.s m sh-s nsw rdi.tw rmn (6) iaby.f mt(ir)r ḥaty f yw irw pa n tay.f (7) qris m gs ḥrw Ir ir(i).tw n.f mḏat tn khr (8) sn-sn f mi ba(w***) nṯrw r ḥḥ hnʿ ḏ.t

(I/1) "inside (of) the lake great (of) Chonsu (2) born of Taykhebyt justified likewise (3) after clasp-ed (two)arms his upon breast his being as wrap-(4)-ped like a book (or roll); the Book of Breathings being written according-to-what is (5) in (the sacred) writings (books) on both inside and outside in linen (of) the king One places (or, is placed) arm (6) left his vicinity of heart his, having-been-done this for his (7) wrapping on (the) side outer If makes one for him book this, then (8) breathes he like souls (of the) gods for time and eternity"

Joseph Smith Translation (of particle ỉw only, in "Egyptian Alphabet and Grammar," pp. F and V, and "Valuable Discovery," p. 11):

"Za Ki on-hish or Kulsidon hish, - The land of the Chaldees[130]
~~Za Ki on hish~~- Ah-brah oam, The father of the faithful

[128] Nibley's inconsistent use of punctuation, () for both breaks and elipses, capitalization of initial words of sentences, and spelling (Hor or Horus for the papyrus owner, Ra, Re or Reʿ) are all here retained, as is his idiosyncratic transliteration. Brackets [...] have been added where Nibley did indicate textual breaks (by x, ° or *) in the transliteration but failed to employ () or [] in the translation.

[129] Nibley (p. 20) has misread the suffix ⸗w as m. This error is retained in Gee, Rhodes and Nibley 2005, p. 35.

[130] So "Egyptian Alphabet and Grammar," p. F; "Chaldeans" on "Valuable Discovery," p. 11. For these texts, see Tanner 1966.

~~the first right ______ unto whom is committed~~"[131]

III. THE MAIN BODY OF THE BREATHING DOCUMENT

(Col. III/1–V/13 = P JS XI.2 + P JS IVA–D [mismounted fragments] + P JS X)[132]

PARAGRAPH I

(III/1) ḥꜣ.t-ꜥ m [šꜥy.t n sns]n ꞽr.t[.n ꜣs.t n sn⸗s Wsꞽr r sꜥnḫ bꜣ⸗f r sꜥnḫ ẖꜣ.t⸗f r srnp ḥꜥ.w⸗f nb] (III/2) m wḥm [r ẖnm⸗f] ꜣḫ.t ḥnꜥ ꞽt⸗f Rꜥ [r sḫꜥ bꜣ⸗f m p.t m ꞽtn n ꞽꜥḥ r psd ẖꜣ.t⸗f m Sꜣḥ m ẖ.t n Nw.t r] (III/3) rdꞽ.t ḫpr m[ꞽ.tt n]n n Wsꞽr Ḥr mꜣꜥ-ḫrw s[ꜣ[133] … Wsꞽr-wr mꜣꜥ-ḫrw ms.n Tꜣy-ḫy-by.t mꜣꜥ.t-ḫrw ḥꜣ]p[134] sp-2 ꞽmn sp-2 (III/4) ꞽmy⸗k r[dꞽ] ꜥš s.(t) s nb ꜣḫ[⸗s n s m ẖr.t-nṯr ꜥnḫ⸗f m wḥm m sšrw] mꜣꜥ ḥḥ n sp[135]

(III/1) Beginning of the [Breath]ing [Document] that [Isis] made [for her brother Osiris in order to revivify his *ba*-spirit, to revivify his corpse, and to rejuvenate all his limbs] (III/2) again, [so that he might unite with] the horizon together with his father Re, [so that his *ba*-spirit might be made to appear gloriously in heaven in the moon disk, so that his corpse might shine in Orion within the

---

[131] With these initial attempts at translation, cf. the opening words of the published "Book of Abraham," Chapter 1.1: "In the land of the Chaldeans, at the residence of my fathers, I Abraham …"

[132] Lacunae restored from P. Louvre 3284 and variants 3121, 3126, and 3291, in de Horrack 1907, pls. 7–13. Suggestions in Nibley 1975, p. 28, and Gee, Rhodes and Nibley 2005, p. 41, n. 31, linking a further patch in P JS VI are incorrect. See Paragraph III, n. 165, below.

[133] Rhodes 2002, p. 28, read ms.[n], contracting the text. The preserved strokes at the left edge are not from ms but s[ꜣ]. Muhlestein 2005, p. 484, n. 32, restated Rhodes' reading but noted the problem thus produced by "extra" space. The common sign that Muhlestein found "extremely difficult to make out" is the egg (over a lost stroke: ♀) following the "w" of ḫrw; see Erman and Grapow 1957, vol. III, p. 408; and Möller 1912, p. 22, no. 238 = Verhoeven 2001, pp. 146–47.

[134] The final traces [ḥꜣ]p sp-2 ꞽmn sp-2 appear on a fragment pasted upside down in the upper left corner of Fragment IV in patch 1/1 (= Baer's Fragment IV a/1). The signs for ꞽmn sp-2 were not visible to me on the earlier photographs, but were read correctly by Rhodes 2002, pp. 37 and 28, and were inserted by the editors in Gee, Rhodes and Nibley 2005, p. 39 (hieroglyphic transcription).

[135] The final words mꜣꜥ ḥḥ n sp appear inverted on patch 1/2 (Baer's Fragment IV a/2).

body of (the sky-goddess) Nut, and so that] (III/3) the same things might be made to happen to the Osiris Hôr, the justified, son [of ... Osorwer, the justified, born of Taikhibit, the justified.] Hide (it)! Conceal (it)! (III/4) Do not let anyone read it![136] [It] is effective [for a man in the necropolis, so that he might live again,] [being proved] truly [effective], millions of times.[137]

Baer 1968 Translation (p. 120):

"Here begins *the Breathing Permit, which* Isis made for her *brother Osiris in order to revive his ba, to revive his corpse, and to make his entire body young* again, *so that* he *might enter* the horizon with his father Re, *that his ba might appear gloriously in heaven in the disk of the moon, and that his corpse might shine in Orion in the belly of Nut—and in order that* the same might happen to Osiris Hôr ... *Keep it secret!* Do not *let* anyone read it. *It* is useful *for a man in the Necropolis, to help him live again, and it has worked* successfully millions of times."

Parker 1968b Translation (p. 98):

"Column II.

1. The beginning [of the Book of Breathings made by Isis for her brother Osiris, to make his soul live, to make his body live, to make young his members]
2. again, [so that he may attain the] horizon with his father Reʿ (the sun), [so that his soul may appear in glory in the sky in the disk of Yah (the moon), so that his body may shine as Sah (Orion) in the body of Nut (the sky), and to]
3. cause [the like of th]is to happen to the Osiris Hor, justified,

---

[136] Commands for secrecy in religious texts were intended to maintain elite privilege not magical efficacy; see Ritner 1993, pp. 202–204.

[137] Compare the translation of the parallel P. Louvre N 3284, 1/1–7, by Mark Smith 2009, p. 469: "Beginning of the letter for breathing which Isis made for her brother Osiris in order to animate his ba, restore life to his corpse, make all his limbs youthful again, unite him with the horizon in the company of his father Re, cause his ba to appear in the sky as the disc of the moon, illuminate his corpse as Orion in the womb of Nut, and to cause the same to happen for the Osiris ... Hide (it), conceal (it). Do not let anyone read it. It is useful for a man in the god's domain, so that he will live again. Truly effective, a million times."

[born of Taykhebyt .... Hide (it), hide (it!)]

4. Don't [allow] any man to read it. [It] is profitable [for a man in the necropolis. He truly lives anew millions of times. Words to be recited]:"

Gee, Rhodes and Nibley 2005 Transliteration and Translation (p. 39, col. 2, lines 1–4):

1 ḥ3.t-ᶜ m [... snsn].w ỉr.t [...]
m wḥmy [...] 3ḫ.t ḥnᶜ ỉt=f Rᶜ [...]
rdỉ.t ḫprw [...] nn n Wsỉr Ḥr m3ᶜ-ḫrw [...]
ỉmỉ=k rdỉ [...] ᶜš s nb 3ḫ [...] ḥḥ n sp

"1 Beginning of [...]s which ... made [...]
anew [...] the horizon along with his father, Re, [...]
to cause to happen [...] things for the Osiris Hor, Justified, [...]
Do not let any man read it! It is beneficial [...] countless times."

Rhodes 2002 Transliteration and Translation (p. 28):

2. ḥ3.t-ᶜ m [šᶜ(.t) sn]sn ỉr.[n[138] 3s.t n sn=s Wsỉr r sᶜnḫ b3=f, r sᶜnḫ ẖ3.t=f, r srnp ḥᶜ.wt=f nb.t] (2) m wḥmy, [r ẖmn[139]=f] 3ḫ.t ḥnᶜ ỉt=f Rᶜ, [r sḫᶜ b3=f m p.t m ỉtn n ỉᶜḥ, r psd ẖ3.t=f m s3ḥ m ẖ.t Nn.t, r] (3) rdỉ(.t) ḫpr [mỉt.t n]n n Wsỉr Ḥr, m3ᶜ-ḫrw, ms.[n[140] T3y-ḫy-by.t, m3ᶜ-ḫrw.]

ḥ3p sp 2, ỉmn sp 2. (4) ỉm=k rdỉ(.t) ᶜš st s nb. 3ḫ[=s n s m ẖr.t-nṯr ᶜnḫ=f m wḥmy m sšrw] m3ᶜ.t ḥḥ n sp

"2. The beginning [of the Document of Breathing], which [Isis] made [for her brother, Osiris to cause his soul to live, to cause his body to live, to rejuvenate all his limbs], (2) again, [so that he might join] the horizon with his father, Re, [to cause his soul to appear in heaven as the disk of the moon, so that his body might shine like Orion in the womb of Nut, and to] (3) cause [the same] thing to happen to the Osiris Hor, justified, [born of Taykhebyt, justified.]

[138] Rhodes 2002, p. 37 copied ỉr.t.[n] but transliterated only ỉr.[n] on p. 28. The mistake was noted by Muhlestein 2005.

[139] Rhodes 2002, p. 37 copied ẖnm but transliterated ẖmn on p. 28.

[140] For the proper reading of these signs as s3 "son of" requiring a longer restoration, see n. 133, above.

Hide (it)! Keep (it) secret! (4) Do not let anyone read it, since [it is] effective [for a man in the god's domain so that he might live again] successfully millions of times."

Nibley 1975 Word-for-Word Transliteration and Translation of Preserved Sections Only (pp. 24–25):

(II/1) Hat-ᶜ m (sn-sn-w ir.t (2) m wḥm(y) akh.t ḥnᶜ it f? Re' (3) rdi.t khpr(w) (khope) nn n Wsir Hr maᶜ-khrw(4) imi.k rdi.(t) ᶜshw.s s nb akh ** .t ḥḥ n sp

(II/1) "Beginning of Breathings made (by ...) (2) a second time [...] horizon with father his Ra (3) to cause to happen [the likes of] this to Osiris Horus justified (4) do-not thou let read it man any beneficial (proven) millions of times"

PARAGRAPH II

(III/5) hy[141] [Wsỉr Ḥ]r mꜣᶜ-ḫrw ms.n Tꜣy[-ḫy-by.t mꜣᶜ.t-ḫrw ỉw=k wᶜb ḥꜣ.ty=k wᶜb ḥꜣ.t=k m] ᶜbw pḥ.ty=k[142] (III/6) m dwr[143] ḥr(y)-ỉb=k m bd [ḥsmn nn ᶜ ỉm=k m ỉsf.t wᶜb] Ws[ỉr Ḥ]r mꜣᶜ-ḫrw ms.n[144] (III/7) Tꜣy-ḫ(by.t)[145] mꜣᶜ.(t)-ḫr[w] m šdy.(t) twy nt[y[146] Sḫ.wt-ḥtp ḥr mḥt.t n.(t) Sḫ.wt snḥm.w] swᶜb tw=k Wꜣḏy.t[147] (III/8) Nḫb.t m

[141] For this interjection in late (and often Theban) texts, see Quaegebeur 1990, pp. 76 and 86.

[142] The final words ᶜbw pḥ.ty=k appear inverted on patch 1/3 (= Baer's Fragment IV a/3).

[143] Written for twr. The loss of the d sound in later Egyptian led to a common conflation of the once distinct consonants d and t.

[144] The final words Ws[ỉr Ḥ]r mꜣᶜ-ḫrw ms.n appear inverted on patch 1/4 (= Baer's Fragment IV a/4).

[145] Misread Rmny-qꜣỉ by Parker 1968b, p. 99; Nibley 1975, p. 26; and Gee 1992, pp. 105 and 108, where it is said to be Hôr's father's name. Gee's article and error are signaled in Coenen 1998, p. 1104. For the abbreviated spelling, see Ritner 2003a, p. 165. Rhodes 2002, pp. 29 and 88, simply read the name as Tꜣy-ḫy-by.(t) without noting the complete ellipse of the final element -by.t. The name is improperly corrected as Tꜣy-ḫy-bỉꜣ.t in Gee, Rhodes and Nibley 2005, p. 40.

[146] As often in Ptolemaic texts, the form nty anticipates the Coptic genitive ⲚⲦⲈ.

[147] The final words swᶜb tw=k Wꜣḏy.t appear inverted on patch 1/5 (= Baer's Fragment IV a/5).

wnw.t 4.t[148] n.t grḥ (m) wnw.t 4.t [n.t hrw my r=k Wsỉr Ḥr m3-ḫrw ms.n T3y-ḫby].t m3ᶜ.(t)-ḫrw ᶜq=k r wsḫ.t[149] (III/9) M3ᶜ.ty ỉw=k[150] wᶜb.tw r ḫww [nb bt3w nb ỉnr n M3ᶜ.t rn=k]

(III/5) "Hail, [Osiris Ho]r, the justified, born of Tai[khibit, the justified! You are pure! Your heart is pure! Your front is in] a state of purity, your rear (III/6) is in a state of cleanliness, and your interior parts consist of soda and [natron. There is no limb of yours in an evil state.] The Os[iris Ho]r, the justified, born of (III/7) Taikhibit, the justified, [has been purified] in this pool of [the Fields of Offerings on the north of the Fields of Locusts.[151]] Edjo and Nekhbet have purified you (III/8) in the fourth hour of night and in the fourth hour [of day. Come, then, Osiris Hôr, the justified, born of Taikhibi] t, the justified! May you enter into the Hall of the (III/9) Two Truths, since you are pure from [all] impurity [and every abomination. 'Rock of Truth'[152] is your name.]"[153]

---

[148] Other versions have the eighth (P. Louvre 3284, Louvre 3291 and British Museum 9995) or the ninth hour of day and night (P. Berlin 3135). Parker 1968, p. 99, read "fourth," and he was followed by Nibley 1975, p. 27, and Rhodes 2002, pp. 28–29 and 37. Baer 1968, p. 120, read "third," and while I followed him in my earlier editions, new photographs have convinced me of the accuracy of Parker's original reading. Muhlestein 2005, p. 485, n. 35, was unable to make a decision.

[149] The final words [T3y-ḫby].t m3ᶜ.(t)-ḫrw ᶜq=k r wsḫ.t appear inverted on patch 1/6 (= Baer's Fragment IV a/6).

[150] The lower portion of the words M3ᶜ.ty ỉw=k appears on patch 2/1 (= Baer's Fragment IV d/1), wrongly pasted below the *ba*-bird vignette in column 2 of Fragment IV.

[151] For the location of these fields north of Heliopolis, see Mark Smith 2009, p. 469, n. 36.

[152] Perhaps a reference to the durability of the deceased's truthfulness; see Mark Smith 2009, p. 470, n. 38.

[153] Compare the translation of the (generally) parallel P. Louvre N 3284, 1/8–16, by Mark Smith 2009, pp. 469–70: "Hail Osiris … You are pure. Your heart is pure. Your front is in a state of purity. Your hindparts are in a clean state. Your middle is (as) pure as *bed*-natron and *hesmen*-natron. No limb of yours is impure. The Osiris … will be purified in this pool of the fields of Hetepet on the north of the fields of locusts. Wadjit and Nekhbet will purify you in the eighth hour of the night and the eighth hour of the day. Come Osiris … You will enter the hall of the two truths, for you are cleansed of all wrongdoing and every sin. Stone of truth is your name." This papyrus substitutes "eighth hour" for "fourth hour."

Baer 1968 Translation (p. 120):

"O *Osiris* Hôr …, *you are pure. Your heart is pure. Your front is in* a state of purity, your back is in a state of cleanliness, and your middle is cleansed with *natron. No part of you is engaged in wrong-doing. Osiris Hôr … has purified himself* in that Pool *of the Field of Offerings to the north of the Field of Locusts.* Uto and Nekhbet have purified you in the third[154] hour of the night and the third hour *of the day. Come, Osiris Hôr …,* that you may enter the Hall of Double Justice. *You* have been purified of *all* impurity *and all sin. True Precious Stone is your name.*"

Parker 1968b Translation (p. 99):

"5. Hail, [Osiris H]or, justified, born of Tay[khebyt .... You are pure; your heart is pure, your front is purified; your back is]
6. cleansed; your middle is in *bd*-natron [and *ḥsmn*-natron. There is no bad member of yours. Purified is the Osiris Hor, justified, born of Taykhebyt, engendered by]
7. Remenykay,[155] justified, with the *šdyt*-water [of the Field of Offerings, north of the Field of Locusts. Have purified you Edjo and]
8. Nekhbet at the fourth hour of the night and the fourth hour [of the day. Come thou, Osiris Hor, justified, born of Taykhebyt, that you may enter the Broad Hall of the]
9. Two Goddesses of Righteousness, you being purified from [all] baseness [and all wrongdoing. Stone of Righteousness is your name.]"

Gee, Rhodes and Nibley 2005 Transliteration and Translation (pp. 40–41, col. 2, lines 5–9):

5 hy Ḥr[156] mꜣꜥ-ḫrw ms.n Tꜣy […] wꜥb pḥwy=k
m twr.t ḥr-ỉb=k m bd […] mꜣꜥ-ḫrw ms.n
Tꜣy-ḫy-bỉꜣ.t mꜣꜥ-ḫrw m šdy.(t) twy nty […] swꜥb.tw=k Wꜣḏ.t
Nḫb.t m wnw.t fdw.t nt grḥ wnw.t [… Tꜣy-ḫy-bỉꜣ].t mꜣꜥ-ḫrw

---

[154] For the improved reading of this number as "fourth," see n. 148, above.

[155] Misread from the abbreviated writing Tꜣy-ḫ(by.t). For the impact of this misreading on subsequent publications, see n. 145, above.

[156] The editors (p. 40) have ignored the space for "[Osiris]" in both the transliteration and translation.

ʿq=k r wsḫ.t
9 mꜣʿ.ty ỉw=k wʿb.tw r ḫww [...]

"5 Hail, Hor, Justified, born of Tay[khebyt ...] with washing, thy back with cleansing water, thine inner parts with *bd* (soda) [...] Justified, born of
Taykhebyt, Justified, in (these) standing waters of [...] have made thee pure Edjo (*Wꜣdy.t*, Uto)
and Nekhbet in the fourth hour of the night, [...] hour [...] Justified, that thou mayest enter into the broad Hall
9 of the Two Maats since thou hast been cleansed from all defilement [...]"

Rhodes 2002 Transliteration and Translation (pp. 28–29):

(5) hy[157] [Wsỉr] Ḥr, mꜣʿ-ḫrw, ms.n Tꜣ[y-ḫy-by.t, mꜣʿ-ḫrw. ỉw=k wʿb.tw.[158] ḥꜣty=k wʿb. ỉb=k wʿb. ḫꜣ.t=k m] wʿb,[159] pḥ.t=k (6) m dwr.t. ḫr-ỉb=k m bt [ḥsmn. nn ʿ.t ỉm=k m ỉsfy.

wʿb Wsỉr Ḥr], mꜣʿ-ḫrw, ms.n (7) Tꜣy-ḫy-by.t, mꜣʿ-ḫrw, m šdy(.t) twy nty sḫ.t[160] [ḥtp.w ḥr mḥt.t n sḫ.t snḥm.] swʿb tw=k Wꜣḏ.t (8) Nḫb(.t) m wnw.t fdw(.nw)t n.t grḥ wnw.t fdw(.nw)t [n.t hrw.

my r=k Wsỉr Ḥr, mꜣʿ-ḫrw, ms.n Tꜣy-ḫy-by.t], mꜣʿ-ḫrw. ʿq=k r wsḫ.t (9) mꜣʿ.ty, ỉw=k wʿb.tw r ḫww [nb btꜣw nb. ỉnr mꜣʿ.t rn=k.]

---

157 Influenced by Nibley 1975, p. 255, Rhodes 2002, p. 37, has copied the wrong determinative (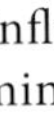); cf. his glossary entry for hy, p. 83 (). The sign is corrected in Gee, Rhodes and Nibley 2005, p. 40.

158 The discussion of a supposed wʿb.tw in Rhodes 2002, p. 28, n. 13, is pointless, as the passage is not preserved, and the Louvre parallel has only wʿb; cf. Rhodes, pp. 52–53, line 9. The older terminations of the Old Perfective/Stative need not be written in Ptolemaic texts; cf. the inconsistent use of wʿb.tw in P. Louvre 3284, col. I, lines 9 and 15 (Rhodes, pp. 52–53).

159 Misread by Rhodes 2002, p. 28, with wʿb for ʿb. Rhodes does not know the reading for this group and misread it again as wʿb in col. I/2; see above. Rhodes' error follows Nibley 1975, p. 25 = Gee, Rhodes and Nibley 2005, p. 40. Here Muhlestein 2005, 485, n. 34, conceded the accuracy of my reading.

160 Rhodes 2002, p. 28, wrongly placed the broken nt[y sḫ.t] completely outside of brackets. His translations of a singular "Field of Offerings" and "Field of the Grasshopper" (p. 29) are incorrect as restorations from the plural "Fields" in P. Louvre N 3284; cf. Rhodes 2002, pp. 52–53, lines 12–13.

"(5) O [Osiris] Hor, justified, born of Ta[ykhebyt, justified, you have been purified. Your heart has been purified. Your front is in] (a state of) purity, and your back (6) is in (a state of) cleanliness. Your midsection is (cleansed) with soda [and natron. There is no part of you (polluted) by sin.

May the Osiris Hor,] justified, born of (7) Taykhebyt, justified, be purified in that pool of [the Field of Offerings to the north of the Field of the Grasshopper.] May Wadjet (8) and Nekhbet purify you in the fourth hour of the night and the [fourth] hour [of the day.

Come, Osiris Hor, justified, born of Taykhebyt], justified. May you enter the Hall (9) of the Two Truths, having been purified from every sin [and misdeed. Stone of Truth is your name.]"

Nibley 1975 Word-for-Word Transliteration and Translation of Preserved Sections Only (pp. 25–27):

(II/5) Hy[161] (H)r maᶜ-khrw ms.n Tay- wᶜb pḥwy.k (6) m t-wr-t[162] ḥr-ib.k m bḏ x x maᶜ-khrw ms.n (7) Rmny-Qai maᶜkhrw m š̱hdy(t) twy nty x x s-waᶜb tw.k Wd̲.t (8) Nkhb.t m wnw.t fdw.t nt grḥ wnw.t xxx ·(Kheby).t maᶜ-khrw ᶜq.k r wskh.t (9) Maᶜt.y iw.k wᶜb tw=ti r khww

(II/5) "Hail (Osiris) Hor justified born to Tay(khebyt) purified back-parts thine (6) by (a) cleansing inner-parts thine with natron [...] justified, born of (7) Rmn-y-qai justified in pool this of [...] makes-clean thee Edjo (8) Nekhbet in hour fourth of night hour [...] Khebyt justified enter(est)-thou into the (broad) hall (9) (of the) Two Maats thou-being purified from sins"

161 The determinative is incorrect ( for ). The sign is corrected in the 2005 re-edition.

162 Wrongly read for dwr. Nibley 1975, p. 26, claimed that "no distinction was made between the writing of -t and -d." The sounds of these letters are conflated, but the written forms are distinct. The error is retained in the 2005 re-edition but not in Rhodes 2002.

PARAGRAPH III

[hy] Wsỉr Ḥr mꜣꜥ-ḫrw ꜥq⸗k[163] (III/10) r dwꜣ.t[164] [m] ꜥbw wr swꜥb tw⸗k [Mꜣꜥ.ty m wsḫ.t[165] ꜥꜣ.t ỉr.tw n⸗k ꜥbw m wsḫ.t Gb swꜥb ḥꜥ].w⸗[k] m wsḫ.t[166] (III/11) Šw ỉw⸗k[167] [ḥ]r mꜣꜣ Rꜥ m ḥtp⸗f ʾI[tm m mšrw ʾImn (ỉ)rm⸗k ḥr dỉ.t n⸗k ṯꜣw Ptḥ ḥr nb](III/12)ỉ [ḥ]ꜥ.w⸗k[168] ꜥq⸗k r ꜣḫ.[t] ḥn[ꜥ] Rꜥ [šsp⸗w bꜣ⸗k r nšm.t ḥnꜥ Wsỉr] (IV/1) [nṯrỉ⸗w b]ꜣ⸗k[169] [m pr Gb ỉw⸗k n mꜣꜥ-ḫrw r nḥḥ ḏ.t]

[Hail,] Osiris Hôr, the justified! May you enter (III/10) into the Underworld [in] a state of great purity. [The Two Truths] have purified you in the [Great Hall. Purification is made for you in the Hall of Geb. Your limb]s [have been purified] in the Hall of (III/11) Shu. You see Re at his setting, A[tum at twilight.[170] Amon is with you, giving you breath. Ptah fashion]s (III/12) your limbs. May you enter into the horizon with Re. [May your *ba*-spirit be received into the *Neshmet*-bark with Osiris.] (IV/1) [May] your *ba*-spirit [be deified

---

[163] The final words Wsỉr Ḥr mꜣꜥ-ḫrw ꜥq⸗k appear inverted on patch 1/7 (= Baer's Fragment IV a/7).

[164] The words r dwꜣ.t appear on patch 2/2 (= Baer's Fragment IV d/2).

[165] The words m wsḫ.t are wrongly said to appear on a misplaced fragment pasted on Fragment VI, upper left corner; see the hand-copy in Nibley 1975, p. 28, top left. The signs copied by Nibley actually are found (upside down) on inverted patch 1/8 (= Baer's Fragment IV a/8), and belong to the conclusion of this line. The error is maintained in Gee, Rhodes and Nibley 2005, p. 41, but Rhodes 2002 has followed my correction. See the following note.

[166] The final words [ḥꜥ].w⸗[k] m wsḫ.t appear inverted on patch 1/8 (= Baer's Fragment IV a/8).

[167] The words Šw ỉw⸗k appear on patch 2/3 (= Baer's Fragment IV d/3).

[168] The words [nb]ỉ [ḥ]ꜥ.w⸗k appear on patch 2/4 (= Baer's Fragment IV d/4). The line insertion III/12 was omitted by accident in my earlier versions. The surviving traces at the beginning of III/12 are ỉ plus otiose w; see the parallel spellings in P. Louvre N 3284, P. BM 9995 and P. Berlin 3135.

[169] The traces that I have read [b]ꜣ⸗k appear on patch 3, an isolated fragment now pasted at the top of Fragment X, column 1 (= Rhodes 2002, p. 38, traces above Ḥr in line 1; and see Charles M. Larson, plate for Fragment X, upper right). My transcription requires that the patch be moved lower and to the right on the same fragment.

[170] Atum is part of the solar trinity, the form of Re at evening.

in the Estate of Geb, since you are justified forever and ever.] [171]

Baer 1968 Translation (p. 121):

"O Osiris Hôr ..., you have entered the Netherworld *in* a state of *purity. The Double Goddess of Justice* has purified you greatly *in the Great Hall. A purification has been made for you in the Hall of Geb. Your body has been purified* in the Hall of Shu. You see Re when he sets and A*tum at twilight. Amon is with you and gives you breath. Ptah shapes* your body, that you may enter the horizon with Re. *Your ba has been welcomed into the Neshmet-bark together with Osiris; your ba has been made divine in the palace of Geb. You are justified forever and ever.*"

Parker 1968b Translation (p. 99):

"9. [Hail, Osiris Hor, justified, born of Taykhebyt! You enter]
10. [the Otherworld] very pure. Have purified you [the Two Goddesses of Righteousness in the great Broad Hall. A cleansing has been made for you in the Broad Hall of Geb and your members have been purified in]
11. [the Broad Hall of Shu. You] see Reʿ when he sets [as Atum in the evening. Amon is with you, giving you well-being and Ptah]
12. [fashions your limbs]. You enter into the horizon with Re'
[... ... ...]"

Gee, Rhodes and Nibley 2005 Transliteration and Translation (p. 41, col. 2, lines 9–12):

Wsỉr Ḥr mꜣꜥ-ḫrw ꜥq=k
r dwꜣ.t [m] wꜥb wr swꜥb.tw=k [...] m wsḫ.t [172]
Šw ỉw=k [ḥr] mꜣꜣ Rꜥ m ḥtp=f [...]

[171] Compare the translation of the parallel P. Louvre N 3284, 1/16–22, by Mark Smith 2009, p. 470: "Hail Osiris ... You will enter the underworld in great purity. The two truths will purify you in the great hall. Cleansing will be performed for you in the hall of Geb. Your body will be purified in the hall of sunlight. You see Re when he sets and Atum in the evening. Amun is with you, giving you breath. Ptah fashions your body. You will enter the horizon together with Re. Your ba will be taken to the *neshmet*-bark in company with Osiris. Your ba will be divinized in the house of Geb. You are justified for ever and ever."

[172] See nn. 165–66, above.

[ỉw ḥ]ᶜ.wt=k ᶜq=k r ꜣḫ.t ḥnᶜ Rᶜ [...]

"The Osiris Hor, Justified. Thou enterest
into the *duat* in perfect (great) purity, which [...] have washed thee
... in the great Hall (Court) of Shu.
Thou art about to behold Re in his coming down, [...]
thy body (members). Thou enterest (*or* that thou mayest enter) the
horizon in company with Re [...]"

Rhodes 2002 Transliteration and Translation (p. 29):

[hy] Wsỉr Ḥr, mꜣᶜ-ḫrw, ᶜq=k (10) r dwꜣ.t [m] wᶜb[173] wr. swᶜb tw=k [mꜣᶜ.ty m wsḫ.t ᶜꜣ.t. ỉr.tw n=k wᶜb m wsḫ.t Gb, swᶜb ḥ]ᶜ.wt=k[174] m wsḫ.t[175] (11) Šw. ỉw=k ḥr mꜣꜣ Rᶜ m ḥtp=f ꜣItm [m mšr. ꜣImn ỉrm=k ḥr dỉ.t n=k ṯꜣw Ptḥ] ḥr nb[ỉw (12) ḥᶜ.wt=k.[176]

ᶜq=k r ꜣḫ.t ḥnᶜ Rᶜ. [šsp=w bꜣ=k r nšm(.t) ḥnᶜ Wsỉr. nṯr=w bꜣ=k[177] m pr Gb,] (13) [ỉw=k m mꜣᶜ-ḫrw r nḥḥ] ḏ.t.

"[O] Osiris Hor, justified, may you enter (10) into the hereafter [in] a state of great purity.[178] [May the two Goddesses of Truth]

[173] As elsewhere, Rhodes 2002, p. 29, misread the word ᶜbw as wᶜb. The error derives from Nibley 1975, p. 28 = Gee, Rhodes and Nibley 2005, p. 41.

[174] Rhodes 2002, p. 29, wrongly omitted the brackets from the suffix pronoun =[k].

[175] See nn. 165–66, above.

[176] Rhodes 2002, pp. 29 and 37, was inconsistent and inaccurate regarding the beginning of line 12, which appears after ḥr nb[ỉw] in the transliteration, but before its translation "is fashioning" where both words are indicated as missing (both p. 29), and yet transcribed on p. 37 as if ḥr [nbỉ]. Rhodes has misread the signs ỉw as ḥr, and misrepresented the spelling of nbỉ; cf. the copy of P. Louvre N 3284 in Rhodes 2002, pp. 52–53, line 21.

[177] Traces of [b]ꜣ=k appear on patch 3, an isolated fragment now pasted at the top of Fragment X, column 1 (= Rhodes 2002, p. 38, traces above Ḥr in line 1). Rhodes 2002, pp. 29 and 39, seems to have ignored this text and placed [nṯr=w bꜣ=k m pr Gb] in the conclusion of line 12, and he began a supposed line 13 with [ỉw=k n mꜣᶜ-ḫrw r nḥḥ] ḏ.t (transliteration), but with [ḏ.t] inconsistently indicated as being lost in the corresponding translation (p. 29) and transcription (p. 37). For further problems with Rhodes' line numbering, see the discussion on the initial words of Paragraph IV, below.

[178] Rhodes translates m wᶜb "in a state of purity" on p. 29, but "in (a state of) purity" on p. 28.

purify you [in the Great Hall. May a purification be performed for you in the Hall of Geb], and may your body [be purified] in the Hall (11) of Shu. You see Re when [he][179] sets and [Atum in the evening. Amon is with you, giving you breath and Ptah (12) is fashioning] your limbs.

May you enter into the horizon together with Re. [May they receive your soul into the Neshmet boat with Osiris. May they make your soul divine in the House of Geb, (13) since you are justified forever and ever.]"

Nibley 1975 Word-for-Word Transliteration and Translation of Preserved Sections Only (pp. 27–28):

(II/9) Wsir Ḥr maꜥ-khrw ꜥq.k (10) r dwa.t (m) wꜥb wr s-wꜥb ṯw.k ○○○ m wskh.t[180] (11) Shw iw.k ḥr maa Reꜥ m hpt.f (12) -yw ḥꜥwt.k x x ꜥq.k r akh.t ḥnꜥ Reꜥ

(II/9) "Osiris Hor justified enter(est) thou (10) into Duat (with) purification great Purify thee [...] in great hall (11) (of) Shu thou art about to see Re in his setting (12) (fashion)ing body thine [...] enter(est) thou into horizon with Reꜥ"

PARAGRAPH IV

[Wsỉr] Ḥr mꜣꜥ-ḫrw ms.n Tꜣy-[ḫy-by.t[181] mꜣꜥ.(t)-ḫrw m]n rn=k ḏ[d] ẖꜣ.t=k rwd sꜥḥ=k[182] [nn šnꜥ.tw=k] (IV/2) [m p.t tꜣ sḥḏ ḥr=k ḫr Rꜥ]

[179] The brackets do not properly correspond to lost text (or the transliteration) in lines 11–13.

[180] These words are misplaced on Nibley 1975, p. 28 (top left); see nn. 165–66, above.

[181] The words Ḥr mꜣꜥ-ḫrw ms.n Tꜣy-[ḫy-by.t] appear on patch 4/1 (= Baer's Fragment IV c/1), mounted upside down in the middle of the plate, between the center vignettes. An image of the patch restored to its proper place appears in Rhodes 2002, p. 38, but with patch 3 wrongly left above it; see nn. 169 and 177, above.

[182] The term "corpse" is written with only the seal logogram ( ); see Erman and Grapow 1957, vol. IV, p. 52; and Möller 1912, p. 40, no. 422 = Verhoeven 2001, pp. 180–81, and col. V/12, below. The term was misprinted as sꜣḥ for sꜥḥ in my earlier editions. Nibley 1975, p. 30, misread the detached elements as rꜥ nb or khr (= ḫr), though he read the sign correctly in col. V/12 (p. 44). Rhodes 2002, pp. 29 and 39, misread sꜥḥ=k as ḫr ( ) but noted (p. 29, n. 15) that his reading was unparalleled. He was thus forced to place the expected sꜥḥ=k in brackets. Like Nibley, he reproduced the same sign properly in col. V/12 (Rhodes 2002, p. 41). Gee, Rhodes and Nibley 2005, p. 43,

ʿnḫ b3=k ḫr ʾImn rn[p[183] ẖ3].t=k ḫr Wsỉr snsn=k r nḥ[ḥ ḏ].t

[Osiris] Hôr, the justified, born of Tai[khibit, the justified! May your name end]ure, may your corpse abide, and may your mummy thrive. [You shall not be turned away] (IV/2) [in heaven or on earth. May your face be illuminated[184] in the presence of Re.] May your *ba*-spirit live in the presence of Amon. May your [cor]pse be rejuvenated in the presence of Osiris. May you breathe forever [and ev]er.[185]

Baer 1968 Translation (p. 121):

"*Osiris* Hôr ..., your name *end*ures, your corpse lasts, and your mummy is permanent. *You have not been repulsed in heaven or on earth. Your face has been gladdened in the presence of Re,* your ba lives in the presence of Amon, and your *corpse* has been rejuv*enated* in the presence of Osiris, that you may breathe *forever and ever.*"

Gee, Rhodes and Nibley 2005 Transliteration and Translation (p. 43, col. 3, lines 1–2):

1 [...] Ḥr m3ʿ-ḫrw ms.n T3y-[ḫy-bỉ3.t ... mn] rn=k ḏd ẖ3.t=k rwd ḫr[186] [...]
[...] ʿnḫ b3=k ḫr ʾImn rn[p ...] ẖ3.t=k ḫr Wsỉr snsn=k r nḥ[ḥ ...]

"1 [...] Hor, Justified, born of Tay[khebyt ... Abiding (is)] thy name, firm and enduring thy flesh (corpse), hale (is)

---

presented an inconsistent mixture of readings, with rʿ nb copied in the transcription but ḫr read in the transliteration. Muhlestein 2005, p. 485, n. 36, did not recognize the writing with the seal: "This is probably a ḫr." He did note my misprint of s3ḥ for sʿḥ in n. 37.

[183] The words ʿnḫ b3=k ḫr ʾImn rn[p] appear on patch 4/2 (= Baer's Fragment IV c/2).

[184] Literal illumination by the sun-god is intended, with the added nuance of "gladden" (sḥḏ-ḥr).

[185] Compare the translation of the parallel P. Louvre N 3284, 2/1–4, by Mark Smith 2009, p. 470: "Osiris ... your name will remain, your corpse will endure, and your mummy will flourish. You will not be turned away in the sky or on earth. Your face will be illuminated before Re. Your ba will live before Amun. Your corpse will be rejuvenated before Osiris. You will breathe for ever and ever." Smith joins §§ 4 and 5.

[186] For the improved reading sʿḥ=k "your corpse" and the misunderstanding of the term in all LDS editions, see n. 182, above.

[…] living is thy ba in the presence of Amon. (Ever) youthful is thy body (corpse) in the presence of Osiris. Thou breathest henceforth for time […]"

Rhodes 2002 Transliteration and Translation (p. 29):

3. [Wsỉr] Ḥr, mꜣᶜ-ḫrw, ms.n Tꜣy-ḫy-b[y.t,[187] mꜣᶜ-ḫrw, mn] rn=k, ḏd ẖꜣ.t=k, rwt.ḫr[188] [sᶜḥ=k. nn šnᶜ=k (2) m p.t tꜣ. sḥḏ ḥr=k ḫr Rᶜ.] ᶜnḫ bꜣ=k ḫr ʾImn. rn[p ẖꜣ.t]=k ḫr Wsỉr. snsn=k r nḥ[ḥ ḏ.t.]

"3. [Osiris] Hor, justified, born of Tay[khebyt, justified, may] your name [endure] and may your body last, then [your mummy] will flourish. [You shall never be turned back (2) from heaven or earth. May you be made happy in the presence of Re.] May your soul live in the presence of Amon. May your [body] be renewed in the presence of Osiris. May you breathe forever [and ever.]"

Nibley 1975 Word-for-Word Transliteration and Translation of Preserved Sections Only (p. 30):

(III/1) Ḥr maᶜ-khrw ms.n Ta-y- * * mn rn.k ḏd ẖa.t.k rwd rᶜnb(or khr?) (2) ᶜnkh ba.k khr Imn rn(p) ẖat.k Wsir sn-sn.k r ḥ(ḥ)

(III/1) "Hor justified born of Tay(khbyt) (en)dures name thine is steadfast corpse thine flourishes every day (2) lives Ba thine before (in the presence of) Amon (is) young corpse thine before (in the presence of) Osiris breathest thou unto eternity"

PARAGRAPH V

(IV/3) [ỉr n⸗k bꜣ⸗k pr.t-ḫrw m t ḥnq.(t) kꜣ.w ꜣpd.w m qbḥw snṯ]r m ẖr.t hrw[189] [n.t rᶜ nb ḥᶜ.w⸗k ḥr] qs.w⸗k[190] mỉ qỉ⸗k ḥr-tp tꜣ ỉsw[r]⸗

---

[187] The words Ḥr mꜣᶜ-ḫrw ms.n Tꜣy-[ḫy-by.t] appear on patch 4/1 (= Baer's Fragment IV c/1), mounted upside down in the middle of the plate, between the center vignettes. Rhodes 2002, p. 38, has scanned an image of the patch restored to its proper place, but he has left unmoved the smaller patch above it with text that I read as [b]ꜣ⸗k earlier in the line (patch 3). His restored photograph thus makes his line 1 in fact line 2.

[188] For Rhodes' misreading of sᶜḥ⸗k "your corpse" (2002, pp. 29 and 39, following Nibley 1975), and the effect on his transliteration, see n. 182, above.

[189] The words [snṯ]r m ẖr.t hrw appear on patch 4/3 (= Baer's Fragment IV c/3).

[190] Of qs.w⸗k, only faint traces remain of the suffix ⸗k. Following Nibley 1975, p. 31,

k[191] m š[n]b=k (IV/4) [wnm=k m r3=k šsp=k] snw ḥnᶜ[192] [b3.w nṯr.w ḫ]w tw=k ᵓInpw ỉr=f s3w=k[193] nn šn[ᶜ.t]w=k[194] m r3.w (IV/5) [n.w dw3.t ỉy n=k Ḏḥwty ᶜ3] sp-2 wr nb Ḫmnw s[š]=f[195] n=k šᶜ.(t) (n) snsn m ḏbᶜ.w=f ḏs=f [s]nsn (IV/6) [b3=k r nḥḥ wḥm=k q]ỉ=k ḥr-tp t3 m-m[196] ᶜnḫ.w ỉ[w]=k nṯrỉ ḥnᶜ b3.w nṯr.w ỉb=k ỉb n Rᶜ ỉwf=k[197]

Rhodes 2002, pp. 29 and 39, misread the determinatives as ỉrw. The final two signs are the looped cloth (borrowed from the similar root "embalm"; the sign is looped and *not* oval: ᛜ) and the flesh determinative (𓂑)—both signs consistently misread by Rhodes. For the looped cloth, see Cols. I/3 and 5 and II/5; and for the flesh determinative, see Cols. II/6 and IV/6. Rhodes, p. 30, n. 18, remarked that "ỉrw here is difficult," and he assumed that the text included a conflation of versions. Gee, Rhodes and Nibley 2005, p. 31, repeated the incorrect reading. Muhlestein 2005, pp. 485–86, n. 38, could not read the signs and ironically praised Rhodes for "the difficulty of dealing with the grapheme and what he has done with it." *Contra* Muhlestein, the text does not contain ỉrw, it is no error that I "left it out," and the misreading by Rhodes is not "preferable."

[191] Metathesis for sỉw[r]=k. Nibley 1975, p. 31, correctly read the order of signs but noted the word as a "spelling stumblingblock." Rhodes 2002, p. 11, suggested that this was an error for sỉrw, but the phonetic writing sỉwr is the common late spelling; see Erman and Grapow 1957, vol. III, p. 428. On both pp. 11 and 29, Rhodes misread the word as ỉsrw. Nibley's better reading was retained in Gee, Rhodes and Nibley 2005, p. 43.

[192] The words snw ḥnᶜ appear in patch 4/4 (= Baer's Fragment IV c/4).

[193] For this aspect of Anubis, see Facsimile 3, col. VIII/8, below.

[194] Cf. P. Louvre N 3284, 2/8.

[195] The words sp-2 wr nb Ḫmnw s[š] appear on patch 4/5 (= Baer's Fragment IV c/5). For the evolution of the epithet of Thoth the Thrice Greatest (here literally, "the doubly great and great"= "Trismegistos") in this and other texts, see Ritner 1981a and 1981b. My citation of the available image of Fragment IV should not be construed as an endorsement of Nibley's scholarship, *contra* the implications of Gee 1992, p. 98, n. 6. For general studies of the Egyptian god and the adaptation of his epithet and role in Greek contexts, see Fowden 1986 and Copenhaver 1992, pp. xv–xvi, citations on p. 292 (Hermes Trismegistus).

[196] The top half of the words [q]ỉ=k ḥr-tp t3 m-m appears in patch 4/6 (= Baer's Fragment IV c/6).

[197] The scribe employs the variant found in P. Louvre N 3291, line 16, with three flesh signs for ỉwf (Erman and Grapow 1957, vol. I, p. 51). Nibley 1975, p. 33, wrongly read ḥᶜt.k, following P. Louvre N 3284, 2/11. Nibley's error is repeated by Rhodes 2002, pp. 29–30 and 39, so that he added an erroneous note to the final word of the previous line ([s]nsn): "There seems to be a third masculine pronoun, mistakenly written

(IV/7) [ỉwf n nṯr ꜥꜣ]

(IV/3) [May your *ba*-spirit make for you an invocation-offering consisting of bread, beer, beef and fowl, and of cool water and incen]se in the course of [every] day. [Your flesh is on] your bones in accordance with the form that you had on earth. May you drink with your throat. (IV/4) [May you eat with your mouth. May you receive] offering bread together with [the *ba*-spirits of the gods.] Anubis has [gua]rded you.[198] He has made your protection. You shall not be turned [away] from the doors (IV/5) [of the Underworld. Thoth], the Thrice [Great]est, Lord of Hermopolis, [has come to you.] He has writ[ten] for you a Breathing Document with his own fingers, so that (IV/6) [your *ba*-spirit] may breathe [forever, and that you might regain the fo]rm that you had on earth among the living, since you are divine together with the *ba*-spirits of the gods. Your heart is the heart of Re; your flesh (IV/7) [is the flesh of the great god.][199]

Baer 1968 Translation (p. 121):

"*Your ba has made invocation offerings for you consisting of bread, beer, cattle and fowl, libations and incense* in the course *of every day. Your flesh is on* your bones just like the shape you had on earth. You

after the verb to breathe, i.e. snsn=f" (p. 30, n. 20). This supposed pronoun is simply the flesh determinative of ỉwf in the line below. Nibley's 1975 translation "flesh" was wrongly omitted in Gee, Rhodes and Nibley 2005, p. 44. Muhlestein 2005, p. 486, n. 39, accepted my reading.

[198] Literally, "Anubis has designated you for protection." The sentence is in clear Late Egyptian with the object pronoun tw⸗k.

[199] Compare the translation of the (generally) parallel P. Louvre N 3284, 2/4–11, by Mark Smith 2009, pp. 470–71: "Your son will make invocation offerings to you consisting of bread, beer, oxen, and fowl, with libations and burning of incense in the course of every day. Your body is attached to your skeleton, exactly like your earthly form. You will drink with your throat and eat with your mouth. You will receive loaves together with the bas of the gods. Anubis will safeguard you. He will effect your protection. You will not be turned away from the doors of the underworld. Thoth the twice greatest, lord of Hermopolis, will come to you. He will write you a letter for breathing with his own fingers. Your ba will breathe for ever. You will resume your earthly form among the living, being divine in company with the bas of the gods. Your heart is the heart of Re. Your flesh is the flesh of the great god." Smith joins §§ 4 and 5 and has mistranslated *ba*-spirit as "son" in 2/4. This papyrus names Thoth only as "doubly great" (2/8).

have drunk with your throat, *eaten with your mouth, and received* offering-cakes together with *the bas of the gods.* Anubis has guarded you and protected you. You have not been turned back from the gates *of the Netherworld. Thoth* Twice *Great,* the Great, Lord of Hermopolis *has come to you* to write for you a Breathing Permit with his own fingers, that *your* ba may breathe *forever. You have assumed again the shape* you had on earth among the living. *You are* divine together with the bas of the gods. Your heart is the heart of Re, and your body *is the body of the Great God.*"

Gee, Rhodes and Nibley 2005 Transliteration and Translation (pp. 43–44, col. 3, lines 3–6):

[…] snṯr m ẖr.t [hrw …] qs=k ỉrw[200] mỉ qỉ=k ḥr tp-tꜣ ỉswr=k m […][201]

4 […] sn.w ḥnꜥ [… ḫ]w tw=k Inp ỉrw=f nḏ=k[202] nn ḫsf [tw=k][203] m rꜣ.w […]

[…] sp-2 wr nb Ḫmnw sš=f n=k šꜥ snsn.w m ḏbꜥ.w=f ḏs=f snsn

[…] tw.t=k ḥr tp-tꜣ m-m[204] ꜥnḫ.w ỉw=k nṯry ḥnꜥ bꜣ.w nṯr.w ỉb=k ỉb n Rꜥ ḥꜥ.t=k[205]

[…]

"incense as the requirements of each [day …] thy bones, like thy very form(s) upon the earth: Thou drinkest with

4 […] (offering) bread, along with […] Anubis [gu]ards thee; he is (*lit.* makes) thy security. There is no turning [thee] away from the gates

[200] For this erroneous reading, see n. 190, above.

[201] The final traces š[n]b=k were ignored in Nibley 1975, p. 31; Rhodes 2002, pp. 29–30 and 39; and Gee, Rhodes and Nibley 2005, p. 43.

[202] The word sꜣw was misread as nḏt in Nibley 1975, p. 32; and in Gee, Rhodes and Nibley 2005, p. 44.

[203] Misread as ḫsf [twk] by Nibley 1975, p. 32; and in Gee, Rhodes and Nibley 2005, p. 44..

[204] Gee and Rhodes repeat Nibley's mistaken assumption of dittography, not recognizing the compound preposition m-m (Erman and Grapow 1957, vol. II, p. 2).

[205] For the proper reading of this word as ỉwf, see n. 197, above.

[…] the Most High (twice great), Lord of Hermopolis, has written for thee a book of breathings with his own fingers so that […] may go on breathing
[…] thy form (as) upon the earth among the living, thous being deified along with the *ba*s of the gods. Thy heart is the heart of Re; thy" [206]

Rhodes 2002 Transliteration and Translation (pp. 29–30):

[ỉrw n=k (3) bꜣ=k pr.t-ḫrw m tꜣ, ḥnq.t, kꜣ, ꜣpd], qbḥ, snṯr[207] m ẖr.t hrw [n.t rꜥ nb. ḥꜥ.t=k ḥr] qs.w<=k> ỉrw[208] mỉ q(ỉ)=k ḥr-tp tꜣ. sỉrw=k[209] m [šnb(.t)=k.[210] (4) wnm=k m rꜣ=k. šsp=k] snw.w ḥnꜥ [bꜣ.w nṯr.w ḫꜣ]w[211] tw=k ꜣInp, ỉrw=f sꜣ=k. nn šn[ꜥ=k][212] m rꜣ.w (5) [n.w dwꜣ.t. ỉỉ n=k Ḏḥwty ꜥꜣ] sp 2 wr, nb Ḫmnw. sš=f n=k šꜥ(.t) snsn m ḏbꜥ.w=f ḏs=f. snsn (6) [bꜣ=k r nḥḥ. wḥm=k] q(ỉ)=k ḥr-tp tꜣ m-m ꜥnḫ, ỉw=k ntry ḥnꜥ bꜣ.w nṯr.w, ỉb=k ỉb n Rꜥ, ḥꜥ.t=k[213] (7) [ḥꜥ.t n nṯr ꜥꜣ.]

"[May (3) your soul make for you invocation offerings of bread, beer, beef, and fowl,] libations and incense during the course [of every day. Your flesh is on] <your> bones, made like your form on earth.[214] May you drink with [your throat. May you eat with your

---

[206] Gee and Rhodes have mistakenly dropped Nibley's term "flesh."

[207] Since Rhodes misread sꜥḥ=k in line 1, his subsequent line division is inaccurate, so that he began line 3 with [bꜣ=k] rather than with the preceding [ỉrw n=k]. The word qbḥ is lost in the break, and only the final traces of snṯr are present on patch 4/3.

[208] For this erroneous reading, see n. 190, above.

[209] For the proper reading of the signs as ỉsw[r]=k (< sỉwr=k), see n. 191, above.

[210] Following Nibley, the preserved traces of š[n]b=k were unrecognized by Rhodes, pp. 29–30 and 39.

[211] Since the P. JS I text writes the verb as ḫw (col. IV/12), Rhodes (pp. 29 and 39) was probably wrong to restore it as ḫꜣw, following the writing of P. Louvre N 3289.

[212] Rhodes (pp. 29 and 39), ignored the surviving final traces of šn[ꜥ.t]w=k and misread šn[ꜥ=k], but cf. Louvre N 3284 in Rhodes 2002, pp. 54–55, line 8.

[213] For Rhodes' misunderstanding of the word ỉwf and his mistaken emendation (p. 30, n. 2), see n. 197, above.

[214] The translation by Rhodes 2002, p. 30, "made like your form on earth" is incorrect as there is no word for "made"; see n. 190 on qs.w=k, above.

mouth. May you receive] (4) offerings with [the souls of the gods. May] Anubis [protect] you and may he guard you. [You] shall not be turned back from the gates (5) [of the hereafter]. May the twice [great] and mighty [Thoth,] Lord of Hermopolis, [come to you.] May he write for you the Document of Breathing with his own fingers. May [your soul] breathe (6) [forever. May you assume again] your form on earth among the living, having been made divine together with the souls of the gods, your heart being the heart of Re, and your limbs (7) [the limbs of the Great God.]"

Nibley 1975 Word-for-Word Transliteration and Translation of Preserved Sections Only (pp. 31–33):

(III/3) sntr m ẖr.t ° ° ° (qs.k?) irw mi k.i.k ḥr tp-ta iswr.k m (4) .snw ḥnᶜ ° ° ° kh)w twk inp irw.f nḏt.k[215] nn khsf (twk)[216] m rw (5) sp-2 wr nb Khnmw s-sh.f n.k shᶜ sn-sn(w) m ḏbaw.f ḏs.f sn-sn (6) twt.k ḥr tp-ta m-m ᶜnkh(w) yw.k nṯry hnᶜ Baw nṯrw ib.k ib n Re ḥᶜt.k

(III/3) "(3) incense as prescribed (daily) [...] (bones thine) or thou being like shape thine (nature) upon earth drinkest thou with (4) (offering) bread with [...] (guard)s thee Anubis makes he protection thine there is no turning thee aside from gates (5) two-times great lord of Hermopolis write(s) he for thee book (of) breathings with fingers his own breath(est) (6) image thine upon-earth among (the) living thou being divine with (the) Spirits (of the) gods heart thine heart of Re flesh thine"

PARAGRAPH VI

[hy Ws]ȉr Ḥr mȝᶜ-ẖrw ʾImn (ȉ)rm=k rᶜ nb m pr Rᶜ[217] wḥm=k ᶜnḫ

[215] Misread from sȝw=k in Nibley 1975, p. 32; and in the 2005 revision, p. 44.

[216] Misread from šn[ᶜ.t]w=k by Nibley 1975, p. 32; and in the 2005 revision, p. 44.".

[217] All other versions have rᶜ nb ḥr wḥm=k, omitting the phrase "in the estate of Re." Baer, p. 122, n. 60, was unable to read the traces between rᶜ "day" and m pr Rᶜ "in the estate/temple of Re." This is simply the expected modifier nb "every" placed to the right of rᶜ, not below it as restored by Nibley 1975, p. 34, who ignored the following sign. The damaged suffix =k fills the space where Nibley restored nb. Nibley's error has been repeated by Rhodes 2002, p. 39; and in Gee, Rhodes and Nibley 2005, p. 44.

wp n≠k Wp-wꜣ.wt wꜣ.t (IV/8) nfr[.t[218] mꜣꜣ≠k m ỉr.ty≠k sḏm≠k m] ꜥnḫ.wy≠k mdw≠k m rꜣ≠k šm≠k m rd(. wy)≠k[219] ỉw bꜣ≠k nṯrỉ m dwꜣ.t [r ỉ]r (IV/9) ḫpr.[w nb r mr≠f ỉr≠k nꜣ šr]šr.w[220] n p(ꜣ) (ỉ)šd šps [...][221] m ꜣIwnw nhs≠k tw[222] rꜥ nb mꜣꜣ≠k nꜣ sty(IV/10)[.wt n Pꜣ-Rꜥ ỉy n≠k ꜣImn ẖr ṯꜣ].w n ꜥnḫ dỉ≠f ỉr≠k sn[sn m][223] ḏbꜣ.t≠k pr≠k r tꜣ rꜥ nb ỉr≠w[224] n≠k šꜥ(IV/11)[y.t n sns]n [n Ḏḥwty m] sꜣw≠k snsn≠k

[218] A small misplaced fragment inserted in lines 9–10 of this column contains the words nfr (patch 5/1) and ḫpr (patch 5/2), which properly begin lines 8 and 9. See Baer, p. 122, n. 62. Nibley 1975, pp. 35–36, did not place the fragment and mistranscribed nfr as a divine determinative. The matter of the fragment with nfr and ḫpr was poorly resolved in Gee, Rhodes and Nibley 2005, p. 45, where the fragment was now correctly placed but ignored in the the transcription and transliteration (see nn. 46 and 48, unchanged from Nibley 1975).

[219] Only one leg is written. The same writing is found in P. Berlin 3135.

[220] P. Louvre N 3284 indicates a vocalization šlšl.w, corresponding to Coptic ϣⲟⲗϣⲗ "shaking" (Crum 1939, p. 561b). Mark Smith 2009, p. 471, n. 39, failed to note the Coptic parallel and translated "breezes."

[221] A gap at this spot was later filled with a fragment (patch 5) torn from the beginnings of lines 8–9, probably covering a hole already present when the papyrus was written; see Baer 1968, p. 122, n. 62. Nothing is expected between šps and m ꜣIwnw. Baer considered the trace of m following the hole to be the conclusion of a second writing of šps (dittography), and his remarks were misinterpreted by Nibley 1975, p. 35, who transcribed the final determinatives of (ỉ)šd as another writing of šps. Had such dittography existed, it would have been in the hole.

[222] Literally, "May you waken yourself." The phrase was misread by Nibley 1975, p. 35, as nhs twk. Misunderstood by Rhodes 2002, p. 30, n. 22, the tw reflects simply the reflexive use of the dependent object pronoun with this verb in contemporary Demotic; see Erichsen 1954, p. 222. Were Rhodes competent in Demotic, he would not have stated that the usage "makes no sense here" (p. 30, n. 22). This error makes his reading of the Demotic numeral 2 in col. II/3 even less likely and is particularly odd since on pp. 7 and 31, n. 27, the form is correctly understood: "You rouse yourself every day" (p. 7), "may you wake yourself" (p. 31). Is this a further, incompletely reworked revision?

[223] The hole in the papyrus is here patched with ḫpr from line 9 (patch 5/2). The lost text of sn[sn m] is too small for the current gap, supporting Baer's suggestion of ancient damage. Slight traces of m or the determinative of ṯꜣw are preserved on tatters to the right of ḏbꜣ.t.

[224] Not attested in other variants, which have a slightly different text: "The Document of Breathing of Thoth is your protection, so that you might breathe by means of it every day." The word (𝟿𝑂) is misread in all LDS editions; see below.

ꞽm=s mꞽ Rꜥ mꜣꜣ ꞽr.t=k sty.(wt) ꞽtn ḏd=w mꜣꜥ.t r=k (IV/12) [m-bꜣḥ Wsꞽr] ꞽr=w m[k.t=k(?)][225] Ḥr Bḥd.t ḫw=f ḏ.t=k nṯrꞽ=f bꜣ=k mꞽ ꞽr[226] nṯr.w nb.w bꜣ n Rꜥ ḥr sꜥnḫ [bꜣ=]k (IV/13) [bꜣ n Šw ḥr ẖnm ms]ty=k

[Hail, Os]iris Hôr, the justified! Amon is with you every day in the Estate of Re, so that you might live again. Wepwawet has opened for you the good way, (IV/8) [so that you might see with your eyes, that you might hear with] your ears, that you might speak with your mouth, and that you might walk with your feet, while your *ba*-spirit is deified in the Underworld [in order to] make (IV/9) [any] transformation[s according to its will. May you cause the rust] lings of the noble persea tree […] in Heliopolis.[227] May you awake every day so that you might see the ray[s (IV/10) of the sun. Amon has come to you bearing the brea]th of life. He has caused that you brea[the in] your sarcophagus so that you might go forth to the earth every day. (IV/11) The [Breath]ing Docu[ment of Thoth] has been made for you [as] your protection, so that you might breathe by means of it like Re, so that your eyes might see the rays of the sun disk, and so that you might be called 'justified' (IV/12) [in the presence of Osiris.] [Your] pro[tection(?)] has been made. Horus the Behdedite[228] has guarded your body and has deified your *ba*-spirit as do all the gods. The *ba*-spirit of Re revivifies your [*ba*-spirit].

[225] Fragment X has a broken, shorter variant than standard texts. The word m[k.t] "protection" is restored following col. V/5, where it also precedes mention of Horus of Behdet. This restoration was first suggested by Baer in his unpublished notes, p. 35. Nibley 1975, p. 37, misread the traces as ꞽt.f. Other texts have sš.w mꜣꜥ-ḫrw ḥr ns=k "They have written 'justified' on your tongue." For "tongue" rather than "body," see Herbin 2008, p. 24, and for the practice, cf. Ritner 1993, p. 88. Rhodes 2002, pp. 30–31 and 39, has copied both the incorrect Nibley reading and the Louvre text, but the former is a misreading and there is no room for the latter, as Rhodes admitted on p. 30, n. 24. Gee, Rhodes and Nibley 2005, p. 46, retain Nibley's misreading as ꞽt=f. Herbin 2008, p. 24, n. 63, suggests reading the initial trace as the man-with-hand-to-mouth determinative of mꜣꜥ-ḫrw followed by ꞽw (= r) for ḥr, but he admits that the following traces cannot be reconciled with the expected ns "tongue."

[226] Other versions read: "Horus, the protector of his father, … has deified your *ba*-spirit like all the gods."

[227] For the mythological associations, see Baer 1968, p. 123, n. 63.

[228] Horus of Edfu.

(IV/13) [The *ba*-spirit of Shu[229] unites with] your [nos]trils.[230]

Baer 1968 Translation (p. 122):

"O Osiris Hôr ..., Amon is with you every day ...[231] in the Temple of Re so that you may live again. Wepwawet has opened the good way for you. *You have seen with your eyes, heard with* your ears, spoken with your mouth, and walked with your feet. Your ba is divine in the Netherworld, *so that* it can assume *any* form *it wishes. You have scat*tered the Noble[232] Ished-tree *in* Heliopolis. You have awakened every day and seen the rays *of the sun. Amon has come to you bringing the breath* of life to let you brea*the in* your sarcophagus. You have gone out to the earth every day. The *Breathing* Permit *of Thoth* has been made *as a protection for* you that you may breathe by means of it like Re. Your eye has seen the rays of the sun's disk. You have been declared just *before Osiris* ... Horus of Edfu has protected your body and made your ba divine as all the other gods do. The ba of Re revives your ba; *the ba of Shu enters* your nostrils."

---

[229] For Shu as god of air, and thus particularly appropriate in this context, see the discussion of "Luft (Luftgott)" in Westendorf 1980, cols. 1098–1102. Cf. also Mark Smith 2009, p. 471, n. 42 on the ba of Shu: "Scil. the wind."

[230] Compare the translation of the (generally) parallel P. Louvre N 3284, 2/12–21, by Mark Smith 2009, p. 471 (his § 5): "Hail Osiris ... Amun is with you every day, making you live again. Wepwaut will open up the beautiful ways for you. You will see with your eyes. You will hear with your ears. You will speak with your mouth. You will walk with your feet, while your ba is divine in the underworld so as to assume any form it wishes. You will enjoy the breezes beneath the venerable balanites tree in Heliopolis. You will awaken each day and look upon the rays of the sun. Amun will come to you bearing the breath of life. He will cause you to breathe within your sarcophagus. You will go forth to the earth every day, with the letter for breathing of Thoth as your protection. You will breathe by means of it daily. You will behold the rays of the sun disc. 'Truth' will be said about you in the presence of Osiris. They will inscribe 'justified' upon your tongue. Horus the protector of his father will keep your body safe. He will divinize your ba like (those of) all the gods. The ba of Re enlives your ba. The ba of Shu unites with your nostrils." Smith's translation "breezes" is discussed in n. 220, above.

[231] For the lack of anything missing here (nb "every" simply shifted to the right), see n. 217, above.

[232] Baer (p. 122, n. 62) considered the trace of m following the hole to be the conclusion of a second writing of šps (dittography), and he restored the required m ("in") in italics. See n. 221, above.

Gee, Rhodes and Nibley 2005 Transliteration and Translation (pp. 44–46, col. 3, lines 7–13):

[…] Wsỉr Ḥr mꜣʿ-ḫrw Imn r-m=[k] rʿ [nb][233] m pr Rʿ wḥm=k ʿnḫ wp n=k Wp-wꜣ.wt[234]

[[235] …] ʿnḫ.wy=k mdw=k m rꜣ=k šm=k m rd.wy=k[236] ỉw bꜣ=k nṯry m dwꜣ.t

[[237] … šr]šr.w n p (ỉ)šd šps m Iwnw nhs.tw=k[238] rʿ nb mꜣꜣ=k stw.t

[…].w n ʿnḫ dỉ=f ỉr.t=sn […] ḫpr […] ḏbꜣ.wt=k pr=k r tꜣ rʿ nb rdỉ.tw[239] n=k šʿ

[…] nḏ.w=k[240] snsn.w=k ỉm=s mỉ Rʿ mꜣꜣ ỉr.t=k stw.t Itn ḏd.w mꜣʿ.t n=k[241]

12 [… ỉnḏ] ỉt=f[242] […] Bḥdty ẖnm.n=f[243] ḏ.t=k nṯr.ty=fy[244] bꜣ=k mỉ ỉrw nṯr.w nb bꜣ n Rʿ ḥr sʿnḫ

[… ms]ty=k

"[… Osi]ris Hor, Justified, born of Taykhebyt, Justified! Amon (is) at (thy) side constantly ([every] day), in the Temple (House)

---

[233] For the presence of nb "every," see n. 217, above.

[234] The word wꜣ.t "way/road" was copied but misread as the conclusion of Wp-wꜣ.wt by Gee, Rhodes and Nibley, p. 44, following Nibley 1975, p. 34.

[235] For the confused and inconsistent omission of nfr[.t], see n. 218, above.

[236] Only one leg is actually written: rd.(wy). The error follows Nibley 1975, p. 34.

[237] For the confused and inconsistent omission of ḫpr[.w], see n. 218, above.

[238] Misread (following Nibley 1975, p. 35) from nhs⸗k tw.

[239] For this misreading of ỉr⸗w, see n. 224, above. Gee, Rhodes and Nibley (p. 45) repeat the error of Nibley 1975, p. 36, but add hatching to indicate lost text.

[240] Misread by Nibley 1975, p. 36, as (nḏ)w.k from sꜣw⸗k. Nibley's error was repeated in Gee, Rhodes and Nibley, p. 45.

[241] On p. 45, Nibley's transliteration was printed as n⸗k, but the transcription changed to r⸗k, while his original note misreading rn⸗k or n⸗k was retained (n. 49)!

[242] For this passage and the misreading ỉt=f, see n. 225, above.

[243] Misread by Nibley 1975, p. 37, as ẖnm.n.f from ḫw⸗f. The error was retained in Gee, Rhodes and Nibley, p. 46.

[244] Misread by Nibley 1975, p. 37, as a sḏm.ty.fy-form (future participle) nṯr.ty.fy from nṯrỉ⸗f. The error was retained in Gee, Rhodes and Nibley, p. 46.

of Re. Thou repeatest life. Wepwawet reports to thee
[...] thy (two) ears, thou speakest with thy mouth, thou walkest with thy two legs. Thy *ba* is deified in the *duat*.
[...] rustlings (whisperings) of the most noble *ished*-tree in Heliopolis (when) thou awakenest every day (and) seest (*or* upon beholding) the ray(s)
[...]s of life, he causes thee to begin (make) breathing thy coffin and come up to earth every day. There is given to thee the book
[...] thy protections, thou breathest by it like Re (when) thine eye beholds the rays of Aton. They call thee (*or* they refer to thee as) Maat
[... protector of] his father [...] Horus the Behdetite embraces (unites with) thy body and deifies thy spirit (*ba*) as all the gods do (*or* in the manner of all the gods). The *ba* of Re is giving life
[...] thy (two) [nost]rils."

Rhodes 2002 Transliteration and Translation (pp. 30–31):

hy [Ws]ỉr Ḥr, mꜣꜥ-ḫrw. ꜣImn ỉrm=k rꜥ nb[245] m pr Rꜥ. wḥm=k ꜥnḫ. wp n=k Wpwꜣ.wt wꜣ.t (8) nfr[.t. mꜣꜣ=k m ỉr.t=k, sḏm=k m] ꜥnḫ.wy=k, mdw=k m rꜣ=k, šm=k m rd.wy=k,[246] ỉw bꜣ=k ntry m dwꜣ.t [r ỉrw] (9) ḫpr[w nb r-mr=f.

ỉr=k nꜣ] šršr.w[247] n p(ꜣ) (ỉ)št šps m ꜣIwnw. nhs=k tw[248] rꜥ nb, mꜣꜣ=k nꜣ sty (10) [n] pꜣ [rꜥ.

ỉỉ n=k ꜣImn ẖr tꜣw] n ꜥnḫ. dỉ=f ỉr=k sn[sn m] ḏbꜣw.t=k. pr=k r tꜣ rꜥ nb, sp-2. ỉrw[249] n=k šꜥ(.t) (11) [snsn n Ḏḥwty m] sꜣ=k. snsn=k

[245] For the copying error in Rhodes, p. 39 (following Nibley), see n. 217, above.

[246] Only one leg is written, *contra* Rhodes, pp. 30 and 39 (following Nibley's error, 1975, p. 34).

[247] Rhodes (p. 31 and n. 26) questioned the meaning of the word, but see n. 220, above.

[248] Rhodes (p. 30, n. 22) could not understand the form that he has adopted; see n. 222, above, for this passage and its implications.

[249] Rhodes (pp. 30 and 39), misread the Demotic past tense passive ỉr⸗w as sp-2 ỉrw. Rhodes' transcription on p. 39 is wrong, as are his paleographic comments (p. 30, n. 23); his superlinear sp is merely part of the verb ỉr, written with the full eye, not the oval pupil. His grammatical comments (pp. 8 and 30, n. 23) suggested a passive sḏm⸗f form for what is simply the contemporary third plural suffix ⸗w—replacing the older suffix ⸗sn as Rhodes noted for two other examples (p. 7).

ỉm=s mỉ Rᶜ. m33 ỉr.t=k sty ỉtn.

ḏd=w m3ᶜ.t r=k (12) [m-b3ḥ Wsỉr. sš=w m3ᶜ-ḫrw ḥr ḏ.t=k. Ḥr nḏty] ỉt=f,[250] Ḥr bḥdt(y), ḫw=f ḏ.t=k, ntr=f b3=k mỉ ỉrw nṯr.w nb, b3 n Rᶜ ḥr sᶜnḫ [b3=k] (13) [b3 n Šw ḥr ẖnm ms]ty=k.

"O Osiris] Hor, justified. Amon is with you every day in the House of Re. May you live again. May Wepwawet open for you the beautiful path. (8) [May you see with your eyes, hear with your] ears, speak with your mouth, and walk with your legs, your soul having been made divine in the hereafter [so that it can assume (9) any] form [it desires.

May you cause] the rustlings(?) of the noble Ished tree in Heliopolis. May you awake every day and see the rays (10) [of] the [sun.

May Amon come to you bearing the breath] of life. May he cause you to breathe [in] your coffin. May you go forth to the earth every day. May the Document (11) [of Breathing of Thoth be made for you for] your protection. May you breathe by means of it like Re. May your eye see the rays of the (sun's) disk.

May they speak truth concerning you (12) [in the presence of Osiris. May "justified" be written upon your body. May Horus, the Avenger] of His Father, (even) Horus of Edfu, protect your body, and may he cause your soul to be divine like all the gods do, while the soul of Re is animating [your soul] and (13) [the soul of Shu is surrounding] your [nos]trils."

Nibley 1975 Word-for-Word Transliteration and Translation of Preserved Sections Only (pp. 34–38):

(III/7) Wsir Ḥr maᶜ-khrw imn r-mᶜ.k[251] rᶜ-nb[252] m pr Reᶜ wḥm.k ᶜnkh wp n.k Wp(wa)wt (8) ᶜnhwy k md(w).k m r.k sh-m.k m

[250] For this passage and the misreading ỉt=f, see n. 225, above.

[251] For the common late conjunction, misunderstood by Nibley (p. 34) as a confusion of r-ᶜ and m-ᶜ, see Erman and Grapow 1957, vol. I, p. 115/17–20. Nibley's error was recognized in Gee, Rhodes and Nibley 2005, p. 44, n. 44.

[252] For Nibley's copying error, p. 34, see n. 217, above.

rdwy.k[253] iw ba.k nṯry m dwt (9) (shr)shr.w n pa (i)sh-d sh-p-ss[254] m[255] ᾽Iwnw nhs.twk[256] rᶜ-nb maa.k na stwt (10) -w n ᶜnkh di.f ir.t sn dbawt.k pr.k r ta rᶜ-nb rdi.tw[257] n.k shᶜk ◦ ◦ (11) (nḏ)w.k[258] sh-sn(w).k im.s mi Reᶜ maa irt.k stwt ỉtn ḏd-w maᶜt n.k[259] (12) (nḏ.ty) it.f[260] Ḥr bḥddty ẖnm.n.f[261] ḏt.k nṯr ty.fy[262] ba.k mi irw nṯrw nb Ba n Reᶜ ḥr sᶜnkh (13) (ms)ty.k

(III/7) "(the) Osiris Hor justified Amon (is) beside thee day every in house (of) Re repeat thou life opens to thee Wepwawet[263] (8) (2) ears thine speakest thou with mouth thine walkest thou with 2 legs thine is Ba thine divine in (the) Duat (9) whisperings (or splittings) of the Ished-tree twice-noble in Heliopolis awakened art thou [or reflexive] every-day seest thou the rays (10) (breath)s of life causes he to make breath(ing) (in) coffin thine goest up thou to earth every-day, given to thee writ(ings) (11) protection thine breathest thou by (in) it like Re sees eye thine rays (of) Aton; they say truth to

[253] Only one leg is written, *contra* Nibley, p. 34. Nibley's error was repeated by Rhodes and Gee, Rhodes and Nibley, p. 45.

[254] For Nibley's misunderstanding of a misplaced fragment here and in line 10, see nn. 218 and 221, above.

[255] Omitted in the hand copy in Nibley 1975, p. 35, but corrected in Gee, Rhodes and Nibley 2005, p. 45.

[256] Misread by Nibley (p. 35) from nhs=k tw. Nibley's error was repeated by Rhodes and Gee, Rhodes and Nibley.

[257] Misread by Nibley (p. 36), from ỉr=w. Nibley's 1975 reading was retained, but hatched as damaged, in Gee, Rhodes and Nibley 2005, p. 45.

[258] Misread by Nibley (p. 36) from sꜣw=k. Nibley's error was repeated in Gee, Rhodes and Nibley 2005, p. 45.

[259] Nibley (p. 37) suggested rn=k or n=k. Nibley's supposed n is the lower stroke of the ovoid r from r=k.

[260] For this passage and the misreading ỉt.f, see n. 225, above.

[261] Misread by Nibley 1975, p. 37, as ẖnm.n.f from ḫw=f. The error was retained in Gee, Rhodes and Nibley, p. 46.

[262] Misread by Nibley 1975, p. 37, as a sḏm.ty.fy-form (future participle) nṯr.ty.fy from nṯrỉ=f. The error was retained in Gee, Rhodes and Nibley 2005, p. 46.

[263] The word wꜣ.t "way/road" was copied but misread as the conclusion of Wp-wꜣ.wt by Nibley, p. 34; and Gee, Rhodes and Nibley 2005, p. 44.

(concerning thee *or:* they call the [*sic* for "thee"]) Maat (12) (avenger of) father his Horus (of) Edfu has enfolded body being about to deify spirit thine as do gods all. Ba of Re shall cause to live (two) nostrils thine"

PARAGRAPH VII

h[ꜣ]y[264] Wsỉr Ḥr mꜣꜥ-ḫrw ms.n Tꜣy-ḫy-b(y.t)[265] mꜣꜥ.(t)-ḫrw snsn bꜣ=k ỉw (= r) [bw] mr=k[266] (V/1) [ỉ]w=k m[267] [Wsỉr Wsỉr Ḫnty-ꜣImnty.w rn=k Ḥꜥpy wr ỉw n=k m ꜣbw mḥ=f ḥtp=k m ḏfꜣ](V/2).w

Hail, Osiris Hôr, the justified, born of Taikhibit, the justified! May your *ba*-spirit breathe wherever it likes, (V/1) since you exist as [Osiris.[268] Osiris Foremost of the Westerners is your name. Hapy the great (the Nile Inundation) has come to you from Elephantine, so that he might fill your altar with (V/2) food offering]s.[269]

---

[264] Here there is room for the fuller form of hy, found clearly in col. V/12 and throughout Louvre N 3284.

[265] For this spelling of the name, see "The Individuals," above.

[266] The signs were ignored by Nibley 1975, p. 38, with mr wrongly included in the photograph of the end of line 12 on p. 37. The photograph has been improved but the reading unchanged in Gee, Rhodes and Nibley 2005, p. 46. Rhodes 2002, p. 31, followed Nibley in considering mr=k lost (placing it in brackets in the transliteration and translation), but in his transcription on p. 39 it has been found. Perhaps another late addition taken from my work, the incomplete revision indicates again the carelessness of the Rhodes volume.

[267] Unread by Nibley 1975, p. 39, and Gee, Rhodes and Nibley 2005, p. 48.

[268] As Rhodes employed only Louvre N 3284 for his restoration here, he has failed to note that this Louvre exemplar is unique and probably corrupt at this point. Louvre N 3291, British Museum 9995 and Berlin 3135 all have "you exist as Osiris. Osiris Foremost of the Westerners is your name." Unlike Rhodes, I have followed the majority of manuscripts in my restoration.

[269] Compare the translation of the parallel P. Louvre N 3284, 3/1–4, by Mark Smith 2009, p. 472 (his § 6): "Hail Osiris ... Your ba will breathe at the place where you desire, for you are Osiris. Osiris foremost of the Westerners is your name. Hapi the great has come to you from Elephantine. He will fill your offering table with provisions." Here Smith has translated the phrase ỉw=k m s.t n Wsỉr "you are in the place of (or 'on the throne of') Osiris" simply as "for you are Osiris." In all variants, the passage stresses the unity of the deceased *as a form of* Osiris, so that the traditional translation "Osiris NN" is correct, *contra* Smith's general rendering "Osiris of NN"; see Ritner 2010, p. 178, n. 26.

Baer 1968 Translation (pp. 122–23):

"O Osiris Hôr …, your ba has breathed *everywhere* you wished, for you have the attributes of *Osiris. Osiris Foremost-of-the-Westerners is your name. The Great Inundation has come to you from Elephantine that it might fill your altar with provisions.*"

Gee, Rhodes and Nibley 2005 Transliteration and Translation (pp. 46 and 48, col. 3, lines 13–4, line 1):

hy[270] Wsỉr Ḥr mꜣʿ-ḫrw ms.n Tꜣy-ḫy-bỉꜣ.t mꜣʿ-ḫrw snsn bꜣ=k ỉw

1 […]

"Hail thou Osiris Hor, Justified, born of Taykhebyt, Justified. Thy *ba* breathes in (any)

1 […]"

Rhodes 2002 Transliteration and Translation (p. 31):

hy[271] Wsỉr Ḥr, mꜣʿ-ḫrw, ms.n Tꜣy-ḫyb.t, mꜣʿ-ḫrw. snsn bꜣ=k ỉw [b(w) mr=k.[272]] 4. (1) [ỉw]=k m [s.t n Wsỉr. Ḫnty-ʾImnty.w rn≠k. Ḥʿpy wr <m> ỉw n=k m ꜣbw mḥ=f ḥtp=k m ḏfꜣw.w.]

"O Osiris Hor, justified, born of Taykhebyt, justified. May your soul breathe [anyplace you want.] 4. (1) You [are] on [the throne of Osiris. Foremost of the Westerners is your name. The Great Hapy has come to you from Elephantine to fill your offering table with provisions.]"

Nibley 1975 Word-for-Word Transliteration and Translation of Preserved Sections Only (p. 38):

(III/13) (ha)y Wsir Ḥr maʿ-khrw ms n Ta-y-khbt[273] maʿ-khrw sn-

---

[270] For the fuller spelling here, see n. 264, above, and the following note.

[271] Following Nibley 1975, p. 38, Rhodes 2002, p. 39, read only hy, though here there is room for the fuller form, found clearly in col. V/12 and throughout Louvre N 3284. Rhodes' glossary on p. 83 does not correspond to his own transcriptions, since he copied the wrong determinative in col. 3/5 (his 2/5).

[272] For Rhodes' inconsistent incorporation of the preserved mr=k, see n. 266, above.

[273] Nibley (p. 38) mistranscribed the final signs, substituting a "t" for the human figure after ḫb. *Contra* Nibley, this is not the "only occurrence of the complete name,"

sn ba.k iw (= r)

(III/13) "Hail Osiris Hor justified born of Taykhebyt justified breathes ba thine unto (IV/1) (illegible)"

PARAGRAPH VIII

Wsỉr Ḥr mꜣꜥ-ḫrw ms.n[274] [Tꜣy-ḫy-by.t mꜣꜥ.(t)-ḫrw ỉw n=k nṯr.w n.w Šmꜥw Mḥw ssm=w tw=k r ꜥrq-ḥḥ[275] ꜥnḫ bꜣ=k šm](V/3)s=k Wsỉr snsn=k (m)-ḫnt Rꜣ-Sṯꜣw [mk tw=k Ḥꜣp(.t)-nb=s ḥnꜥ nṯr ꜥꜣ ẖꜣ.t=k ꜥnḫ m] (V/4) Ḏdw Ṯꜣw-wr bꜣ=k ꜥnḫ m p.t [rꜥ] nb

Osiris Hôr, the justified, born of [Taikhibit, the justified! The gods of Upper and Lower Egypt have come to you so that they might guide you to Alkhah. May your *ba*-spirit live,[276] may you] (V/3) serve Osiris, may you breathe within Rostau. ["She-who-hides-her-Lord"[277] and the great god have protected you. Your corpse lives in] (V/4) Busiris and the Thinite nome.[278] Your *ba*-spirit lives in heaven every [day].[279]

---

nor is its meaning "unknown." Nibley himself noted the full writing in col. II/2 (p. 20). Other unbroken writings of the mother's name appear in cols. I/3 and III/7. Nibley's treatment skipped col. I and misread col. III/7 (p. 26). Nibley's transcription has been improved (but still with a nonexistent "t") in Gee, Rhodes and Nibley 2005, p. 46. The "t" was properly omitted in Rhodes 2002, p. 39.

[274] Lines 1–2 were dismissed as illegible by Nibley 1975, p. 39, and Gee, Rhodes and Nibley 2005, p. 48. Aside from the first signs of line 1, they were also ignored in Rhodes 2002, pp. 31 and 41, so that most of his text for these lines is placed in brackets and the lines wrongly divided.

[275] For the writing of ꜥrq-ḥḥ, see Erichsen 1954, p. 68; and Erman and Grapow 1957, vol. I, p. 213.

[276] The majority of the text traditions begin a new sentence ꜥnḫ bꜣ=k "May your *ba*-spirit live." Louvre N 3284 has ḥnꜥ bꜣ=k "with your *ba*-spirit," and this was followed in Rhodes 2002, pp. 31 and 41.

[277] Alkhah is the specific burial site of Osiris at Abydos, Rostau is a generic term for burial ground (originally just for Saqqara), and "She-who-hides-her-Lord" (Hapetnebes) is the name of the necropolis at Abydos.

[278] The province of Egypt that includes Abydos.

[279] Compare the translation of the (generally) parallel P. Louvre N 3284, 3/4–8, by Mark Smith 2009, p. 472 (his § 7): "Osiris … the gods of Upper and Lower Egypt will come to you. They will conduct you to Alkhai in company with your ba. You will

Baer 1968 Translation (p. 123):

"Osiris Hôr …, *the gods of Upper and Lower Egypt have come to you in order to show you how to spend millions of years*[280] *in all together with your ba*. You have *accompanied* Osiris and breathed in Rostau. *Hapetnebes and the Great God have protected you. Your corpse lives* in Busiris and the Thinite Nome; your ba lives in heaven every *day*."

Gee, Rhodes and Nibley 2005 Transliteration and Translation (p. 48, col. 4, lines 2–4):

[…]
[šmš]=k Wsỉr snsn=k ḫnty[281] Rꜣ-sṯꜣw […]
m Ḏdw Ṯꜣ-wr bꜣ=k ꜥnḫ m p.t [rꜥ]-nb […]

"[…]
thou [mayest follow] Osiris and breathe in Rostau […]
in Busiris of the Thinite nome (while) thy *ba* lives in heaven all the time (every day) […]"

Rhodes 2002 Transliteration and Translation (p. 31):

[Wsỉr Ḥr (2) mꜣꜥ-ḫrw, ms.n[282] Tꜣy-ḫy-by.t, mꜣꜥ-ḫrw. ỉỉ n=k nꜣ nṯr.w n.w Šmꜥw Tꜣ-mḥw, sšm=w tw=k r ꜥrq-ḥḥ ḥnꜥ bꜣ=k. šms] (3) =k Wsỉr, snsn=k ḫnt Rꜣ-stꜣw. [mk tw=k Ḥꜣp(.t)-nbs=s ḥnꜥ nṯr ꜥꜣ, ẖꜣ.t=k <ḥr> ꜥnḫ] (4) m Ḏd(w) Tꜣ-wr, bꜣ=k <ḥr> ꜥnḫ m p.t rꜥ nb.

"[Osiris Hor, (2) justified, born of Taaykhebyt, justified. May the gods of Upper and Lower Egypt come to you and guide you to the Alchaꜥa together with your soul. May] you [accompany] (3) Osiris and may you breathe within Rostau. [May Hapetnebes protect you

---

follow Osiris and you will breathe in the necropolis. 'The one who conceals her lord' will protect you along with the great god. Your corpse lives in Busiris and the nome of Abydos. Your ba lives in the sky every day."

[280] Baer (p. 123) failed to recognize the name of the cult site of Osiris, Alkhah, and he adopted the copying error of P. Louvre N 3284 for the following word (ḥnꜥ for ꜥnḫ).

[281] Nibley 1975, p. 39, read "M or khnti" with a missing footnote. The reading was changed to ḫnty in Gee, Rhodes and Nibley, p. 48.

[282] Rhodes (pp. 31 and 41) was unable to read the surviving traces in line 2. His line divisions are thus incorrect, shifting a bracketed "Osiris Hor" to the lost end of line 1.

together with the Great God, while your body is living] (4) in Busiris and the Thinite nome, and your soul is living in heaven every day."

Nibley 1975 Word-for-Word Transliteration and Translation of Preserved Sections Only (p. 39):

(IV/3) (shms).k Wsir sn-sn.k M or khnti[283] r-stw (4) m ḏdw ṯa-wr ba.k ʿnkh m pt (rʿ)-nb

(IV/2) "(illegible) (3) (followest) thou Osiris breathest thou in Rostau (4) in Busiris (of) Thinite nome ba thine lives in heaven every-(day)"

PARAGRAPH IX

[Wsỉr Ḥr mȝʿ-ḫrw ms.n Tȝy-ḫy-by.t mȝʿ.(t)-ḫrw sḫm Sḫm.t m wȝw.w ỉm⸗k Ḥr] (V/5) ʿȝ ỉb ḥr ỉr mk.t⸗(k) Ḥr Bḥd.t [ḥr ỉr ỉb⸗k Ḥr-Mr.ty ḥr sȝw ḏ.t⸗k ḏd⸗k m] (V/6) ʿnḫ wḏȝ snb ỉw⸗k mn.tw ḥr ns.t⸗k m tȝ ḏsr [m]y [r⸗k Wsỉr Ḥr mȝʿ-ḫrw ms.n Tȝy-ḫy-by.t mȝʿ.(t)-ḫrw ỉw⸗k] (V/7) ḫʿ.tw m qd⸗k[284] twt m ẖkr.w⸗k sḏr⸗k[285] m ʿnḫ [wrš⸗k m snb šm⸗k snsn⸗k] (V/8) r[286] bw nb wbn Rʿ ḥr tpḥ.t⸗k[287] mỉ Wsỉr snsn⸗k [ʿn]ḫ[⸗k m sty.w⸗f ʾImn-Rʿ sʿnḫ⸗f] (V/9) kȝ⸗k swȝḏ⸗f

[283] Nibley (p. 39) had intended to insert a footnote here, but it was not printed.

[284] Nibley 1975, p. 41, mistranscribed ḫʿ as ḫn and misread qd⸗k as tyt.k. Yet another example of uncredited borrowing probably appears here in Rhodes 2002, which duplicated Nibley's error as tỉ.t=k in the transliteration (p. 32), but (re?)-transcribed the words in accordance with my comments as qd⸗k on p. 41! In Gee, Rhodes and Nibley 2005, p. 49, ḫn was changed to ḫʿ, but tyt=k was retained. Muhlestein 2005, p. 486, n. 40, detected Rhodes' inconsistency and error.

[285] Nibley's insistence, 1975 p. 41, that "the sign … is *not* sḏr but grg" shows ignorance of late hieratic and Demotic forms. See Möller 1912, p. 37, no. 384B = Verhoeven 2001, pp. 174–75, and Erichsen 1954, p. 480 (bottom). The form is now read sḏr in Rhodes 2002, pp. 32, 41 and 87, but is still translated as if grg on p. 32: "May you be established in life." This seems yet a further example of incomplete, and uncredited, reworking from my edition. In Gee, Rhodes and Nibley 2005, p. 49, only sḏr was now transcribed, but the contradictory, older note on grg retained (n. 57), and grg used for the translation "prepared while you were alive."

[286] By typographical error, this obvious r was placed within the brackets of col. V/7 in my earlier versions. The position was correctly noted by Baer, Nibley and Rhodes.

[287] "Cavern" signifies "tomb"; see Erman and Grapow 1957, vol. V, p. 365/5. Other versions have ḥw.t "mansion" with the same nuance. The word is misread in all LDS editions.

tw⸗k[288] m šꜣ.t[289] snsn šms⸗k Wsỉr [Ḥr nb ḥnw ỉw⸗k m nṯr ꜥꜣ ḫnty] (V/10) nṯr.w ꜥnḫ ḥr⸗k nfr ms.w⸗k rn⸗k rwd rꜥ nb [m]y[290] [ꜥ]q⸗k r [sḥ]-nṯr[291] [wr sp-2] (V/11) m Ḏdw mꜣꜣ⸗k Ḫnty-ʾImnty.w m ḥb Wg[ꜣ] nḏm sty⸗k m ḥwn[292] [ꜥꜣ rn⸗k m] (V/12) sꜥḥ[293] šps

[Osiris Hôr, the justified, born of Taikhibit, the justified! Sakhmet has overpowered those who would conspire against you. Horus] (V/5) the steadfast makes (your) protection. Horus the Behdedite [performs your wishes. Hormerty guards your body, so that you

---

[288] Nibley 1975, p. 42, garbled this passage, misreading swꜣḏ⸗f tw⸗k as "ꜥnkh nd (wḏa?)-snb or m swḏa.tw.k." As elsewhere, Nibley's "transliteration" does not follow standard conventions. Rhodes 2002, pp. 32 and 41, has repeated Nibley's error, in confusing the initial s of swꜣḏ as ꜥnḫ, the following sign wꜣḏ as wḏꜣ, and the man-with-hand-to-mouth determinative as wꜣḏ and reading ꜥnḫ wḏꜣ snb (s)wꜣḏ.tw⸗k. This example of Demotic tw⸗k is otherwise found in cols. III/7, 10; and IV/4; see Rhodes 2002, p. 7. For the supposed writing of ꜥnḫ wḏꜣ snb following kꜣ⸗k in this line, as suggested by Nibley and Rhodes, cf. the actual writing in col. V/6. In Gee, Rhodes and Nibley 2005, p. 49, the passage was changed to ꜥnḫ wḏꜣ snb swꜣḏ.tw⸗k. Muhlestein 2005, p. 486, n. 41, has again followed Rhodes and criticized me for failing to "account for all the signs." In consideration of the general inaccuracy of his remarks, it is apparent that Muhlestein was unable to provide an informed critique of the editions.

[289] The scribe has written šꜣ.t in error for šꜥ.t.

[290] The parallels alternate between my⸗k and ꜥq⸗k. Thus P. Louvre N 3284 has my⸗k (Rhodes 2002, pp. 56–57, line 17). As suggested by Baer in his notebooks, p. 51, the Smith version combines both variants.

[291] The words [ꜥ]q⸗k r [sḥ]-nṯr appear on patch 6/1 (= Baer's Fragment IV b/1), inserted upside down at the upper left of the *ba*-bird vignette. All extant versions have sḥ-nṯr, but Nibley 1975, p. 43, restored [ḥr.t]-nṯr. Baer translated "Great Divine Council," but the term refers specifically to the embalming booth of Anubis. Rhodes 2002, pp. 32 and 41, misunderstood the traces and identified the surviving "r" with the phonetic complement of wr. In so doing, he has ignored the surviving portion of the following [sḥ]-nṯr. The expected wr sp-2 can only be placed in the lost section at the end of the line. Gee, Rhodes and Nibley 2005, p. 50, have changed Nibley's transcription to accord with that of Rhodes, hatching the traces on Fragment IV that Nibley had transcribed correctly in 1975.

[292] The words ⸗k m ḥwn appear in patch 6/2 (= Baer's Fragment IV b/2). The final sign is the child determinative, not plural strokes as transcribed by Nibley 1975, p. 43 (mistyped as ḥnn.w). All other versions have nḏm sty⸗k mỉ ỉmꜣḫ.w "May your scent be sweet like the revered ones." Rhodes 2002, p. 41, has followed my revision of Nibley, but the reading is unchanged in Gee, Rhodes and Nibley 2005, p. 50.

[293] The word was misprinted as sꜣḥ in my earlier editions.

are permanently in] (V/6) life, prosperity and health, enduring upon your throne in the sacred land. Come, [then, Osiris Hôr, the justified, born of Taikhibit, the justified,] (V/7) appearing gloriously in your proper form, complete in your ornaments! May you spend the night in life; [may you spend the day in health. May you travel and may you breathe] (V/8) in any place. May Re shine upon your cavern like that of Osiris, so that you might breathe and [live by means of his rays. Amon-Re has revivified] (V/9) your *ka*-spirit and has made you flourish by means of the Breathing Document. May you serve Osiris [and Horus, Lord of the *Henu*-bark, since you exist as the Great God, Foremost] (V/10) of the gods. May your face live; may your forms be perfect. Your name thrives every day. [Come,] may you enter into the very great embalming [booth] (V/11) in Busiris. May you see the Foremost of the Westerners in the *Wag*-Festival.[294] May your scent be sweet as a youth. [May your name be great as] (V/12) an august noble.[295]

Baer 1968 Translation (pp. 123–24):

"*Osiris Hôr ..., Sekhmet has prevailed over those that plotted against you. Horus* the Steadfast protects [you]. Horus of Edfu *carries out*

[294] The *Wag*-festival was one of Egypt's most ancient celebrations, attested from the Old Kingdom onwards. Perhaps originally a festival of the moon, it became closely linked with Osiris and Orion.

[295] The term "noble" also indicates "mummy." This passage is paralleled by P. Louvre N 3291, line 29. Other versions have "be great among the nobles/mummies." Compare the translation of the (generally) parallel P. Louvre N 3284, 3/8–19, by Mark Smith 2009, pp. 472–73 (his §§ 8 and 9): "Osiris ... Sekhmet will prevail over those who have conspired against you. Horus the great-hearted safeguards you. Horus the Crocodopolite carries out your desire. Horus Merti protects your body. You will be perpetually in a state of life, prosperity, and health, remaining on your throne in the Sacred Land. Come Osiris ... appearing in your form, perfect in your regalia. You will spend the night in a state of vitality. You will pass the day in a state of well-being. You will go, breathing, to every place. Re will shine on your mansion, Osiris. You will breathe and live thanks to his sunbeams. Amun-Re will enliven your ka. The letter for breathing will make you flourish. You will follow Osiris and Horus master of the *henu*-bark. You are a great god pre-eminent among the gods. Your countenance will be alive. <Your> children will be happy, while your name flourishes daily. You will enter the very great god's booth in Busiris. You will see the Foremost in the West during the Wag feast. Your perfume will be pleasant like that of the revered ones. Your name will be prominent among the nobles."

your wishes. Hormerti guards your body. Your life, prosperity, and health *have become permanent,* and you will remain in your position in the Sacred Land. Come, *Osiris Hôr …,* for you have appeared in your glorious form, and your appurtenances are complete. You have spent the night alive *and the day in health. You have gone and breathed* everywhere. Re has shined on your cavern as he did on that of Osiris, that you might breathe *and live by his rays. Amon-Re has caused your ka to live* and made you flourish by means of the Breathing Permit. You have accompanied Osiris *and Horus, the Lord of the Henu-bark, for you have the attributes of the Great God, the Foremost* of Gods. Your face is alert and your form perfect. Your name endures always. *Come,* that you may enter the *Great* Divine Council in Busiris! That you may see the Foremost of the Westerners at the Wag-festival. Your smell is pleasant like that of a young man, *and your reputation is as great as that of a* functionary of high rank."

Gee, Rhodes and Nibley 2005 Transliteration and Translation (pp. 48–50, col. 4, lines 5–12):

ꜥꜣ ỉb.w ḥr ỉrw mk.t Ḥr Bḥdty […]
6 ꜥnḫ wḏꜣ snb ỉw=k mn.tw ḥr ns.t=k m tꜣ-ḏsr […]
ḫꜥ.tw m ty.t=k[296] tw.t m ẖkr.w=k sḏr.n=k[297] m ꜥnḫ […]
r bw nb wbn Rꜥ ḥr tp.t=k[298] mỉ Wsỉr snsn […]
kꜣ=k ꜥnḫ wḏꜣ snb swꜣḏ.tw=k[299] m šꜣ.t snsn šms=k[300] Wsỉr […]

[296] For the misreading of qd⸗k, see n. 284, above.

[297] For this edition's inconsistent reading of sḏr and grg, see n. 285, above.

[298] Nibley 1975, p. 41, mistranscribed the ḥ of tpḥ.t as a stroke to read tp.t. Rhodes 2002, pp. 32, 41, followed Nibley's reading error (but not his translation), which was retained in Gee, Rhodes and Nibley, p. 49.

[299] For the misreading of swꜣḏ⸗f tw⸗k in all LDS editions, see n. 288, above.

[300] Although perfectly legible, šms was placed in hatching in Gee, Rhodes and Nibley, p. 49, and Rhodes 2002, p. 41. The erroneous hatching is not found in Nibley 1975, p. 42.

10 nṯr.w[301] ꜥnḫ ḥr=k nfr ms.t=k rn=k rwd rꜥ nb […][302] ꜥq=k r [ẖr.t]- nṯr […][303]
m Ḏdw mꜣꜣ=k ḫnty-ỉmnty.w m ḥb wg[304] nḏmy sty=k m ḥwn.w[305] […]
sꜥḥ šps

"Great of Heart is providing (making) thy protection; Horus the Behdetite […]
6. life, prosperity, health, remaining upon thy throne in the holy land (Deseret). […]
Thou appearest in glory in thy proper and perfect form in thy full ceremonial regalia, (which) you prepared while you were alive (*or* having made preparation in life) […]
everywhere. Re shines upon thy high place (as for) Osiris, that thou mayest (*or* mayest thou) breathe […]
thy *ka,* living, protecting (*or* prospering) to flourish in (*or* by) the Book of Breathings. Thou art following Osiris […]
10. the gods. Thy countenance liveth; beautiful (perfect) is thy form (*or* are thine offspring); thy name shall be firmly established (*or* flourish) henceforward (every day). […] Enter into the god's [domain …]
in Busiris to see the Chief of the Westerners at the *wag*-festival Pleasant is thine odor as (*or* among) the young men […]
very Elect."

Rhodes 2002 Transliteration and Translation (p. 32):

[Wsỉr Ḥr, mꜣꜥ-ḫrw, ms.n Tꜣy-ḫy-by.t, mꜣꜥ-ḫrw. sḫm Sḫm.t m

[301] This line begins only with nṯr.w. Rhodes 2002, pp. 32 and 41, wrongly placed ḫnty (in hatching) at the beginning of col. V/10, and Gee, Rhodes and Nibley, p. 50, have added empty hatching before nṯr.w to accommodate the possibility of this insertion (which was not made in the text itself).

[302] For the restoration [m]y "Come," see n. 290, above.

[303] Wrongly restored for [sḥ]-nṯr, following Nibley 1975, p. 43. See n. 291, above.

[304] The traces and space for the final ꜣ are ignored in Nibley 1975, p. 43, followed by Gee, Rhodes and Nibley, p. 50. It is inserted in Rhodes 2002, pp. 32, 41.

[305] For this misreading as a plural (following Nibley 1975, p. 43), see n. 292, above. The editors have corrected Nibley's ḫnn.w without comment.

wȝ.w ỉm=k, Ḥr] (5) ʿȝ ỉb.w ḥr ỉrw mk(.t)=k, Ḥr bḥdty [ḥr ỉrw ỉb=k, Ḥr mrw.ty ḥr sȝw ḏ.t=k. ḏd=k m] (6) ʿnḫ, wḏȝ, snb, ỉw=k mn.tw ḥr ns.t=k m tȝ ḏsr.

[mỉ r=k Wsỉr Ḥr, mȝʿ-ḫrw, ms.n Tȝy-ḫy-by.t, mȝʿ-ḫrw. ỉw=k] (7) ḫʿ.tw m tỉ.t=k,[306] twt.tw m ẖkr.w=k. sdr=k[307] m ʿnḫ. [wrš=k m snby. šm=k snsn=k] (8) r b(w) nb. wbn Rʿ ḥr tp.t=k[308] mỉ Wsỉr. snsn[=k, ʿnḫ=k m sty.w=f.

ʾImn-Rʿ sʿnḫ=f] (9) kȝ=k, ʿnḫ, wḏȝ, snb. <s>wȝḏ.tw=k m šȝ.t snsn.ty. šms=k[309] Wsỉr, [Ḥr nb ḥnw. ỉw=k m nṯr ʿȝ,] (10) ḫnty[310] nṯr.w. ʿnḫ ḥr=k, nfr ms.t=k, rn=k rwd rʿ nb. ʿq=k r sḥ-nṯr wr[311] [sp 2] (11) m Ḏdw, mȝȝ=k Ḫnty-ʾImnty.w m ḥb wgȝ. nḏmy sty=k m ḥwnw. [ʿȝ rn=k m] (12) sʿḥ šps.

"[Osiris Hor, justified, born of Taykhebyt, justified. May Sekhmet have power over those who conspire against you, while Horus,] (5) Great of Hearts, is protecting you, Horus of Edfu [is doing what you want, and Horus of the Two Eyes is guarding your body. May you endure in] (6) life, prosperity, and health, having been established upon your throne in the Sacred Land.

[Come now Osiris Hor, justified, born of Taykhebyt, justified. You] (7) have arisen in your form, complete in your royal regalia.

---

[306] For Rhodes' questionable reading qd=k *and* tyt=k, see n. 284, above.

[307] For Rhodes' inconsistent reading of sḏr *and* grg, see n. 285, above. Cf. the glossary entry for this term, p. 87 ("to spend the night") and his translation, p. 32: "May you be established in life." "Be established" derives from Nibley's false reading grg.

[308] Rhodes (pp. 32, 41), followed Nibley's error (1975, p. 41) in misreading tpḥ.t "cavern" as tp(ḥ).t, but he has selected the correct translation.

[309] Although perfectly legible, šms was placed in hatching in Rhodes, p. 41, and Gee, Rhodes and Nibley 2005, p. 49.

[310] Col. V/10 properly begins only with nṯr.w. For the form, see Verhoeven 2001, pp. 176–77 (R8a). Rhodes (pp. 32, 41) misread the traces, wrongly shifting ḫnty (in hatching) from the lost conclusion of col. V/9. The correct transcription was copied by Rhodes, p. 56, line 16 (for P. Louvre N 3284).

[311] Rhodes (p. 41) made numerous errors in reading this line. He ignored the traces of [m]y, placed the following ʿq=k r sḥ-nṯr in hatching as if lost (but inserted the patch with the preserved text back into position on the photo), confused the surviving preposition r in the patch with the final letter of the lost word wr, and failed to recognize the initial sign of [sḥ]-nṯr. For the proper reading of the text, see nn. 290–291, above.

May you be established in life. [May you spend your time in health. May you walk and breathe] (8) anywhere. May Re shine in your cave like (he did upon) Osiris. May [you] breathe [and live on his rays.

May Amon animate] (9) your *ka*, may it live, prosper, and be healthy. May the Document of Breathing cause you to flourish. May you accompany Osiris and [Horus, Lord of the Henu boat. You are the Great God,] (10) Foremost among the Gods. May your face live and your form be beautiful, while your name endures every day. May you enter into the god's [very] great hall (11) in Busiris, and may you see the Foremost of the Westerners at the Wag festival. May your odor be as pleasant as a young man's. [May your name be as great as] (12) an august noble."

Nibley 1975 Word-for-Word Transliteration and Translation of Preserved Sections Only (pp. 40–44):

(IV/5) ʿa ib(w) ḥr ir(w) mʿkt Ḥr bḥdt(y) (6) ʿnkh wḏa snb iw.k mn (tw) ḥr nst.k m ta-ḏsr (7) khʿ.tw m tyt.k[312] twt m ẖkr.k grg(sḏr).n.k[313] m ʿnkh (8) r bw nb wbn Reʿ ḥr tp(ḥ).k[314] mi Wsir sn-sn (9) ka.k ʿnkh nd (wḏa?)-snb or m s-wḏa.tw.k m shaʿt sn-sn shms.k Wsir (10) nṯrw ʿnkh hr.k nfr msw.k rn.k rwd rʿ-nb ʿq.k r (ẖrt)-nṯr[315] (11) m Ḏdw maa.k hnty imnty(w) m ḥb wg[316] nḏmi sṯy k m ḥnn-w[317] (12) sʿḥ shps

(IV/5) "great (or of greatness) of heart is making protection(s) Horus the Behdetite (6) life-prosperity-health thou being firm upon throne thine in land holy (7) risen-in-glory thou in form-thine proper natural in adornments thine prepared (slept) hast thou in life (8) to

[312] Nibley (p. 41) mistranscribed ḫʿ.tw as ḫn.tw and misread qd=k as tyt.k; see n. 284, above.

[313] For Nibley's misreading of sḏr for grg, see n. 285, above.

[314] Nibley (p. 41) mistranscribed the ḥ of tpḥ.t as a stroke to read tp.t "top-place/roof." The misreading is retained in all LDS editions.

[315] Nibley, p. 43, wrongly restored [ẖr.t]-nṯr for [sḥ]-nṯr.

[316] The traces and space for the final ȝ are ignored in Nibley, p. 43, and in Gee, Rhodes and Nibley 2005, p. 50.

[317] Misread for ḥwn; see n. 292, above.

place every. Shines Re upon top-place thine as (for) Osiris. Breathes (9) Ka thine living and protecting [*or:* may it live, be prosperous, be healthy!] Made to flourish art thou in (by) Book (of) Breathing(s), followest-thou Osiris (10) (of the gods) living face-thine fair offspring-thine, name-thine flourishes every-day enterest thou into (the gods' domain) (11) in Busiris seest-thou head, chief president (of) the West in festival Wag- (i.e. Wag-festival) pleasant odor thine as (or, together with) youths (12) noble (elect) august one."

PARAGRAPH X

hꜣy Wsỉr Ḥr mꜣꜥ-ḫrw ꜥnḫ bꜣ=k m šꜥy.t snsn[318] [ẖnm=k m mỉ.tt] (V/13) bꜣ[319] ꜥq=k r dwꜣ.t nn wn ḫfty.w=k ỉw=k m ꜣḫ[320] nṯrỉ [m Ḏdw ỉb=k n=k nn ḥrỉ=f r=k ỉr.ty=k n=k wn rꜥ nb]

Hail, Osiris Hôr, the justified! May your *ba*-spirit live by means of the Breathing Document, [and may you be united by the same manner with] (V/13) the *ba*-spirit. May you enter into the Underworld. There are no enemies of yours, for you exist as a divine, effective spirit [in Busiris. Your heart belongs to you; it will not be far from you. Your eyes belong to you, being open every day."][321]

---

[318] The words [šꜥ]y.t snsn appear in patch 6/3 (= Baer's Fragment IV b/3).

[319] Texts differ considerably here. P. Louvre N 3284 has ẖnm=k m mỉt.t "may you be joined likewise," while Louvre N 3291 has ẖnm=k m šꜥ.t n snsn "may you be joined by means of the Breathing Document." Goyon 1972, p. 222, noted examples of "you are united with Shu, son of Re." Rhodes 2002, pp. 32 and 41, restored [ẖnm=k m] bꜣ(=k) "May you be united with (your) soul."

[320] Other versions have bꜣ nṯrỉ "divine ba," and Nibley 1975, p. 45, wrongly followed that reading, ignoring the remarks of Baer, p. 124, n. 85. For the hieratic sign, see Möller 1912, p. 19, no. 204 (with back tick) = Verhoeven 2001, pp. 140–41, clearly distinct from no. 208 (bꜣ) and the writing of bꜣ found at the beginning of this line and throughout the text. Rhodes 2002, pp. 32, 41, has adopted ꜣḫ, but translated the word as "soul" (as he translated bꜣ; cf. p. 80) rather than as "spirit" (as he translated ꜣḫ; cf. p. 77). A further example of incomplete conversion?

[321] Compare the translation of the (generally) parallel P. Louvre N 3284, 3/19–22, by Mark Smith 2009, pp. 473: "Hail Osiris … Your ba will live by virtue of the letter for breathing. You will be united with the same. You will enter the underworld. Your enemies will not exist. You are a divine ba in Busiris. Your heart belongs to you, without being distant from you. Your eyes are yours, open every day."

Baer 1968 Translation (pp. 124):

"O Osiris Hôr ..., your ba lives by means of the Breathing Permit, *and you have joined* the ba *by the same means.* You have entered the Netherworld. You have no enemies, for you are a divine akh *in Busiris. You have possession of your heart; it will not leave you. You have possession of your eyes, which are open every day.*"

Gee, Rhodes and Nibley 2005 Transliteration and Translation (p. 50, col. 4, lines 12–13):

hy[322] Wsꞽr Ḥr mꜣꜥ-ḫrw ꜥnḫ bꜣ=k m šꜥy snsn [...]
bꜣ ꜥq=k r dwꜣ.t nn wn ḫfty.w=k ꞽw=k m bꜣ nṯr [...]

"Hail, Osiris Hor, Justified. Thy *ba* lives by the Book of Breathings, [...] a *ba*. Thou enterest (*or* Enter thou) into the *duat;* thine enemies do not exist, for thou art a deified *ba* [...]"

Rhodes 2002 Transliteration and Translation (p. 32):

hy[323] Wsꞽr Ḥr, mꜣꜥ-ḫrw. ꜥnḫ bꜣ=k m šꜥꞽ.t snsn. [ẖnm=k m] (13) bꜣ<=k>.[324] ꜥq=k r dwꜣ.t, nn wn ḫfty.w=k. ꞽw=k m ꜣḫw[325] ntry [m Ḏdw. ꞽb=k n=k. nn ḥrw=f r=k.]

"O Osiris Hor, justified. May your soul live by means of the Document of Breathing. [May you join with] (13) <your> soul. May you enter into the hereafter without your enemy. You are a divine soul [in Busiris. You have your heart. It will not be far from you.]"

Nibley 1975 Word-for-Word Transliteration and Translation of Preserved Sections Only (pp. 44–45):

(IV/12) ha-y[326] Wsir Hr naꜥ-khrw ꜥnkh ba.k m shaꜥi-t n sn-sn (13) ba ꜥq.k r dwa nn wn khft.w.k iw.k m ba[327] nṯri

[322] Misread from hꜣy by Nibley 1975, p. 44, and followed by Rhodes 2002, pp. 32 and 41, and in Gee, Rhodes and Nibley, p. 50.

[323] Misread from hꜣy by Rhodes (pp. 32 and 41), following Nibley 1975, p. 44.

[324] For the restoration, see n. 319, above.

[325] For the reading and Rhodes' inconsistent translation of it, see n. 320, above.

[326] Though he vocalized the word as ha-y, Nibley (p. 44) miscopied hy for hꜣy.

[327] Misread (p. 45) from ꜣḫ; see n. 320, above.

> (IV/12) "Hail Osiris Hor justified lives ba thine in book of breathing(s) (13) spirit. Enterest thou into Duat (do)not exist enemies thine thou-being as (a) ba divine"

This marks the end of the preserved text. Paragraphs XI–XIV are lost, comprising approximately two columns (cols. VI–VII).

The papyrus concludes with a vignette preserved only in a poorly rendered engraving at the end of the Book of Abraham, labeled as showing that "Abraham is reasoning upon the principles of Astronomy, in the king's court." The "Explanations" of Facsimile 3 offered by Joseph Smith are fanciful in the extreme[328] and are now abandoned in the Mormon-sponsored publication by Rhodes.[329] As several of Smith's explanations state explicitly that they are based on his understanding of texts "given in the characters above his head," "as written above the hand," or "as represented by the characters above his hand," Facsimile 3 provides indisputable evidence that Smith *had absolutely no abilities* to read or translate Egyptian, or even derive accurate information from Egyptian images. He could not distinguish deities from humans, females from males or even human from animal figures![330]

---

[328] A simple table of offerings is "explained" by Smith as: "Fig. 3. Signifies Abraham in Egypt as given also in Figure 10 of Facsimile No. 1."

[329] Rhodes 2002, pp. 23–25.

[330] Smith mistook Osiris, Isis, Maat and Anubis as human rather than gods, Isis and Maat as male, and the jackal Anubis as human. Anubis was also mistaken as human in Facsimile 1, and Smith frequently misidentified images of Ta-sherit-Min as male in P. Joseph Smith 2 (and see P. Joseph Smith 4). In the Book of Abraham Smith's explicit references to texts in the Facsimiles and his use of the subtitle "Translated from the Papyrus, by Joseph Smith," can mean only that he misrepresented or did not understand the concept of translation. There is no other choice, and I have no reason to regret my earlier description of his "translations" as "outlandish," "nonsense," "hopeless" and "uninspired fantasies." These are factual assessments derived from scholarly analysis, not "partisan language" as asserted in the truly partisan (i.e. based on pre-existing religious bias) defense by Morris 2004, p. 360, and Muhlestein 2005, p. 479, n. 22. As I noted in 2003 (2003a, p. 162), true "personal attack and vituperative language" (in the words of Muhlestein, p. 479) was the hallmark of Nibley's anti-Egyptological approach now adopted by FARMS. In sum, Smith's pseudo Egyptological work (rather than his person) deserves no greater respect than that of Charles Piazzi Smyth (*Our Inheritance in the Great Pyramid*), Immanuel Velikovsky (*Oedipus and Akhnaton*, etc.), Erich von Däniken (*Chariots of the Gods*) and John Anthony West (*Serpent in the Sky*, etc.), which have all been rightly disparaged by scholars.

Baer conservatively chose to translate only the most obvious of these passages,[331] but additional readings are possible and have been attempted here, with uncertainties noted. The scene, as already recognized by Baer, is the well-attested conclusion of the older judgment scene associated with Book of the Dead 125.[332] Having attained justification, the deified Hôr is brought by Maat and Anubis before the altar of the enthroned Osiris, behind whom stands Isis. Comparable scenes open Papyrus Hague 42/88 (Denon) and Tübingen 2016.[333] The origin of these vignettes in the classic judgment scene is shown conclusively by the final vignette of the comparable Breathing Document Florence 3666 + Vienna 3850, in which Maat and Anubis escort the deceased to the scales, enthroned Osiris and Isis.[334] The iconography of Facsimile 3 has been discussed most reasonably

[331] Baer 1968, p. 127, and n. 110.

[332] Baer 1968, pp. 126–27. Baer's statement that it is "similar to but not identical with scenes showing judgment of the deceased before Osiris" (p. 126) and "is not a judgment scene" (his quoted letter to Nibley in Gee 1992, p. 100) means only that the actual process of judgment is not shown. This image *does,* however, form part of standard judgment scenes, see the following notes. [This Gee citation was wrongly linked to his *A Guide to the Joseph Smith Papyri* (2000a) in Ritner 2002, pp. 113–14, nn. 116–17, and in 2003a p. 175, nn. 125–26.] Gee 2005 insists that the scene is properly linked to Book of the Dead 30B, but the association with Chapter 125 long predates the Hôr papyrus; see the description in Allen 1974, pp. 40 and 101, and even Gee 2000a, pp. 10 and 18. Gee's statement that Facsimile 3 "came from the middle of a long roll" is a fantasy as are the supposed surviving words "Beginning of the Book of ..." (2005, p. 96, and cf. 2000a, p. 10). For these supposed traces, see the introductory discussion of the original size of this papyrus, above.

[333] See Coenen and Quaegebeur 1995, figs. 3–5; and Brunner-Traut and Brunner 1981, pls. 12–13. These and other examples eliminate the doubt once expressed by Baer that "parallels may be hard to find" (quoted letter to Nibley in Gee 1992, p. 100). Gee failed to quote the remainder of Baer's assessment: "But one must not exaggerate in the other direction. I doubt that one could find many instances of exactly identical scenes in Egyptian art" (Baer files, quoted by permission, unlike the unauthorized use by Gee, ibid., pp. 98, n. 15 and 100, n. 22). The inclusion of Thoth recording the judgment and the "Swallowing Monster" Amyt further stress the derivation of this scene from Book of the Dead 125 vignettes, as in the Papyrus of Hunefer illustrated in Faulkner 1985, pp. 34–35. For Book of the Dead 125 and its vignette, see further the edition of P. Joseph Smith 3 in this volume.

[334] Marc Coenen 1999b, 98–103, especially plate 21.

by Stephen E. Thompson.[335] This scene depicts events in the underworld court of Osiris, not a funeral re-enactment with human actors.[336]

CONCLUDING VIGNETTE, COL. VIII

(= FACSIMILE 3 OF THE BOOK OF ABRAHAM)

- **Label for Osiris (Fig. 1 of Facsimile 3)**[337]
  (VIII/1) ḏd-mdw ỉ(n) Wsỉr Ḫnty-ỉmnty.w (VIII/2) nb(?) ꜣbḏw(?) pꜣ nṯr ꜥꜣ (VIII/3) r ḏ.t nḥḥ(?)[338]

  (VIII/1) Recitation by Osiris, Foremost of the Westerners, (VIII/2) Lord of Abydos(?), the great god (VIII/3) forever and ever(?).

- **Label for Isis (Fig. 2 of Facsimile 3)**[339]
  (VIII/4) ꜣs.t wr.(t) mw.t nṯr

  (VIII/4) Isis the great, the god's mother.[340]

- **Label for Maat (Fig. 4 of Facsimile 3)**[341]
  (VIII/5) Mꜣꜥ.t ḥnw.t nṯr.w

---

[335] Thompson 1995. Gee's brief—and bizarre—rebuttal (Gee 2000, pp. 40, 67, n. 17) is unacceptable. Reference to a costumed private individual in the Roman procession of Isis *is not evidence* that the figure of Isis here (no. 2) is "King Pharaoh, whose name is given in the characters above his head," as published by Joseph Smith. For the Facsimiles, see further Ashment 1979.

[336] Gee 2000, p. 66, wrongly conflated this Anubis with masked Anubis-priests at funerals. Actors did not, however, impersonate Maat, Osiris, and Isis at funerals. Gee's suggestion was not repeated in Rhodes 2002, pp. 23, 25.

[337] Joseph Smith explained the figure of Osiris as follows: "Fig. 1 Abraham sitting upon Pharaoh's throne, by the politeness of the king, with a crown upon his head, representing the Priesthood, as emblematical of the grand Presidency in Heaven; with the scepter of justice and judgment in his hand."

[338] My suggestion of nḥḥ follows the first Ptolemaic spelling noted in Erman and Grapow 1957, vol. II, p. 299.

[339] Joseph Smith could not recognize even the gender of this figure, which he explained as: "King Pharaoh, whose name is given in the characters above his head." As elsewhere (cf. Abraham 1:25), Smith confused the title "Pharaoh" with a personal name.

[340] The same (common) label appears in P. Tübingen 2016 for the figure of Isis.

[341] Smith has again confused genders in his supposed explanation: "Prince of Pharaoh, King of Egypt, as written above the hand."

(VIII/5) Maat, mistress of the gods.

- **Label for Hôr (Fig. 5 of Facsimile 3)**[342]
  (VIII/6) Wsỉr Ḥr (VIII/7) mꜣꜥ-ḫrw r ḏ.t

  (VIII/6) The Osiris Hôr, (VIII/7) justified forever.

- **Label for Anubis (Fig. 6 of Facsimile 3)**[343]
  (VIII/8) ḏd-mdw ỉ(n) ꜥInpw ỉr sꜣ[344] (VIII/9) ḫnty[345] sḥ-nṯr(?) (VIII/10) …[346]

  (VIII/8) Recitation by Anubis, who makes protection, (VIII/9) foremost of the embalming booth(?)(VIII/10) …

[342] Joseph Smith could not recognize that this central figure was being conducted into the presence of the enthroned deity and misinterpreted him as a simple attendant: "Fig. 5. Shulem, one of the king's principal waiters, as represented by the characters above his hand." Hôr's label, like the invocation on his behalf below the scene, faces left.

[343] Surely because of the black color of the jackal Anubis (misunderstood as a human!), Joseph Smith explained him as follows: "Olimiah, a slave belonging to the prince." Anubis, who follows Hôr, is also provided with a label facing left.

[344] Or, less likely, nb dwꜣ.t "Lord of the Underworld." The epithet ỉr sꜣ appears in a comparable scene in Papyrus McClung Museum: 98.11.1; see Evans 2002, at n. 3 (using my reading). Anubis is said to have "made your protection" in Paragraph V of the Breathing Document (col. IV/4). Rhodes 2002, pp. 24–25, has copied my reading without credit, while failing to correct his own initial guess. On p. 24, the signs for ỉr sꜣ are mistakenly placed by Rhodes to the right of their column, while his own transcription r //// still remains in its proper place. Clearly a late substitution was intended, but bungled. Rhodes' copy now reads: ḏd-mdw ỉn ꜥInpw r … nb p.t ḫnty ỉr sꜣ (p. 24), which does not correspond to his transliteration (p. 25).

[345] The unclear lines might read nb p.t nṯr ꜥꜣ ḫnty sḥ-nṯr "Lord of heaven, great god, foremost of the embalming booth."

[346] Possibilities include ỉmy-wt "who is in the mummy bandages," pꜣ nṯr ꜥꜣ "the great god," or sꜣ Wsỉr "son of Osiris. Rhodes 2002, pp. 24–25, suggested ỉmnt.t "West," which is possible.

- **Invocation below scene**
  (VIII/11) ỉ[347] n(ꜣ) nṯr.w ẖr.t-nṯr[348] nṯr.w qrr.wt nṯr.w rsy mḥt ỉmnt.t ỉꜣb.t swḏꜣ Wsỉr Ḥr mꜣꜥ-ḫrw ỉr.n Tꜣy-ḫy-by.t[349]

  (VIII/11) "O gods of the necropolis, gods of the caverns, gods of the south, north, west and east, grant salvation to the Osiris Hôr, the justified, born by Taikhibit."

Baer 1968 Translation (p. 127):

- **Label for Hôr (Fig. 5 of Facsimile 3)**
  "Osiris Hôr, justified forever."

- **Invocation below scene**
  "O gods of …, gods of the Caverns, gods of the south, north, west, and east, grant well-being to Osiris Hôr, justified, …"

Rhodes 2002 Transcription, Transliteration and Translation (pp. 24–25):

- **Label for Isis (Fig. 2 of Facsimile 3)**
  ꜣIs.t wr.t, mw.t nṯr

  "The great Isis, mother of the god."

- **Label for Osiris (Fig. 1 of Facsimile 3)**
  (1) ḏd mdw ỉn Wsỉr, ḫnty imnty.w: (1) mn=k, Wsỉr Ḥr (3) m ns.t ꜥꜣ.t=f

  "(1) Words spoken[350] by Osiris, the Foremost of the Westerners:

---

[347] This invocation by Hôr or Anubis to the gods of the underworld reads from left to right, oriented toward the direction of these figures as they enter from the right of the scene and address the gods at the left.

[348] The word was unread by Baer 1968, p. 127. Rhodes 2002, pp. 24–25 read ỉmn.t "west," which is highly unlikely since the gods of the west are invoked in the following clause.

[349] Unread by Baer, p. 127, the signs ỉr.n Tꜣy-ḫby.t can be recognized, including the figure with upraised arms (ḫy), shifted to the end as in col. I/2. See also P. Louvre N 3207 for the use of ỉr.n … Tꜣy-ḫ(bỉ.t) "born by … Taikhi(bit)." Rhodes 2002, pp. 24–25, duplicated my reading while ignoring the Louvre parallel and adding a common dictionary reference.

[350] A common, but inaccurate, rendering that would require mdw.t ḏdd.wt. The expression means literally "the saying of words" or "recitation."

(2) May you, Osiris Hor, abide at (3) the side of the throne of his greatness."[351]

- **Label for Maat (Fig. 4 of Facsimile 3)**
  Mꜣꜥ.t, ḥm.t[352] ỉmnt.t

  "Maꜥat, Lady of the West."

- **Label for Hor (Fig. 5 of Facsimile 3)**
  (1) Wsỉr, Ḥr, pꜣ (2) mꜣꜥ-ḫrw r ḏ.t.

  "(1) Osiris Hor, the (2) justified forever."

- **Label for Anubis (Fig. 6 of Facsimile 3)**
  (1) ḏd mdw ỉn ʾInp ỉr sꜣ[353] (2) nb p.t, ḫnty[354] (3) ỉmnt.t

  (1) "Words spoken by Anubis who makes protection (2) Lord of heaven, Foremost of (3) the Westerners."

- **"Bottom line"**
  ỉn[355] nṯr.w ỉmn.t, nṯr.w qrty.w, nṯr.w rsy, mḥty, ỉmn.t, ỉꜣb.t: swḏꜣ

---

[351] For col. VIII/2–3, Rhodes ("To the right of Osiris," lines 2–3), confusingly read mn=k Wsỉr Ḥr m ns.t ꜥꜣ.t=f, but translated the phrase as if it were mn=k Wsỉr Ḥr r gs ns.t ꜥꜣ.t=f "May you, Osiris Hor, abide *at the side of* the throne of his greatness" (emphasis added). Rhodes has thus read variously Ḥr or Ḥr r, m or gs, without any attempt at consistency between the text copy and translation. This seems a further sign of the haste employed in rushing this manuscript to press, already noted with regard to incomplete textual revisions. In either version, Rhodes' interpretation is unusual, and the supposed spelling of ns.t "throne" lacks a determinative.

[352] Rhodes misread ḥm.t "woman/wife," which he translated as though it were ḥnw.t "Lady/Mistress."

[353] Again, Rhodes' hieroglyphic hand copy does not match his translation. For Rhodes' uncredited and incomplete borrowing from my published translation (of a rare phrase), see n. 344, above. Rhodes failed to insert his revised "patch" over an original hatching, adding it only at the side.

[354] Rhodes' reading cannot account for the two vertical strokes following the possible p.t "heaven." These strokes may be nṯr ꜥꜣ "great god," see n. 345, above.

[355] Rhodes 2002, pp. 24–25, wrongly transcribed the passage into hieroglyphs, with a supposed lacuna following "caverns" that is neither justified by Facsimile 3 nor indicated in his transliteration and translation. Moreover, his edition placed the initial vocative ỉ plus standing-man-with-upraised-hand determinative (see Erman and Grapow 1957, vol. I, p. 25: ) at the end of the line (a further sign of rushed

Wsỉr, Ḥr, mꜣꜥ ḫrw, ỉr n Tꜣy-ḫy-by(.t).

"The gods of the West, the gods of the cavern,[356] the gods of the south, north, west, and east say: May Osiris Hor, justified, born of Taykhebyt, prosper."

Here the papyrus ended. The general wording, implications, basic symbolism and intent of the text are certain.[357] Despite claims to the contrary, no extended portions of this papyrus are missing that might have held the Book of Abraham, which is explicitly tied to this text as indicated by the vignettes/Facsimiles.[358] While the link between the

---

publication?). Rhodes ignored the lexical distinction between the hieroglyph for the vocative and the man-with-hand-to-mouth, and read ỉn "so say" for what must be ỉ n(ꜣ). For the ellipse of ꜣ in the definite article, cf. Cols. II/6 and IV/9: p(ꜣ); noted also in Rhodes 2002, p. 8. For polemical reasons, Rhodes wished to avoid a prayer to the gods in this text, so that he reversed speaker and audience; see n. 84 on col. I/4, above, and the defensive remarks by Morris 2004, p. 361. The direction of the writing is oriented *toward not from* Osiris and the gods of the underworld.

[356] Rhodes has wrongly deleted the plural.

[357] *Contra* Nibley's nihilistic quibbling on the impossibility of true translation (1975, pp. 47 ff.). Where precisely the great pool of Khonsu was located does not change the meaning, significance, or use of the text, none of which is in doubt. In response to Morris 2004, p. 362, I have selected the terms "nihilistic quibbling" here with good reason and no regret; the term "quibble" was already used by Gee to describe his own writings (1996), and its implication of bickering well suits the content of Nibley's objections, which dispute the very nature of translation and so are "nihilistic" (denying an objective ground of truth). Nibley can only defend Smith's use of the term "translation" by undercutting the very meaning of the term.

[358] Given the indisputable mismatch between the wording of the "Breathing Document" and the Book of Abraham, explicitly "translated from the papyrus," it has become fashionable among Mormon apologists to posit the existence of a lost section of this papyrus that held the Book of Abraham; see Gee 2000, pp. 10, 12–13, who wished to double the size of the Hôr papyrus, and my response in Ritner 2003a, p. 166, n. 33. As noted above, Rhodes 2002, p. 4, was intentionally ambiguous in his description of the Hôr papyrus. For the approach of the Mormon group Foundation for Apologetic Information and Research (FAIR), see the remarks of its president, Scott Gordon (2003, p. 2): "Dr. Ritner sheds no new light on the subject, stating what LDS scholars have been saying since 1967: the rediscovered scroll fragments are *not* the source of the Book of Abraham. The simple answer is that the Book of Abraham was translated from the papyri, which we assume were destroyed in the museum fire." An alternate approach has been to dispute the meaning of the term "translation"; see the previous note.

papyrus and the Book of Abraham is indisputable on a rational basis, that conclusion does not serve apologetic ends. In his preface to the 2005 revision of Nibley's work, Gee has attempted to exploit a semantic distinction in the term "source" to deny this obvious association: "Still, there is no reason to assume that Papyrus Joseph Smith I + IX + X is the source of the Book of Abraham. The Church of Jesus Christ of Latter-day Saints has had no official position on the issue, and most members of the church do not believe that it is. The Egyptologists are adamant that it is not, and so everyone seems to be in agreement on that issue."[359]

Gee's glib remarks on supposed Egyptological agreement suppress the very subtitle of Baer's basic study of the text, "A Translation of the Apparent Source of the Book of Abraham."[360] Egyptologists have been adamant that the Book of Abraham *does* derive from P. Joseph Smith 1, which was its *purported source* according to Smith himself. The fact that Smith's published interpretation of the papyrus is pure fantasy is indication not of a lost papyrus or section, but of the *ultimate source* of Smith's wording—his imagination. Since *there is agreement* that Smith could not translate accurately the hieroglyphs on Facsimile 3[361]—despite his published claims to the contrary—there is no reason to believe that he could have translated any supposedly lost section of the papyrus with greater accuracy. Here there is no question of a lost, "extra text," but a portion of the Breathing Document itself, surviving in Smith's copy and interpreted fallaciously by Smith himself.

Whether this assessment will have any impact beyond the world of scholarship is questionable, since Gee has noted that "Members of the Church of Jesus Christ in general have no pretensions about holding any dialogue with critics. They simply do not, for the most part, care what their critics say."[362] While that may well be true for many, it does not

---

[359] Gee, Rhodes and Nibley 2005, pp. xxi–xxii.

[360] Baer 1968, Contents page and p. 109, and see the explicit comments of Nibley 1975, p. 1 = Gee, Rhodes and Nibley 2005, p. 1.

[361] See the complete disagreement of the translations published by Rhodes 2002, pp. 23–25, with the interpretations published by Smith. The failure by Rhodes to cite the Smith translations is in itself eloquent—and damning. Note also Nibley's recognition that Smith's "Egyptian Alphabet and Grammar" was evidence of his "independent thinking and speculation" (1968, p. 100).

[362] See Gee 2003, pp. 81–85. In the same publication, my entire 2002 edition of P.

account for the extraordinary interest in the Joseph Smith Papyri among Mormons of all opinions, as evidenced by email, chatrooms, web postings, and the continued publications of Nibley, Rhodes and Gee himself. Clearly FARMS has taken a direct interest in the Egyptological opinions concerning these papyri, and it aspires to scholarly acceptance,[363] but where faith and scholarship are irreconcilable, the apologists defer to faith. I prefer scholarship. The reader may choose for himself.

Joseph Smith I is bizarrely dismissed in n. 1 as a "summary" supposedly "out-of-date" at the time of its appearance—well before the secondary work of Rhodes.

[363] Thus is explained not only the 2002 appearance of Rhodes at the convention of the American Research Center in Egypt, but the detailed commentaries provided by Nibley and his successors. Certainly on some level a dialogue with scholars is desired, but the results are unappreciated.

PAPYRUS JOSEPH SMITH 1: THE BREATHING PERMIT OF HÔR

(Fragments I, XI and X with patches in Fragment IV)

PART TWO: CONSECUTIVE TRANSLATION

The following consecutive translation is provided for the reader wishing to read the content of the Breathing Permit of Hôr with minimal distractions or additions. For notes on individual readings or interpretations, see the previous section detailing the comparative transliterations and translations of P. JS 1.

I. INTRODUCTORY VIGNETTE WITH ADDRESS TO HÔR

(Fragment I)

(I/1) ["Osiris, the god's father], prophet of Amon-Re, King of the Gods, prophet of Min who slaughters his enemies, prophet of Khonsu, the [one who exercises] authority in Thebes, (I/2) [...] ... Hôr, the justified, son of the similarly titled overseer of secrets and purifier of the god, Osorwer, the justified, born by the [housewife and sistrum-player of] (I/3) [Amon]-Re, Taikhibit, the justified!

May your *ba*-spirit live among them, and may you be buried on the west [of Thebes]."

(I/4) ["O Anubis(?), ...] justification(?). (I/5) [May you give to him] a good and splendid burial on the west of Thebes as on the mountains of Ma[nu]."

II. DIRECTIONS FOR USE

(Fragment XI.1)

[(II/1) Osiris shall be towed in]to the great lake of Khonsu, (II/2) and likewise [the Osiris Hôr, the justified,] born of Taikhibit, the justified, (II/3) after his two arms have been [placed] at his heart, while (II/4) the Breathing Document, being what (II/5) is written on its interior and exterior, shall be wrapped in royal linen and placed (under) his left arm at the midpoint of his heart. The remainder of his (II/7) wrapping shall be made over it.

As for the one for whom this book is made, (II/8) he thus breathes like the *ba*-spirit[s] of the gods, forever and (II/9) ever.

III. THE MAIN BODY OF THE BREATHING DOCUMENT

PARAGRAPH I

(Fragment XI.2 + Patch 1 on Fragment IV)

(III/1) Beginning of the [Breath]ing [Document] that [Isis] made [for her brother Osiris in order to revivify his *ba*-spirit, to revivify his corpse, and to rejuvenate all his limbs] (III/2) again, [so that he might unite with] the horizon together with his father Re, [so that his *ba*-spirit might be made to appear gloriously in heaven in the moon disk, so that his corpse might shine in Orion within the body of (the sky-goddess) Nut, and so that] (III/3) the same things might be made to happen to the Osiris Hôr, the justified, son [of … Osorwer, the justified, born of Taikhibit, the justified.] Hide (it)! Conceal (it)! (III/4) Do not let anyone read it! [It] is effective [for a man in the necropolis, so that he might live again,] [being proved] truly [effective], millions of times.

PARAGRAPH II

(Fragment XI.2 + Patches 1–2 on Fragment IV)

(III/5) "Hail, [Osiris Hô]r, the justified, born of Tai[khibit, the justified! You are pure! Your heart is pure! Your front is in] a state of purity, your rear (III/6) is in a state of cleanliness, and your interior parts consist of soda and [natron. There is no limb of yours in an evil state.] The Os[iris Hô]r, the justified, born of (III/7) Taikhibit, the justified, [has been purified] in this pool of [the Fields of Offerings on the north of the Fields of Locusts.] Edjo and Nekhbet have purified you (III/8) in the fourth hour of night and in the fourth hour [of day. Come, then, Osiris Hôr, the justified, born of Taikhibi]t, the justified! May you enter into the Hall of the (III/9) Two Truths, since you are pure from [all] impurity [and every abomination. 'Rock of Truth' is your name.]

PARAGRAPH III

(Fragment XI.2 + Patches 1–2 on Fragment IV + Patch 3 on Fragment X.1)

[Hail,] Osiris Hôr, the justified! May you enter (III/10) into the Underworld [in] a state of great purity. [The Two Truths] have purified you in the [Great Hall. Purification is made for you in the Hall of Geb. Your limb]s [have been purified] in the Hall of (III/11) Shu. You see Re at his setting, A[tum at twilight. Amon is with you, giving you breath. Ptah fashion]s (III/12) your limbs. May you enter into the horizon with Re. [May your *ba*-spirit be received into the *Neshmet*-bark with Osiris.] (IV/1) [May] your *ba*-spirit [be deified in the Estate of Geb, since you are justified forever and ever.]

PARAGRAPH IV

(Fragment X.1 + Patch 4 on Fragment IV)

[Osiris] Hôr, the justified, born of Tai[khibit, the justified! May your name end]ure, may your corpse abide, and may your mummy thrive. [You shall not be turned away] (IV/2) [in heaven or on earth. May your face be illuminated in the presence of Re.] May your *ba*-spirit live in the presence of Amon. May your [cor]pse be rejuvenated in the presence of Osiris. May you breathe forever [and ev]er.

PARAGRAPH V

(Fragment X.1 + Patch 4 on Fragment IV)

(IV/3) [May your *ba*-spirit make for you an invocation-offering consisting of bread, beer, beef and fowl, and of cool water and incen]se in the course of [every] day. [Your flesh is on] your bones in accordance with the form that you had on earth. May you drink with your throat. (IV/4) [May you eat with your mouth. May you receive] offering bread together with [the *ba*-spirits of the gods.] Anubis has [gua]rded you. He has made your protection. You shall not be turned [away] from the doors (IV/5) [of the Underworld. Thoth], the Thrice [Great]est, Lord of Hermopolis, [has come to you.] He has writ[ten] for you a Breathing Document with his own fingers, so that (IV/6) [your *ba*-spirit] may breathe [forever, and that you might regain the fo]rm that you had on earth among the living, since you are divine together with the *ba*-spirits of the gods. Your heart is the heart of Re; your flesh (IV/7) [is the flesh of the great god.]

Paragraph VI

(Fragment X.1 + Patch 5 on Fragment X)

[Hail, Os]iris Hôr, the justified! Amon is with you every day in the Estate of Re, so that you might live again. Wepwawet has opened for you the good way, (IV/8) [so that you might see with your eyes, that you might hear with] your ears, that you might speak with your mouth, and that you might walk with your feet, while your *ba*-spirit is deified in the Underworld [in order to] make (IV/9) [any] transformation[s according to its will. May you cause the rust]lings of the noble persea tree [...] in Heliopolis. May you awake every day so that you might see the ray[s (IV/10) of the sun. Amon has come to you bearing the brea]th of life. He has caused that you brea[the in] your sarcophagus so that you might go forth to the earth every day. (IV/11) The [Breath]ing Docu[ment of Thoth] has been made for you [as] your protection, so that you might breathe by means of it like Re, so that your eyes might see the rays of the sun disk, and so that you might be called 'justified' (IV/12) [in the presence of Osiris.] [Your] pro[tection(?)] has been made. Horus the Behdedite has guarded your body and has deified your *ba*-spirit as do all the gods. The *ba*-spirit of Re revivifies your [*ba*-spirit]. (IV/13) [The *ba*-spirit of Shu unites with] your [nos]trils.

Paragraph VII

(Fragment X.1–2)

Hail, Osiris Hôr, the justified, born of Taikhibit, the justified! May your *ba*-spirit breathe wherever it likes, (V/1) since you exist as [Osiris. Osiris Foremost of the Westerners is your name. Hapy the great (the Nile Inundation) has come to you from Elephantine, so that he might fill your altar with (V/2) food offering]s.

Paragraph VIII

(Fragment X.2)

Osiris Hôr, the justified, born of [Taikhibit, the justified! The gods of Upper and Lower Egypt have come to you so that they might guide you to Alkhah. May your *ba*-spirit live, may you] (V/3) serve Osiris, may you breathe within Rostau. ['She-who-hides-her-Lord' and the great god have protected you. Your corpse lives in] (V/4) Busiris and the Thinite nome. Your *ba*-spirit lives in heaven every [day].

PARAGRAPH IX

(Fragment X.2 + Patch 6 on Fragment IV)

[Osiris Hôr, the justified, born of Taikhibit, the justified! Sakhmet has overpowered those who would conspire against you. Horus] (V/5) the steadfast makes (your) protection. Horus the Behdedite [performs your wishes. Hormerty guards your body, so that you are permanently in] (V/6) life, prosperity and health, enduring upon your throne in the sacred land. Come, [then, Osiris Hôr, the justified, born of Taikhibit, the justified,] (V/7) appearing gloriously in your proper form, complete in your ornaments! May you spend the night in life; [may you spend the day in health. May you travel and may you breathe] (V/8) in any place. May Re shine upon your cavern like that of Osiris, so that you might breathe and [live by means of his rays. Amon-Re has revivified] (V/9) your *ka*-spirit and has made you flourish by means of the Breathing Document. May you serve Osiris [and Horus, Lord of the *Henu*-bark, since you exist as the Great God, Foremost] (V/10) of the gods. May your face live; may your forms be perfect. Your name thrives every day. [Come,] may you enter into the very great embalming [booth] (V/11) in Busiris. May you see the Foremost of the Westerners in the *Wag*-Festival. May your scent be sweet as a youth. [May your name be great as] (V/12) an august noble.

PARAGRAPH X

(Fragment X.2 + Patch 6 on Fragment IV)

Hail, Osiris Hôr, the justified! May your *ba*-spirit live by means of the Breathing Document, [and may you be united by the same manner with] (V/13) the *ba*-spirit. May you enter into the Underworld. There are no enemies of yours, for you exist as a divine, effective spirit [in Busiris. Your heart belongs to you; it will not be far from you. Your eyes belong to you, being open every day."]

PARAGRAPHS XI–XIV ARE LOST

(Cols. VI–VII)

CONCLUDING VIGNETTE, COL. VIII

(Preserved only as Facsimile 3)

- **Label for Osiris:**

(VIII/1) Recitation by Osiris, Foremost of the Westerners, (VIII/2)

Lord of Abydos(?), the great god (VIII/3) forever and ever(?).

- **Label for Isis:**
  (VIII/4) Isis the great, the god's mother.
- **Label for Maat:**
  (VIII/5) Maat, mistress of the gods.
- **Label for Hôr:**
  (VIII/6) The Osiris Hôr, (VIII/7) justified forever.
- **Label for Anubis:**
  (VIII/8) Recitation by Anubis, who makes protection(?),(VIII/9) foremost of the embalming booth(?)(VIII/10) …
- **Invocation below scene:**
  (VIII/11) "O gods of the necropolis, gods of the caverns, gods of the south, north, west and east, grant salvation to the Osiris Hôr, the justified, born by Taikhibit."

PAPYRUS JOSEPH SMITH 2: BOOK OF THE DEAD OF TA-SHERIT-MIN

(Fragments IX, VII, VIII, V, VI, IV and II with pp. 12 and 14 of "Valuable Discovery" in Joseph Smith's Egyptian Grammar and Alphabet)

Classed as "Document B" in John Wilson's summary report on the Joseph Smith Papyri,[1] the Book of the Dead of the lady Ta-sherit-Min is probably to be dated to the second half of the Ptolemaic Period (ca. 100 BC) on the basis of paleography.[2] Although thus contemporary with the "Breathing Permit of Hôr" (P. Smith 1), the funerary document for Ta-sherit-Min is more traditional and closely parallels the later manuscripts of this composition that first dates to Egypt's New Kingdom.[3] Ta-sherit-Min ("The daughter of Min") has no titles, and only the name of her mother Nes-Khonsu ("The one belonging to Khonsu") is noted in the text. Portions of 8 columns of the original papyrus still exist, and either by hand copy or original manuscript, surviving evidence of Ta-sherit-Min's papyrus

---

A new edition of this text by Michael D. Rhodes reached me (February 25, 2011) while my manuscript was in press, too late to be incorporated in the present study.

[1] John Wilson 1968, pp. 68–69 and 71–85.

[2] Baer 1968, p. 111.

[3] For translations of the Book of the Dead (hereafter BD), see Allen 1974, Faulkner 1985, and Verhoeven 1993. The chapter arrangement of the Ta-sherit-Min papyrus generally corresponds to that of the late Ptolemaic Turin papyrus published by Lepsius in 1842, while many of its textual variations are paralleled by the Chicago Ryerson Papyrus (R in Allen 1960). See the assessment of John Wilson (1968, p. 71): "In particular, Allen's Document R is very close to our Document B." Restorations and variations from the Lepsius Turin papyrus and P. Ryerson are noted throughout the following edition of P. JS 2.

includes Book of the Dead chapters 1–7, 10–14, 16, 53–54, 57, 59(?), 63, 65, 67, 70, 72, 74–77, 83, 86–89, 91, 100–101, 103–106, 110 and 125.[4]

"Once the longest papyrus in the collection,"[5] P. Joseph Smith 2 is now broken into several sheets and many smaller fragments pasted unsystematically onto the larger pieces. As noted by Wilson, "the sections of Document B have been mounted with a brusque disregard for handwriting, continuity, or the grain of the papyrus. Pieces of the same manuscript have been wrongly moved in to fill holes, sometimes upside down, and there is at least one patch from another document."[6] The papyrus was certainly in much better condition when acquired by Smith, as he made extensive hand copies in his "Egyptian Alphabet and Grammar"[7] of portions now lost. These hand copies serve as a base—or even as the sole witness—for several of the spells translated below, and running transliterations of pages 12 and 14 of the Smith manuscript are included as appendices to this chapter. For the same manuscript, Smith also reassembled newly broken sections into a mock papyrus sheet: the so-called Church Historian's Fragment, otherwise known as "Fragment IX."

Unlike the other eleven papyrus leaves given the designation "Fragment" by Hugh Nibley, the so-called "Fragment IX"[8] is not a single section of an original papyrus (with or without intrusive additions pasted into it), but rather a conglomeration of many patches joined randomly to produce a disordered and artificial sheet, which even includes a hand copy by Smith[9] upside down in the lower right corner.[10] While other "fragments" contain

[4] Cf. the incomplete (and partially incorrect) chapter lists in John Wilson 1968, p. 72, and Parker 1968b, p. 87.

[5] John Wilson 1968, p. 68.

[6] Ibid., p. 69.

[7] Tanner 1966.

[8] Green 1968, p. 40, and Todd 1968, p. 40H. Note that Nibley's fragments are styled P. for "Papyrus" by Baer 1968 (thus Fragment IV = Baer's P JS IV). Baer's system has been adopted by myself in Ritner 2003a and 2002, and by Gee, Rhodes and Nibley 2005, plates 1–7. Within the present volume, only the originally independent documents (composed of one or more fragments) are labeled P(apyrus).

[9] Throughout this chapter, I have designated the hand copy as done by Smith, who oversaw the work but was assisted by "scribes." For these and their individual handwritings, see the discussion by H. Michael Marquardt in this volume.

[10] I have made no attempt to decipher this hand copy, as it contains only words and signs jumbled and even reversed.

some intrusive patches (VIII, VI and V), and such patches are particularly numerous (and disfiguring) in Fragment IV,[11] "Fragment IX" more closely resembles a modern work of "decoupage" than an ancient manuscript. The following translation does incorporate more portions of this pastiche than previously attempted, particularly in chapters 3 through 7 and 10 through 13, but without access to the original document one must echo Wilson's early assessment: "Probably more exhaustive—and exhausting—research would identify further pieces of the Church Historian's fragment."[12]

Despite its unfortunate state of preservation, "Fragment IX" does provide critical clues regarding the original condition of the Joseph Smith papyri and their subsequent damage. This "fragment" was not one of the papyrus sections that passed through many hands before being acquired by the Metropolitan Museum of Art in New York in 1947.[13] Rather, it was rediscovered in the Church Historian's office in Utah and "apparently has always been in the Church's hands" since it was "part of the manuscript of the Egyptian Alphabet and Grammar prepared by Joseph Smith preparatory to the translation of the Book of Abraham."[14] A comparison of the latter manuscript with the "The Church Historian's Fragment" reveals that the "fragment" served as page 9 of Smith's "Valuable Discovery of hiden [*sic*] reccords [*sic*] that have been obtained from ancient buring [*sic*] place of the Egyptitiens [*sic*]," while an extended hand copy of the same text appears on the final page (14).[15]

What is striking, however, are the differences between the two versions. The hand copy is no facsimile, as it introduces line divisions according to the width of Smith's copying paper, not the original text.

[11] Designations of patches on Fragment IV belonging properly to P. JS 1 only were noted by Baer 1968, plate III. Other patches were ignored by Baer, but some were labeled in unpublished personal notes by John Wilson (now in the Oriental Institute Archives). The current patch numbers are indicated in the plates that accompany this volume.

[12] John Wilson 1968, p. 85.

[13] Todd 1968. The papyri were given by Joseph Smith's mother (Lucy Mack Smith), ca. 1855, to his remarried widow (Emma Smith Bidamon) and her son (Joseph Smith) and then sold in 1856 to a Mr. A. Combs. By 1918 the papyri belonged to Mrs. Alice C. Heusser, daughter of Combs' housekeeper, a resident of Brooklyn.

[14] Todd 1968, p. 40A.

[15] Published in facsimile in Tanner 1966. The cover of "Valuable Discovery" is taken as page 1, following Wilson 1968. A full transliteration of this page appears as Appendix III to this chapter, below.

Examination of surviving patches on "Fragment IX" proves that distinct papyrus lines are often joined on the hand copy while, in contrast, single lines on the papyrus were on occasion subdivided by Smith. Nevertheless, the hand copy seems otherwise generally faithful to the original papyrus manuscript at Smith's disposal.[16] The papyrus must already have suffered some damage, as the hand copy continues seamlessly across parts of the spells and incomplete names whose continuation no longer existed. Smith either failed to recognize or chose to ignore these gaps when making his hand copy. The existence of similar injuries was already noted in an 1837 account by William S. West, who reported that the papyri were damaged when they were removed from the mummies purchased by the Mormons: "These records were torn by being taken from the embalming salve which contained them, and some parts entirely lost."[17] Further damage must certainly have been produced by Smith or others handling the material for the church.

Many hieratic signs required by Book of the Dead parallels are included in his hand copy but now lost on "Fragment IX." As the patchwork "Church Historian's Fragment" not only lacks the signs but any space for them, the loss of these textual elements can only have occurred between the time of Smith's initial hand copy and the later assemblage of broken segments to form "Fragment IX." Even clearer is the fate of the vignette for Chapter 16 of Ta-sherit-Min's Book of the Dead. The vignette was sufficiently well preserved to be copied with baboons, priest and text intact on "Valuable Discovery," p. 14, yet these scenes are reduced to mismatched scraps on the "Church Historian's Fragment" (IX), with the base line of the second baboon pasted at the far upper left (patch 11), pieces of the 2 baboons pasted at the far right (patches 9–10), and unrelated text pasted haphazardly in the middle. This destruction occurred during the time of the composition of the "Valuable Discovery" manuscript.

Since both the hand copy by Smith and the assemblage of fragment IX form part of "Valuable Discovery" (pp. 9 and 14), the damage was unquestionably done during Smith's own work on the fragile papyrus. Moreover, the sort of jumbled patching that characterizes the "Church

[16] Smith's hand copies do include some discrepancies, however, particularly where he copied the same chapter on more than one page of his "Valuable Discovery." Perhaps these variations represent the deteriorating condition of the papyri as he continued to work on them. See the remarks in Appendix II to this chapter, below.

[17] John A. Larson 1994, p. 169.

Historian's Fragment"—with obvious ignorance of paleographic, textual, pictorial, spatial or even directional matters—is similar to that found on the other papyrus fragments that did pass to the Metropolitan Museum. The present, disordered state of all the papyri can thus probably be attributed to Smith and his circle, and not to any later owners. Repeated viewings of the original materials by curious visitors to Smith's home may have contributed to the damage[18] and necessitated the unprofessional repairs.

Color photographs of P. Joseph Smith 2 appear in Charles M. Larson 1992, p. 34 (folded color plate of "The Untranslated Book of Joseph Papyrus Scroll"; omitting Fragment IX and the "Valuable Discovery" hand copies); with older, sepia-toned images in Green 1968, pp. 40, and Todd 1968, pp. 40·A through 40·H. Sepia photos of vignette details are found in Nibley 1975.[19] Color photos of Fragments II, IV, V and VI appear in Gee, Rhodes and Nibley 2005, plates 4 and 6–7. The proper alignment of published fragments has been inconsistent. Fragments V and VI are properly oriented in Larson 1992 (plate = p. 34), but not in the subsequent publication by Gee, Rhodes and Nibley 2005 (plate 7), which reproduces the fragments as currently mounted.[20] The alignment of Fragments IV and VI is incorrect in all previous publications; Fragment IV should be one line lower in relation to Fragment VI. The join between Fragments II and IV is shown properly in Larson 1992 (plate = p. 34), but with the lowering of Fragment IV, Fragment II must be shifted correspondingly to maintain the join. These alignments have now been corrected in the plates accompanying this volume.

Only John Wilson has attempted an extensive, if partial, translation of P. JS 2.[21] As a result of the poor quality of the photos then available, Wilson's

[18] See the accounts given in John A. Larson, ibid., pp. 164ff. The possible gift by Smith of papyrus fragments to Potawatomi Indians is noted in Todd 1968.

[19] Pp. 81 (Fragment IV, BD 89), 129 (Fragment IV, BD 106), 136 (Fragment IV, BD 100 and 101), 142 (Fragment IV, BD 104), 143 (Fragment IV, BD 105), 144 (Fragment II, BD 110), and 181 (Fragment IV, BD 74 and 75), with hand copies on pp. 101 (BD 100), 102 (BD 101), and 117 (BD 105). These now appear as black and white images in Gee, Rhodes and Nibley 2005, pp. 112 (BD 89), 186 (BD 105), 237 (BD 104) and 318 (BD 74 and 75); with reconstructed hand copies of vignettes on pp. 209 (BD 106), 223 (BD 100 and 101), 240 (BD 105), and 242 (BD 110).

[20] See the obvious join between Fragments V and VI in Chapter 86 (V.2+VI.1/x+9) at the rubric: ḫprw n [m]n.t ḏd-md.w ỉn Wsỉr Tꜣ-šr.t-Mnw [...]. The mounted papyrus places Fragment V two lines too low in Gee, Rhodes and Nibley 2005, plate 7.

[21] John Wilson 1968, pp. 73–85. I thank John A. Larson, Oriental Institute Archivist,

translations rely heavily upon Allen's edition of the Chicago Ryerson papyrus and do not always reflect the precise state of the Smith papyrus (regarding misplaced patches, lost words or passages) or its deviations from the Chicago exemplar. Nor did Wilson attempt a translation of the hand copies in "Valuable Discovery," though he recognized their significance.[22] Wilson's brief and often dismissive commentary indicates clearly his lack of sensitivity or sympathy for Egyptian religion.[23] While Book of the Dead manuscripts are notorious for scribal errors, modern misinterpretations of anciently revised passages have not helped comprehension: "I adorn my intestines at the landing of the ferryboat" (Chapter 53); "O my spirit, you should not make a head which you weigh in yourself(?)" (Chapter 105).[24] Aside from Wilson's publication, two brief phrases were noted by Nibley.[25]

Joseph Smith and his circle misidentified the Book of the Dead of Ta-sherit-Min as a companion to the supposed Book of Abraham. Variously called the "writings of Joseph of Egypt," "the book of Joseph" or "Joseph's record," the apocryphal translation was never produced, although the vignette of Ta-sherit-Min before the serpent in Chapter 74 (Fragment V) was said to represent "Eve talking to the serpent."[26] This vignette was

for permission to republish the extensive commentary of John Wilson.

[22] John Wilson 1968, p. 73: "Because I always want to see with my own eyes, I shall limit myself to the six photos and the Historian's Fragment, omitting comment on the copied texts which are i and ii above." Wilson's section i is "Valuable Discovery," p. 12 and section ii is p. 14.

[23] E.g., "This again is a little baffling" (John Wilson 1968, p. 74); "The best that can be said for that is that the western desert burial ground was hot and dry" (ibid., pp. 74–75); "I should be happy if I could explain how this spell gave the deceased the power of infinite transformation" (ibid., p. 78); "Out of that tangle of myth, I can only say that the deceased became very flexible in form …" (ibid., p. 79); etc.

[24] Both translations are by John Wilson, but cf. Allen 1960, p. 133: "(I) festoon (my) intestines at joining the ferryboat" (Chapter 53); and p. 180: "(O) my spirit, let not (my) head {be taken away} from {me}" (Chapter 105). Those lines are here translated "May I rejoice over my bowels in joining the rowers" (within a discussion of sanitary eating habits on the solar boat in Chapter 53), and "O my ka-spirit, may you not act on the two arms of the balance at which you are" (within a discussion of truthfulness of the weighing of the heart in Chapter 105).

[25] Nibley 1975, pp. 129 (BD 106) and 144 (BD 110).

[26] Baer 1968, p. 111, n. 5, with reference to "Joseph Smith's Egyptian Alphabet & Grammar," pp. 1 ("writings of Joseph of Egypt") and 3 ("the book of Joseph" or "Joseph's record").

clearly of interest to Smith, as he recopied it on p. 6 of "Valuable Discovery" adjacent to texts copied from the distinct papyrus of Amenhotep (P. Joseph Smith 4). From the vignette of three gods in Ta-sherit-Min's Chapter 104 (Fragment IV) may derive the suggestion by Oliver Cowdery that in "Joseph's record" the "god-head—three, yet in one, is curiously drawn to give simply, though impressively, the writers [*sic*] views of that exalted personage."[27] In Cowdery's same letter, he included in Joseph's record a judgment scene that could be either the lost vignette of Chapter 125 from P. Joseph Smith 2 or—much more likely—the comparable, but surviving, scene from P. Joseph Smith 3.[28]

The source of P Joseph Smith 2 may be the mummy "No. 1" described in the *Painesville Telegraph* of 27 March 1835: "4 feet 11 inches, female, supposed age 60; arms extended, hands side by side in front; the head indicating motherly goodness. There was found with this person a roll or book, having a little resemblance to birch bark; language unknown. Some linguists however say they can decipher 13–36, in what they term an epitaph; ink black and red, many female figures."[29] If correctly identified, this would be the best surviving description of Ta-sherit-Min's lost remains.

THE CURRENT EDITION

Passages originally written in red ink ("rubrics") are indicated in the following edition by the use of all capital letters. Red ink served to highlight titles and directions, but because of the link between red, blood and Seth, only black ink is used for the names of Osiris, other favorable deities and the deceased.[30] Red ink was also used by Smith in his hand copies in "Valuable Discovery"; such instances (and deviations) are indicated in the translations and notes below. As noted previously, Ashment and others have assigned a decimal number for the papyrus components of P. JS 2, in the order of their original position within the now-divided papyrus. Thus Fragment IX is P. JS 2.1, Fragment VII is P. JS 2.2, Fragment VIII is P. JS 2.3, Fragment V is P. JS 2.4, Fragment VI is P. JS 2.5, Fragment IV is P. JS 2.6, and Fragment II is P. JS 2.7.

---

[27] See Howard 1968, p. 89; and Baer 1968, p. 111, n. 5.

[28] Howard 1968, p. 89.

[29] Wolfe and Singerman 2009, p. 109.

[30] See the discussion and references in Ritner 1993, pp. 147–48.

The scholarly apparatus of line divisions within transliterations and translations serves primarily to facilitate identifications between the modern edition and the original papyrus manuscript. Normally, this is done with respect to "columns" of text, whether surviving or reconstructed. This is the pattern adopted above for P. JS 1, which consists of only a few columns now divided over three adjacent "fragments." The situation presented by P. JS 2, however, is far more complex. The shattered papyrus is reconstructed from lost sections recorded in hand copies, multiple large sections arbitrarily subdivided and mounted (the "fragments"), numerous misplaced patches scattered among these larger sections and reconstructions based on parallels. While I have superimposed a system of columns over this framework, that is far less convenient for easy reference than the now-entrenched notation of fragments. Despite initial misgivings, I have designated the parenthetical transliteration and translation divisions below by reference to the standard numbering of fragments—not columns. Thus the surviving traces of Chapter 57 begin in (VIII.1/x+1), which indicates Fragment VIII, col. 1, first preserved line after a gap of uncertain size. It is hoped that this concession will simplify consultation of the surviving papyrus.

Preserved columns are, however, also noted below for those who wish to cite the papyrus in the expected scholarly format of column and line number. No certain column assignment can be made for the initial chapters 1 and 2 which are attested only in hand copies. "column x + 1" (beginning within Chapter 3) corresponds to a patch on Fragment IX, "column x + 2" (beginning at Chapter 53) corresponds to the righthand column of Fragments VII + VIII, "column x + 3" (beginning at Chapter 63) corresponds to the lefthand column of Fragments VII + VIII, "column x + 4" (beginning within Chapter 72) corresponds to the righthand column of Fragment V, "column x + 5" (beginning at Chapter 83) corresponds to the lefthand column of Fragment V + righthand of VI, "column x + 6" (beginning within Chapter 89) corresponds to the lefthand column of Fragment VI + righthand of IV, "column x + 7" (beginning at Chapter 103) corresponds to the lefthand column of Fragment IV, and "column x + 8" (beginning at Chapter 110) corresponds to Fragment II.

Chapter 1. This chapter contains the proper Egyptian title, "Going Forth by Day," of the document now styled the Book of the Dead, as well as the introductory spell to be recited on the day of burial. In the text, the blessed Ta-sherit-Min both invokes Osiris and is assimilated to him as "the Osiris

Ta-sherit-Min."[31] Chapter 1 is partially preserved only in hand copy on "Valuable Discovery," p. 12, lines 1–15. Line numbers of the hand copy of p. 12 appear in () and sections not in the hand copy are placed in []. Restorations are based on Lepsius 1842, plates 1–2.

[ḥꜣ.(t)-ꜥ m rꜣ.w n.w pr m hrw s͟ts ꜣḫ.w m ẖr.t-nṯr ḏd.tw hrw qrἰs ꜥq m-ḫ.t pr ἰn Wsἰr Tꜣ-šr.t-Mnw mꜣꜥ-ḫrw ms n Ns-Ḫnsw mꜣꜥ-ḫrw]

(1) ἰ Wsἰr kꜣ ἰ[mnt.t ... ἰnk wꜥ m nn n nṯr.w ḏꜣḏꜣ.t] (2) smꜣꜥ ḫrw Wsἰr r [ḫfty.w=f hr](3)w pwy n wḏꜣ md.wt [... wnn=ἰ r-ḥnꜥ Ḥr hrw ḥb n Wsἰr Wn-nfr mꜣꜥ-ḫrw ἰr.t ꜥꜣb.wt n.t Rꜥ hrw 6-n.t dnἰ] (4) n ꜣIwnw ἰnk wꜥb m Ḏdw sbq m [ꜣbḏw ...] (5) [ἰnk] stm m ἰry.w=[f] ἰnk wr ḫrp ḥmww.t rdἰ [ḥny ḥr mfḫ ... ἰ stkn bꜣ.w mnḫ.w m pr Wsἰr stkn=tn bꜣ n Wsἰr Tꜣ-šr.t-Mnw] (6) [mꜣꜥ-ḫrw] ms n Ns-Ḫnsw mꜣꜥ-ḫrw ḥnꜥ=tn r pr Wsἰr mꜣꜣ(?)[=f mἰ mꜣꜣ=tn ... dἰ=tn t ḥnq.t r tr n Wsἰr] (7) Tꜣ-šr.t-Mnw mꜣꜥ-ḫrw ms n Ns-Ḫnsw mꜣꜥ-ḫrw ḥnꜥ=tn [... ἰ wp mtn.w n bꜣ.w mnḫ.w m pr Wsἰr ... wp=tn mtn.w n Wsἰr Tꜣ-šr.t-Mnw mꜣꜥ-ḫrw ms n] (8) Ns-Ḫnsw mꜣꜥ-ḫrw ḥnꜥ=tn ꜥq=f m rꜣ pwy [m pr Wsἰr ... pr=f] (9) mr.tw[32] smꜣꜥ ḫrw[=f] ἰr.tw wḏ.t[=f] m pr Wsἰr šm[=f] md.wt[=f] ḥ[nꜥ=tn šm Wsἰr Tꜣ-šr.t-Mn](10)w [mꜣꜥ-ḫrw ms n] Ns-Ḫn[sw mꜣꜥ-ḫrw ...][33] sἰp.tw m rꜣ.w ꜥšꜣ sꜥḥꜥ bꜣ=k r ḫ[ft-ḥr gm.tw=f wḏꜣ rꜣ tp tꜣ ... wnn=ἰ mἰ] (11) [w]ꜥ [ἰm=tn] s͟ts nmt.t m Ḥr-ꜥḥꜣ mꜣꜣ.n=ἰ Sꜣḥ [... ἰnḏ-ḥr=k ḫ](12)nty ἰmnt.t Wsἰr ḥry-ἰb Ṯꜣw-wr dἰ=k hꜣ=ἰ r ἰmnt.t ššp [wἰ nb.w tꜣ ḏsr ...] (13) pr.n=ἰ m-bꜥḥ Wn-nfr mꜣꜥ-ḫrw šms=ἰ Ḥr m Rꜣ-s[ṯꜣ.w Wsἰr m Ḏdw ... ἰr rḫ mḏꜣ.t tn ḥr-tp tꜣ ἰw=f ἰr=s m sš ḥr qrἰs] (14) [r]ꜣ-pw ἰw=[f] pr=f m hrw nb mr=[f ḥ]nꜥ [ꜥ]q r ḥw.[t]=f nn [šnꜥ.tw=f ...] (15) [wn]n=f wꜣḏ mἰ [w] nn=f ḥr-tp tꜣ

[BEGINNING OF THE SPELLS OF GOING FORTH BY DAY AND OF EXALTING BLESSED SPIRITS IN the necropolis, SAID on the day of burial and on entering after going forth by the Osiris

[31] For this traditional interpretation, recently questioned by Mark Smith, see the remarks of Ritner 2010, p. 178, n. 26, and the edition of P. JS 1, Paragraph VII, in the current volume.

[32] Signs copied on line 9 beyond mr.tw are very indistinct and transcribed here tentatively on the basis of the Lepsius parallel (1842, plate 1, line 15).

[33] The "Valuable Discovery" hand copy jumps directly from the initial signs of the mother's name to a later portion of the spell, omitting sections in the Lepsius parallel. This jump may indicate damage to the papyrus when copied.

Ta-sherit-Min, the justified, born of Nes-Khonsu, the justified.] (1) "O Osiris, bull of the W[est ... I am one of these gods of the tribunal] (2) who justified Osiris against [his enemies on] (3) this [da]y of judgment. [... I am together with Horus on the day of festival for Osiris the Perfect Being (Onnophris), and in making the offerings of Re on the 6th-day festival and the 5th-day festival] (4) in Heliopolis.[34] I am a pure priest in Busiris, a cleansed one in [Abydos, ...,] (5) [I am] a *setem*-priest in [his] duties; I am the chief master-craftsman (high priest of Ptah) who placed [the barque of Sokar on the sledge.... O you who introduce excellent *ba*-spirits in the house of Osiris, may you introduce the *ba*-spirit of the Osiris Ta-sherit-Min,] (6) [the justified,] born of Nes-Khonsu, the justified, together with you into the house of Osiris. [He] sees [even as you see ... May you give bread and beer per season to the Osiris] (7) Ta-sherit-Min, the justified, born of Nes-Khonsu, the justified, together with you. [... O you who open the roads for excellent *ba*-spirits in the house of Osiris, ... may you open the roads for the Osiris Ta-sherit-Min, the justified, born of] (8) Nes-Khonsu, the justified, together with you. May he enter by this door [in the house of Osiris ... May he go forth] (9) beloved, [his] voice having been justified, while [his] command is performed in the house of Osiris. May [he] go while his words are w[ith you. May the Osiris Ta-sherit-Min], (10) [the justified, born of] Nes-Kh[onsu, the justified, go ...], being examined by multiple mouths. May your *ba*-spirit be elevated when [it is found sound of speech on earth ... I exist just like] (11) [on]e [among you], being exalted of stride in Kheraha,[35] since I have seen Orion. [... Hail to you,] (12) Foremost of the West, Osiris resident in the nome[36] of Abydos. May you cause that I go down to the West while [the lords of the sacred land] receive [me ...] (13) I have gone forth in the presence of the Perfect Being, even as I follow Horus in Ro[setau and Osiris in Busiris ..."]

[AS FOR THE ONE WHO KNOWS THIS BOOK on earth, or makes it in writing on the coffin,] (14) he goes forth on any day [that

[34] The Biblical city of On.

[35] Egyptian Babylon, now Old Cairo.

[36] A province of Egypt. Here the Thinite nome is meant; see P. JS I, Paragraph VIII (col. V/4).

he] desires, and enters into his mansion without [his being repelled …] (15) He exists soundly just as he was on earth.

Chapter 2. The title alone can be recovered from this short spell on P. Joseph Smith 2. In the lost sentences, the deceased invokes the deity of the moon for membership in his retinue, so that the blessed spirit might do "whatever he may wish on earth among the living." A variant survives in P. Joseph Smith 2 as the initial portion of Chapter 65. Chapter 2 is partially preserved only in hand copy on "Valuable Discovery," p. 12, line 15. Line numbers of the hand copy of p. 12 appear in () and sections not in the hand copy are placed in []. Restorations are based on Lepsius 1842, plate 2.

(15) rꜣ n pr m hrw ꜥnḫ m-ḫ[t mt ḏd-md.w ỉn Wsỉr Tꜣ-šr.t-Mnw mꜣꜥ-ḫrw ms n Ns-Ḫnsw mꜣꜥ-ḫrw …]

(15) SPELL FOR GOING FORTH BY DAY living after [DEATH. RECITATION BY the Osiris Ta-sherit-Min, the justified, born of Nes-Khonsu, the justified. "…"]

P. JS 2 PRESERVED COLUMN (x+) 1

FRAGMENT IX (= P. JS 2.1)

Chapter 3. Designed to give the deceased powers similar to those in the previous spell, Chapter 3 invokes the solar creator Atum and the twin lion of the horizon, Ruty. Chapter 3 is partially preserved on Fragment IX, patch 7/x+1 (upper right, second patch), and in hand copy on "Valuable Discovery," pp. 12, lines 16–19, and 14, line 1. Restorations are based on Lepsius 1842, plate 2.

[ky rꜣ mỉt.t=f ḏd-md.w ỉn Wsỉr[37] Tꜣ-šr.t-Mnw mꜣꜥ-ḫrw ms n Ns-Ḫnsw mꜣꜥ-ḫrw ỉ ꜣItm wr m Nnw(?) ꜣḫ m rw.ty[38] … wḏ md.wt=k

[37] Signs probably corresponding to [k]y rꜣ mỉt[.t=f] ḏ[d-m]d.w [ỉ]n Wsỉr are found on line 16 of "Valuable Discovery," page 12.

[38] The signs for [w]r m Nnw(?) ꜣḫ m rw.[ty] appear on line 17 of "Valuable Discovery," p. 12. Traces of a leaning man with staff(?) and divine determinative would correspond to [w]r, with a horizontal "m" before nnw(?) and ꜣḫ with divine determinative and abusive plural strokes (as is common). The Lepsius text (1842, plate 2) has instead m-ẖnw mw "within the water" for "in Nun/the Abyss." Earlier versions have wr hnhnw with similar meaning.

n][39] (x+1) ỉs.t n Rᶜ m mšrw [ᶜnḫ Wsỉr m-ḫt mt mỉ Rᶜ rᶜ nb ỉn[40] ḥm ms Rᶜ m sf ms Wsỉr T3-šr.t-Mnw m3ᶜ-ḫrw ms n Ns-Ḫnsw m3ᶜ-ḫrw ... ỉnk Ḏḥwty pr=f m ḥw.t sr wr m ʾIwnw[41]]

[ANOTHER SPELL, SIMILAR TO IT. RECITATION BY the Osiris Ta-sherit-Min, the justified, born of Nes-Khonsu, the justified. "O Atum, the great one in the Abyss, blessed as Ruty ... Give your command to] (x+1) the crew of Re in the evening [so that Osiris might live after death like Re, every day. It was assuredly the one who bore Re yesterday who bore the Osiris Ta-sherit-Min, the justified, born of Nes-Khonsu, the justified.... I am Thoth[42] when he goes forth from the great Mansion of the Prince in Heliopolis."]

Chapter 4. In this spell, the deceased insists on his cosmic role, determining the flood, and—like Thoth—separating Horus from Seth ("the two combatants"). Chaper 4 is partially preserved on Fragment IX, patch 7/x+2–3 (upper right, second patch), and in hand copy on "Valuable Discovery," p. 14, lines 1–2. Restorations are based on Lepsius 1842, plate 2.

[ky r3 n snỉ ḥr w3.t ḥry(t) t3 ḏd-md.w ỉn Wsỉr] (x+2) T3-šr.t-Mnw m3ᶜ-ḫrw ms n Ns[-Ḫnsw[43] m3ᶜ-ḫrw ... ỉnk tš 3gb wp] (x+3) [r]ḥ.wy ỉy.n=ỉ dỉ.n=ỉ 3ḥ.wt [n[44] Wsỉr ...]

[ANOTHER SPELL FOR PASSING BY THE ROAD above the earth. RECITATION BY the Osiris] (x+2) Ta-sherit-Min, the justified, born of Nes-[Khonsu, the justified.... "I am one who limits

---

[39] The signs for md.wt=k n ỉs.t n Rᶜ m mšrw are found in line 1 of "Valuable Discovery," page 14.

[40] The signs for ᶜ[nḫ Wsỉr m]-ḫt mt mỉ Rᶜ rᶜ nb ỉn appear on line 18 of "Valuable Discovery," p. 12.

[41] The signs for [s]r wr m ʾIwnw appear on line 19 of "Valuable Discovery," p. 12.

[42] Other texts have "Ptah."

[43] The signs for Wsỉr T3-šr.t-Mnw m3ᶜ-ḫrw ms n Ns-[Ḫnsw] appear on line 1 of "Valuable Discovery," p. 14. The "Valuable Discovery" hand copy skips directly from ms n Ns- to rḥ.wy ỉy.n=ỉ, perhaps indicating that the papyrus already had gaps when copied by Joseph Smith. The phrase ỉy.n=ỉ spans lines 1–2 of "Valuable Discovery," but appears on a single line (IX.1/x+6) on the surviving papyrus, thus proving that the hand copy is not a precise facsimile of the original manuscript.

[44] The signs for ỉy.n=ỉ dỉ.n=ỉ 3ḥ.wt n appear on lines 1–2 of "Valuable Discovery," p. 14.

the flood pool, who separates] (x+3) the two combatants. I have returned after I have given fields [to Osiris …"]

Wilson 1968 Translation (p. 84):

"'[I am one … who judged] the two [companions.] I have come that I might give the fields [to Osiris].'"

Chapter 5. This spell serves as a less common variant for the ushebti spell that follows. Chapter 5 is partially preserved on Fragment IX, patch 7/x+4 (upper right, second patch), and in hand copy on "Valuable Discovery," pp. 12, lines 19–21, and 14, line 2. Restorations are based on Lepsius 1842, plate 2.

[rꜣ n[45] tm di͗.t i͗r s kꜣ.t m[46] ẖr.t-nṯr ḏd-md.w i͗n Wsi͗r Tꜣ-šr.t-Mnw[47] mꜣꜥ-ḫrw ms n Ns-Ḫnsw mꜣꜥ-ḫrw i͗nk ḏꜥr bꜣ nni͗ pr][48] (x+4) m Wnw.t ꜥnḫ m bsk[.w ꜣꜥꜥn.w]

[SPELL FOR NOT MAKING A MAN DO WORK IN THE NECROPOLIS.[49] RECITATION BY the Osiris Ta-sherit-Min, the justified, born of Nes-Khonsu, the justified. "I am one who has sought out the *ba*-spirit of the Weary One, who has gone forth] (x+4) from Hermopolis, who lives on the entrail[s of the baboons."]

Wilson 1968 Translation (p. 84):

"'[I am the seeker of the weary one, who came forth from] Hermopolis, who lives on the entrails [of baboons.]'"

---

[45] The signs for rꜣ n appear in red ink on line 19 of "Valuable Discovery," p. 12.

[46] The signs for [t]m rdi͗.t i͗r s kꜣ.t m nṯr (with honorific transposition of ẖr.t-nṯr) appear in red ink on line 20 of "Valuable Discovery," p. 12. The hand copy's stroke and dots that should correspond to tm must indicate that the word was broken when copied.

[47] The signs for ẖr.t-[nṯr] ḏd-md.w i͗n Wsi͗r Tꜣ-šr.t-Mnw appear on line 21 of "Valuable Discovery," p. 12. Red ink is used for all signs except Osiris Ta-sherit-Min. Although these words join the rubric of Chapter 5, they may also be copied from Chapter 6.

[48] The signs for [nn]i͗ pr m Wnw.t ꜥnḫ m bsk appear on line 2 of "Valuable Discovery," p. 14.

[49] The signs for ẖr.t-nṯr are copied in red ink on lines 20–21 of "Valuable Discovery," p. 12, contrary to the usual practice of placing the word "necropolis" in black ink. As the text always resumes in red ink, Smith (or his scribes) may have failed to switch inks for this word. However, cf. the inconsistent use of ink (black for red) in the preserved opening of Chapter 12, below.

Chapter 6. This spell is commonly inscribed both on papyrus and on individual servant figures (ushebtis or "answerers") who act as substitute workers for the deceased. Chapter 6 is partially preserved on Fragment IX, patch 7/x+5–6 (upper right, second patch), and in hand copy on "Valuable Discovery," pp. 12, line 22, and 14, lines 2–3. Restorations are based on Lepsius 1842, plate 2.

> [rꜣ n rdỉ.t ỉry wšbty kꜣ.t m ẖr.t-nṯr ḏd-md.w ỉn Wsỉr Tꜣ-šr.t-Mnw[50] mꜣꜥ-ḫrw] (x+5) [m]s [n] Ns-Ḫnsw mꜣꜥ-ḫrw[51] [ỉ wšbty ỉpn ỉr ỉp.tw Wsỉr Tꜣ-šr.t-Mnw mꜣꜥ-ḫrw ms n Ns-Ḫnsw mꜣꜥ-ḫrw r kꜣ.t nb.(t) ỉr.t ỉm m ẖr.t-nṯr ỉs ḥwỉ.tw sḏb.w ỉm=f m s r ẖr.wt=f mk wỉ kꜣ=tn[52] sỉp=tn r nw nb ỉr.t ỉm r srwd sḫ.wt] (x+6) [r smḥw wḏb].w [r] ẖnty [šꜥ[53] n ỉmnt.t r ỉꜣbt.t mk wỉ kꜣ=tn]
>
> [SPELL FOR CAUSING A USHEBTI TO DO WORK IN the necropolis. RECITATION BY the Osiris Ta-sherit-Min, the justified,] (x+5) born of Nes-Khonsu, the justified. [" O this ushebti, if the Osiris Ta-sherit-Min, the justified, born of Nes-Khonsu, the justified, is assigned to any work which might be done there in the necropolis, for indeed obstacles are set for him as a man regarding his duties, 'Behold, here I am,' so you will say. May you be assigned at any time to act there, whether to cultivate fields,] (x+6) [to irrigate the shore]s, [or to] convey [sand from the west to the east, 'Behold, here I am,' so you will say."]

Chapter 7. This spell ensures that the deceased will escape the demonic serpent Apep, who threatens the barque of Re each night. The description of Apep as being of wax refers to common rituals that destroy the demon by melting wax images.[54] Chapter 7 is partially preserved only in hand copy on "Valuable Discovery," pp. 12, lines 23–25, and 14, lines 3–4. Line

---

[50] Signs for ẖr.t-[nṯr] ḏd-md.w ỉn Wsỉr Tꜣ-šr.t-Mnw appear on line 21 of "Valuable Discovery," p. 12, but seem to join the rubric of Chapter 5 rather than the parallel in Chapter 6.

[51] The signs for (T)ꜣ-šr.t-Mnw mꜣꜥ-ḫrw ms n Ns-Ḫnsw mꜣꜥ-ḫrw appear on lines 2–3 of "Valuable Discovery," p. 14.

[52] The signs for [ỉ]m=f m s r ẖr.wt=f mk wỉ kꜣ=tn appear on line 22 of "Valuable Discovery," p. 12.

[53] The signs for r [s]mḥw wḏb.w r ẖnty šꜥ appear on line 3 of "Valuable Discovery," p. 14.

[54] Ritner 1993, pp. 157–58, 184 and 211.

numbers of the hand copy of p. 12 appear in () and sections not in that hand copy are placed in []. Line numbers of the hand copy of p. 14 appear in the notes. Restorations are based on Lepsius 1842, plate 3.

> [rꜣ n snỉ ḥr ṯs.w ꜥꜣpp qsn pw ḏd-md.w ỉn Wsỉr] (23) Tꜣ-[šr.t]-Mnw mꜣꜥ-ḫrw ms n Ns-Ḫnsw mꜣꜥ-[ḫrw[55] ỉ wꜥ (n) mnḥ ḥꜣq ỉṯ m ꜥwꜣy ꜥnḫ] (24) m nnỉ.w nn nnỉ=ỉ n=k nn [ꜥ]q [mtw.t=k m ꜥ.wt=ỉ ỉptn ỉnk wꜥ ḥr ḫnty Nwn[56] ... ỉnk štꜣ] (25) rn.w wr m[57] ḏsr s.wt r ḥḥ.[w ...]

> [SPELL FOR PASSING BY THE VERTEBRAE OF APEP. IT IS DANGEROUS. RECITATION BY the Osiris] (23) Ta-[sherit]-Min, the justified, born of Nes-Khonsu, the just[ified. "O one of wax, plunderer, who seizes by robbery, who lives] (24) on the weary ones, I shall not be weary for you. [Your poison] will not enter [into these limbs of mine. I am the unique one who is preeminent in the Abyss ... I am one secret] (25) of names, the great one in the holiest of places for million[s (of years). ..."]

Chapter 10. Ensuring defeat of one's enemies, this spell contrasts the fate of the justified with that of the overturned enemies, whose bodily functions are reversed in punishment (cf. Chapter 53, below). Chapter 10 is partially preserved on Fragment IX, patch 8/x+1–2 (third patch at the upper left), and in hand copy on "Valuable Discovery," pp. 12, line 26, and 14, lines 4–5. Restorations are based on Lepsius 1842, plate 3.

> [rꜣ n pr m mꜣꜥ-ḫrw ḏd-md.w ỉn Wsỉr Tꜣ-šr.t](x+1)-Mnw mꜣꜥ-ḫrw ms n Ns-Ḫnsw [mꜣꜥ-ḫrw pr=ỉ[58] m mꜣꜥ-ḫrw r ḫfty.w=ỉ ... wbꜣ.n=ỉ tꜣ šꜣỉs.n=ỉ r nmt.t=f[59] ... wnm=ỉ m rꜣ=ỉ fgn](x+2)=ỉ m ꜥr.w(t)=ỉ ḥr-nt.t

---

[55] "Valuable Discovery," p. 14, lines 3–4, preserves the extract differently: [Tꜣ-šr.t](3)-Mnw mꜣꜥ-ḫrw ms n (4) Ns-Ḫnsw mꜣꜥ-ḫrw.

[56] The signs for m ꜥ.t=ỉ ỉptn ỉnk wꜥ ḥr ḫnty Nwn appear on line 4 of "Valuable Discovery," p. 14.

[57] The addition wr m does not appear in the parallels but is suggested by the hand copy.

[58] The signs for -Mnw mꜣꜥ-ḫrw ms n appear on line 4 of "Valuable Discovery," p. 14, while the originally contiguous signs for Ns-Ḫnsw mꜣꜥ-ḫrw pr appear on line 5.

[59] The signs for [wb]ꜣ.n=ỉ tꜣ šꜣỉs.n=ỉ r nmt.t=f appear on line 26 of "Valuable Discovery," p. 12. Following šꜣỉs.n=ỉ, the hand copy omits tꜣ as do versions noted in Allen 1974, p. 10.

ỉnk n[ṯr nb[60] dwꜣ.t …]

[SPELL FOR GOING FORTH IN JUSTIFICATION. RECITATION BY the Osiris Ta-sherit](x+1)-Min, the justified, born of Nes-Khonsu, [the justified. "May I go forth in justification against my enemies … As I have opened the earth, so I have traveled at his steps … May I eat with my mouth while] (x+2) I [defecate] with my hindquarters, because I am a god, [lord of the underworld …"]

Chapter 11. Providing a further protection against earthly and demonic enemies, Chapter 11 is partially preserved on Fragment IX, patch 8/x+3–4 (third patch at the upper left) and in hand copy on "Valuable Discovery," pp. 12, lines 27–28, and 14, lines 5–6. A section may be preserved in unplaced patch 30 (Fragment V.1). Restorations are based on Lepsius 1842, plate 3.

[rꜣ n pr r ḫfty.w=f m ẖr.t-nṯr ḏd-md.w ỉn Wsỉr Tꜣ-šr.t-Mnw[61] mꜣꜥ-ḫrw ms n Ns-Ḫnsw mꜣꜥ-ḫrw … ỉnk Rꜥ pr m ꜣḫ.t r][62] (x+3) ḫfty.w=ỉ nn nḥm=f m-ꜥ=ỉ [… nn rdỉ.t[63] n=ỉ dr ky-ḏd ḫr[64] m-ꜥ=ỉ ḫfty pwy rdỉ.n=f n=ỉ[65] nn nḥm=f m-ꜥ=ỉ ꜥḥꜥ.n=ỉ[66] m Ḥr ḥms.n=ỉ m Ptḥ … šm.n=ỉ] (x+4) m rd.wy=ỉ mdw=ỉ m rꜣ=ỉ ḥḥ[=ỉ[67] ỉm=f …]

[SPELL FOR GOING FORTH AGAINST HIS ENEMIES IN the necropolis. RECITATION BY the Osiris Ta-sherit-Min, the justified, born of Nes-Khonsu, the justified.… "I am Re, who has gone forth from the horizon against] (x+3) his enemies. There is no

[60] The signs for [fgn]=ỉ m ꜥr.w(t)=ỉ ḥr-nt.t ỉnk nṯr nb appear on line 5 of "Valuable Discovery," p. 14.

[61] The signs for ḫfty.w=f m ẖr.t-nṯr ḏd-md.w ỉn Wsỉr Tꜣ-šr.t-[Mnw] appear on line 27 of "Valuable Discovery," p. 12.

[62] The signs for m ꜣḫ.t r are copied on line 5 of "Valuable Discovery," p. 14.

[63] The signs for nn rdỉ.t appear on line 28 of "Valuable Discovery," p. 12.

[64] If the text followed only the alternate version (rdỉ.t n=ỉ ḫr), preserved traces may appear on the unplaced patch 30 on Fragment V.1.

[65] The signs for ḫfty pwy rdỉ.n=f n=ỉ appear on line 28 of "Valuable Discovery," p. 12.

[66] The signs for ḫfty.w=ỉ nn nḥm=f m-ꜥ=ỉ ꜥḥꜥ.(n)=ỉ appear on line 6 of "Valuable Discovery," p. 14.

[67] The signs for [šm].n=ỉ m rd.wy=ỉ mdw=ỉ m rꜣ=ỉ ḥḥ=ỉ appear on line 6 of "Valuable Discovery," p. 14.

rescuing him from me. [... There is no driving away from me—otherwise said, letting fall from my hand—this enemy whom he has given to me, there is no rescuing him from me. As I have stood as Horus, so I have sat down as Ptah ... I have gone] (x+4) on my two feet, speaking with my mouth and seeking [him (ie. the enemy) ..."]

Chapter 12. This brief spell invokes rituals performed for the earth god Geb and the weighing of the heart. Chapter 12 is partially preserved on Fragment IX, patch 8/x+5–6 (third patch at the upper left), and in hand copy on "Valuable Discovery," pp. 12, lines 29–30, and 14, line 7. Restorations are based on Lepsius 1842, plate 3.

(x+5) rꜣ n [ꜥq pr ỉn Wsỉr] T[ꜣ]-šr.t-Mnw [mꜣꜥ-ḫrw ms n] (x+6) Ns-[Ḫnsw mꜣꜥ]-ḫrw ḏd-[md.w[68] ỉꜥnw n=k Rꜥ mk ẖr sštꜣ.w n dwꜣ.t[69] ḥr ỉꜣ.t twy n.t Gb ḥr mḫꜣy.(t) twy n.t Rꜥ fꜣỉ=f Mꜣꜥ.t ỉm=s rꜥ nb mk wỉ bꜣ.n=ỉ tꜣ dỉ=k[70] ỉw=ỉ m nḫḫ]

Spell[71] for [entering and going forth by the Osiris] T[a]-sherit-Min, [the justified, born of] (x+6) Nes-[Khonsu, the justi]fied. RECITATION. ["Hail to you, Re who gives protection for the secrets of the underworld concerning this mound of Geb and concerning this balance of Re in which he weighs Truth every day. Behold, I have hacked the earth. May you cause that I come as an aged one."]

Chapter 13. Like the previous spell, this allows the unhindered movement of the deceased, but it includes additional directions for a protective amulet. Two words only survive on Fragment IX, patch 8/x+7 (third patch at the upper left), with more extensive sections in hand copy on "Valuable Discovery," pp. 12, lines 31–32, and 14, lines 7–8. Restorations are based on Lepsius 1842, plate 4.

[rꜣ n ꜥq m-ḫt pr ỉn Wsỉr Tꜣ-šr.t-Mnw mꜣꜥ-ḫrw ms n Ns-Ḫnsw

[68] The signs for Wsỉr Tꜣ-šr.t-Mnw mꜣꜥ-ḫrw ms n Ns-Ḫnsw [mꜣꜥ-ḫrw] ḏd-md.w appear on line 29 of "Valuable Discovery," p. 12.

[69] The signs for Rꜥ mk ẖr sštꜣ.w n dwꜣ.t appear on line 7 of "Valuable Discovery," p. 14.

[70] The signs for fꜣỉ=f Mꜣꜥ.t ỉm=s rꜣ nb mk wỉ bꜣ.n=ỉ tꜣ dỉ=k appear on line 30 of "Valuable Discovery," p. 12.

[71] Although most versions place the introduction in red ink, the traces on P. JS 2 are here in black. Cf. the inconsistency noted in the hand copy of Chapter 5, above.

mꜣʿ-ḫrw ḏd-md.w[72] ... nṯr dwꜣ ỉr n=ỉ wꜣ.t dwꜣ=ỉ Rʿ m ỉmnt.t nfr.t nš šnw[73] n Wsỉr nw ṯsm.w Ḥr ỉr n=ỉ wꜣ.t dwꜣ=ỉ Wsỉr ḏd-](x+7) [md].w ḥr [bnn.(t) n.(t) ʿnḫ-ỉmy rdỉ.t[74] (m) msḏr wnm n ꜣḫw rdỉ.t[75] k.t bnn.(t) n sšd n pgꜣ (< pꜣq.t) ỉr.t rn n Wsỉr Tꜣ-šr.t-Mnw mꜣʿ-ḫrw ms n Ns-Ḫnsw mꜣʿ-ḫrw ḥr=f m hrw qrỉs][76]

[SPELL FOR ENTERING AFTER GOING FORTH BY the Osiris Ta-sherit-Min, the justified, born of Nes-Khonsu, the justified. RECITATION. "... God of the morning (star), make a path for me so that I might adore Re in the goodly West. Hairdresser of Osiris, binder of the hounds of Horus, make a path for me so that I might adore Osiris."]
(x+7) [RECITA]TION OVER [a pellet of the "Life-therein-plant." Place (in) the right ear of a blessed spirit. Place another pellet in a strip of fine linen. Write the name of the Osiris Ta-sherit-Min, the justified, born of Nes-Khonsu, the justified, on it on the day of burial.]

Chapter 14. Chapter 14, designed to avert any god's anger at the deceased, is partially preserved only in hand copy on "Valuable Discovery," pp. 12, lines 33–34, and 14, line 9. Line numbers of the hand copy of p. 12 appear in () and sections not in that hand copy are placed in []. Line numbers of the hand copy of p. 14 appear in the notes. Restorations are based on Lepsius 1842, plate 4.

[rꜣ n dr šp.t m ỉb n Wsỉr Tꜣ-šr.t-Mnw mꜣʿ-ḫrw ms n Ns-Ḫnsw mꜣʿ-ḫrw ḏd-md.w ỉʿnw n=k hb ꜣ.t ḫnty štꜣ.w nb.w mk ḏd md.wt r Wsir Tꜣ-šr.t-Mnw mꜣʿ-ḫrw ms n] (33) Ns-Ḫnsw mꜣʿ-ḫrw nn nṯr šp[t r=f

[72] The signs for Wsỉr Tꜣ-šr.t-Mnw mꜣʿ-ḫrw ms n Ns-Ḫnsw mꜣʿ-ḫrw ḏd-md.w appear on line 7 of "Valuable Discovery," p. 14.

[73] The signs for ỉr n=ỉ wꜣ.t dwꜣ=ỉ Rʿ m ỉmnt.t nfr.t nš[š]nw appear on line 31 of "Valuable Discovery," p. 12.

[74] The signs for Wsỉr ḏd-md.w ḥr bnn.(t) n.(t) ʿnḫ-ỉmy rdỉ.t are copied on line 8 of "Valuable Discovery," p. 14.

[75] The signs for [ʿnḫ]-ỉmy rdỉ.t (m) msḏr wnm n ꜣḫw rdỉ.t appear on line 32 of "Valuable Discovery," p. 12.

[76] The signs for [Ns-Ḫn]sw mꜣʿ-ḫrw ḥr=f m hrw qrỉs conclude line 8 of "Valuable Discovery," p. 14.

... d̲r dr.n=ỉ nkn ỉm=f d̲w smꜣ nt̲r m Mꜣꜥ.t r dr sd̲b.w=f n ky nt̲r[77] ... ỉn=(ỉ)] (34) n=k sḥtp.w ꜥnḫ=k ỉm=f ꜥnḫ W[sỉr Tꜣ-šr.t-Mnw mꜣꜥ-ḫrw ms n Ns-Ḫnsw mꜣꜥ-ḫrw ỉm=f ...]

[SPELL FOR AVERTING ANGER AT THE HEART of the Osiris Ta-sherit-Min, the justified, born of Nes-Khonsu, the justified. RECITATION. "Hail to you, one who sends the striking power, preeminent of all secrets! Behold, words have been said against the Osiris Ta-sherit-Min, the justified, born of] (33) Nes-Khonsu, the justified, without a god being angry [at him.... since I have averted injury from him, the evil that god unites with Truth in order to divert his ill-will to another god ... I have brought] (34) to you propitiatory offerings so that you might live by means of it and so that the O[siris Ta-sherit-Min, the justified, born of Nes-Khonsu, the justified,] might live [by means of it ..."]

Chapter 16. Although designated by Wilson[78] as Chapter 15, the vignette depicting baboons adoring the rising sun and the deceased receiving water offerings has traditionally been labeled Chapter 16.[79] Two baboons with an adjacent label are shown on "Valuable Discovery," p. 14, and fragments of the figures remain on Fragment IX in both the upper right (patches 9–10) and upper left (patch 11, the base line of the second baboon). Below the baboons on "Valuable Discovery" is a drawing of a priest offering water. For the composition, cf. Lepsius 1842, plate 6, left. Line numbers of the hand copy appear in () and sections not in the hand copy are placed in [].

Label for the baboons: (1) [...] (2) [...] Wsỉr(?) [nb(?)] (3) D̲d[w[80] ...]
(1) [...] (2) [...] Osiris(?), [lord of(?)] (3) Busiris [...]

[77] The signs for [sm]ꜣ nt̲r m Mꜣꜥ.t r dr sd̲b.w=f n ky nt̲r comprise line 9 of "Valuable Discovery," p. 14.

[78] Wilson 1968, pp. 72 and 85.

[79] Faulkner 1985, p. 43, considered this standard designation "incorrect," but cf. Chapter 110, typically reduced to a vignette with labels (110c) in late versions (the "Saite Recension") of the Book of the Dead. See Chapter 110 below and Verhoeven 1993, vol. I, p. 110, and vol. III, cols. 48–49.

[80] Traces of D̲d[w] and the baseline of the second baboon (originally left of patch 10) are preserved in patch 11—now pasted at the opposite side of Fragment IX from Patch 10.

Label for the priest: (1) [...] qbḥ.w[81]
(1) [Offering] cool water.

FRAGMENTS VII (= P. JS 2.2) + VIII (=P. JS 2.3)

Fragment VII is composed of two distinct papyrus sections that do not directly join each other, but which are now mounted side by side. The first, or righthand, column would have continued below to join the first (righthand) column of Fragment VIII, whose spells precede those of the second (lefthand) columns of Fragments VII and VIII. All previous treatments of P. Joseph Smith 2 have discussed the sequence of spells on Fragments VII and VIII out of order, as though all chapters in Fragment VII preceded those in Fragment VIII.[82] Chapters 53 and 54 are followed by a lost section of text between Fragments VII and VIII. Then Chapter 57 is followed by one or more uncertain—and largely lost—spells. After this damage, the papyrus continued on the lefthand column on Fragment VII with chapters 63 and 65, with a further gap before chapters 67, 70 and 72 on Fragment VIII.

P. JS 2 PRESERVED COLUMN (x+) 2

Chapter 53. The first spell to survive on the larger, original papyrus "fragments," Chapter 53 is designed to ensure sanitary food supply in the underworld—in contrast to the situation with the damned, whose fate is to be literally overturned so that the processes of eating and defecation are reversed.[83] For this reason, reciters insist that they are companions of the gods, who do not go upside-down, and who may thus be happy about the state of their digestion—and chances of survival—as they join the solar boat. The distasteful aspect noted by Wilson (1968, p. 74) is precisely what the spell prohibits. No intestines are "adorned" in the text of the spell. The vignette shows the deceased Ta-sherit-Min seated at a proper table of offerings and holding a cup.[84]

[81] The upper portion of the ḥ of qbḥ.w is still preserved below the baboon on Patch 10.

[82] See John Wilson 1968, pp. 74–75; and Parker 1968, p. 87.

[83] Kadish 1979, pp. 203–17. *Contra* John Wilson 1968, p. 74, the Egyptologist is not poorly informed about the reasons for this fear and its associations with reversal; see further R. Ritner 1993, pp. 168–72.

[84] Cf. the vignette for Chapter 49 in P. Ryerson in Allen 1960, plate 22.

(VII.1/x+1–x+2)[85] [rꜣ n tm wnm ḥs swr wsš m ẖr.t-nṯr ḏd-md.w ỉn Wsỉr Tꜣ-šr.t-Mnw mꜣꜥ-ḫrw ms n Ns-Ḫnsw mꜣꜥ-ḫrw ỉnk kꜣ dm ḥn.ty sšm p.t nb ḫꜥ.w p](VII.1/x+3).t s(VII.1/x+4)[ḥḏ wr pr m bḫḫ] ḥr tr (VII.1/x+5) [ꜣw rw rdỉ tꜣ šm ꜣ]ḫ.w bw.t⸗ỉ pw[86] ḥs nn sỉw⸗ỉ (VII.1/x+6) [wsš nn šm⸗ỉ m sḫ]d [ỉn]k nb t m ʾIwnw[87] ỉw t⸗ỉ r p.t ḫr (VII.1/x+7) [Rꜥ ỉw t⸗ỉ r tꜣ ḫr Gb ỉn Skt.t] ỉn[88] s[89] n⸗ỉ m pr nṯr ꜥꜣ m ʾIwnw wn(VII.1/x+8)[f⸗ỉ qꜣb⸗ỉ m smꜣ m ẖn(y).t ḏꜣ]⸗ỉ r ỉꜣb.t n.t p.t wnm⸗ỉ m (VII.1/x+9) [wnm⸗sn ꜥnḫ⸗ỉ m ꜥnḫ⸗sn wn]m.n⸗ỉ t m ꜥ.t nb ꜥꜣb.wt

(VII.1/x+1–x+2) [SPELL FOR NOT EATING EXCREMENT OR DRINKING URINE IN the necropolis. RECITATION BY the Osiris Ta-sherit-Min, the justified, born of Nes-Khonsu, the justified. "I am the bull with sharp horns, the guide of heaven, the lord of appearances of heav]en, (VII.1/x+3) the [great] ill(VII.1/x+4) [uminator, who has gone forth as a scorching flame], who honors (VII.1/x+5) [expansiveness,[90] the lion who gave the earth, so that

---

[85] The tail ends of two lines are visible above the offering table to the right of the seated Ta-sherit-Min. These may belong either to spell 53 or to the preceding spell (probably spell 52). By comparison with the adjacent spell 65, 6 lines may have occupied the space above the groundline of the vignette. The beginning of the spell (in red ink) is completely lost, and the black traces of two lines could both correspond to flourishes at the end of the letter "m." Where these traces correspond to the lost text is uncertain, and I have not attempted to fix the divisions of lines 1/x+1 and 1/x+2, nor the beginning of line 1/x+3, which ends with the determinative of p.t "heaven" and the first "s" of sḥḏ "illuminator."

[86] P. JS 2 uses more "Ptolemaic" spellings than P. Ryerson, its close parallel. Here the letter "p" is written with the spitting mouth. In both papyri, the following verb "to drink" (old swr) is written with contemporary vocalization reflecting the loss of the final "r" (cf. Coptic **ⲥⲱ** and **ⲥⲉⲩ**-).

[87] For the unusual hieratic writing, which occasionally appears in P. Ryerson, see the references in Allen 1960, p. 23; and cf. P. London and Leiden cols. 6/20 and 11/7 and 13, writings gathered in Griffith and Thompson 1921, p. 8.

[88] For the hieratic form, see Griffith and Thompson 1921, p. 8 (cols. 3/33, 21/10, 14 and 15).

[89] Placed in () by John Wilson in his 1968 translation, p. 74, but written.

[90] Derived from Coffin Text Spell 218, BD 53 recasts earlier wording, one version of which is: [wn]f ḥtr.w fꜣw "who loosens the bonds of the magnificent." John Wilson 1968, p. 74, translated the Smith passage as "who honors [length of years]," while Allen 1960, p. 132, translated the Ryerson parallel as: "who values long (life)." No

the] blessed spirits[91] [might walk.] Excrement is my abomination. I shall not drink (VII.1/x+6) [urine. I shall not go upside-]down. I am a possessor of bread in Heliopolis. My bread is in heaven with (VII.1/x+7) [Re. My bread is on earth with Geb. It is the solar evening barque] that brings it to me from the house of the great god in Heliopolis. May [I] rejoice over[92] (VII.1/x+8) [my bowels in joining the rowers as] I [cross over] to the east of heaven. May I eat of (VII.1/x+9) [that which they eat. May I live on that from which they live.] I have eaten bread specifically from the chamber of the lord of offerings."

Wilson 1968 Translation (p. 74):

"[The speech for not eating dung or drinking urine in the necropolis. Words to be spoken by the Osiris T-N: 'I am the sharp-horned bull, the guide of the sky, the lord of festivals of the sky, the great] illu[minator, who went forth as a flame,] who honors [length of years, the lion who gave the earth, so that the sun's rays go.] Dung is my abomination. I will not drink [urine. I will not walk upside-down. I am] a possessor of bread in Heliopolis. My bread is at the sky with [Re. My bread is at the earth with Geb. It is the evening-barque (of the sun) which] brings (it) to me from the house of the great god in Heliopolis. I ad[orn my intestines at the landing of the ferryboat. I cross] to the east of heaven. I eat of [that which they eat; I live on that (on which) they live. I have eaten] bread in the room of the possessor of offerings.'"

---

explicit word for "years/life" appears in the texts.

[91] Late Books of the Dead have changed the wording of Coffin Text spell 218 from "to whom the movements of the sunshine were given," substituting tꜣ "land" for n=f "to whom" and ꜣḫ.w "illuminated spirits" for šw "sunshine." Allen and Wilson ignore the latter substitution as elsewhere the synonym (ỉ)ꜣḫ.w "sunlight" can be written abusively with a divine spirit determinative; see the comment of Allen 1960, p. 137, n. h, and cf. the translations of the same section of BD 65 (with human determinative) as "blessed " by Allen 1960 (p. 141) and "the sun's rays" by John Wilson 1968, p. 75.

[92] The deceased asks to take comfort in the absence of digestive problems. In seeking the meaning of wnf, Allen (1960, p. 133) and John Wilson (1968, p. 74) produce unlikely translations: "I adorn/festoon my intestines." Faulkner 1985, p. 65, translated: "I am loosed from my windings."

Chapter 54. Egyptian biological notions stress the critical function of the "breath of life," which is here given again to the deceased as to the chick in the cosmic egg of Amon, the Great Cackler. The vignette shows the deceased standing and holding a (now lost) sail, the hieroglyphic symbol for air and breath.[93] As only a brief section of the lengthy spell is preserved in P. Smith 2, and the text need not have paralleled P. Ryerson in all respects, the full text is not translated here.

> (VII.1/x+10)[94] [rꜣ n rdꞽ.t ṯꜣw n s m ẖr.t-nṯr ḏd-md.w ꞽn Wsꞽr Tꜣ-šr.t-Mnw mꜣꜥ-ḫrw ms n Ns-Ḫnsw mꜣꜥ-ḫrw ꞽ Ꞽtm ꞽmy n⸗ꞽ ṯꜣw nḏm n šry.ty⸗k ꞽnk swḥ.t twy n.t (n)gg wr ꞽw sꜣw.n⸗ꞽ swḥ.t twy] (VII.1/x+11) ꜥꜣ.t wp.t Gb (VII.1/x+12) [r tꜣ ꜥnḫ⸗ꞽ ꜥnḫ⸗s ṯs-pẖr nḫḫ⸗ꞽ nḫḫ⸗s snꞽ⸗ꞽ ṯꜣw snꞽ⸗s ṯꜣw[95] ...]

> (VII.1/x+10) [SPELL FOR GIVING BREATH TO A MAN IN the necropolis. RECITATION BY the Osiris Ta-sherit-Min, the justified, born of Nes-Khonsu, the justified. "O Atum, give to me the sweet breath of your nostrils! I am this egg of the Great Cackler. I have guarded this] (VII.1/x+11) great [egg] which separated Geb (VII.1/x+12) [from the earth. As I live, so it lives, and vice-versa. As I grow old, so it grows old. As I breathe the air, so it breathes the air ..."]

Wilson 1968 Translation (p. 74):

> "[The speech for giving breath to a man in the necropolis. Words to be spoken by the Osiris T-N: 'O Atum, give me the sweet breath of your nostrils! I am that egg of the great honker. I guarded that] great [egg] which separated Geb [from earth. If I live, it lives, and vice versa. ...]'"

[A lost section of papyrus will have contained other, intervening spells].

---

[93] Cf. the vignette for P. Milbank, Chapter 54 in Allen 1960, plate 69 and P. Ryerson, chapters 56 and 60 in Allen 1960, plate 23.

[94] The precise number of lines is unknown between the lost beginning of 1/x+10 and the preserved conclusion of what I have designated as 1/x+11. The restoration of 1/x+10 surely included more than one line. The minor traces at the end of line 1/x+12 could correspond to the sail of ṯꜣw "air," but this is far from certain.

[95] P. Ryerson is defective in this passage, omitting both nḫḫ⸗s and snꞽ⸗s ṯꜣw. Probably for that reason Wilson chose to halt his translation before these sentences.

Chapter 57. After a gap, the papyrus continues on Fragment VIII with the remains of a spell for ensuring access to air and water. No trace of the vignette remains, but earlier examples showed the deceased standing in a pool, surrounded by streams of water and holding the sail hieroglyph for air.[96] The initial half of the spell is lost,[97] and the surviving text begins with a later version of the second section (57b).

[rꜣ n snỉ ṯꜣw sḫm m mw m ẖr.t-nṯr ḏd-md.w ỉn Wsỉr Tꜣ-šr.t-Mnw mꜣꜥ-ḫrw ms n Ns-Ḫnsw mꜣꜥ-ḫrw ...]
(VIII.1/x+1) [ỉw rꜣ n Wsỉr Tꜣ]-šr.t-Mnw mꜣꜥ-ḫrw (VIII.1/x+2) [ms n Ns-Ḫnsw mꜣꜥ-ḫrw n-t=f[98] šrỉ.(t)=f wn.tw m Ḏdw] ḥtp=f m ꜥIwnw[99] (VIII.1/x+3) [pr=f qd n=f Sšꜣ.t sꜥḥꜥ n=f Ḫnmw sbt].t=f ỉr ỉw p.t (VIII.1/x+4) [m mḥṯ.t ḥms=f m rsy ỉr ỉw p.t n rs.t ḥ]ms=f n mḥt.t (VIII.1/x+5) [ỉr ỉw p.t m ỉmnt.t ḥms=f m ỉꜣbt.t ỉr ỉw p].t m ỉꜣbt.t ḥms=(VIII.1/x+6)[f n ỉmnt.t ỉtḥ ỉnḥ.wy=f ḥr šrỉ.ty=f Wsỉr] Tꜣ-šr.t-Mnw (VIII.1/x+7) [mꜣꜥ-ḫrw ms n Ns-Ḫnsw mꜣꜥ-ḫrw wbꜣ=s r bw] nb[100] mr=s (VIII.1/x+8) [ḥms=s ỉm]

[SPELL FOR BREATHING AIR AND HAVING POWER OVER WATER IN the necropolis. RECITATION BY the Osiris Ta-sherit-Min, the justified, born of Nes-Khonsu, the justified. ...]
(VIII.1/x+1) ["The mouth of the Osiris Ta]-sherit-Min, the justified, (VIII.1/x+2) [born of Nes-Khonsu, the justified, belongs to him, his nose being open in Busiris.] May he rest in Heliopolis, (VIII.1/x+3) [his house that Seshat built for him, and] whose wall [Khnum erected for him.] If the sky comes (VIII.1/x+4) [in a north wind, let him sit in the south. If the sky comes in a south wind,] let him sit in the north. (VIII.1/x+5) [If the sky comes in a west wind, let him sit in the east. If the] sky [comes] in an east wind, let [him] sit (VIII.1/x+6) [in the west, his eyebrows having been drawn together over his nostrils. The Osiris] Ta-sherit-Min, (VIII.1/x+7) [the justified, born of Nes-Khonsu, the justified, let her penetrate into] any [place in

[96] See Faulkner 1985, p. 91 = Naville 1886 (reprinted 1971), vol. 1, plate 70.

[97] Noted by John Wilson 1968, p. 75.

[98] The form in P. Ryerson, col. 40, l. 23, is a late phonetic rendering of older m ḏr.t=f "in his possession," misunderstood by Allen 1960, p. 135.

[99] The scribe returns to the use of the late hieratic form of Heliopolis.

[100] The modifier "every" is not in P. Ryerson.

which] she[101] desires (VIII.1/x+8) [to sit."]

Wilson 1968 Translation (p. 75):

"[the speech for breathing air and having control of water in the necropolis.... A mouth belongs to the Osiris] T-[N. His is a nose which is open in Busiris.] He rests in Heliopolis, [his house which Seshat built for him, and whose wall Khnum set up for him.] If the sky comes [with north winds, he sits in the south. If the sky comes with south winds,] he sits in the north. [If the sky comes with west winds, he sits in the east. If the sky comes] with east winds, [he] sits [in the west. His eyebrows are knitted over his nose, the Osiris] T-[N. He has freedom for] any [place where] she wishes to sit."

Chapter 59(?).[102] The identification of this fragmentary spell is quite uncertain. If correctly identified, the vignette would have shown the deceased receiving food and water from the goddess of the sycamore tree. A further, isolated portion of text appears on the patch (patch 12, col. 1/x+1) misplaced at the top right of Fragment IV.[103]

(VIII.1/x+8) [rꜣ n snỉ ṯꜣw m ẖr.t-nṯr(?) ḏd-md.w] ỉn Wsỉr (VIII.1/x+9) [Tꜣ-šr.t-Mnw mꜣꜥ-ḫrw ms n Ns-Ḫnsw mꜣꜥ-ḫrw ...]

(VIII.1/x+8) [SPELL FOR BREATHING AIR IN the necropolis(?). RECITATION] BY the Osiris (VIII.1/x+9) [Ta-sherit-Min, the justified, born of Nes-Khonsu, the justified. ...]

Wilson 1968 Translation (p. 75):

"Traces of another chapter are visible below this, but I have not been

[101] As noted by John Wilson 1968, p. 75, the scribe here changes the gender of the pronoun to agree with the female owner of the papyrus. I have made the same change in the lost beginning of this sentence.

[102] Unrecognized by John Wilson 1968, pp. 75 and 78, the papyrus as currently mounted includes patch 13 with lines from BD 75, 76 and 77, aligned to match the traces of the *in situ* rubric (ỉn Wsỉr) below Spell 57. The patch properly belongs at the lower right of Fragment V, where it joins the remainder of Spells 75 and 76. BD Spell 57 is followed by Spell 59 in P. Ryerson, but the scant surviving traces below BD 57 ("by the Osiris") on P. JS 2 are so generic that they could also belong to any other spell. P. JS 2 does not reproduce the order of P. Ryerson, as is proved by the order of spells 67, 70 and 72 in the former.

[103] The brief traces of ỉw⸗s(?) correspond to about line x+15 of Fragment VIII and should belong to this or a subsequent spell.

able to identify it."

[A lost section of papyrus will have contained other, intervening spells.]

P. JS 2 PRESERVED COLUMN (x+) 3

Chapter 63. As the rudder of the solar barque is unburnt and has ready contact with water, so the deceased shall not be parched nor thirst.[104] The vignette shows the deceased pouring water offerings before a flaming brazier.[105]

(VII.2/x+1)[106] [rꜣ n sỉw mw tm ꜥgꜣ[107] m sḏ.t ḏd-md.w ỉn Wsỉr Tꜣ-šr.t-Mnw mꜣꜥ-ḫrw ms n Ns-Ḫnsw mꜣꜥ-ḫrw ỉ kꜣ ỉmnt.t rdỉ.n=(ỉ) wỉ n=k ỉnk mỉwḥ pwy n Rꜥ ẖnw=f ỉ]ꜣw(VII.2/x+2)[.w=f ỉm=f nn ꜥgꜣ=ỉ nn nwḫ=ỉ[108] ỉ]nk Bꜣby (VII.2/x+3) [sꜣ tp(y) n Wsỉr ꜥbỉ=f nṯr n=f m ẖnw] ỉr.t=f m ꜣIwnw ỉnk ỉwꜥw tp(y) (VII.2/x+4) [n wr kfꜣ wrd rw]d Wsỉr (n) rn=f[109] nḥm=f ꜥnḫ=k ỉm=f [ky-ḏd] (VII.2/x+5) [ỉnk mỉwḥ pw ꜥpr ẖnw] Rꜥ ỉm=f ẖnw ỉꜣw.w m ṯs rd[w] (VII.2/x+6) [n Wsỉr Tꜣ-šr.t-Mnw mꜣꜥ-ḫrw] ms n Ns-Ḫnsw[110] ẖnw.n=f ỉw n=f ỉw[ty] (VII.2/x+7) [ꜥgꜣ n=f ḥfd.n=ỉ ꜣḫw Ḥnmw ḫn]ty sšr ḫm ḥsk ḫm ỉ[w=k(?)][111] (VII.2/x+8) [šꜣs m-sꜣ wꜣ.t tn pr.(t).n=ỉ ỉm=s]

(VII.2/x+1) [SPELL FOR DRINKING WATER AND NOT BEING PARCHED BY FIRE. RECITATION BY the Osiris Ta-sherit-Min, the justified, born of Nes-Khonsu, the justified. "O bull of the

[104] In the dismissive assessment of John Wilson 1968, 75, the spell "somehow related the dead person to mythological forces who could not be burnt up by dryness."

[105] Cf. the vignette for P. Ryerson, Chapter 57 in Allen 1960, plate 23.

[106] The restored line designated as col. 2/ x+1 may include several lost lines. Traces visible behind the vignette are not Egyptian and derive from the nineteenth-century backing applied to the papyrus.

[107] Following P. Ryerson; for earlier ꜥwg.

[108] P. Ryerson omits nn nwḫ=ỉ.

[109] The writing of rn=f for n rn=f is common in contemporary Demotic documents and likely here.

[110] Unread by John Wilson 1968, p. 74.

[111] P. JS 2 here deviates from the text of P. Ryerson, which does not repeat ḫm and continues with rw(ỉ) "go forth." The fragmentary word here restored as ỉw=k ("may you go") begins with walking legs and could represent a textual corruption, preserving only the determinative of one of the following verbs of motion.

West, to you I have given myself. I am that rudder of Re by which he rowed his] elders. (VII.2/x+2) [I shall not be parched. I shall not be scorched.] I am Babi, (VII.2/x+3) [the first son of Osiris, when he united the god to himself within] his eye in Heliopolis.[112] I am the first heir (VII.2/x+4) [of the unwrapped great one, the weary one.] May Osiris flourish (by) his name. May he save your life by means of it.

[Otherwise said:] (VII.2/x+5) [I am this equipped rudder] by which Re [rows] and the elders row in raising up the efflux (VII.2/x+6) [of the Osiris Ta-sherit-Min, the justified,] born of Nes-Khonsu, when he has rowed the boatless one belonging to him, to which[113] there is no (VII.2/x+7) [parching, though I have ascended the solar rays. O Khnum,] foremost of the shrine, seize and decapitate the one who should be seized. [May you] come(?); (VII.2/x+8) [travel along this road on which I have gone forth!"]

Wilson 1968 Translation (p. 74):

"[The speech for drinking water and not being parched by fire .... ' I shall not be parched; I shall not be baked. I am Ba]bi, [the first son of Osiris, who united to himself every god within] his eye in Heliopolis. I am the first heir [of the great unwrapped one, the weary one.] Osiris and his name have flourished. He has rescued your life by it.'

"[Another version. ' I am that decorated oar] with which Re [rows] and the elders row who lift up [the decay of Osiris,] ... when he has rowed his marooned one, who has not [become parched. I have climbed the sun's rays O you who preside over] the sanctuary, seize and behead what is seized, [travelling along this road on which I have gone forth.]' "

Chapter 65. Aside from the title, the spell for unhindered movement and overcoming enemies more closely resembles Book of the Dead Chapter 2 and Coffin Text Spell 93. This recitation begins a series of spells (65–75) for ensuring free movement between the tomb, the underworld, selected

[112] Unlike in col. 1/x+6 and 7, the scribe here uses the more traditional hieratic writing of Heliopolis.

[113] The antecedent is "this rudder."

sacred sites and the earth in general. The vignette shows the deceased striding with a staff.

(VII.2/x+8) rꜣ n pr m hrw sḫm m ḫfty.w=f ḏd-md.w ỉn (VII.2/x+9) [Wsỉr Tꜣ-šr.t-Mnw mꜣʿ-ḫrw ms n Ns-Ḫ]nsw (VII.2/x+10) [mꜣʿ-ḫrw ỉ wbn m ỉʿḥ psd m ỉʿ]ḥ pr=k (VII.2/x+11) [m ʿšꜣ.w=k r rw.ty] wḥʿ=k wỉ (VII.2/x+12) [ỉmy.w ꜣḫ.w w]n dwꜣ.t (VII.2/x+13) [ỉst wỉ pr.kwỉ m hrw] pn ꜣḫ.kwỉ (VII.2/x+14) [rdỉ n=ỉ ꜣḫ.w=ỉ ʿnḫ=ỉ] ỉn.t[w] n=ỉ ḫfty=ỉ qꜣỉs[114] m ḏꜣḏꜣ.t [ḥ]t(VII.2/x+15)[p[115] kꜣ n mw.t=ỉ ỉm]=f mꜣꜣ=ỉ[116] ʿḥʿ.kwỉ m rd.wy=ỉ mdw=ỉ m ḏr.t=ỉ m (VII.2/x+16) [nbw šʿt=ỉ ḥ]ʿ.w ʿnḫ=ỉ[117] m mn.ty Spd.t nḫn [m] (VII.2/x+17) [ḥtp=sn]

(VII.2/x+8) SPELL FOR COMING FORTH BY DAY AND HAVING POWER OVER HIS ENEMIES. RECITATION BY (VII.2/x+9) [the Osiris Ta-sherit-Min, the justified, born of Nes-Kh] onsu, (VII.2/x+10) [the justified. "O one who rises as the moon, one who shines as the mo]on, when you go (VII.2/x+11) [outside among your multitude], may you release me. (VII.2/x+12) O one who is among the blessed, open the underworld! (VII.2/x+13) [Indeed, I have gone forth on] this [day], being blessed. (VII.2/x+14) [May my blessed ones grant to me that I live] and that my enemy be brought to me, being bound, in the tribunal. (VII.2/x+15) [May the soul of my mother be sat]is[fied with] it (at) seeing me standing on my two feet, my staff in my hand being (VII.2/x+16) [of gold. May I cut the lim]bs so that I might live at the thighs of Sothis, a child [by] (VII.2/x+17) [their grace]."

Wilson 1968 Translation (p. 75):

"The speech for coming forth by day and having power over one's enemies. Words to be spoken [by the Osiris T-N: 'O you who rise

[114] P. JS 2 here deviates from P. Ryerson, which writes qꜣm < qmꜣ "overthrown."

[115] The spelling of ḥtp is split between lines as in P. Ryerson, with the edge of the "t" visible.

[116] Allen 1960 (pp. 141–42, n. f) and Wilson 1968 (p. 75) emend the text to "when (she) sees me," but the identical text in P. Ryerson and P. JS 2 is comprehensible as written and is not an error but a variant tradition.

[117] Allen 1960 and John Wilson 1968 treat the seated man as a determinative for "living one," but as Allen notes (p. 142. n. g), the text refers to the cutting of the umbilical cord so that the deceased may be reborn.

as the moon and shine as the moon,] when you go forth [in your throng,] may you release me. [You who are in the sun's rays,] open up the underworld. [See, I have gone forth on] this [day,] being blessed. [My blessed (relatives) grant to me that I live.] My enemies are brought to me, tied up, in the council. [The spirit of my mother is satisfied with] it, when (she) sees me standing on my two feet, with my staff in (my) hand, of [gold. I cut off] the body of a living one at the thighs of Sothis, a child by [their graciousness].'"

Chapter 67. Designed to allow free movement from the tomb, the spell equates the deceased with a messenger of Re. The vignette, to the left of the spell, depicts the deceased Ta-sherit-Min striding.[118]

(VIII.2/x+1) [rꜣ n pr r ḥ]ꜣ [ḏd-md]w ỉn (VIII.2/x+2) Wsỉr Tꜣ-šr.t-Mnw mꜣ^c-ḫrw ms n Ns-Ḫnsw mꜣ^c-ḫrw (VIII.2/x+3) wn tpḥ.wt[119] n ỉmy.w Nwn sfḫ (VIII.2/x+4) n ỉmy.w ꜣḫ.w wn tpḥ.wt (n) Šw (VIII.2/x+5) pr.n=ỉ m rw.ty hꜣb=ỉ m wỉꜣ n Rꜥ

(VIII.2/x+1) [SPELL FOR GOING OUT]SIDE. [RECITATION] BY (VIII.2/x+2) the Osiris Ta-sherit-Min, the justified, born of Nes-Khonsu, the justified. (VIII.2/x+3) "Open the caverns for those who are in the Abyss! Unfasten (VIII.2/x+4) for those who are among the blessed![120] Open the caverns (for) Shu! (VIII.2/x+5) I have gone outside precisely because I was sent from the barque of Re."

Wilson 1968 Translation (p. 75):

"[The speech for going outside. Words to be spoken by] the Osiris T-N: 'The cavern is opened for those who are in the abysmal waters, freed for those who are in the sun's rays. The cavern is opened (for) Shu, and I have gone out-of-doors. I have been sent in the boat of Re.'"

Chapter 70. The spell continues the theme of unhindered movement and has no vignette.

---

[118] A fragment of a vignette now placed above the spell preserves a section of the kilt of the deceased, and seems to match the now missing section of this vignette.

[119] As in P. Ryerson, the original plural strokes are replaced by a "w" before the determinative.

[120] Or "those who are within the solar rays," but the determinative suggests "blessed spirits." For the ambiguity, see n. 91, above.

(VIII.2/x+5) k(y) rꜣ d̲d(VIII.2/x+6)-md.w ỉn Wsỉr Tꜣ-šr.t-Mnw mꜣꜥ-ḫrw ms n Ns-H̱nsw mꜣꜥ-ḫrw n[n m]nỉ(VIII.2/x+7)=ỉ n ḥry ry.(t)[121] sš wd̲ꜣ ỉb ḥt[p Wsỉ]r ḥq=f Ddw wnn=ỉ (VIII.2/x+8) ḥr ỉdb=f sns=ỉ[122] ỉꜣbt.t ḥr d̲ꜣd̲ꜣ=f ḫfꜣ.(n)=ỉ mḥt.t ḥr ḥ[nk](VIII.2/x+9)s.ty=f ḫfꜥ.n=ỉ ỉmnt.t ḥr msq=f pẖr.n=ỉ p.t ḥr qꜥḥ.(w)=s r[sy] (VIII.2/x+10) ḥr gmḥ.w=f dỉ=ỉ t̲ꜣw n ỉmꜣḫ.w ỉmy.(w) wnm.(w) t ỉr rḫ md̲ꜣ.t tn [tp tꜣ] (VIII.2/x+11) ỉw=f pr m hrw wn n=f šm.t ḥr tꜣ ỉmy ꜥnḫ.w nn sk=f[123] r ḥḥ

(VIII.2/x+5) ANOTHER SPELL. (VIII.2/x+6) RECITATION BY the Osiris Ta-sherit-Min, the justified, born of Nes-Khonsu, the justified. "I shall not moor (= "die") (VIII.2/x+7) for the master of decay, (being) a scribe sound of heart. As Osiris is satisfied when he rules Busiris, so I exist (VIII.2/x+8) on his shore, while I smell the east wind on its head. As I have grasped the north wind on (VIII.2/x+9) its tresses, so I have grasped the west wind on its skin. I have encircled heaven on its sides,[124] and the south wind (VIII.2/x+10) on its eyelashes, just so that I might give breath to the revered ones among the eaters of bread."
AS FOR THE ONE WHO KNOWS THIS BOOK [ON EARTH,] (VIII.2/x+11) he will go forth by day, possessing movement on earth among the living. He will not be destroyed forever.

Wilson 1968 Translation (pp. 75–76):

"Another speech. Words to be spoken by the Osiris T-N: 'I shall not come to rest, one who is over an abscess, a scribe sound of heart. (Osiris) is satisfied, as he rules Busiris, when I am on his bank. I breathe the east wind by its head; I grasp the north wind by its hair; I have grasped the west wind by its skin. I have encircled the sky by its shoulder, and the south wind by (its) eyelashes. I (give) breath to the revered ones among the eaters of bread.'
"As for the one who knows this speech, he may go forth by day,

[121] P. JS 2 varies from both earlier versions and P. Ryerson in determining ry.t as "decay/pus" rather than the homonym "judgment hall."

[122] P. JS 2 is here more traditional than P. Ryerson, which substitutes: "when I exist on his teeth (ỉbḥ.w)." Ryerson also uses the later spelling of "smell" (snỉ for sns).

[123] P. Ryerson adds rn "name": "His name will not be destroyed forever."

[124] The term derives from "shoulder," the translation employed by Wilson.

while he walks among the living on earth, without his perishing forever."

Chapter 72.[125] The spell again ensures passage from the tomb and concludes with directions for ritual practice and a testimonial extolling its value. The vignette shows the deceased standing before what is probably a highly schematic drawing of a tomb or shrine with its projecting cavetto cornice rendered as a triangle.[126] This chapter continues from Fragment VIII to the top right of Fragment V, but a long gap of lost text separates the two sections. A portion of this gap is filled by patch 12 now misplaced at the top of Fragment IV and long misidentified as a unique variant of Chapter 99.[127] The patch originally belonged at the bottom of Fragment VIII.2.

(VIII.2/x+12) rꜣ n pr m hrw[128] wbꜣ ỉmḥ.t ỉmnt.t ḏd-md.w ỉn Wsỉr Tꜣ-šr.t-Mnw mꜣ^c-ḫrw (VIII.2/x+13) ms n Ns-Ḫnsw mꜣ^c-ḫrw ỉnḏ-ḥr(VIII.2/x+14)=tn nꜣ nb.w Mꜥꜣ.t šw m ỉsf.t (VIII.2/x+15) wn.w[129] ꜥn[ḫ r ḥ]ḥ sp[-2] ḥn.(VIII.2/x+16)ty sp-2 ḏ.t wbꜣ t[n][130] (VIII.2/x+17) ḥry.t tꜣ tw=ỉ ꜣḫ.kw[ỉ][131] (VIII.2/x+18) [m ỉr.w=t]n sḫm.kwỉ m ḥk[ꜣ.w=tn[132] ...]

(VIII.2/x+12) SPELL FOR GOING FORTH BY day AND OPENING

[125] The text spans P. JS 2.3 to 2.4 (Fragments VIII and V).

[126] Cf. Naville 1886, vol. 1, plate 84.

[127] John Wilson 1968 translation (p. 81): "'[... Hail to you, good of person, lords of truth, who continue to live forever to the limits] of eternity! I have access [to you ...]'" The false identification was based on the duplicate phrase ḥn.ty sp-2 ḏ.t wbꜣ, but see the subsequent remarks by Wilson, p. 81: "After that one sees scattered traces, but it is difficult to fit them into the text as known from other papyri."

[128] The similarity of hrw "day" to Rꜥ "Re" has led the scribe to write this word in black ink. See similarly Lepsius 1842, plate 27.

[129] The lower traces of line x+15 appear on line 1 of the misplaced patch 12 (col. 2) at the top right of Fragment IV.1.

[130] The line appears as line 2 of the misplaced patch 12 (col. 2) at the top right of Fragment IV.1.

[131] The line appears as line 3 of the misplaced patch 12 (col. 2) at the top right of Fragment IV.1.

[132] The line appears as line 4 of the misplaced patch 12 (col. 2) at the top right of Fragment IV.1.

THE underworld of the West. RECITATION BY the Osiris Tasherit-Min, the justified, (VIII.2/x+13) born of Nes-Khonsu, the justified. "Hail to (VIII.2/x+14) you, the lords of Truth, free from falsehood, (VIII.2/x+15) who exist alive forever and [ever] (to) the limits (VIII.2/x+16) of eternity! Open, O you, (VIII.2/x+17) the sky and the earth! I am effective (VIII.2/x+17) [by means of] your forms. I am powerful by means of [your] magic. [...]

P. JS 2 PRESERVED COLUMN (x+) 4

FRAGMENT V (= P. JS 2.4)

This section contains two patches incorrectly placed: the first above the end of line 1/x+3 (patch 29) and the second above the next vignette, between lines 1/x+7 and 1/x+8 (patch 30).

(V.1/x+1) [dỉ⸗tn pr.(t)-ḫrw m t ḥnq.t kꜣ.w ꜣpd.w šs mnḫ.t mrḥ.t ḫ.t nb.t nfr.(t) wʿb.(t) ʿ]nḫ.t nṯr ỉm⸗s[n wnn⸗ỉ] (V.1/x+2) [mn.kwỉ ḏ.t m ḫprw nb n mrw.t⸗ỉ ḫd⸗ỉ ḫnty⸗ỉ r mrw.t⸗]ỉ ḫd⸗ỉ r sḫ.wt [ỉꜣnr.w] (V.1/x+3) [ḫnty⸗ỉ r sḫ.wt ḥtp.w ẖ]nm.n⸗ỉ Mꜣʿ.ty ỉ[n]k[133] r[w](V.1/x+4) [.ty ỉ]r ỉr.tw n⸗f mḏꜣ.t tn [tp tꜣ] ỉr.tw m sš ḥr qrỉs (V.1/x+5) [rꜣ-pw ỉw]⸗f pr⸗f m hrw m ḫprw nb [n mrw.t⸗f ḥ]nʿ ʿq r ḥw.t⸗f nn šnʿ.(V.1/x+6) [t⸗f ỉw dỉ.tw] n⸗f t ḥnq.t wr n [ỉwf ḥr ḫ]ꜣw.t n.t Wsỉr ỉw⸗f (V.1/x+7) [pr⸗f r sḫ].wt ỉꜣnr.[w[134] ỉw dỉ.tw] n⸗f bd.t ỉt ỉm ḫr wn(V.1/x+8)[⸗f wḏꜣ mỉ] wnn⸗f[135] ḥr-tp tꜣ ỉw⸗f ỉ[r⸗f mrw.t⸗f nb mỉ] nn n nṯr.w nty.(w) ỉm⸗s m šs (V.1/x+9) m[ꜣʿ].t ḥḥ n sp

(V.1/x+1) [May you grant invocation offerings consisting of bread, beer, oxen, fowl, alabaster, clothing, oil and everything good and pure] on which a god lives [and that I exist,] (V.1/x+2) [enduring forever in any form of my desire. May I go downstream and may I go upstream according to] my [desire]. May I go downstream to the Fields of [Reeds,] (V.1/x+3) [may I go upstream to the Fields of Offerings,] having joined the Two Truths. I am the Double (V.1/x+4) [Lion.]

[133] Above the traces of this word is a misplaced patch of text (unplaced patch 29). A diagonal stroke of the following rw.ty "Double Lion" indicates that the word began on this line.

[134] In this lacuna is now unplaced patch 30 with two fragmentary lines, extending into 1/x+8.

[135] P. Ryerson has the ungeminated wn⸗f.

IF THIS BOOK IS PERFORMED FOR HIM [ON EARTH] [or] made in writing on the coffin, (V.1/x+5) he goes forth by day in any form [of his desire and] enters into his mansion without [his] being repulsed. (V.1/x+6) [There is given] to him bread, beer, and a large portion [of meat on the] altar of Osiris. He (V.1/x+7) [goes forth to the Field]s of Reed[s. There is given] to him emmer and barley therein. Thus [he] exists (V.1/x+8) [soundly just as] he was on earth. He [does all that he wishes like] these gods who are there. Effective, (V.1/x+9) truly, millions of times![136]

Wilson 1968 Translation (pp. 76–77):

"The speech for going forth by day and opening up the underworld in the west. Words to be spoken by the Osiris T-N: 'Hail to you, those lords of truth, free from falsehood, who remain alive forever, (to) the limits [of eternity]! … '"

"' … [I go upstream as I wish.] I go downstream to the Field [of Reeds. I go upstream to the Field of Offerings.] I have joi[ned] the Two Truths. [I am the Double-lion god.]'

"[If] this scroll is [put on earth] for him, or is set in writing upon his coffin, [it is a speech] (whereby) he goes forth by day in any form [which he wishes,] as well as entering his house without being checked. [There are given] to him bread, beer, and a large piece of [meat from] the altar of Osiris. He [goes forth to] the Field of Reeds. [There are given to him] barley and wheat there. So [he continues to thrive as] he did on earth, [and he does all that he wants] like those gods who are therein. (A charm) with a true value a million times."

Chapter 74. Sokar, god of inertness,[137] is compelled to allow the deceased free passage to heaven. The vignette shows the deceased standing with a staff before a serpent striding on two legs. Wilson notes that the serpent is "a symbol of the earth, since snakes live underground."[138] Joseph Smith

[136] Literally, "in true value, millions of times" as in John Wilson 1968, pp. 77 and 81.

[137] For the role of Sokar as a mortuary and cthonic deity, see Brovarski 1984b, cols. 1055–74.

[138] John Wilson 1968, p. 77. Note also the Egyptian expression "son of the earth" (sꜣ-tꜣ) for serpents in Chapter 87. Though atypical for this vignette, snakes with legs are common in the book of Amduat ("What Is in the Netherworld?").

was clearly taken with this imagery, and the vignette is also copied in "Valuable Discovery" on p. 6 near text from P. JS 4. During a visit to his Nauvoo Museum on May 15, 1844, by Josiah Quincy and Charles Francis Adams, Smith was asked about the scene. "When Quincy questioned him about a drawing of a serpent walking about on a pair of legs, he expanded heartily: 'Why that's as plain as a pikestaff. Before the Fall snakes always went about on legs, just like chickens. They were deprived of them in punishment for their agency in the ruin of man.' "[139]

> (V.1/x+9) rꜣ n wn.t[140] rd.wy p[r m tꜣ ḏd] (V.1/x+10) [md]w ỉn Wsỉr Tꜣ-šr.t-Mnw mꜣꜥ-ḫrw ms n (V.1/x+11) Ns-Ḫnsw mꜣꜥ-ḫrw ỉr⸗k ỉr.wt⸗k n⸗ỉ[141] (V.1/x+12) [S]kr sp-2 ỉmy qr.ty⸗f ỉmy rd.wy⸗ỉ m (V.1/x+13) ẖr.t-nṯr[142] psd⸗ỉ m ḥry wꜥr.t (V.1/x+14) twy n.t p.t[143] ḥfd⸗ỉ ḥr ꜣḫw ỉ nn.kwỉ sp-2 šm.n⸗(ỉ) nn.kwỉ (V.1/x+15) sp-2 m ẖr.t-nṯr ḥr ỉdb.w ṯꜣỉ rꜣ⸗sn m ẖr.t-nṯr ỉw bꜣ⸗ỉ mꜣꜥ-ḫrw (V.1/x+16) m pr ʾItm nb ʾIwnw

> (V.1/x+9) SPELL FOR STRIDING WITH THE LEGS AND FOR [GOING FORTH FROM THE EARTH.] (V.1/x+10) RECITATION BY the Osiris Ta-sherit-Min, the justified, born of (V.1/x+11) Nes-Khonsu, the justified. "May you do what you do to me, (V.1/x+12) Sokar, Sokar who is in his cavern, my impeder in (V.1/x+13) the necropolis. May I shine as the master of this district (V.1/x+14) of heaven. May I ascend the solar rays. O I am weary, weary! I have gone although weary, (V.1/x+15) weary, in the necropolis on the shores of the one who seizes their speech in the necropolis. My *ba*-spirit is justified (V.1/x+16) in the house of Atum, lord of Heliopolis."

Wilson 1968 Translation (p. 77):

> "The speech for stretching the legs [and going forth from earth. Words to be spoken] by the Osiris T-N: 'You will do what you should do [against him,] O Sokar, Sokar, who is in his cave, who is the obstructor in the necropolis. I shine as the one who is over this

---

[139] See Adams 1952. Quotation in Brodie 1945, p. 293.

[140] P. Ryerson has reinterpreted the verb as "to open."

[141] P. Ryerson has r⸗f "against him."

[142] The honorifically written sign for "god" (nṯr) appears at the end of line 1/x+12.

[143] P. Ryerson adds pr⸗ỉ r p.t, "may I go forth to heaven."

district of heaven. I climb upon the sun's rays, being weary, weary. I have gone, being weary, weary, in the necropolis, upon the banks of taking away their speech in the necropolis. My soul is triumphant in the house of Atum, lord of Heliopolis.'"

Chapter 75. The spell allows the deceased to travel to the sacred sites of Heliopolis and Edfu, in addition to Pe and Dep within Buto. The vignette shows the deceased striding with her staff toward the pillar hieroglyph that represents Heliopolis.

(V.1/x+16) rꜣ n šm r ꜣIwnw šsp s.t ỉm d̲d-md.w ỉn Wsỉr (V.1/x+17) Tꜣ-šr.t-Mnw mꜣꜥ-ḫrw ms n Ns-Ḫnsw mꜣꜥ-ḫrw (V.1/x+18) [p]r.n=ỉ m dwꜣw.t ỉw.n=ỉ m d̲rw.w tꜣ (V.1/x+19) [šs]p=ỉ mw sỉꜣw=ỉ r bsk(V.1/x+20).w ꜣꜥꜥn.w šsp.n=ỉ wꜣ.wt r (V.1/x+21) sbḫ.wt d̲sr.w sḫnw=ỉ s.wt (V.1/x+22) wꜥb.(w) ỉmy.(w) D̲bꜣ[144] ḫbḫb.[n]=ỉ ḥw.wt Rꜣmrꜣm pḥ.n=ỉ s.t (V.1/x+23) ꜣIḫssf bs.n=ỉ sn.w d̲sr.(w) ḫn.n D̲ḥwty[145] ḥr=s m sḥtp(V.1/x+24)=f[146] ꜥḥꜣ.wy-ḥr ḫp=(ỉ) sp-2 r P ỉy=ỉ r Dp

(V.1/x+16) SPELL FOR GOING TO Heliopolis and taking a place there. RECITATION BY the Osiris (V.1/x+17) Ta-sherit-Min, the justified, born of Nes-Khonsu, the justified. (V.1/x+18) "As I have gone forth from the underworld, so I have come from the ends of the earth (V.1/x+ 19) so that I might take[147] water and that I might understand regarding the entrails (V.1/x+20) of the baboons.[148] I have taken the roads to the (V.1/x+21) the sacred portals just so that I might alight upon the places (V.1/x+22) of the pure ones who are in Edfu. As I have broken into the mansions of Remrem, so I have reached the seat of (V.1/x+23) Ikhsesef.[149] I have penetrated the

[144] This term is understood in earlier versions as "rewards" and in P. Ryerson as "shrouds/tailed kilts." The house and divine determinatives of P. JS 2 suggest the place name Edfu.

[145] Written here and in P. Ryerson in "Ptolemaic" spelling.

[146] The tail of the "f" is visible on line 1 of patch 13 on Fragment VIII (at 1/x+7).

[147] Reinterpreted from P. Ryerson, which has "illumine the water," with a solar determinative on šsp. Both versions have šsp "take" in the following sentence.

[148] In BD Chapter 5, the deceased seeks the "weary one from Hermopolis, who lives on baboon's entrails."

[149] A deity who "controls the judgment hall and is first among the westerners," see Allen 1960, p. 149, n. e.

sacred precincts on which Thoth trod when he pacified (V.1/x+24) the two combatants, so that I might proceed, that I might proceed to Pe, so that I might come to Dep."

Wilson 1968 Translation (p. 78):

"The speech for going forth to Heliopolis and taking a place there. Words to be spoken by the Osiris T-N: 'I have gone forth from the underworld. I have come from the limits of the earth. I shine upon the water. I understand about the entrails of a baboon. I have taken the ways to the holy gates. I occupy the places [of the pure ones] who are in [shrouds.] I break into the houses of Remrem. I have reached the seat of Ikhsesfi. I have penetrated the sacred areas upon which Thoth stepped in pacifying the two warriors. I go, I go to Pe; I come to Dep.'"

Chapter 76.[150] Forming a transition between the spells for movement and the next series, Chapter 76 is the first of 14 spells in the Book of the Dead that enable the deceased to make transformations into other spirits, animals or plants. As properly noted by Wilson, "this was not transmigration of souls; this was the power to make powerful or pleasing transformations."[151] Following the pattern for the previous series, the vignette to the left of the spell depicts the deceased striding with a staff.

(V.1/x+24) rꜣ n ỉrw[152] ḫprw (V.1/x+25) nb n mr⸗f[153] ḏd-md.w ỉn Wsỉr Tꜣ-šr.t-Mnw mꜣꜥ-ḫrw ms n (V.1/x+26) Ns-Ḫnsw[154] mꜣꜥ-ḫrw snỉ.n⸗ỉ ḥr pr-ny-sw.t ỉn ḥby[155] ỉn tw n⸗ỉ[156] ỉnḏ-ḥr⸗k pꜣy r p.t (V.1/

---

[150] The spell is completed by a patch of 6 line fragments (patch 13) currently mis-mounted at the lower right of Fragment VIII, over lines x+8 through x+13.

[151] John Wilson 1968, p. 78.

[152] Written simply with the pupil of the eye and a coiled w. P. Ryerson has ḫpr m "transforming into."

[153] The words nb n mr⸗f appear on line 2 of patch 13 on Fragment VIII (at 1/x+8).

[154] The signs Ns-Ḫn appear on line 3 of patch 13 on Fragment VIII (at 1/x+9). The conclusion of the name is preserved at the beginning of V.1/x+26.

[155] The final y and determinative appear on line 4 of patch 13 on Fragment VIII (at 1/x+10).

[156] P. JS 2 follows older tradition in writing "who brought you to me," unlike P. Ryerson, which writes ỉn wỉ "who brought me."

x+27) [s]ḥḏ[157] sbꜣ.w sꜣw ḥḏ.t[158] wnn≈f ỉm≈k dmd (V.1/x+28) n≈k nṯr[159] ꜥꜣ ỉry n≈ỉ wꜣ.t snỉ≈ỉ ḥr≈k

(V.1/x+24) SPELL FOR MAKING ANY TRANSFORMATION (V.1/x+25) OF HIS DESIRE. RECITATION BY the Osiris Ta-sherit-Min, the justified, born of (V.1/x+26) Nes-Khonsu, the justified. "I have passed by the palace. It is the fowler who has brought you to me. Hail to you, who have flown up to heaven, (V.1/x+27) who has illuminated the stars, who has guarded the white crown. He is within you, being united (V.1/x+28) to you. O great god, make a path for me so that I might pass by you!"

Wilson 1968 Translation (p. 78):

"The speech for going into [any] form [that he wishes. Words to be spoken by] the Osiris T-[N: 'I have passed] by the palace. It was the fowler [who brought me]. Hail to you who flies to heaven, [who illuminates the] stars, the protected white crown. He is in you, united [to you. O great god], make a way for me, so that I may pass by you.'"

Chapter 77. Following the generic spell for making any transformation, this recitation is for assuming the specific form of a falcon. The vignette depicts a falcon on a stand with a flail, a hieroglyphic symbol for "god."

(V.1/x+28) rꜣ n ỉr ḫprw n bỉk (V.1/x+29) n n[b]w[160] ḏd-md.w ỉn Wsỉr Tꜣ-šr.t-Mnw mꜣꜥ-ḫrw (V.1/x+30) [ms n Ns]-Ḫnsw mꜣꜥ-ḫrw ỉw≈ỉ ḫꜥ.kwỉ m bỉk (V.1/x+31) [ꜥꜣ] pr m swḥ.t pꜣy.n≈ỉ m bỉk (V.1/x+32) [m mḥ 4 ḥ]r psd≈f dnḥ.w m wꜣḏ.w (V.1/x+33) [Šmꜥw pr m ꜥfd] Skt.t ỉw ỉn.n≈ỉ ỉb(V.1/x+34)[≈ỉ m ḏw ỉꜣbt.t] ḫnd.n≈ỉ m ꜥdty (< Mꜥnḏ.t) ỉw n≈ỉ ỉmy.w pꜣ[wty.w](V.1/x+35) [≈sn m ksw] snỉ tꜣ d[ỉ]≈sn n≈ỉ ỉꜣwy ḫꜥ[.kwỉ] (V.1/x+36 ff.) [dmd.kwỉ m bỉk nfr n nbw tp≈ỉ n bnw ꜥq Rꜥ r sḏm md.wt≈f ...]

[157] The word [s]ḥḏ appears on line 5 of patch 13 on Fragment VIII (at 1/x+11).

[158] The text uses honorific transposition (and the change of older sbꜣ.w to sỉꜣ.w) to produce the visual and vocal pun: sḥḏ sỉꜣ.w ḥḏ sꜣw.

[159] The determinative of dmd, the phrase n≈k and the initial "n" of nṯr appear on line 6 of patch 13 on Fragment VIII (at 1/x+12).

[160] The determinatives of bỉk, the genitive n and the upper portion of nbw appear on line 7 of patch 13 on Fragment VIII (at 1/x+13).

(V.1/x+28) SPELL FOR MAKING A TRANSFORMATION AS a falcon (V.1/x+29) of gold. RECITATION BY the Osiris Ta-sherit-Min, the justified, (V.1/x+30) [born of Nes]-Khonsu, the justified. "I have appeared as a [great] falcon (V.1/x+31), gone forth from the egg. As a falcon [of four cubits] (V.1/x+32) on his back have I flown, with my wings of malachite (V.1/x+33) [of Upper Egypt, having gone forth from the cabin of the solar evening barque. I have brought away [my] heart (V.1/x+34) [from the mountain of the East,] which I traversed in the solar morning barque.[161] May those who are among [their] primeval [ones] come to me (V.1/x+35) [in bowing] and kissing the ground while they give me praise since I have appeared (V.1/x+36 ff) [united as a goodly falcon of gold, with my head as a phoenix, whose words Re enters to hear ..."]

Wilson 1968 Translation (p. 78):

"The speech for taking the form of a falcon [of gold. Words to be spoken] by the Osiris T-[N]: 'I have appeared as [a great] falcon which came forth from his egg. I have flown as a falcon [of four cubits across] his back, while the wings were of greenstone [of Upper Egypt, who came forth from the hold of the] evening-barque. (My) heart has been brought to me [from the eastern mountain.] I have trodden in the [morning]-barque. There come to me those who are among the prime[val beings of them, bowing down] and kissing the ground. They give me praise [as I] appear ... '"

P. JS 2 PRESERVED COLUMN (x+) 5

FRAGMENT V (= P. JS 2.4) + VI (= P. JS 2.5)

Chapter 83. The spell continues the transformation into birds. As the phoenix is itself a transformation of the solar creator, so identification with the bird allows the deceased the full range of the creator's manifestations.[162] The partially preserved vignette represented the phoenix as a

---

[161] The two solar barques appear here in their traditional roles, with the *Sektet*-barque representing the evening ship and the *(M)andjet*-barque that of the morning—as the latter's association with the "mountain of the East" proves. In late texts, their roles are often reversed, but that does not apply to this New Kingdom composition. The traditional interpretation is also retained in Verhoeven 1993, p. 173. For the late reversal, see Mark Smith 1987, p. 85.

[162] Thus is answered the curious remark by John Wilson 1968, p. 79: "Out of that tangle of myth, I can only say that the deceased became very flexible in form, just as

crested heron, whose two head feathers, back and tail are faintly preserved to the left of an intrusive patch of 4 lines (patch 18) mounted upside down. This patch preserves sections of Chapter 100, and belongs on Fragment IV.[163] Two additional patches now wrongly adjoin the top and bottom of this larger patch. The lowest of these patches (patch 17), now just above Chapter 86 (V.2+VI.1/x+9), contains the lefthand water baseline of the vignette for Chapter 100 and a portion of the adjacent Chapter 105. The uppermost patch (patch 31) contains the baseline of a different vignette, pasted upside down.

(V.2+VI.1/x+1) [rꜣ n ỉr ḫprw n bn]w[164] ḏ]d-m[d.w ỉn Wsỉr Tꜣ-šr.t-Mnw mꜣꜥ-ḫrw ms n Ns-Ḫns](V.2+VI.1/x+2)w mꜣꜥ-[ḫrw[165] pꜣy.n⸗ỉ m pꜣw.tyw ḫpr.n⸗ỉ m Ḫpr]ỉ rd.n⸗ỉ m rd[166] (V.2+VI.1/x+3) [štꜣ.n⸗ỉ m štꜣ dgꜣ n nṯr nb rḫ ḥr.wt] (V.2+VI.1/x+4) ẖ.t⸗sn ỉ[n]k [sf pn n ỉfd n ꜥrꜥy.wt] (V.2+VI.1/x+5) ỉptn m ḫpr[w m tꜣ ḥr Wr sḥḏ m-m ḏ.t⸗f] (V.2+VI.1/x+6) m nṯr pw Sw[ty Ḏḥwty ỉmy.tw⸗sn m wpy.t ỉ Ḫn.t] (V.2+VI.1/x+7)y-Ḫm [ḥnꜥ bꜣ.w ʾIwnw nwy ỉmy.tw](V.2+VI.1/x+8)⸗sn ỉy⸗(ỉ) [m hrw pn ḫꜥ.kwỉ ḫꜥ.kwỉ m-m nṯr.w ỉnk Ḫn]sw

(V.2+VI.1/x+1) [SPELL FOR MAKING A TRANSFORMATION AS a] phoenix. RECITATION BY the Osiris Ta-sherit-Min, the justified, born of Nes-Khon](V.2+VI.1/x+2)su, the justified. ["As I have flown as the primeval ones, so I have transformed as Khepri.] As I have grown as a plant, (V.2+VI.1/x+3) [so I have clad (myself) as a turtle, the fruit of every god, who knows the necessities] (V.2+VI.1/x+4) of their bodies. I am [that yesterday of] these [four

---

the phoenix was supposed to change."

[163] Patch 18 was noted by John Wilson 1968, p. 78, but he was unable to assign it to its proper location: "Then somebody mounted an intrusive fragment of text upside down in the upper right corner of photo 4. Its handwriting is the same as the rest of Document B. I have not identified it."

[164] Patch 14 of two lines, now placed at the top of this column on Fragment V, retains the traces of what may be the determinative of bnw "phoenix" and the rubric ḏd-md.w "Recitation"—if the patch is properly to be placed here in the chapter. If so, the patch is too low and too far to the right. Alternatively, the rubric may be the remains of a lost title rꜣ n "Spell for … ."

[165] The second line of patch 14 (at the top of this column) contains the determinatives of a personal name and the feather of mꜣꜥ-ḫrw "justified."

[166] These traces, unrecognized by Wilson, appear in their original position above and to the left of the vignette on Fragment VI.

uraeus-serpents] (V.2+VI.1/x+5) as a form [in the earth, the face of the Great One, who illuminates throughout his body] (V.2+VI.1/x+6) as this god Seth, [with Thoth between them in judgment. O (Horus), foremost] (V.2+VI.1/x+7) of Letopolis, [together with the souls of Heliopolis and the flood water that is between] (V.2+VI.1/x+8) them, let me come [on this day, having appeared, having appeared among the gods. I am Khon]su."

Wilson 1968 Translation (p. 79):

"[The speech for taking the form of a phoenix … ' … I am the fruit of every god, who knows the requirements of] their bodies. I am [this yesterday of] these [four uraeus-serpents,] as a form [in the earth, the elder Horus, who illuminates within his body,] as this god Se[th, Thoth being between them in the trial of him who] presides over Letopolis, [together with the Souls of Heliopolis, water being between] them, as I come [today, having appeared among the gods. I am Khon]su.'"

Chapter 86. As Spell 77 allowed the deceased to become the falcon hieroglyph for "god," this spell equates the deceased with the swallow hieroglyph for "great" (wr) and concludes with a testimonial. The vignette shows a swallow on a mound (not "some object" as described by Wilson 1968, p. 79).[167] Most published photos of this section are out of alignment (as in Gee, Rhodes and Nibley 2005, plate 7), but see the adjusted plates in C. M. Larson 1992, p. 34.

(V.2+VI.1/x+8) rꜣ n ꞽr.t (V.2+VI.1/x+9) ḫprw n [m]n.t ḏd-md.w ꞽn Wsꞽr Tꜣ-šr.t-Mnw [mꜣꜥ-ḫrw ms n Ns-Ḫ]nsw mꜣꜥ-ḫrw ꞽnk (V.2+VI.1/x+10) mn.t sp-2 ꞽnk ꞽrf ḥḏḏ.t sꜣ.t Rꜥ ꞽ nṯr.w nḏm.wy sty⸗[t]n [nsr].t pr m ꜣḫ.t (V.2+VI.1/x+11) ꞽ nty m nꞽw.t ꞽn.n⸗ꞽ sꜣw q(ꜣ)b[168] ꞽmy n⸗ꞽ ꜥ⸗k wrš⸗ꞽ m ꞽw ns(V.2+VI.1/x+12)r.t šm.n⸗ꞽ m wp.t ꞽy.n⸗ꞽ ẖr smꞽw (V.2+VI.1/x+13) ꞽ-wn n⸗ꞽ ꞽḫ ḏd{.n}⸗ꞽ mꜣꜣ.n⸗ꞽ ꞽw Ḥr m ḫrp (V.2+VI.1/x+14) n wꞽꜣ ꞽw rdꞽ.t(w) n⸗f ns.t ꞽt⸗f ꞽw Stš pwy (V.2+VI.1/x+15) sꜣ Nw.t m ꞽnty.t ꞽr⸗f r⸗ꞽ ꞽw sꞽpy.n⸗ꞽ nty m Ḫ(V.2+VI.1/x+16) m qꜥḥw.n⸗ꞽ ꜥ.wy⸗ꞽ n Wsꞽr šm.n⸗ꞽ m (V.2+VI.1/x+17) wp.t ꞽw.n⸗ꞽ ꞽw (= r) ḏd ꞽmy snꞽ⸗ꞽ smꞽw⸗ꞽ wp.t ꞽnk ꜥq ꞽpt{n} tnw (V.2+VI.1/

[167] The order of the spells does not follow that of P. Ryerson, but for the contiguity of 83 and 86, see Faulkner 1985, p. 81. For the mound, see Allen 1974, p. 73, n. 145.

[168] P. Ryerson has q(ꜣ)b⸗f "his bend."

x+18) ḥr sbꜣw pwy n Nb-r-ḏr wꜥb=ỉ ḥr wꜥr.t twy ꜥꜣ.t wr.(t)[169] dr.n=ỉ ḏw.w(V.2+VI.1/x+19)=ỉ ḫm.n=ỉ ỉsfy.w ḫsr.n=ỉ ḏw.w=ỉ ỉry=ỉ r tꜣ ỉry.w-ꜥꜣ ỉr[y] (V.2+VI.1/x+20) n=ỉ wꜣ.t ỉnk ỉs mỉ.ty=tn pr=ỉ m hrw ỉy.n=ỉ šm=ỉ ḥr rd.wy=[ỉ] sḫm.[kwỉ] m nmt.wt[170] (V.2+VI.1/x+21) ꜣḫ.w ỉw=ỉ rḫ.kwỉ wꜣ.wt štꜣ.w(t) sbꜣ.w n.w sḫ.wt ỉꜣnr.w wn(V.2+VI.1/x+22)=ỉ ỉm mk wỉ ỉy.kwỉ sḫr.n=ỉ ḫfty.w=ỉ ḥr-tp tꜣ ẖꜣ.[t=ỉ ỉ]w qrỉs(V.2+VI.1/x+23).tw=s ỉr rḫ mḏꜣ.t tn ỉw=f pr=f m hrw m ẖr.t-nṯr ꜥq=f m-ḫt pr=f ỉr [ḫm](V.2+VI.1/x+24).tw rꜣ [p]n nn ꜥq=f m-ḫt pr=f ḫm pr m hrw

(V.2+VI.1/x+8) SPELL FOR MAKING (V.2+VI.1/x+9) A TRANSFORMATION AS a swallow. RECITATION BY the Osiris Ta-sherit-Min, [the justified, born of Nes-Kh]onsu, the justified. "I am (V.2+VI.1/x+10) a swallow. I am a swallow. I am, indeed, a scorpion, the daughter of Re.[171] O gods, how sweet is your fragrance, [the flame] that has gone forth from the horizon! (V.2+VI.1/x+11) O he who is in Thebes, I have brought the protector of the bend. Give to me your hand so that I might spend the day in the Island of Flame. (V.2+VI.1/x+12) As I have gone on business, so I have returned bearing a report. (V.2+VI.1/x+13) Open to me! May I say what I have seen. Horus is the controller (V.2+VI.1/x+14) of the barque. The seat of his father has been given to him. This Seth, (V.2+VI.1/x+15) the son of Nut, is in fetters when he acts against me. I have inspected the one in Letopolis, (V.2+VI.1/x+16) having bent my arms to Osiris. As I have gone on (V.2+VI.1/x+17) business, so I have returned to speak. Let me pass so that I might report the business. I am one who enters, reckoned and counted, (V.2+VI.1/x+18) at this portal of the lord of the universe, since I am pure in this very great district. As I have expelled evils (V.2+VI.1/x+19) of mine, so I am ignorant of wrongdoing, having cast to the ground the evils of mine that had pertained to me. Doorkeepers, make (V.2+VI.1/x+20) a path for me. I am indeed one like you. Let me go forth by day. I have returned, walking on [my] feet, having power over the steps (V.2+VI.1/x+21) of the blessed. I know the secret roads and the gates of the Fields of Reeds, so that I might exist (V.2+VI.1/x+22) there. Behold, I have

[169] Not found in P. Ryerson.

[170] The damaged P. JS 2 text could have wꜣ.wt "paths," but P. Ryerson's clear writing shows nmt.wt "steps."

[171] For the scorpion as the daughter of Re, see Ritner 1998, pp. 1027–41.

come, having overthrown my enemies on earth. As for my corpse, it is buried."

(V.2+VI.1/x+23) AS FOR THE ONE WHO KNOWS THIS BOOK, he goes forth by day from the necropolis, entering after he goes forth. If one [does not know](V.2+VI.1/x+24) [this] spell, he will not enter after he goes forth; being ignorant of how to go forth by day.

Wilson 1968 Translation (pp. 79–80):

"The speech for taking the form of [a swallow. Words to be spoken by the Osiris T-]N: 'I am a swallow; I am a swallow. I am really a scorpion, the daughter of Re. O gods, how sweet is the fragrance [of you, the fire] which went up from the horizon. O you who are in the city, I bring him who guards his district. Give me your hand, as I spend the day in the Island of Flaring-up. I went on an errand; I returned with a report. Open for me, so that I might tell what I have seen. Horus is the controller of barques. The throne of his father has been given to him. That Seth, the son of Nut, is in fetters, when he would act against me. I have taken stock of what is in Letopolis. I have folded my arms for Osiris. I went on an errand; I returned to tell. Let me pass so that I may report the errand. I am one who goes in accounted and numbered by that gate of the Supreme Lord. I have become pure in that great district. I have driven away my evils. I know no falsehood. I have completely dispelled my evils which were on me. O doorkeepers, make a way for me. I am indeed one like unto you. I come and go [on foot, having] control of the course of the sun's rays. I know the secret ways and the gates of the Field of Reeds, so that I may be there. See, I have come. I have completely overthrown my enemies. My corpse is buried.'

"As for the one who knows this scroll, he may go forth by day in the necropolis and go back in after he has gone forth. If this speech is not known, he will not go back in after he has gone forth, being unable to go forth by day."

Chapter 87. The transformation spells now move from creatures of the air to those of land and water. Combining images for this and the following Spell 88, the vignette depicts the deceased as a human-headed serpent and as a standing, mummified crocodile.[172]

[172] Cf. the adjoining vignettes in Faulkner 1985, p. 86.

(V.2+VI.1/x+24) rꜣ n ỉr.t ḫprw m (V.2+VI.1/x+25) sꜣ-tꜣ [ḏd]-md.w ỉn Wsỉr Tꜣ-šr.t-Mnw mꜣꜥ-ḫrw ms n Ns-(V.2+VI.1/x+26)Ḫnsw [mꜣꜥ-ḫrw ỉnk sꜣ-t]ꜣ ꜣw rnp.wt sḏr ms rꜥ nb ỉnk (V.2+VI.1/x+27) sꜣ-tꜣ [m ḏrw.w] p.t[173] sḏr.kwỉ ms.kwỉ mꜣw.kwỉ (V.2+VI.1/x+28) rnp[.kwỉ rꜥ nb]

(V.2+VI.1/x+24) SPELL FOR MAKING A TRANSFORMATION as (V.2+VI.1/x+25) a son-of-the-earth serpent. RECITATION BY the Osiris Ta-sherit-Min, the justified, born of Nes-(V.2+VI.1/x+26) Khonsu, [the justified. "I am a son-of-the-earth] serpent, long of years, who sleeps and is born every day. I am (V.2+VI.1/x+27) a son-of-the-earth serpent [at the limits] of heaven, sleeping, reborn, renewed (V.2+VI.1/x+28) and rejuvenate[d every day]."

Wilson 1968 Translation (p. 80):

"The speech for taking the form of a son of earth. Words to be spoken by the Osiris T-N: '[I am a son of earth,] long of years, who sleeps and is reborn every day. I am a son of earth [at the ends of the earth,] as I sleep, am reborn, become new, and become young [every day.]'"

Chapter 88. The text concludes the series of transformation spells. As noted above, the vignette is combined with that of Chapter 87.

(V.2+VI.1/x+28) [r]ꜣ n ỉr.t ḫprw n msḥw (V.2+VI.1/x+29) ḏd-md.w ỉn [Wsỉr Tꜣ-šr.t]-Mnw mꜣꜥ-ḫrw ms n Ns-Ḫnsw mꜣꜥ-ḫrw (V.2+VI.1/x+30) ỉnk Sbk [ḥr-ỉb nry=f ỉ]nk Sbk m ỉw bꜣ=f m rmt.w ỉnk Sbk ỉn m ꜥwꜣ(V.2+VI.1/x+31)y ỉn[k rmw Ḥr ꜥ]ꜣ m Km.(t) ỉnk nb ks(V.2+VI.1/x+32)w m Ḫm

(V.2+VI.1/x+28) SPELL FOR MAKING A TRANSFORMATION as a crocodile. RECITATION BY [the Osiris Ta-sherit]-Min, the justified, born of Nes-Khonsu, the justified. (V.2+VI.1/x+30) "I am Sobek [in the midst of his terror.] I am Sobek[174] when his *ba*-spirit returns from among mankind. I am Sobek who snatches by

[173] P. Ryerson has ḏrw.w tꜣ "at the limits of the earth."

[174] The form of the crocodile (with extended tail, Gardiner Sign-List I 3) is identical to that used in the writing of the simple word "crocodile" (msḥw) in VI.1/x+28, but followed by a divine determinative. The second writing of Sobek in the spell shows the crocodile with inward curved tail (Gardiner Sign-List I 5) and divine determinative.

robbery. (V.2+VI.1/x+31) I am [the fish of Horus] here in Egypt. I am the possessor of obeisance (V.2+VI.1/x+32) in Letopolis."

Wilson 1968 Translation (p. 80):

"[The speech for] taking the form of a crocodile. Words to be spoken by [the Osiris] T-N: 'I am Sobek [in the middle of his terror.] I am a crocodile, when his soul returns from his people. I am Sobek who carries off by robbery. I am [the fish of Horus] here in Egypt. I am the possessor of obeisance in Letopolis.'"

Chapter 89. The spell begins a new series designed to protect the mobile *ba*-spirit of the deceased, ensuring its proper return (Chapter 89), its freedom of movement (Chapter 91) and contentment (Chapter 100). The vignette depicts the deceased's winged *ba*-spirit clutching the hieroglyph for eternity and hovering above her corpse on the traditional lion bier, long misidentified in Mormon literature as a sacrificial altar.[175] A lengthy section of the continuation of the spell is lost following the end of Fragment VI.2 (line x+37), before resuming at the top of Fragment IV. The uppermost section of Fragment IV.1 is now distorted by the presence of the intrusive patch 12 with lines from Chapter 72 (formerly misidentified as Chapter 99).

(V.2+VI.1/x+32) [rꜣ n rd.t] dmꞽ.t bꜣ n s r ẖꜣ.t⸗f m (V.2+VI.1/x+33) ẖr.t-nṯr ḏd-[md.w ꞽn Wsꞽr] Tꜣ-šr.t-Mnw mꜣꜥ-ḫrw ms n Ns-Ḫ[n] (V.2+VI.1/x+34)s[w mꜣꜥ-ḫrw ꞽ ꞽny.w ꞽ ḥ]rr ꞽmy sḥ⸗f nṯr ꜥꜣ dꞽ⸗k (V.2+VI.1/x+35) [ꞽw] n⸗ꞽ bꜣ[⸗ꞽ m bw nb nty ꞽw⸗f ꞽm] ꞽr [w]dfꜣw.t(w) ꞽn⸗k (V.2+VI.1/x+36) [n⸗ꞽ] bꜣ⸗ꞽ [m bw nb nty ꞽw⸗f ꞽm g]m⸗k [ꞽr.t Ḥ]r ꜥḥꜥ.tw r⸗k (V.2+VI.1/x+37) [mꞽ nfꜣ nn(?)] sḏr [sḏr.w(?) n]ḏr.w[176] m ʾIwnw tꜣ m ḫꜣ.w n dmꞽ ꞽm⸗f

(V.2+VI.1/x+32) [SPELL FOR CAUSING] the *ba*-spirit of a man TO ADHERE TO his corpse in (V.2+VI.1/x+33) the necropolis. RECITATION BY the Osiris Ta-sherit-Min, the justified, born of Nes-(V.2+VI.1/x+34)Khonsu, [the justified. "O bringers, O de]layer who is in his hall, the great god, may you cause that (V.2+VI.1/

[175] As in the vignette for the "Breathing Permit of Ḥor" (P. JS 1), the lion couch is *not* a sacrificial altar.

[176] Here the text of P. JS 2 does not follow P. Ryerson, and many variants exist. The determinatives of the unbracketed sḏr (cloth) and [n]ḏr.w (man with stick) are clear, but the restoration is conjectural.

x+35) [my] *ba*-spirit [come] to me [from any place in which it is.] If there is delay when you bring (V.2+VI.1/x+36) [to me] my *ba*-spirit [from any place in which it is,] may you find the [Eye of] Horus standing against you (V.2+VI.1/x+37) [like those without(?)] sleep, [the sleeping ones(?)] who are seized in Heliopolis, while land in the thousands is for the one who adheres to him.

P. JS 2 PRESERVED COLUMN (x+) 6

FRAGMENT VI (= P. JS 2.5) + IV (= P. JS 2.6)

All previously published photos of this section are out of alignment. Fragment IV should be one line lower in relation to Fragment VI.

[ỉw ỉṯ.n=ỉ b3=ỉ 3ḫw=ỉ ḥnᶜ=f m b nb nty ỉw=f ỉm m nw ỉr=k ỉry.w p.t n b3=ỉ ỉr wdf3.tw dỉ=k m33=ỉ b3=ỉ ẖ3.t=ỉ gm=k ỉr.t Ḥr ᶜḥᶜ.tw r=k mỉ nf3 ỉ nṯr.w sṯ3.w wỉ3 n nb ḥḥ.w ỉn.w ḥry.t r dw3.t sḥr.w w3.t n Nwn.t stkn b3.w r sᶜḥ.w ᶜ.wy=sn mḥ ẖr ᶜq3.w 3mm=tn ẖr mt3ỉ.w(t)=tn dr=tn ḫfty.w ḥᶜᶜ wỉ3 wḏ3 nṯr ᶜ3 m ḥtp ỉs rdỉ=tn b3 pn ẖr ḫp]
(VI.2+IV.1/x+1)d[=tn[177] m 3ḫ.t ỉ3bt.t n.t p.t r]
(VI.2+IV.1/x+2) šms[178] [r b=f nb ẖr=f n sf m ḥtp sp-2 ḫr ỉmnt.t m33=f]
(VI.2+IV.1/x+3) ẖ3.t=f [ḥtp=f ḥr sᶜḥw=f nn sk=f nn ḥtm](VI.2+IV.1/x+4)=f n [ḏ.t ḏ.t ỉr rḫ] r3 pn nn sk [n ẖ3.t=f nn rwỉ3 n]
(VI.2+IV.1.x+5) b3=f r ẖ3.[t]=f

[I have taken my *ba*-spirit, my blessed spirit being with it in every place in which it is. Behold this, then, guardians of heaven, for my *ba*-spirit. If there is delay when you let me see my *ba*-spirit and my corpse, may you find the Eye of Horus standing against you like those. O gods who drag the barque of the Lord of Millions, who bring the sky to the underworld, who expel from the road to the lower heaven, who cause *ba*-spirits to approach mummies, while their arms are filled with guide ropes, may you grasp your spears and may you drive off the enemies. The barque rejoices, even as the god proceeds in peace.

---

[177] The preserved "d" at the beginning of VI.2/x+1 might belong to an earlier word (or may be an isolated patch), so that the division of the line is tentative.

[178] Signs now following šms on Fragment IV.1 (ỉw=s?) derive from the intrusive patch 12 with a section of Chapter 72. Relevant traces of Chapter 89 begin on Fragment IV.1 only in line x+4 (r3 pn nn sk).

Now then, may you place this *ba*-spirit be](VI.2+IV.1/x+1)hind [you[179] in the eastern horizon of heaven in order to] (VI.2+IV.1/x+2) follow [to every place that it was yesterday in peace, in peace, before the West, while it sees] (VI.2+IV.1/x+3) its corpse [and rests on its mummy. It will not be destroyed.] (VI.2+IV.1/x+4) It [will not be exterminat]ed in [body forever."]
As for the one who knows this spell, there is no destruction [for his corpse. There is no removal of] (VI.2+IV.1.x+5) his *ba*-spirit from his corpse.

Wilson 1968 Translation (p. 80):

"[The speech for causing that] the soul of a man join his corpse in the necropolis. [Words] to be spoken [by the Osiris] T-N: '[O you who bring, O] runner who is in his hall, O great god, may you let [my soul come to me from any place where it may be.] If there be delay in your bringing [me my] soul [from any place where it may be, you will find the (sacred) Eye standing against you like those watchers over the sleeper in Heliopolis. Land] by the thousands belongs to the one who joins [to him.] … '"

Chapter 91. Like the earlier series of spells for unhindered movement, this recitation grants such power to the *ba*-spirit. The vignette, of the fluttering *ba*-spirit of Ta-sherit-Min, is in its original position in Fragment IV, with 2 detached sections of the wing (on the viewer's left) now pasted below their original position (patches 15 and 16).[180] Wilson, misled by patch 12 of 4 lines from Chapter 72 (misidentified by him as Chapter 99), assumed that the vignette was misplaced, and he failed to recognize the adjoining text of Chapter 91, which he deemed "not otherwise visible in our document."[181]

(VI.2+IV.1/x+5) [rꜣ n tm rdꞽ.t] ḫnꞽ.tw bꜣ [n s m ẖr.t-nṯr] (VI.2+IV.1/x+6) [ḏ]d-md.w ꞽn [Wsꞽr Tꜣ-šr.t-M]nw mꜣꜥ-[ḫrw] (VI.2+IV.1/x+7) [ms n] Ns-Ḫnsw [mꜣꜥ-ḫrw ꞽ] qꜣ=f (VI.2+IV.1/x+8) {tw}[182] dwꜣ.[tw=f wr bꜣ.w] bꜣ ꜥꜣ (VI.2+IV.1/x+9) šfy.t [rdꞽ] nr[ꞽ=f n nṯr.w] ḫꜥ ḥr

---

[179] Literally, "under your buttocks."

[180] The feathers of patch 16 are rotated 90 degrees clockwise.

[181] John Wilson 1968, p. 81.

[182] P. JS 2 here blends the forms found in P. Ryerson (qꜣ.tw=f) and other versions (Lepsius 1842, plate 33: qꜣ tw).

(VI.2+IV.1/x+10) s.t=f wr.t [kꜣ ỉry=k wꜣ].t [n] bꜣ=ỉ (VI.2+IV.1/x+11) šw.t=ỉ ỉw=ỉ [ꜥpr.kwỉ] ỉnk ꜣḫw [ỉry n=ỉ wꜣ.t r b nty Rꜥ ꜣItm] (VI.2+IV.1/x+12) Ḫprỉ Ḥ[w].t-Ḥr [ỉm ỉr rḫ] rꜣ pn [ỉw=f ḫp]r=f m-m ꜣḫw.w [ꜥpr.w m ẖr].t-[nṯr]

(VI.2+IV.1/x+5) [SPELL FOR NOT LETTING] the *ba*-spirit [of a man] BE RESTRAINED [in the necropolis.] (VI.2+IV.1/x+6) RECITATION BY [the Osiris Ta-sherit]-Min, the justified, (VI.2+IV.1/x+7) [born of] Nes-Khonsu, [the justified. "O] may he be high, (VI.2+IV.1/x+8) may [he be] praised, [the one great of wrath], the *ba*-spirit great of (VI.2+IV.1/x+9) respect, [who placed] terror [of himself among the gods], who has appeared on (VI.2+IV.1/x+10) his great throne! [Then may you make a road for] my *ba*-spirit (VI.2+IV.1/x+11) and my shadow, since I am [equipped.] I am a blessed spirit. [Make a a road for me to the place where Re, Atum,] (VI.2+IV.1/x+12) Khepri and Hathor [are!]
[As for the one who knows] this spell, [he] comes to be among the [equipped] blessed spirits [in the necro]polis.

Chapter 100. The spell confers upon the *ba*-spirit the power to join the eternal circuit of the solar journey. The term in the late version of the title here translated "be satisfied" has the additional nuance of "to alight" or "to rest" in the barque. Ritual directions and a testimonial follow the spell. Preserved on Fragment IV.1, the vignette depicts the deceased rowing in a papyrus boat with the sun god Re as a passenger, while Osiris[183] watches from the shore. The spell is completed by at least three misplaced patches. A fragment of the lower lefthand base of the vignette (patch 17) is now pasted in column 1 of Fragment VI, just above line x+9. A second, larger patch (patch 18) is now pasted—but inverted—just above that (VI, 1/x+5 through 1/x+8). A third patch (patch 19) is placed in the middle of spell 100 on Fragment IV not far from its original position, but turned upside down.

(VI.2+IV.1/x+13) rꜣ n rdỉ.t [ḥt]p[184] [bꜣ n ꜣḫw rdỉ].t hꜣ=f r wỉꜣ n Rꜥ ḥnꜥ ỉmy.w-ḫt=f (VI.2+IV.1/x+14) ḏd-m[d.w ỉ]n Wsỉr [Tꜣ-šr.t-Mnw

[183] Wrongly identified as Ptah in John Wilson 1968, p. 81.

[184] The papyrus Fragments VI and IV join with only a slight gap of lost text between them. The words rꜣ n rdỉ.t [ḥt]p appear in red ink in the second column of Fragment VI, and the sentence continues in black ink in the first column of Fragment IV.

mꜣꜥ-ḫrw ms n Ns-Ḫns]w mꜣꜥ-ḫrw ḏꜣ.n=ỉ m bnw r ꜣbdw (VI.2+IV.1/x+15) Wsỉr r Ḏd[w snỉ.]n=ỉ (VI.2+IV.1/x+16) tpḥ.t Ḥꜥpy [ḫsr].[185] (VI.2+IV.1/x+17)n=ỉ wꜣ.t n ỉ[tn sṯꜣ.n=ỉ] Skr (VI.2+IV.1/x+18) ḥr tmm[=f sws]r.(VI.2+IV.1/x+19)[n=ỉ Wr].t m ꜣ[.t=s šms.n=ỉ dwꜣ.n=ỉ ỉ]tn[186] (VI.2+IV.1/x+20) [smꜣ].n=ỉ m ỉ[my.w h]tt ỉnk pw wꜥ ỉm=sn ỉr.n=ỉ 2-nw[187] [n ꜣs.t swsr.] (VI.2+IV.1/x+21)[n=ỉ m][188] ꜣḫ[w=sn ṯs].n=ỉ ꜥ[qꜣ] ḫsf.[189] (VI.2+IV.1/x+22)[n]=ỉ [ꜥꜣp]p [sḥm.n=ỉ nmt.t]=f[190] [r]dỉ [n=ỉ Rꜥ ꜥ.wy=f nn] ḫsf wỉ ỉs.t=f[191] (VI.2+IV.1/x+23) wsr=ỉ w[sr Wḏꜣ.t ṯs-pẖ]r[192] ỉr tnỉw.tw=ỉ m wỉꜣ n Rꜥ[193] (VI.2+IV.1/x+24) tnỉ.tw s[wḥ.t ḥnꜥ ꜣbdw] ḏd-md.w ḥr qꜥḥ[194] [n] šww sš[195] (VI.2+IV.1/x+25) rꜣ pn ḥr=s [ḥnꜥ sš sšm] pn nty m sš[196] m dgꜣ n ḥm.t (VI.2+IV.1/x+26) wꜣḏ šb[n ḥr ꜥntyw rdỉ.t n] ꜣḫw pn ḥr šnb.t=f rdỉ.t(w) ẖnm=f ḥnꜥ nṯr.w (VI.2+IV.1/x+27) ỉmy.w-ḫt [Rꜥ sḥḏ.n=f

---

[185] Traces of the determinative appear on Fragment IV, behind the crown of Osiris.

[186] Traces survive at the right lower edge of the vignette. The text follows the tradition of naming the solar disk Aton, rather than Atum as in P. Ryerson.

[187] Traces of 2-nw are visible below the water baseline of patch 17, col. 1/1, on Fragment VI, at col. 1/x+9.

[188] Faint traces seem to correspond to the restored signs.

[189] The signs for n=ỉ ꜥ[qꜣ] ḫsf appear upside down on the large inverted patch 18 (col. 1/1) on Fragment VI, at col. 1/x+8.

[190] The signs for =f [r]dỉ appear upside down on the inverted patch 19 (line1) pasted below the vignette of Chapter 100. The patch should be moved farther to the left and flipped.

[191] The signs for ḫsf wỉ ỉs.t=f appear upside down on the large inverted patch 18 (col. 1/2) on Fragment VI, at col. 1/x+7.

[192] The signs [ṯs-pẖ]r ỉr tnỉw appear upside down on the inverted patch 19 (line 2) pasted below the vignette of Chapter 100.

[193] The signs for tw=ỉ m wỉꜣ n Rꜥ appear upside down on the large inverted patch 18 (col. 1/3) on Fragment VI, at col. 1/x+6.

[194] The signs for ḏd-md.w ḥr qꜥḥ appear upside down on the inverted patch 19 (line 3) pasted below the vignette of Chapter 100.

[195] The signs for šww sš appear upside down on the large inverted patch 18 (col. 1/4) on Fragment VI, at col. 1/x+5. The determinative for sš then follows on the main portion of the fragment.

[196] The signs for pn nty m sš appear upside down on the inverted patch 19 (line 4) pasted below the vignette of Chapter 100. The determinative for sš then follows on the main portion of the fragment.

tꜣ.wy] ḫft=sn ỉw=f pr=f r wỉꜣ n Rꜥ m ẖr(VI.2+IV.1/x+28).t hrw n.t rꜥ nb [ỉw ḥsb sw Ḏḥwty m] šs mꜣꜥ.t ḥḥ n sp

(VI.2+IV.1/x+13) SPELL FOR CAUSING TO BE SATISFIED [the *ba*-spirit of a blessed one and for causing] that he go down into the barque of Re together with those who are in his following. (VI.2+IV.1/x+14) RECITATION BY the Osiris [Ta-sherit-Min, the justified, born of Nes-Khons]u, the justified. "As I have crossed as a phoenix to Abydos, (VI.2+IV.1/x+15) with Osiris bound for Busiris, so I have [passed] (VI.2+IV.1/x+16) the cavern of Hapy. As I have [cleared] (VI.2+IV.1/x+17) the path for the solar disk, [so I have dragged] Sokar (VI.2+IV.1/x+18) on [his] sledge. [As I have empowered] (VI.2+IV.1/x+19) the Great One in [her moment, so I have praised the] solar disk, (VI.2+IV.1/x+20) having [joined] with [those who are among the] baboon chorus. I am one among them. As I have acted as a companion [to Isis, so I have given power] (VI.2+IV.1/x+21) [by means of their[197]] spells. As I have [tied] the rope, so I [have] repelled (VI.2+IV.1/x+22) Apep. [I have driven back] his [stride, even while Re] gives [his hands to me.] His crew [will not] repel me. (VI.2+IV.1/x+23) As I am strong, so [the Sound Eye is strong, and vice]-versa. If I am blocked from the barque of Re, (VI.2+IV.1/x+24) then the [egg and *Abdju* fish are blocked.]

RECITATION OVER a sheet [of] papyrus. Write (VI.2+IV.1/x+25) this spell on it, [and draw] this inscribed [image] in powder of (VI.2+IV.1/x+26) green glaze, mixed [with myrrh. Place on] this blessed one on his breast,[198] so that it is caused that he be united with the gods (VI.2+IV.1/x+27) who are in the following of [Re when he has illuminated the Two Lands] before them. He goes forth to the barque of Re in the course (VI.2+IV.1/x+28) of every day. [Thoth takes account of him.] Effective, truly, millions of times!

Wilson 1968 Translation (p. 81):

"The speech for [causing that the soul of a blessed one be satisfied

[197] "Their" refers to Isis and her companion, Nephthys.

[198] John Wilson 1968, p. 81, wrongly repeats the extended version of P. Ryerson. P. JS 2 collapses two mentions of "this blessed one," omitting "at his feet, without letting it come near his body. Ennobled is (this blessed one)."

and for causing] that he go down into the barque of Re, together with his retinue. [Words to be spoken by the Osiris T-N]: ‘I have ferried the phoenix over to Abydos, Osiris to Mendes.... [I have joined those who are among] the worshipping baboons. It is I, one of them. I have formed [the companion of Isis … As I am strong] the Sacred Eye is strong [and vice versa. As] for him who keeps me away [from the barque of Re, the egg and the *abdju*-fish] are (thus) kept away.’

“[Words to be spoken over] a sheet [of papyrus,] upon which this speech [is written, together with a picture of this god, which has been drawn] with the powder of green fayence, mixed [with myrrh, and placed on this blessed one at his feet, without letting it come near his body. Ennobled is] this blessed one over his breast, and caused to join the gods who are in the retinue [of Re, when he has illuminated the Two Lands in the presence of] them. He goes up into the barque of Re each and every day. [Thoth takes account of him. With] true value a million times.”

Chapter 101. The text now moves from joining to protecting the solar barque. A testimonial ends the spell. The vignette depicts Re, flanked by sacred Wedjat-Eyes, enthroned before an offering stand in his barque. Only the initial third of the spell is preserved in Fragment IV, column 1, with the concluding line of the directions for the spell preserved at the top of Fragment IV, column 2 (unrecognized by Wilson).[199]

(VI.2+IV.1/x+28) rꜣ n mk.t wꞽꜣ (VI.2+IV.1/x+29) n Rꜥ ḏd-md.w [ꞽn Wsꞽr Tꜣ-šr.t] (VI.2+IV.1/x+30)-Mnw mꜣꜥ-ḫrw [ms n Ns-Ḫnsw] (VI.2+IV.1/x+31) mꜣꜥ-ḫrw ꞽ ꞽꜣ[t mw pr] (VI.2+IV.1/x+32) m ḥbb.(t) [ḥfd ḥr mꜣ{ḥ}w] (VI.2+IV.1/x+33) [n wꞽ]ꜣ⸗f [wḏꜣ ꞽr⸗k r rꜣ-ꜥ⸗k n sf] (VI.2+IV.1/x+34?)[200] [ḥfd⸗k ḥr mꜣ{ḥ}w n wꞽꜣ⸗k ꞽw] (VI.2+IV.1/x+35?) [ẖnm.n⸗ꞽ m ꞽs.t⸗k ꞽnk ꜣḫ ꞽqr] (VI.2+IV.1/x+36?) [ꞽ Rꜥ m rn⸗k pwy n] Rꜥ ꞽr snꞽ⸗k ḥr wḏꜣ.t (VI.2+IV.1/x+37) [m mḥ 7 ḏfḏ⸗s n mḥ 3 1/2 kꜣ swḏ]ꜣ⸗k wꞽ ꞽnk [ꜣ]ḫ ꞽqr (VI.2+IV.1/x+38) [wḏꜣ⸗k wḏꜣ⸗ꞽ …] [… ꞽn Ḏḥwty ꞽr nw ḏs⸗f n ḥm (n) Wsꞽr r rdꞽ.t]

---

[199] Note Wilson’s reasonable comments (1968, p. 81): “One would like to work at the left hand column of photo 3 with a pair of tweezers, to remove the intrusive pieces.”

[200] Line divisions are only approximate for the beginnings of VI.2+IV.1/34, 35 and 36. Given the spacing, about three brief lines separate line 32 from the visible traces of text below the vignette (line 36).

(IV.2/x+1) [wbn] šw ḥr ẖꜣ.t=f m šs mꜣꜥ.t ḥḥ n sp

(VI.2+IV.1/x+28) SPELL FOR PROTECTING the barque (VI.2+IV.1/x+29) of Re. RECITATION BY the Osiris [Ta-sherit] (VI.2+IV.1/x+30)-Min, the justified, [born of Nes-Khonsu,] (VI.2+IV.1/x+31) the justified. "O traver[ser of water who has gone forth] (VI.2+IV.1/x+32) from the floodwater, [who takes a seat on the stern] (VI.2+IV.1/x+33) of his [barque, proceed, then, to your position of yesterday.] (VI.2+IV.1/x+34?) [May you take your seat on the stern of your barque.] (VI.2+IV.1/x+35?) [I have joined with your crew. I am an excellent blessed one.] (VI.2+IV.1/x+36?) [O sun, in this your name of] Re, if you pass by the Sound Eye (VI.2+IV.1/x+37) [of seven cubits, with its pupil of 3 1/2 cubits, then] you [shall make] me [sound]. I am an excellent blessed one. (VI.2+IV.1/x+38) [As you are sound, so I am sound …"]
[… It was Thoth who did this himself for the Majesty of Osiris to cause]
(IV.2/x+1) [that] the sunlight [shine] on his corpse. Effective, truly, millions of times!

Wilson 1968 Translation (p. 81):

"The speech for [protecting] the barque of Re. Words to be spoken [by the Osiris T-N]: 'O stri[der over the water, who comes forth] from the floods [and sits on the stern of this barque, go to your position of yesterday.... O Re, in this your name of Re,] if you pass by the Sacred Eye [of seven cubits, its pupil of three and a half cubits, then you shall make me sound. I am a blessed one,] excellent … '"

P. JS 2 PRESERVED COLUMN (x+) 7

Chapter 103. Although early versions of this chapter are entitled "Spell for existing beside Hathor," later texts substitute the homophonous verb "open" for "exist."[201] The vignette for the spell, showing the deceased opening a shrine of Hathor, originally occupied the space between lines 2 through 6, now taken by the misplaced and inverted patch 1 from P. Joseph Smith 1. Traces of the bottom of the vignette (the shrine base) appear above the vignette for the following Chapter 104. The back of the

[201] See Lepsius 1842, plate 38; and Allen 1960, p. 179 (changing wnn "to exist" to wn "to open.").

figure of Ta-sherit-Min can still be seen at the left of these lines, while the righthand edge of the scene appears on patch 20, misplaced and inverted at the beginning of line 3.[202] A further inverted patch (patch 21) now marring Chapter 105 contains the outline of Hathor's torso and her arms holding a staff and an ankh.[203] The text addresses Ihy, the son of Hathor.

(IV.2/x+1) [rȝ n wn r-gs Ḥw.t-Ḥr] (IV.2/x+2) ḏd-md.w ỉn Wsỉr Tȝ-šr.t-Mnw mȝᶜ-ḫrw (IV.2/x+3) [ms n] Ns-Ḫnsw mȝᶜ-ḫrw ỉnk snỉ (IV.2/x+4) [w]ᶜb ỉ ʾIḥy sp-2 wnn[=ỉ m] (IV.2/x+5) šms.w Ḥw.t-Ḥr

(IV.2/x+1) [SPELL FOR OPENING BESIDE Hathor.] (IV.2/x+2) RECITATION BY the Osiris Ta-sherit-Min, the justified, (IV.2/x+3) [born of] Nes-Khonsu, the justified. "I am one who passes, (IV.2/x+4) being pure. O Ihy, Ihy, [I] exist specifically [among] (IV.2/x+5) the followers of Hathor."

Wilson 1968 Translation (p. 82):

"[The speech for being beside Hathor. Words to be spoken by the] Osiris T-N: 'I am one who has passed by, pure. O Ihi, Ihi, [I shall be in] the retinue of Hathor.'"

Chapter 104. The spell allows the deceased to join the gods, here reduced to three to express "plurality." Found to the left of the spell, the vignette depicts the deceased sitting on a mat before a group of three gods on a shrine. This illustration has led to the Mormon designation of "Trinity papyrus" for Fragment IV.[204]

(IV.2/x+5) rȝ n [ḥms ỉmy-tw] (IV.2/x+6) nṯr.w ᶜȝ.w ḏd-md.w ỉn [Wsỉr] (IV.2/x+7) Tȝ-šr.t-Mnw mȝᶜ-ḫrw ms n [Ns-Ḫnsw mȝᶜ-ḫrw ḥms=ỉ] ỉmy.tw[205] (IV.2/x+8) nṯr.w ᶜȝ.w swȝ.n=ỉ ḥ[r] (IV.2/x+9) pr Skt.t (ỉn) wbȝ (IV.2/x+10) ỉn n=ỉ Ḥr sȝ ȝs.t[206] ỉy.n=ỉ (IV.2/x+11)

[202] Originally above (now inverted below) the word ỉmy-tw in line 7.

[203] Unrecognized by Wilson 1968, p. 82: "The usual vignette, the deceased before the goddess Hathor, is not visible."

[204] Green 1968, p. 40; and cf. Nibley 1975, p. 142. The "trinitarian" feature of Egyptian solar religion has long been recognized, but *contra* Green, the designation "Trinity papyrus" derives from remarks by Cowdery, not from Egyptologists.

[205] The word ỉmy-tw is found on the inverted patch 20 now mounted at the start of line 3 of this column.

[206] Other versions have Osiris.

m wp.t n Rᶜ ḥw k3.w (IV.2/x+12) r s.t ỉr(y)=w r sḏf3w (IV.2/x+13) p3w.wt n nṯr.w ᶜ3(IV.2/x+14).w ỉn ḥby ỉn.n=f ỉr rḫ r3 pn ỉw=f ḥms=f ỉmy.tw nṯr.w (IV.2/x+15) ᶜ3.w[207]

(IV.2/x+5) Spell for [sitting among] (IV.2/x+6) the great gods. RECITATION BY [the Osiris] (IV.2/x+7) Ta-sherit-Min, the justified, born of [Nes-Khonsu, the justified. "May I sit] among (IV.2/x+8) the great gods. I have passed by (IV.2/x+9) the house of the solar evening barque.[208] (It is) the butler (IV.2/x+10) who has brought to me[209] Horus the son of Isis. I have come (IV.2/x+11) on the business of Re, with sustenance and food (IV.2/x+12) at their proper places in order to provision (IV.2/x+13) the offering cakes of the great gods. (IV.2/x+14) It is the fowler whom he has brought."
As for the one who knows this spell, he sits among the (IV.2/x+15) great gods.

Wilson 1968 Translation (p. 82):

"[The speech for sitting among] the great gods. Words to be spoken [by the Osiris] T-[N: 'I sit among] the great gods. [I] have passed [by] the house of the evening-barque. It is a butler, the porter of Horus, son of Isis, who comes to me on business of Re. Food and sustenance are at the proper place, to provision the offering-bread for the great gods. It is a fowler whom he has brought.'
"As for the one who knows this speech, he sits among the [great] gods."

Chapter 105. The text is badly damaged, and much of the initial space is now filled by the inverted, intrusive patch 4 from P. Joseph Smith I, in addition to various smaller (unnumbered) patches. The vignette shows the deceased in adoration before a standard representing food (k3.w). As noted by Wilson (p. 83), the text incorporates wordplay, but this is employed to indicate not humor, but inherent cosmological links between words and

[207] The word ᶜ3.w is found on patch 22 (line 1) now misplaced in Chapter 100 on Fragment IV, at col. 1/x+23. The word is followed on the next line by "the Osiris Tasherit-[Min]" from Chapter 105.

[208] For the retention of the traditional role of the *Sektet*-barque here, see the comments on Chapter 77, n. 161, above, and Verhoeven 1993, p. 209.

[209] Allen and Wilson translate "the porter of Horus," but the text of P. JS 2 certainly treats ỉn as a participle "who has brought."

concepts: spirit, bull and food (all kꜣ), and green, amulet and flourishing health (all wꜣḏ). By offering food (kꜣ) to her own spirit (kꜣ), Ta-sherit-Min will not become a sacrificial "bull" (kꜣ), and her control of the green papyrus amulet (wꜣḏ) ensures that she flourishes (wꜣḏ). The spell makes explicit reference to the weighing of the heart, otherwise associated with Chapter 125.

> (IV.2/x+15) [rꜣ n sḥtp kꜣ n] s m ẖr.t-[nṯr] ḏd-md.w ỉn (IV.2/x+16) Wsỉr Tꜣ-šr.t-Mnw m[ꜣꜥ-ḫrw[210] ms n] (IV.2/x+17) [Ns-Ḫnsw mꜣꜥ-ḫrw ỉnḏ]-ḥr=k (IV.2/x+18) [kꜣ=ỉ ꜥḥꜥ]w=ỉ mk wỉ (IV.2/x+19) ỉy.[kwỉ][211] ḫr=k ḫꜥ.kwỉ (IV.2/x+20) bꜣ.k[w]ỉ[212] wsr.kwỉ (IV.2/x+21) bs.[kwỉ[213] ỉn=ỉ] n=k bd snṯr swꜥb.tw ỉm=sn swꜥb[214](IV.2/x+22)=ỉ nt[t[215]=k ỉm]=sn snỉ n=k ḏꜣỉs pfy ḏw (IV.2/x+23) w[ꜥꜣ(?)][216] pwy ḏw ḏd.n=ỉ ꜥb pwy ḏw ỉr.n=ỉ (IV.2/x+24) nn rdỉ n=ỉ[217] n=sn ỉnk ỉs wꜣḏ pwy wꜣḏ ỉry ḫḫw n Rꜥ (IV.2/x+25) wꜣḏ=ỉ[218] wꜣḏ=sn wꜣḏ kꜣ=ỉ wꜣḏ=sn wꜣḏ ꜥḥꜥw=ỉ (m) mỉt.t=sn (IV.2/x+26) ḏfꜣw kꜣ=ỉ (m) mỉt.t=sn fꜣ(ỉ)

---

[210] The signs for Wsỉr Tꜣ-šr.t are found on patch 22 (l. 2) now misplaced in Chapter 100 on Fragment IV, at col. 1/x+24, below the word ꜥꜣ.w that properly concludes Chapter 104. The following -Mnw m[ꜣꜥ-ḫrw] appears on the further misplaced patch 23, now pasted at an angle to the left of the vignette of spell 100 (in the midst of spell 105).

[211] The word ỉy appears on patch 17, col. 2/1 (now pasted in Fragment VI), left of the lefthand water baseline of Chapter 100.

[212] The upper traces of bꜣ are preserved on patch 17, col. 2/2, and the lower traces of bꜣ.kw are preserved on the inverted patch 18 (col. 2/1) at the upper right of Fragment VI that also contains four lines of Chapter 100. The following ỉ remains in proper position on the papyrus.

[213] The signs for bs are preserved on the inverted patch 18 (col. 2/2) at the upper right of Fragment VI that also contains 4 lines of Chapter 100.

[214] The proper location of a patch misplaced over the end of this line (and extending two lines above) remains to be determined. See unplaced patch 37, below.

[215] The signs for =ỉ nt[t] are preserved on the inverted patch 18 (col. 2/3) at the upper right of Fragment VI that also contains four lines of Chapter 100.

[216] Traces of the initial word are preserved on the inverted patch 18 (col. 2/4) at the upper right of Fragment VI that also contains 4 lines of Chapter 100. P. Ryerson has only ḏꜣỉs pfy ḏw ḏd.n=ỉ "that evil statement which I have said."

[217] Error also in P. Ryerson for nn rdỉ.t=ỉ "without giving me."

[218] *Contra* John Wilson 1968, pp. 82–83, the word "Re" is present, but there is no room for the restoration of P. Ryerson's "which was given to those who are in the horizon." P. JS 2 continues directly with "As I am sound/flourish."

mḫꜣ.t qꜣ (IV.2/x+27) Mꜣꜥ.t r fnḏ n Rꜥ m hrw kꜣ=ἰ ἰmy=[k] ἰr.t ḥr rmn.wy ἰm=k ἰnk (IV.2/x+28) ἰr.t mꜣꜣ msḏr=ἰ sḏm nn ἰnk ἰs kꜣ (IV.2/x+29) ḫry nn pr.(t)-r-ḫrw ἰm=ἰ n [ḥry].w (IV.2/x+30) Nw.t

(IV.2/x+15) [SPELL FOR SATISFYING the *ka*-spirit of] a man in the necropolis. RECITATION BY (IV.2/x+16) the Osiris Ta-sherit-Min, the just[ified, born of] (IV.2/x+17) [Nes-Khonsu, the justified. "Hail] to you, (IV.2/x+18) [my *ka*-spirit,] my [lifetime!] Behold, I have (IV.2/x+19) [come] before you, having appeared, (IV.2/x+20) having become a *ba*-spirit, being powerful, (IV.2/x+21), being initiated, [bringing] to you natron and incense by which one is purified so that I might purify (IV.2/x+22) [your] bodily fluids [by means of] them. Disregard that evil statement or (IV.2/x+23) this evil re[proach(?)] which I have said, or this evil impure act which I have done (IV.2/x+24) without giving me over to them. Mine is[219] indeed this green papyrus amulet attached to the neck of Re. (IV.2/x+25) As I flourish, so they[220] flourish. As my *ka*-spirit flourishes, so they flourish. May my lifetime flourish as the like of theirs, (IV.2/x+26) with the provisions of my *ka*-spirit as the like of theirs. O weigher of the balance, may (IV.2/x+27) Truth be as high as the nose of Re by day.[221] O my *ka*-spirit, may [you] not act on the two arms of the balance at which you are.[222] Mine is (IV.2x+/28) an eye which sees, while my ears hear. I am not a bull (IV.2/x+29) for sacrifice. There is no invocation offering deriving from me for those [who are in charge of] (IV.2/x+30) Nut.

[219] Or: "I am, indeed, this green papyrus amulet … ." as understood by Wilson. For the common use of the independent pronoun to indicate either identity or possession, see Gardiner 1957, pp. 54 §65 and 89 §114.3. The possessive use is also adopted here (and below: "I have an eye that sees") by Janák 2003, pp. 193, 199 and cf. 203. The same translation choices are made by Verhoeven 1993, vol. I, p. 210.

[220] In reference to "those in the horizon" (dropped from the text in P. JS 2).

[221] The deceased urges that Truth (Maat) rise to the height of midheaven to be inhaled by the sun god Re.

[222] Wilson's confused translation of this sentence follows Allen 1960 and P. Ryerson: ἰmy=k ἰr.t tp rmn.wy ἰm=k, taking tp as "head" rather than a preposition. For the phrase ḥr rmn.wy or tp rmn.wy and the link to the arms of the balance, see Erman and Grapow 1957, vol. II, p. 418/6–10. Earlier versions had: "Let my head not be taken away from me."

Wilson 1968 Translation (pp. 82–83):

"[The speech for satisfying the spirit of a man] in the nec[ropolis. Words] to be spoken by [the Osiris T-N: 'Hail to you, my spirit, my lifetime! See, I have come to you.... I have brought to you natron] and incense, so that (I) might purify you with them, and purify [your spittle with them.] Overlook that evil arguing and the evil [speech] which I have spoken and this evil arrogance which I have shown, without giving me over to them. I am really this green papyrus-amulet which is at the throat of [Re, which was given to those who are in the horizon. As they flourish] I flourish. As they flourish my spirit flourishes. As they flourish my lifetime flourishes, like unto them. The provisioning of my spirit is like unto theirs. O weigher of the scales, truth is as high as the nose of Re by day. O my spirit, you should not make a head which you weigh in yourself(?). Mine is an eye that sees, my ears hear. I am not really a bull of the sacrifices. From me there will be no mortuary offerings to those who are over Nut.'"

Chapter 106. The vignette depicts Ta-sherit-Min offering the hieroglyphs for ꜣw.(t)-ỉb "joy" to Ptah, chief deity of Memphis. Although Wilson blandly described the presentation as consisting of hieroglyphs for "offering," Nibley 1975, p. 129, correctly recognized this common idiom (literally, "expansion of heart"), which he translated as "rejoicing."

(IV.2/x+30) rꜣ n rdỉ.t ꜣw.(t)-ỉb m Ḥw.t-(IV.2/x+31)kꜣ.w-Ptḥ[223] ḏd-md.w ỉn Wsỉr Tꜣ-šr.t-Mnw (IV.2/x+32) mꜣꜥ-ḫrw ms n Ns-Ḫnsw mꜣꜥ-ḫrw [ỉ] wr (IV.2/x+33) smsw nb tfꜣw ỉ wr ḫnty pr.w ḥry.w dỉ=tn n=ỉ t (IV.2/x+34) ḥnq.t yꜥ(w)=ỉ [m ḫntb] m-ꜥb [sšr] ỉ mẖnty n Wsỉr[224] (IV.2/x+35) m sḫ.t ʾIꜣ[nr.w ỉn n=ỉ nw n t wꜥr.t=k mỉ] (IV.2/x+36) ỉt=k wr sb[ỉ m tp.(t)]-nṯr pr m hrw m-ḫt mnỉw]

(IV.2/x+30) SPELL FOR GIVING JOY in Memphis (IV.2/x+31). RECITATION BY the Osiris Ta-sherit-Min, (IV.2/x+32) the justified, born of Nes-Khonsu, the justified. "[O] great one, (IV.2/x+33) and elder, lord of provisions! O great one, foremost of the upper houses!

[223] Written honorifically, as Ptḥ-Ḥw.t-(IV.2/31)kꜣ.w.

[224] John Wilson 1968, p. 83, did not see the preserved conclusion of IV.2/x+34, and restored the deceased's name after Osiris. Though common in other papyri, the personal name is omitted here in P. JS 2.

May you (plural) give to me bread (IV.2/x+34) and beer, since my breakfast [consists of a joint of meat] together with [toasted bread.] O ferryman of Osiris (IV.2/x+35) in the Field of R[eeds, bring to me this bread of your district, like that of] (IV.2/x+36) your father, the great one who has departed [in the divine boat, going forth by day after mooring."]

Wilson 1968 Translation (p. 83):

"[The speech for giving offerings] in Memphis. [Words] to be spoken [by] the Osiris T-N: 'O great one and elder, lord of provisions, O great one presiding over the upper houses, may you give me bread and beer! My breakfast [is a joint of meat, together with cakes. O ferryman of the Osiris T-N] in the Field of Reeds, [bring me these loaves of bread to your district, as to] your father, the great one who went [away in the ship of the god, going forth by day after coming to rest.]'"

P. JS 2 PRESERVED COLUMN (x+) 8

FRAGMENT II (= P. JS 2.7)

The proper relation of Fragments II and IV (with connecting framing lines) is shown on the folding plate in C. M. Larson 1992, p. 34.[225]

Chapter 110. This chapter consists primarily of a map of paradise, with activities in the Field of Reeds accompanied by brief labels.[226] Only sections of the elaborate vignette are preserved. In the upper register, the deceased is shown sailing and in adoration (broken at the right), while in the lower register she is plowing and scattering seeds. A schematic drawing with minor restorations appears in Gee, Rhodes and Nibley 2005, p. 242.

Preserved labels for the agricultural scene include:

skꜣ "Plowing"

and a description of the dimensions of the region:

p.t ꜣw=f "Its extent is the sky."[227]

---

[225] The join between Fragments II and IV was noted also by John Wilson 1968, p. 84 (as photos 3 and 8), but corrected his reference to "The Improvement Era, Feb. 1968, p. 50-D" to p. 40-D.

[226] See the comments in n. 79, above.

[227] For the full meaning of the text, see the corresponding vignette label in Naville 1886, plate 123: ꜣw p.t ꜣw=f "Its extent is the extent of heaven." Cf. also Coffin Text spell 466, § XI.

In his 1968 translation, Wilson (p. 84) included both "Plowing" and (reversing subject and predicate) "The sky is its length." In 1975, Nibley misinterpreted the latter passage as pt (r) aw.f "The heaven to its entire extent."[228] The erroneous translation is repeated in Gee, Rhodes and Nibley 2005, p. 242.

Two patches now misplaced in Fragment IV (lower right) preserve the names of individual territories within paradise. In patch 24, below the broken word sḫ[.t] "field" (line 1) are the names D̲f(ꜣ).t "Foodstuffs" (line 2) and [W]s[r].t "Powerful" (line 3), placed within ovals.[229] In patch 25, a third name within an oval is misplaced below these, rotated from horizontal to vertical. While quite unclear, the name may be Wr.t "The Great One."[230] Behind the head of Ptah in the vignette for Chapter 106 (Fragment IV.2), patch 26 with the single word mnḫ.t "clothing" may derive from a further label at the lower right of Chapter 110.[231]

Chapter 125. This pivotal chapter is discussed more fully in the edition of P. Smith 3, where the vignette alone survives. In P. Smith 2, the chapter is represented by only a few phrases from the "Negative Confession," statements 8, 9 and 10, now preserved in patch 27 at the top of the second artificial "column" of Fragment IX:

(x+1) [ỉ nbỉ ḥr pr m ḫtḫt pr m ꜥIwnw nn] t̲ꜣỉ=ỉ ḫ.wt n nt̲r
(x+2) [ỉ sd qs.w pr m Nn-ny-sw.t nn] d̲[d]=ỉ grg
(x+3) [ỉ t̲ꜣw=f m sd̲.t pr m Ḥ.wt-kꜣ-Ptḥ nn nḥm=ỉ wnm.]t[232]

(IX.1/x+1) ["O Fiery-Faced-One, who has gone forth backwards, who has gone forth from Heliopolis, I have not] stolen the property of a god."
(IX.1/x+2) ["O Smasher-of-Bones, who has gone forth from Heracleopolis,] I have not said lies."

---

[228] Nibley 1975, p. 144, photo caption.

[229] See the corresponding images in P. Ryerson, plate 31, lower register, top left oval. Cf. Coffin Texts spell 466, §§ XVIII and XII.

[230] Cf. P. Ryerson, plate 31 (as nỉw.t wr.t) and Coffin Texts spell 466, § III.

[231] For the word in similar vignettes, see Naville 1886, plate 123, lower right ("offering clothing to the scribe NN") and Lepsius 1842, plate 41, lower right as the concluding word in the name of an island.

[232] Only final traces of the word remain below and to the left of grg in the previous line.

(IX.1/x+3) ["O He-Whose-Breath-is-of-Fire, who has gone forth from Memphis, I have not seized foo]d."

Wilson 1968 Translation (p. 84):

"'[O Fiery-of-Face, who came forth from Heliopolis, I have not] stolen the property of a god!'"

"'[O Breaker-of-Bones, who came forth from Heracleopolis, I have not told] a lie!'"

APPENDIX I. UNPLACED PATCHES IN P. JS 2

1) Patch 28 in Fragment VIII, above col. 2. The patch derives from a lost vignette, and contains a section of Ta-sherit-Min's dress.

2) Patch 29 in Fragment V.2, above line x+3:
[Wsỉr Tꜣ-šr.t-Mn]w[233] mꜣ[ꜥ ḫ]rw [ms] n [Ns-Ḫnsw mꜣꜥ-ḫrw]
"[the Osiris Ta-sherit]-Min, the justified, [born] of [Nes-Khonsu, the justified]"

3) Patch 30 in Fragment V.1, above the head of Ta-sherit-Min in the vignette for Chapter 74, pasted upside down. The words may derive from Chapter 11, line x+3, as noted above.
(x+1) [...].n=ỉ ḫr [...] (x+2) [...]=ỉ ... [...]
(x+1) "[...] to me [...] fallen [...] (x+2) [...] I ... [...]"]

4) Patch 31 in Fragment VI.1, uppermost righthand patch. The patch preserves part of the baseline of a lost vignette.

5) Patch 32 in Fragment IV.1, at the right edge of at least 3 adjoining patches above and to the right of the barque of Re in the vignette for Chapter 101:
(x+1) [...] ... [...] (x+2) [...] Wsỉr [...] (x+3) [...] wḏ[234] ... [...]
(x+1) "[...] ... [...] (x+2) [...] Osiris [...] (x+3) [...] command ... [...]"

6) Patch 33 in Fragment IV.1, one of at least 3 adjoining patches above and to the right of the barque of Re in the vignette for Chapter 101, left of patch 32 and inverted:

---

[233] The patch preserves the seated woman determinative, the lower sections of mꜣ[ꜥ ḫ]rw and the genitive n. There are many possibilities for the original location of this often repeated phrase.

[234] Written with the "cord wrapped on a stick" (wḏ) and a phonetic complement (w), followed by a vertical stroke.

(x+1) [... b]ꜣ=k(?) [...] (x+2) [...]=f(?)[235] ... [...] (x+3) [...] tꜣ ... [...]
(x+4) [...] r=f ỉy [...] (x+5) [...] ... r ... [...] (x+6) [...] ... [...]
(x+1) "[...] your *ba*-spirit(?) [...] (x+2) [...] his ... [...] (x+3) [...] the [...] (x+4) [...] against/regarding him/it. [...] come [...] (x+5) [...] ... [...] (x+6) [...] ... [...]"

7) Patch 34 in Fragment IV.1, the lowest of at least 3 adjoining patches above and to the right of the barque of Re in the vignette for Chapter 101, turned horizontally, 90 degrees clockwise:
(x+1) [...] ỉr.n=k wḥm [ꜥnḫ(?) ...] (x+2) [...] ỉmy (x+3) [... S]ꜣḥ(?)[236]
(x+4) [...] ... [...]
(x+1) "[...] you have made a repetition [of life(?) ...] (x+2) [...] within (x+3) [...] Orion(?) (x+4) [...] ... [...]"

8) Patch 35 in Fragment IV.1, left of the barque of Re in the vignette for Chapter 101, pasted on an angle:
(x+1) [...]f(?)[237] [...] (x+2) [...] n(?) Rꜥ(?) pr [...]
(x+1) "[...] he(?) [...] (x+2) [...] of Re(?)[238] gone forth [..."]

9) Patch 36 in Fragment IV.2, lower left of the vignette for Chapter 100, rotated 90 degrees counter-clockwise and written in cursive hieroglyphs. The patch is probably from a different manuscript.
(x+1) [...][239] m kꜣ [...]
(x+1) "[coming/going] forth as a *ka*-spirit [...]"

10) Patch 37 in Fragment IV.2, lower left of the vignette for Chapter 105, pasted over the frame line:
(x+1) [... Tꜣ-šr.t-Mn]w mꜣꜥ-(ḫrw)[240] ms n [Ns-Ḫnsw mꜣꜥ-ḫrw ...]

---

[235] Or flesh determinative.

[236] The text ends with a vertical stroke and a star determinative. Other readings are possible.

[237] Or m or w.

[238] The word ends with a clear divine determinative. It is possible that this is one of the invocations in the "Negative Confession," where the names of a few judges might have such a determinative.

[239] The first sign preserved is a "walking legs" determinative (ỉy or pr?).

[240] There is no room for ḫrw, and such an omission would be unusual in this papyrus.

(x+2) […] … [241] ỉy(?)[…] (x+3) […] st[w.t(?)[242] …]
(x+1) "[Ta-sherit]-Min, the justified, born of [Nes-Khonsu, the justified …] (x+2) […] … come(?) […] (x+3) […] ray[s(?) …]"

11) Patch 38 in Fragment IX, an inverted vertical strip with only sections of individual words:

(x+1) […] n(?) […] (x+2) […].w[243] […] (x+3) […] r(?) […] (x+4) […] šꜥ[…] (x+5) […] … […] (x+6) […] … [244] […] (x+7) [… R]ꜥ wbn […] (x+8) […]f … w[245] … […] (x+9) […] ꜥꜣ(?) […] (x+10) […] … […] (x+11) […] … […]
(x+1) "[…] to/for(?) […] (x+2) […] … […] (x+3) […] toward(?) […] (x+4) […] … […] (x+5) […] … […] (x+6) […] … […] (x+7) […] Re shines […] (x+8) […] … […] (x+9) […] door panel(?) […] (x+10) […] … […] (x+11) […] … […]"

12) Patch 39 in Fragment IX, below patch 7 and unplaced patch 38 in the second artificial column:

(x+1) […]ẖ-sw[246] pr m […] (x+2) [… Wsỉr Tꜣ-šr.t-Mn]w mꜣꜥ-ḫrw ms n [Ns-Ḫnsw mꜣꜥ-ḫrw …] (x+3) […] … [247][…]
(x+1) "[… (spirit)] who […] himself, gone forth from […] (x+2) [… the Osiris Ta-sherit]-Min, the justified, born of [Nes-Khonsu, the justified …] (x+3) […] … […]"

13) Patch 40 in Fragment IX, below patch 11 (second upper left patch):

(x+1) [… Tꜣ-šr.t-Mn]w mꜣꜥ-[ḫrw ms n] Ns-Ḫnsw mꜣꜥ-ḫrw … […] (x+2) […] … […] (x+3) [… Tꜣ-šr.t-Mn]w mꜣꜥ-ḫrw ms n Ns-Ḫnsw [mꜣꜥ-ḫrw …]
(x+1) "[… Ta-sherit]-Min, the justi[fied, born of] Nes-Khonsu, the justified … […] (x+2) […] … […] (x+3) [… Ta-sherit]-Min, the justified, born of Nes-Khonsu, [the justified …]"

[241] The unclear traces resemble kỉ + flesh determinative.

[242] Or Ḏ[d] or Ḏ[dw] "stability/Busiris"? Cf. Möller 1912, pp. 15 (no. 167) and 52 (no. 541) = Verhoeven 2001, pp. 130–31 and 176–77.

[243] The final traces suggest plural strokes.

[244] Traces of two signs may conclude with walking legs or k.

[245] The traces end with plural strokes.

[246] The spirit's name does not have a divine determinative, so Ḫ[n]sw is excluded.

[247] The traces end with a water determinative.

14) Patch 41 in Fragment IX, patch at right, below the baboons and rotated 180 degrees counter-clockwise. The patch derives from a lost vignette, and contains the shoulder and arm of Ta-sherit-Min, striding with a staff.[248]

15–16) Illegible patch 42 and patch 43 are, respectively, pasted beside and below unplaced patch 39. At least four illegible patches (44–47) now pasted to the right of the baboons in Fragment IX may contain the remains of vignettes.

APPENDIX II. THE TRANSLITERATION OF SMITH'S "VALUABLE DISCOVERY," P. 12, CONTAINING PORTIONS OF SPELLS 1, 2, 3, 6, 7, AND 10–14

Omitted portions of text are placed in []. Chapter sections are noted within \\.

Overlap between "Valuable Discovery," pp. 12 and 14, is evident, but the copied text is inconsistent, with neither page having the better preservation. Cf.

1) Chapter 7, extracted differently on p. 12, line 23: Tꜣ-[šr.t]-Mnw mꜣꜥ-ḫrw ms n Ns-Ḫnsw mꜣꜥ-[ḫrw] and p. 14, lines 3–4: [Tꜣ-šr.t](3)-Mnw mꜣꜥ-ḫrw ms n (4) Ns-Ḫnsw mꜣꜥ-ḫrw. (Page 12 is fuller for the deceased's name; p. 14 is fuller for that of her mother.)

2) The rubric of Chapter 13, extracted differently on p. 12, line 32 [ꜥnḫ]-ỉmy rdỉ.t and p. 14, line 8 ꜥnḫ-ỉmy rdỉ.t (Page 14 is fuller.)

These variations may reflect continued deterioration of the papyri as Smith worked upon them or simply his inattention to details.

1) \Chapter 1\ ỉ Wsỉr kꜣ ỉ[mnt.t ...]

2) smꜣꜥ ḫrw Wsỉr r [ḫfty.w=f hr]

3)w pwy n wḏꜣ md.wt [... wnn=ỉ r-ḥnꜥ Ḥr hrw ḥb n Wsỉr Wn-nfr mꜣꜥ-ḫrw ỉry ꜥꜣb.wt n.t Rꜥ hrw 6-n.t dnỉ]

4) n ꜣIwnw ỉnk wꜥb m Ḏdw sbq m [ꜣbḏw ...]

5) stm m ỉry.w=[f] ỉnk wr ḫrp ḥmww.t rdỉ [ḥny ḥr mfḫ ... ỉ stkn bꜣ.w mnḫ.w m pr Wsỉr stkn=tn bꜣ n Wsỉr Tꜣ-šr.t-Mnw]

---

[248] For the generic nature of such a vignette, see the remarks of Allen 1974, p. 11, n. 22.

6) [mꜣꜥ-ḫrw] ms n Ns-Ḫnsw mꜣꜥ-ḫrw ḥnꜥ⸗tn r pr Wsỉr mꜣꜣ(?)[⸗f mỉ mꜣꜣ⸗tn … dỉ⸗tn t ḥnq.t r tr n Wsỉr]

7) Tꜣ-šr.t-Mnw mꜣꜥ-ḫrw ms n Ns-Ḫnsw mꜣꜥ-ḫrw ḥnꜥ⸗tn [… Wsỉr Tꜣ-šr.t-Mnw mꜣꜥ-ḫrw ms n]

8) Ns-Ḫnsw mꜣꜥ-ḫrw ḥnꜥ⸗tn ꜥq⸗f m rꜣ pwy [m pr Wsỉr … pr⸗f]

9) mr.tw smꜣꜥ ḫrw[⸗f] ỉr.tw wḏ.t[⸗f] m pr Wsỉr šm[⸗f] md.wt[⸗f] ḥ[nꜥ⸗tn šm Wsỉr Tꜣ-šr.t Mn]

10)w [mꜣꜥ-ḫrw ms n] Ns-Ḫn[sw mꜣꜥ-ḫrw] sỉp.tw[249] m rꜣ.w ꜥšꜣ sꜥḥꜥ bꜣ⸗k r ḫ[ft-ḥr gm.tw⸗f wḏꜣ rꜣ tp tꜣ … wnn⸗ỉ mỉ]

11) [w]ꜥ [ỉm⸗tn] sṯs nmt.t m H̱r-ꜥḥꜣ mꜣꜣ.n⸗ỉ Sꜣḥ [… ỉnḏ-ḥr⸗k ḫ]

12) nty ỉmnt.t Wsỉr ḥry-ỉb Ṯꜣw-wr dỉ⸗k hꜣ⸗ỉ r ỉmnt.t ššp [wỉ nb.w tꜣ ḏsr …]

13) pr.n⸗ỉ m-bꜥḥ Wn-nfr mꜣꜥ-ḫrw šms⸗ỉ Ḥr m Rꜣ-s[ṯꜣ.w Wsỉr m Ḏdw … ỉr rḫ mḏꜣ.t tn ḥr-tp tꜣ ỉw⸗f ỉr⸗s m sš ḥr qrỉs]

14) [r]ꜣ-pw ỉw⸗[f] pr⸗f m hrw nb mr⸗[f ḥ]nꜥ [ꜥ]q r ḥw.[t]⸗f nn [šnꜥ.tw⸗f …]

15) [wn]n⸗f wꜣḏ mỉ [w]nn⸗f ḥr-tp tꜣ \Chapter 2\ rꜣ n pr m hrw ꜥnḫ m-ḫ[t mt ḏd-md.w ỉn Wsỉr Tꜣ-šr.t-Mnw mꜣꜥ-ḫrw ms n Ns-Ḫnsw mꜣꜥ-ḫrw …]

16) \Chapter 3\ [k]y rꜣ mỉt[.t⸗f] ḏ[d-m]d.w [ỉ]n Wsỉr

17) [w]r m Nnw(?) ꜣḫ m rw.[ty]

18) ꜥ[nḫ Wsỉr m]-ḫt mt mỉ Rꜥ rꜥ nb ỉr

19) [ḥw.t s]r wr m ʾIwnw \Chapter 5\ rꜣ n

20) [t]m dỉ.t ỉr s kꜣ.t m

21) ẖr.t-nṯr[250] ḏd-md.w ỉn Wsỉr Tꜣ-šr.t-Mnw

22) \Chapter 6\ [ỉ]m⸗f m s r ẖr.wt⸗f mk wỉ kꜣ⸗tn

23) \Chapter 7\ Tꜣ-[šr.t]-Mnw mꜣꜥ-ḫrw ms n Ns-Ḫnsw mꜣꜥ-[ḫrw]

[249] The "Valuable Discovery" hand copy jumps directly from the initial signs of the mother's name to a later portion of the spell. This jump may indicate damage to the papyrus when copied.

[250] Written with honorific transposition, with nṯr at the end of line 20. The hand copy shows the title all in red ink from rꜣ n (line 19) to ḏd md.w ỉn (line 21).

24) m nnỉ.w nn nnỉ≈ỉ n≈k nn [ʿ]q

25) rn.w wr m d̲sr s.wt r ḥḥ.[w]

26) \Chapter 10\ [wb]ꜣ.n≈ỉ tꜣ šꜣỉs.n≈ỉ r nmt.t≈f

27) \Chapter 11\ ḫfty.w≈f m h̲r.t-nt̲r d̲d-md.w ỉn Wsỉr Tꜣ-šr.t-[Mnw]

28) nn rdỉ.t ḫfty pwy rdỉ.n≈f n≈ỉ

29) \Chapter 12\ Wsỉr Tꜣ-šr.t-Mnw mꜣʿ-ḫrw ms n Ns-Ḫnsw [mꜣʿ-ḫrw] d̲d-md.w

30) fꜣỉ≈f Mꜣʿ.t ỉm≈s rꜣ nb mk wỉ bꜣ.n≈ỉ tꜣ dỉ≈k

31) \Chapter 13\ ỉr n≈ỉ wꜣ.t dwꜣ≈ỉ Rʿ m ỉmnt.t nfr.t nš[š]nw [n Wsỉr]

32) [ʿnḫ]-ỉmy rdỉ.t (m) msd̲r wnm n ꜣḫw rdỉ.t

33) \Chapter 14\ Ns-Ḫnsw mꜣʿ-ḫrw nn nt̲r šp[t]

34) [ỉn≈ỉ] n≈k sḥtp.w ʿnḫ≈k ỉm≈f ʿnḫ W[sỉr]

APPENDIX III. THE TRANSLITERATION OF SMITH'S "VALUABLE DISCOVERY," P. 14, CONTAINING PORTIONS OF SPELLS 3–7 AND 10–14

Omitted portions of individual words are placed in (). Chapter sections are noted within \\.

1) \Chapter 3\ (md).wt≈k n ỉs.t n Rʿ m mšrw \Chapter 4\ Wsỉr Tꜣ-šr.t-Mnw mꜣʿ-ḫrw ms n Ns-(Ḫnsw) \Chapter 4\ (r)ḥ.wy ỉy

2).n≈ỉ dỉ.n≈ỉ ꜣḥ.wt n (Wsỉr) \Chapter 5\ (nn)ỉ pr m Wnw.t ʿnḫ m bsk(.w) \Chapter 6\ (T)ꜣ šr.t-Mnw mꜣʿ-ḫrw ms n Ns-

3)Ḫnsw mꜣʿ-ḫrw \Chapter 6\ r (s)mḥw wd̲b.w r h̲nty šʿ \Chapter 7\ (Tꜣ-šr.t)-Mnw mꜣʿ-ḫrw ms n

4) Ns-Ḫnsw mꜣʿ-ḫrw \Chapter 7\ m ʿ.t≈ỉ ỉptn ỉnk wʿ ḥr ḫnty Nwn \Chapter 10\ (Tꜣ-šr.t)-Mnw mꜣʿ-ḫrw ms n

5) Ns-Ḫnsw mꜣʿ-ḫrw pr \Chapter 10\ (fgn)≈ỉ m ʿrw≈ỉ ḥr-nt.t ỉnk nt̲r nb \Chapter 11\ m ꜣḫ.t r

6) ḫfty.w≈ỉ nn nḥm≈f m-ʿ≈ỉ ʿḥʿ.(n)≈ỉ \Chapter 11\ (šm).n≈ỉ m rd.wy≈ỉ mdw≈ỉ m rꜣ≈ỉ ḥḥ≈ỉ

7) \Chapter 12\ Rᶜ mk ẖr sštꜣ.w n dwꜣ.t \Chapter 13\ Wsỉr Tꜣ-šr.t-Mnw mꜣᶜ-ḫrw ms n Ns-Ḫnsw mꜣᶜ-ḫrw ḏd-md.w

8) \Chapter 13\ Wsỉr ḏd-md.w ḥr bnn.(t) n.(t) ᶜnḫ-ỉmy rdỉ.t \Chapter 13\ (Ns-Ḫn)sw mꜣᶜ-ḫrw ḥr=f m hrw qrỉs

9) \Chapter 14\ (sm)ꜣ nṯr m Mꜣᶜ.t r dr sḏb.w=f n ky nṯr

PAPYRUS JOSEPH SMITH 3: BOOK OF THE DEAD CHAPTER 125 VIGNETTE OF NEFER-IR-NEBU

(Fragment III/A–B)

Only the vignette of a single, if pivotal, Book of the Dead chapter survives from this funerary composition for the lady Nefer-ir-nebu.[1] The papyrus was designated as "Document C" in Wilson 1968, p. 68, and briefly discussed in Parker 1968a, pages 87–88, with photos 5–6. Images of the papyrus appear also in Gee, Rhodes and Nibley 2005, plate 5 (color photo) and page 402, figure 130 (reconstructed drawing); Nibley 1975, pages 226–27 (sepia photo); and Green 1968, pages 40, 40.B and 40.C (photos within the article by Jay M. Todd). Aside from these few remarks and illustrations, the papyrus has not been edited previously.

The text of Chapter 125 contains the "negative confession," or protestation of innocence, declared by the deceased before Osiris, as chief judge, and an underworld tribunal of forty-two gods who correspond to the like-numbered provinces ("nomes") of Egypt. Although not explicitly mentioned in the text of Chapter 125, the recitation serves as a preliminary purification prior to the weighing of the deceased's heart (*psychostasis*), which must balance precisely the feather of Maat, goddess of truth and justice.[2] The vignette of Chapter 125 regularly depicts this judgment scene, with Osiris and the forty-two judges presiding over the weighing.[3]

A new edition of this text by Michael D. Rhodes reached me (February 25, 2011) while my manuscript was in press, too late to be incorporated in the present study.

[1] The name means "What the Golden One (= Hathor) does is good." For a similar name, see Ranke 1935, p. 195, no. 10: Nfr-ỉr.t-Ḥ.t-Ḥr "What Hathor does is good."

[2] For a translation and introduction to the usual text, see Ritner 2000, pp. 59–64.

[3] For the association of this scene with Chapter 125, see Allen 1974, p. 101. Less frequent examples associate it with Chapter 30B; see ibid, p. 40. The association is

The extended recitation of Chapter 125 does not survive for P. Smith 3, but its accompanying scene (with brief labels) is the sole evidence of an otherwise lost papyrus.

Within Smith's inner circle, this papyrus was probably conflated with P. Joseph Smith 2 as part of the apocryphal, and unpublished, "Joseph's record."[4] In describing this roll, Oliver Cowdery stated:

> The inner end of the same roll, (Joseph's record,) presents a representation of the judgment: At one view you behold the Savior seated upon his throne, crowned, and holding the sceptres of righteousness and power, before whom also, are assembled the twelve tribes of Israel, the nations, languages and tongues of the earth, the kingdoms of the world over which satan is represented as reigning.[5]

"Joseph's record" is otherwise associated with P. Joseph Smith 2, but any distinction between these papyri will not have been recognized by Smith and his followers, just as they included the hypocephalus of Sheshonq with the separate "Breathing Permit of Hôr" in the Book of Abraham.

The P. Joseph Smith 3 vignette preserves fourteen of the original forty-two judges in the upper register. As several of these judges are faint, they probably correspond to Cowdery's "twelve tribes." In the main scene, Osiris (Cowdery's Savior) holding scepters sits enthroned on a dais decorated with the hieroglyphs for "life" (ꜥnḫ) flanked by pairs of hieroglyphs indicating "dominion" (wꜣs). Before Osiris is the *wt*-symbol of embalming, a Nile lily blossom atop which stand the four sons of Horus (protectors of the internal organs) and below which are two plant-draped wine jars. To the right of the Nile lily are two human-headed birth-bricks, Meskhenet and Shai, representing the ordained fortune of the deceased.[6]

---

confirmed by Gee 2000a, pp. 10 and 18, *contra* his discussion 2005.

[4] See Baer 1968, p. 111, n. 5, with reference to *Joseph Smith's Egyptian Alphabet & Grammar,* pp. 1 ("writings of Joseph of Egypt") and 3 ("the book of Joseph" or "Joseph's record").

[5] Howard 1968, p. 89. The scene might also refer to a lost vignette from P. Joseph Smith 2. Satan is not capitalized in the original citation.

[6] In Nibley 1975, p. 227, these bricks are termed "an unusual symbol that designates the place as the Hall of the Two Maats." For a similar birth-brick, see the comparable vignette from the Papyrus of Ani, published in (among other places) Russmann 2001, p. 198.

Beyond the lily is the actual weighing of the heart of Nefer-ir-nebu by Horus and Anubis, while the Devouring Monster (Cowdery's satan) sits in frustration on the side, and Thoth records the favorable verdict. At the far right, Nefer-ir-nebu is conducted into the judgment hall by Maat and another goddess, probably a second figure of Maat.[7]

- **Label for Osiris, facing right:**
  ḏd-[mdw ỉ]n Wsỉr ḫnty ʾImnt.t (2) nṯr ꜥꜣ ḥ[qꜣ] ḏ.t
  Recitation by Osiris, foremost of the West, (2) the great god, ruler of eternity.

- **Label for Sons of Horus, facing left:**
  ḏd-mdw ỉn ʾIms[t] (2) Ḥpy (3) Dwꜣ-mw.t=f Qbḥ-sn.(w)=f
  Recitation by Imsety, Hapy, Duamutef, and Qebehsenuef.

- **Label for Thoth. facing left:**
  [ḏ]d-[md]w (2) ỉn [Ḏḥ]wty [nṯr] (3) ꜥꜣ nb (4) Ḫmnw sš Mꜣꜥ.t psḏ.t dỉ=f ḥb.w
  Recitation (2) by Thoth,[8] the (3) great [god], lord (4) of Hermopolis, scribe of Maat for the Ennead.[9] "May he give festivals."

- **Label for Horus at balance, facing left:**
  Ḥr sꜣ[10] ꜣs.t
  Horus, the son of Isis.

- **Label for Anubis at balance, facing left:**
  ʾIn[pw] ỉmy-wt
  Anubis, who is in the embalming bandages.

- **Label for Maat, facing right:**
  ḏd-mdw ỉn Mꜣꜥ.t sꜣ.t Rꜥ

[7] The name of the judgment hall itself is "The Hall of the Two Truths," reflecting the Egyptian preference for duality and probably corresponding to the dual nature of the tribunal, with deities of both Upper and Lower Egypt. For scenes of two Maat figures at the judgment, see the illustrations in Bleeker 1929, pp. 59, 61 (deceased between two Maat-figures as in P JS 3) and 76, and the general discussion in Seeber 1976, pp. 63–64 and 139–47.

[8] Only scant traces remain of the "Recitation by Thoth."

[9] Cf. Thoth's title in Spell 125 of the Papyrus of Ani: "Thoth who determines Truth (wp Mꜣꜥ.t) for the great Ennead."

[10] Reduced to a single stroke.

Recitation by Maat, daughter of Re.

- **Label for Nefer-ir-nebu, facing left:**
  ḏd-mdw ỉn Wsỉr ỉḥỉ.t n (2) ʾImn-Rʿ Nfr-ỉr.(t)-nbw.(t) mʿꜣ.(t)-ḫrw (3) ms [(n) …]n(?)[11] mꜣʿ.(t) ḫrw sp-2(?)
  Recitation by the Osiris, musician of (2) Amon-Re, Nefer-ir-nebu, the justified, (3) born [of … .] the justified!

- **Label beside Nefer-ir-nebu, facing left:**
  ỉy.(t) ẖr Mꜣʿ.t
  Coming bearing Truth.

[11] Traces include a bird (m?), a concluding horizontal stroke (n?) and a seated person determinative (whether male or female remains unclear as the upper half is lost).

PAPYRUS JOSEPH SMITH 4: BOOK OF THE DEAD OF AMENHOTEP

(from "Valuable Discovery")

The papyrus, now lost, is known only from Smith's nineteenth-century hand copy in "Valuable Discovery," pp. 2, 3, 6 and 7(?), and corresponds to Wilson's "Document G."[1] The chapters of the papyrus have not been identified or analyzed previously, although a portion of the text was used by Smith for his "translation" of the narrative of "Princess Katumin."[2] Smith's misinterpretation of the papyrus as the tale of a princess was at least partly inspired by his misidentification of male figures in the vignettes as women.[3] Wolfe and Singerman have suggested that the Amenhotep of this papyrus might be linked to a supposed "Princess Amenhotep," formerly among the mummies of the Niagara Falls Museum,[4] but the preserved female mummy is not an Amenhotep, and the Amenhotep of P JS 4 is male.

Chapter 18, 19 or 20(?). Preserved only in hand copy on "Valuable Discovery," p. 2, col. 1. The only certain passages refer to "his enemies,"

---

[1] Tanner 1966 (for "Valuable Discovery") and Wilson 1968, p. 68. Wilson's suggestion that the papyrus might include Facsimile 3 of the "Pearl of Great Price" (his "Document F") is incorrect, as that scene belongs to the "Breathing Permit of Hôr" (P. JS 1).

[2] See the following Book of the Dead Chapter 46 ("Valuable Discovery," p. 6). Wilson ignored "Valuable Discovery," p. 7 in his discussion of the Joseph Smith Papyri.

[3] See "Valuable Discovery," pp. 2 ("femaul" [*sic*]) and 6 ("woman").

[4] Wolfe and Singerman 2009, pp. 131 and 136, but cf. 129 (where the name of the "princess Amenhotep" is corrected to Iaw-tays-heref). For reasons explained in Wolfe and Singerman, the mummy may be one of those once owned by Smith, but the link to this papyrus is unlikely, and the museum's fanciful choice of the popular name "Amenhotep" is coincidence.

a phrase too common for specific identification of the spell. Smith noted that a vignette of two figures appeared above the spell.

(1/1) ... Wsỉr ỉmn-ḥtp mꜣʿ-ḫrw ms n (1/2) Nꜣy-Nbw[5] mꜣʿ-ḫrw r ḫfty.w=f ... tn (1/3) ḫnty(?) ... nty ʿḥꜣ(?)[6] ... (1/4) ... r(?) ḫfty.w=f m ... (1/5) ... m-sꜣ ... ḥwn(?)[7] ... (1/6) ḥr ỉr.t nn[8] ... (1/7) ... (1/8) ...

(1/1) ... the Osiris Amenhotep, the justified, born of (1/2) Nai-Nub, the justified, against his enemies ... you (plural) ... (1/3) foremost(?) ... who fights(?) ... (1/4) ... against(?) his enemies in ... (1/5) ... after ... youth ... (1/6) doing this ... (1/7) ... (1/8) ...

Chapter 45. Preserved only in hand copy on "Valuable Discovery," p. 2, col. 2. Smith noted that a vignette of two figures appeared above the spell, one male and the other supposedly female. The standard vignette, probably misunderstood by Smith, depicts Anubis with the deceased's mummy.

(2/1) rꜣ n tm ḥwꜣ.t ỉn[9] Wsỉr ỉmn-ḥtp (2/2) mꜣʿ-ḫrw ms n Nꜣy-Nbw mꜣʿ-ḫrw wrd (2/3) sp-[2] m Wsỉr wrd (2/4) ʿ.t m Wsỉr nn wrd=f nn ḥwꜣ=f (2/5) nn tꜣỉ=f nn bn=[f] ỉr=tn n Ws(2/6)ỉr ỉmn-ḥtp mꜣʿ-ḫrw ms n (2/7) Nꜣy-Nbw mꜣʿ-ḫrw Wsỉr ỉmn-ḥt(2/8)p[10] (mỉ) qd=[f] ntf Wsỉr ỉr rḫ (2/9) rꜣ pn nn ḥwꜣ=[f] m ẖr.t-nṯr

(2/1) Spell for not rotting. By the Osiris Amenhotep, (2/2) the justified, born of Nai-Nub, the justified.
"Does the weary (2/3) one weary, being Osiris? Is there wearying in (2/4) a member of Osiris? He will not weary. He will not rot. (2/5) He will not give off discharge. [He] will not be bloated. May you act for the (2/6) Osiris Amenhotep, the justified, born of (2/7) Nai-Nub,

[5] For the rare name, see Ranke 1935, p. 169, no 23.

[6] Or read ỉmn-ḥtp mꜣʿ-ḫrw ms n Nꜣy-Nbw ?

[7] The initial vertical stroke is unclear; read simply wn "to be" ?

[8] Or garbled hand copy from Chapter 18: ḥr ỉr.t ỉkb "in the act of mourning"? See Lepsius 1842, p. 13, line 11.

[9] The copy before "Osiris" is largely illegible, but can correspond to the expected title of the spell. For the parallel text, see Lepsius 1842, plate 20; and Naville 1886 (reprinted 1971), vol. 1, plate 45.

[10] The scribe has copied the name Amenhotep twice. Perhaps the second instance should be interpreted as "[son of] Amenhotep." The father of Amenhotep is not otherwise noted in the sections that I have deciphered.

the justified, the Osiris Amenhotep, (2/8) like(wise). He is Osiris."
As for the one who knows (2/9) this spell, [he] will not rot in the necropolis.

Chapter 46. Preserved only in hand copy on "Valuable Discovery," pp. 2, col. 2, and p. 6. Smith's note on p. 6 regarding the presence of "the figure of a woman" refers to the vignette of the *male* owner, Amenhotep, who would have appeared between the title (p. 2) and the body of the spell (p. 6).[11] The drawings actually copied on "Valuable Discovery," p. 6, are all out of place and derive from the vignettes of P. JS 1 (the winged figure—probably of Isis—above and to the right of the bier of Osiris and the falcon-headed canopic jar of Qebehsenuef, from below the bier) and from P. JS 2 (Chapter 74, the figure of Ta-sherit-Min standing with a staff before a serpent striding on two legs). Copies of Chapter 46 vary significantly as do the published translations.[12]

(2/10) rꜣ n tm sk wnn ꜥnḫ (2/11) m [ẖr.t]-nṯr
(6/1): ḏd[13] md.w ꞽn Wsꞽr ꜣImn-ḥtp mꜣꜥ-ḫrw ms n(?)
(6/2): Nꜣy-Nbw mꜣꜥ-ḫrw ꞽ ḥwn.w Šw[14]
(6/3): sḫm m (s)šd⸗f m ꜣḫ.w ꞽmy dwn m (< n) d(6/4)wn

(2/10) Spell for not perishing and for being alive in the necropolis.
(6/1) Recitation by the Osiris Amenhotep, the justified, born of (6/2) Nai-Nub, the justified.
"O youths of Shu, (6/3) who have power over his fillet among the blessed spirits, give a rising to the one who rises."

JOSEPH SMITH TRANSLATION

The body of Chapter 46 (cols. 6/1–4) was explicitly "translated" by Smith in two versions on pp. 4–5 of "Valuable Discovery." Specific hieratic signs are copied (some in mirror image) before English passages on p. 4, with a running "translation" (minus the hieratic) on p. 5, preceding the copied text of

[11] Smith misidentifies the figure as that of a woman.

[12] Note the variants in Allen 1974, p. 50; Allen 1960 p. 129; and Faulkner 1985, p. 64.

[13] Garbled copies of what must correspond to this word appear at the beginning of this line and twice more at the right of the page, above and below a drawing of the falcon-headed canopic jar of P. JS I. The same signs appear on "Valuable Discovery," p. 4, marking the beginning of the supposed narrative of a "Princess Katumin" (pp. 4–5).

[14] The final traces of the divine name may include a solar sign and a seated deity.

p. 6. On p. 4, Smith inserted just the initial hieratic signs of line 1 from p. 6, indicating the supposed correspondence between the Egyptian script and his English translation.[15] In the following transcription of Smith's notes, the hieratic source of the English is inserted in transliteration within parentheses (). Words subsequently deleted by Smith are placed in {}.

P. 4: (d̲d) Katumin, Princess, daughter of On-i-tas[16] {Pharaoh} King of Egypt, (mdw ỉn[17]) who began to[18] reign in the year of the world 2962.
(Wsỉr[19]) Katumin was born in the 30th year of the reign of her father, and died when she was 28 years old, which was the year 3020.

P. 5: A Translation of the next page
Katumin, Princess, daughter of On-i-tas King[20] of Egypt, who {reigned} began to reign in the year of the world, 2962. Katumin was born in the 30th year of the reign of her father, and deid[21] when she was 28 years old, which was the year[22] 3020.

Unidentified Chapters. Preserved only in "Valuable Discovery," p. 3. Only a few words are recognizable. A second spell may begin in line 5.

(1) [...] h̲r.t-[nt̲r ... ʾImn-ḥtp mȝʿ-]ḫrw ms n [Nȝy]-Nbw mȝʿ-ḫrw ... pr=k m ...
(2) ... Ddw Wsỉr ...

[15] Thus Smith's elaborate translation corresponds to only the first four words of 6/1: d̲d mdw ỉn Wsỉr "Recitation by the Osiris."

[16] Transcribed as "On-i-tos" in *Joseph Smith's Egyptian Alphabet & Grammar.* For the introduction of this figure into the lectures of Lucy Mack Smith, Joseph Smith's mother, when the mummies were displayed in her home, see Wolfe and Singerman 2009, pp. 117–18 and 120.

[17] The signs are copied in inverted order from the hieratic copy of p. 6.

[18] The words "began to" are inserted above the line.

[19] The partial writing of Osiris (throne and sun disk, minus the divine determinative) is copied backwards from the hieratic copy on p. 6.

[20] The word "King" is inserted above the line.

[21] So misspelled.

[22] The words "the year" are inserted above the line.

(3) … [Imn]-ḥtp mꜣʿ-ḫrw ms n Nꜣy-Nbw mꜣʿ-ḫrw …
(4) …
(5) … rꜣ n …
(6) … nb … ʾInp … md.w …
(7) …

(1) […] the necropolis [… Amenhotep, the justi]fied, born of [Nai-] Nub, the justified. … May you go forth from … (2) … Busiris. Osiris … (3) [Amen]hotep, the justified, born of Nai-Nub, the justified, … (4) … (5) … Spell for[23] … (6) … lord/all … Anubis … words … (7) …

Chapters 77–78(?). Preserved only in "Valuable Discovery," p. 7 (copied upside down). Only a few words are recognizable. If correctly deciphered from the nineteenth-century copy, the text preserves sections of chapters 77 and 78, as the latter portion of Chapter 77 contains mention of a "good falcon of gold" (bỉk nfr n nbw),[24] while 78 includes (in order) the phrases "disorder/go astray" (tḫtḫ),[25] "in the house of darkness" (m pr kkw),[26] "those in the underworld" (ỉmy.w dwꜣ.t),[27] and after a short section in the same line (perhaps lost at the time of the copy of P JS 4), "the Osiris" (Wsỉr) and personal name.[28]

(1) …
(2) bỉk(?) nfr n nbw(?) …
(3) … tḫtḫ(?) …
(4) … kkw(?) [29]
(5) …
(6) … ỉmy.w(?) dwꜣ.t … Wsỉr(?) ʾImn-ḥtp(?) …
(7) …

[23] Or "mouth of …"

[24] See Lepsius 1842, plate 28, line 3, and Allen 1960, p. 150 and plate 25, lines 19–20.

[25] Ibid., plate 28, line 1.

[26] Ibid., plate 28, line 3.

[27] Ibid., plate 28, line 6.

[28] Ibid., plate 28, line 6. The copyist of the Turin papyrus has left blank the space for the following personal name.

[29] The line ends with the determinative of a star suspended from heaven, probably from kkw "darkness" or grḥ "night."

(1) …
(2) … good falcon(?) of gold(?) …
(3) … disorder(?) …
(4) … darkness(?)
(5) …
(6) … those who are in the underworld … the Osiris(?) Amenhotep(?) …
(7) …

HYPOCEPHALUS OF SHESHONQ

("Valuable Discovery," p. 13, reworked as Book of Abraham Facsimile 2)

Designated by Wilson as Fragment E,[1] the "hypocephalus" derives its modern name from a Greek phrase meaning "under the head."[2] Shaped like the solar disk, it is an amulet placed beneath the head to restore bodily warmth and corresponds to the document noted in Book of the Dead Chapter 162 and variants, which date from Dynasty 21 to the Ptolemaic period.[3] The texts are typically written in cursive hieroglyphs, not true hieratic, and read from right to left. The Smith hypocephalus was prepared for an individual named Sheshonq.[4] Now lost, the papyrus disk was

[1] See Wilson 1968, p. 68. Illustrations of Facsimile 2 are common, including: Nibley 1975, pp. 136 and 138; and Gee, Rhodes and Nibley 2005, pp. 206, 223 and 227. It is telling that the editors of the 2005 edition (with "numerous changes" inserted into Nibley's manuscript; see p. xx) chose to add an illustration of Facsimile 2, known to be inaccurate, rather than the undoctored hand copy in "Valuable Discovery," p. 13 (Tanner 1966). Such failure to adhere to "meticulous detail in epigraphic and facsimile work" is in Gee's words "both disgraceful and inexcusable" (Gee 1996, at n. 20, complaining of John A. Larson's reprinting of inferior *LDS-published* woodcuts *in an historical context!*). See also n. 7, below.

[2] The modern name was given by Champollion; see Varga 1961, p. 235. Rare examples are inscribed on the head of the mummy mask itself; see Gestermann 2001 (p. 110 for the three known examples).

[3] The title of the spell reads: "Spell for providing heat under the head of the blessed one, NN." Directions indicate that spell 162 is "to be said over a figure of the heavenly cow made of fine gold and placed at the throat of the corpse, or put into writing on a new sheet of papyrus placed under his/her head. Much heat will envelop her/him like one who is on earth (= "alive")." See Allen 1974, pp. 157–58.

[4] A male name of Libyan origin most famous in the form Shishak, used in the Bible for the first king of Dynasty 22. The name remained popular in Egypt into

already damaged when first copied by Smith in "Valuable Discovery," and missing sections were improperly "restored" for the Book of Abraham, Facsimile 2.[5]

For the artificial restorations published first in *Times and Seasons* 3 (March 13, 1842) and then in the Book of Abraham, see the study by Grant S. Heward and Jerald Tanner 1968, pp. 96–98. Smith's "Fig. 3" was a gap, restored by him by recopying the vignette of Chapter 101 from the Book of the Dead of Ta-sherit-Min, found on P. Smith 2 (Fragment IV, bottom right, as already noted by Heward and Tanner). Similarly, sections of Smith's figures 1, 12–15, 18 and 22–23 were improved for publication. See the remarks of the LDS author Richley Crapo: "It would seem indisputable that the Facsimile Number 2 is indeed a copy of a damaged hypocephalus and has been 'restored' from other of the Joseph Smith Papyri. This is another etically discovered fact which must be dealt with by L.D.S. scholars in arriving at a satisfactory analysis of the papyri and their significance for L.D.S. scriptures and doctrines."[6] In addition, official Mormon reproductions have varied in minor aspects.[7] For the Smith hypocephalus, see the discussion by Edith Varga 1998b, pp. 31–33 and fig. 2 (with conflicting history of the Smith materials), and the student publication by G. E. Freeman 1974, pp. 4–9.

Since a version of the Hypocephalus of Sheshonq was published as a section *from the Book of Abraham itself,* this document joins the Breathing Permit of Hôr (Papyrus Joseph Smith 1) in having elicited more discussions and translations than the lesser-known Smith Papyri 2–4. In addition to Smith's own discussion, some tentative attempts at translation appear in the work by Freeman. Michael D. Rhodes has offered a partial translation on three occasions and identifications have been proposed for individual figures.[8] Again for the sake of historical comparison, the

---

the Ptolemaic period.

[5] Cf. the false "improvement" of the vignette of P. Smith 1 (Facsimile 1).

[6] See Crapo 1970, pp. 27–29 and 35, quote on p. 29. In this paper, Crapo defines "etic" approaches as those employing classifications (appropriate to the natural and physical sciences and Egyptology), "validated by the 'natural' structure of the phenomena under study" (p. 26).

[7] See Gee 2000a, p. 7.

[8] See Freeman 1974, p. 6, and Rhodes 1977, 1994 and 1997. A few translations of labels from other hypocephali appear in Gee 2001, pp. 332–34.

analysis and translation offered here are followed by the translations of Rhodes, Freeman and Smith.

In the Book of Abraham, Smith provided an "explanation" for 21 "figures" (a term he used haphazardly to include both images and text passages). Although it could be argued that his explanations were not intended as "translations," Smith did specifically label them as such in his concluding remarks in the explanation of Facsimile 2: "The above *translation* is given as far as we have any right to give at the present time" (emphasis added). Since Smith provided a common explanation for nos. 12 through 21, that explanation is repeated for each of these sections, which are not adjacent groupings below. This minor repetition has seemed preferable to continued cross-references for the reader interested in specific sections. As will be seen, Smith's numbering indicates that he could not recognize the usual order of the texts (right to left), nor could he distinguish texts written upside down (Figs. 16–17) and oriented to the inverted scene below them (Figs. 5–7). Since Facsimile 2 contains distortions clearly introduced by Smith, who further added revelatory "translation" and "explanation" for the artificial insertions, apologists are caught between reproducing the false but "traditional" image or defending its flawed content.[9] Given the obvious discrepancy revealed between the Smith and modern interpretations, Rhodes' conclusion is startling from any scholarly perspective: "It should come as no surprise to members of the Church that as we gain more understanding of Egyptian matters, we find an increasing number of Joseph Smith's explanations of Facsimile 2 are in accord with that increased understanding."[10]

For a comprehensive study of the historical development of hypocephali, see Edith Varga 1998a.[11] Varga includes the Sheshonk example as figure 2,

---

[9] Note that Gee, ibid., p. 327, n. 18, admits that the Smith Facsimile 2 is "inaccurate" (and thus doctored as shown by Heward and Tanner 1968). Gee's complaint that "the more inaccurate versions are generally reproduced" applies most significantly to editions of the Book of Abraham, rather than to scholarly reproductions of that published version by Varga or John A. Larson (cited in Gee's note). Strikingly, the incorrect version was reproduced in the most recent translation by Rhodes (1997, expressly assisted by Gee) and see also note 1, above, for the Gee, Rhodes and Nibley reuse of the same reworked image in 2005. In each of his translations, Rhodes clearly adopts the conclusions of Heward and Tanner but fails to acknowledge their work (1997, p. 2 = 1994, p. 2, 1977, pp. 3–4).

[10] Rhodes 1994, p. 1 = 1997, p. 1.

[11] Comments on typology appear in Gee 2001, pp. 325–34.

pairing it with a comparable example in the Rijksmuseum van Oudheden, Leiden (AMS 62 = fig. 1).

The hypocephalus preserves sections of three registers of vignettes, accompanied or separated by texts. The orientation of the text and images is divided into two opposite directions. The order of the individual sections is disputed,[12] but the following discussion presents the sections from the top downward. The top of hypocephali is clearly indicated by the text of the outer rim, which regularly begins its invocation above the center of the first register, with the opposite position having only the continuation of phrases. Since the original hypocephalus is lost and the engraving of texts poorly done, the translation is necessarily problematic in places, as is indicated by the notes.

I. Outer rim inscription (Smith's "Fig. 18"). Lost sections were wrongly restored with hieratic passages recopied (upside down!) from the Breathing Permit of Hôr (P. Smith 1).[13]

> ỉnk[14] ḏbꜣ.ty m Ḥw.t Bn[b]n m ʾIwnw q(ꜣ) sp-2 [ꜣḫ][15] sp-2 kꜣ nk ỉw.ty sn-nw=f nṯr pwy ꜥꜣ m Ḥw.t Bnbn m ʾIwnw [... my n Wsỉr Ššnq mꜣꜥ-ḫrw sꜣ[16] ...][17] ntf nṯr pf ꜥꜣ m Ḥw.t Sr

[12] See Gee, ibid., p. 331.

[13] See Heward and Tanner 1968, pp. 96–97.

[14] Other texts begin the invocation with the vocative ỉ "O"; see Varga 1961, p. 244 and 1998b, p. 30. Textual variants are common in surviving hypocephali and are not listed exhaustively below.

[15] Freeman read "very splendid," but all traces of the word are missing in Smith's "Valuable Discovery" and a tear is clearly indicated. The signs now placed in the "restored" version are a garbled repeat of wnn=k from Smith's "Fig. 21." The restoration of ꜣḫ "effective" is based on parallels, cf. Varga 1961, p. 244, fig. 5; and Haslauer 2001, pp. 173–74.

[16] For a restoration based on parallels, see Varga 1961, p. 244, fig. 5 (for my n Wsỉr NN) and Haslauer 2001, pp. 173–74 and 176–77 (for nts/ntf nṯr pf ꜥꜣ m Ḥw.t Sr).

[17] The later hand copy has inserted two sections from The Breathing Permit of Hôr, col. II/3: ꜥ.wy=f 2 r ḥꜣ.ty=f ỉw=w qr (extracted from "his two arms are at his heart, while there will be wra[pped]") and II/2: ḫy-by.t (extracted from the mother's name Taikhibit). The hieratic sections are upside down with respect to the cursive hieroglyphs of the hypocephalus and were inserted left to right when the actual text runs right to left. The copy of ꜥ.wy=f 2 r again indicates no correction from a supposed original ꜥ.wy=f ḥr; see the discussion of P. JS 1, col. II/3, n. 102, above.

"I am the punisher[18] in the Mansion of the Benben[19] in Heliopolis, greatly exalted, greatly [effective], the copulating bull who has no equal,[20] this great god in the Mansion of the Benben in Heliopolis, [... Come to the Osiris Sheshonq, the justified, son of ...]. He is that great god in the House of the Noble."[21]

Rhodes 1997, p. 5 = 1994, p. 4:

"I am the Provider in the Sun Temple in Heliopolis. [I am] most exalted and very glorious. [I am] a virile bull without equal. [I am] that[22] Mighty God in the Sun Temple in Heliopolis. <May the Osiris Shishaq live forever> with that Mighty God in Heliopolis.[23]

Rhodes 1977, p. 4:

"I am Djabty in the House of the Benben in Heliopolis, so exalted and glorious. [I am] a copulating bull without equal. [I am] that Mighty God in the House of the Benben in Heliopolis ... that Mighty God."

Freeman 1974, p. 6:

"I am the robing-room in the Sun-Temple in Heliopolis, very joyful, very splendid; the virile bull who has no equal; the great ... in the Sun-Temple in Heliopolis; ... that great god."

Smith's Explanation/Translation:

Figures 12, 13, 14, 15, 16, 17, 18, 19, 20, and 21 will be given in the own due time of the Lord.

II. In the upper field, a two-headed deity strides with the standard of the god Wepwawet (Smith's "Fig. 2"). The god wears a crown of double-plumes

[18] For the term, see Penelope Wilson 1997, p. 1232. Varga and Haslauer translated "adorned one"; see Haslauer 2001, p. 174. Freeman's translation "I am the robing-room" (p. 6) makes little sense.

[19] The primordial solar mound.

[20] Other variants have nṯr wꜥ ỉw.ty sn-nw≈f "the unique god who has no equal." See Haslauer 2001, pp. 173–74.

[21] A shrine at Heliopolis. Haslauer 2001, p. 174, read ḥw.t wr.

[22] Rhodes often confused the demonstratives "this" and "that," cf. section II.

[23] Rhodes wrongly read the conclusion [ḥ]nꜥ nṯr pf ꜥꜣ m ꜣIwnw.

and sun-disk over horizontal horns, and jackal heads protrude from both of his shoulders. No images to the right of this figure were present in the "Valuable Discovery" hand copy, and the altar of Facsimile 2 is a fabrication by Smith.[24] A vertical label for the deity appears to the left of the figure. Smith's interpretation of the deity as being "called by the Egyptians Oliblish" is nonsense, and the discussion of Kolob here and in other explanations links the hypocephalus to the "translated" text of the Book of Abraham chapter 3.

> rn n nṯr pf ꜥꜣ [...]
> "The name of that great god [...]."
>
> *Rhodes 1997, p. 6 = 1994, p. 4 = 1977, p. 4:*
> "The name of this Mighty God."
>
> *Freeman 1974, p. 6:*
> "the name of that god is ..."
>
> *Smith's Explanation/Translation:*
> Fig. 2. Stands next to Kolob, called by the Egyptians Oliblish, which is the next grand governing creation near to the celestial or the place where God resides; holding the key of power also, pertaining to other planets; as revealed from God to Abraham, as he offered sacrifice upon an altar, which he had built unto the Lord.

III. This lost section (Smith's fig. 3) often contains two registers of barques, with Isis and Nephthys in a boat flanking the *ba*-spirit of Osiris on a shrine in the upper field, and a solar barque with Re and the scarab Khepri below.[25] As noted above, nothing survived of the original hypocephalus at this location, and Smith's irrelevant fig. 3 was adapted from P. Smith Fragment IV. Since the entirety of Smith's scene "Fig. 3" was created by him or his engraver for the Book of Abraham, Nibley was either

[24] See Gestermann 2001, p. 104 (fig. 1), where the two-headed deity carries a Wepwawet staff as in the Sheshonq example and cf. Charron 2002, p. 110, number 47, where the god has four heads and carries a *was*-scepter. Nothing is placed beside the god in either example.

[25] Cf. Varga 1961, pp. 238, 240 and 244; idem 1998, p. 30; and Haslauer 2001, pp. 173 and 176. The passengers differ in the two boats found in Gestermann 2001, p. 104 (fig. 1).

ignorant of the extent of this falsification—or chose to ignore it years after it had been proved—when he defended the Facsimile 2 image because it had an inscription not found with the original scene in P. Smith Fragment IV.[26] The single, illegible line in fig. 3 is necessarily a further insert from elsewhere;[27] see the area of damage in "Valuable Discovery," p. 13. Though irrelevant to the original hypocephalus, Smith's fig. 3 is critical for his interpretation of the document regarding priesthood and "key words." Rhodes read the intrusive text[28] as if it were properly present:

> *Rhodes 1997, p. 6 = 1994, p. 5:*
> "Divine ship."
>
> *Smith's Explanation/Translation:*
> Fig. 3. Is made to represent God, sitting upon his throne, clothed with power and authority; with a crown of eternal light upon his head; representing also the grand Key-words of the Holy Priesthood, as revealed to Adam in the Garden of Eden, as also to Seth, Noah, Melchizedek, Abraham, and all to whom the Priesthood was revealed.

IV. Label of 3 vertical columns to the left of the deity in the upper register (Smith's Figs. 21, 20 and 19, numbered by him in reverse order, wrongly assuming a reading order of left to right). The text copy in "Valuable Discovery" differs from the published woodcut, and the signs for line 2 (end) and 3 are uncertain.

> (1) ỉw wnn≈k[29] (2) m nṯr ỉwty(?) (3) ḫsf(?) ḏ.t(?)

[26] Nibley 1975, p. 136; repeated in Gee, Rhodes and Nibley 2005, p. 223. Note that Nibley's 1968 article "Phase One" immediately follows that of Heward and Tanner, but he responded to few of their objections and not this one (p. 103).

[27] The copy (at the shoulder of Re) seems to begin with ỉ; cf. Smith's rendering of the final reed-sign of pwy in "Valuable Discovery," p. 12, line 8 (end). If so, the borrowed line of fig. 3 may be a partial copy of ỉ Wsỉr "O Osiris," found (even less clearly) in "Valuable Discovery," p. 12, line 1. Alternatively, the line may be a garbling of the name Ns-Ḫnsw, mother of Ta-sherit-Min in P. Smith 2; cf. an inverted parallel(?) in section VIII = Smith's fig. 12. Above this intrusive line is the Wedjat-Eye repeated (out of alignment) from P. Smith Fragment IV (Book of the Dead Chapter 101).

[28] Rhodes read dp.t-nṯr.

[29] The earlier hand copy strongly resembles wnn≈k here, but variant hypocephali have ỉw n≈k b3≈k m b3 8 "You have your *ba*-spirit as 8 *ba*-spirits"; see Haslauer 2001, p. 175,

"You are (2) even as the god who is not(?) (3) repelled(?) forever(?)."

Rhodes 1997, p. 5 = 1994, p. 5:
"You shall ever be as that God, the Busirian."[30]

Rhodes 1977, p. 4:
"You shall be as that God, the Busirian."

Smith's Explanation/Translation:
Figures 12, 13, 14, 15, 16, 17, 18, 19, 20, and 21 will be given in the own due time of the Lord.

V. Smith's "Fig. 4" is a standard image of the mummiform god Sokar in his barque and here bears no inscription. Other copies add variants of the epithet bꜣ bꜣ.w bꜣ bꜣ.w bꜣ.w nn thꜣ "*ba*-spirit of *ba*-spirits, *ba*-spirit of *ba*-spirits, powerful manifestation without injury."[31] Nibley sought to defend Smith's "explanation" of this figure by reference to the solar boat (not the depicted Sokar barque) as being "a ship of 1000 cubits" and thus "a numeral figure, in Egyptian signifying one thousand."[32] Neither barque, however, is used in Egyptian texts as a "numeral figure," and the more common designation of the solar boat is in fact "the barque of millions"—not 1,000.[33] As elsewhere, Nibley did not evaluate Smith's statements objectively, but sought out any possible defense, no matter how farfetched.

Smith's Explanation/Translation:
Fig. 4. Answers to the Hebrew word Raukeeyang, signifying expanse, or the firmament of the heavens; also a numerical figure,

---

n. 11. A less likely interpretation of the Smith hypocephalus requires emendation: ꞽw bꜣ⸗k {n}n⸗k "You have your *ba*-spirit…." or ꞽw wn n⸗k [bꜣ⸗k], with the same meaning.

[30] Rhodes read ꞽw wnn⸗k m nṯr pf ḏd.wy

[31] So on the Meux hypocephalus illustrated in Freeman 1974, plate 5. Other variants are noted by Gee 2001, p. 332, but these common epithets (also found in the Greek and Demotic magical papyri as "Bibao" or "Bibiou") need not invalidate the identification of the falcon as Sokar. For the magical name, see Preisendanz 1941, pp. 218 and 251; and Griffith and Thompson 1904, pp. 54–55 (col. 6/26).

[32] Nibley 1975, p. 138; Gee, Rhodes and Nibley 2005, p. 227.

[33] Erman and Grapow 1957, vol. III, p. 153/15: wꞽꜣ n ḥḥ.w.

in Egyptian signifying one thousand; answering to the time of Oliblish, which is equal with Kolob in its revolution and in its measuring of time.

VI. In the central field, a seated figure of Re-Atum (originally with four ram heads and complex crown and scepters)[34] is worshipped by two apes crowned by lunar disks (Smith's Figs. 1, 22 and 23). A snake appears to the left of Re-Atum, and a slight trace in the upper left may be the remains of the standard legend: [dwꜣ nṯr] p[n]"[Worshipping] th[is god.]" The earlier copy in "Valuable Discovery," p. 13, is damaged at this location, and Smith simply copied the heads and shoulders (with jackal extensions) of the double-headed god in the upper register (his fig. 2). In addition, garbled traces of rn n nṯr pf ꜥꜣ ("the name of that great god") were wrongly duplicated between figs. 1 and 22 of the revised Facsimile 2 published in the Book of Abraham. The central figure is not Kolob in Egyptian terms, nor is he the "first creation, nearest to the celestial, or residence of God." Rather, the image is the creator god himself, not simply a figure *near god*. The equation of a day to a cubit is specious, and the Egyptian terms for "earth" do not include the barbaric Jah-oh-eh.[35] Smith discussed Figures 22 and 23 within the explanation of Figure 5: "Kli-flos-is-es, or Hah-ko-kau-beam, the stars represented by numbers 22 and 23, receiving light from the revolutions of Kolob." As elsewhere, these outlandish names are not Egyptian.

Smith's Explanation/Translation:

Fig. 1. Kolob, signifying the first creation, nearest to the celestial, or the residence of God. First in government, the last pertaining to the measurement of time. The measurement according to celestial time, which celestial time signifies one day to a cubit. One day in Kolob is equal to a thousand years according to the measurement of this

[34] Cf. Haslauer 2001, pp. 173–74, and Gestermann 2001, p. 104 (fig. 1).

[35] Apologists Michael Rhodes and John Gee have sought to defend Smith's explanation of "Jah-oh-eh" as "O the earth" (ỉ ꜣḥ.t), although this is impossible both by phonetics (with three hs) and sense (ꜣḥ.t "arable field" is not used to indicate the whole earth), *contra* Gee 1992, p. 114, n. 58; and Rhodes 1997, p. 8. Smith vacillated slightly on this interpretation, as noted in Rhodes 1997, p. 8. His statement in Facsimile 2 that the Egyptians *name* the earth Jah-oh-eh would preclude the vocative "O" that he had once suggested in *Times and Seasons* 4 (13 November 1843), p. 373. In any case, the proposed Egyptian etymology is impossible.

earth, which is called by the Egyptians Jah-oh-eh.

VII. Text of four horizontal columns (Smith's Figs. 11, 10, 9 and 8, again numbered by him in reverse order). Contrary to Smith's assertion, the writings can now be revealed, and the phrase "cause the *ba*-spirit of the Osiris Sheshonq to live" (fig. 8) is hardly a secret of "the Holy Temple of God."

(1) ỉ nṯr šps m sp (2) tpy nṯr ꜥꜣ nb p.t tꜣ (3) dwꜣ.t mw [ḏw.w][36] (4) sꜥnḫ[37] bꜣ (n) Wsỉr Ššnq[38]

(1) "O noble god from the beginning of time,[39] (2) great god, lord of heaven, earth, (3) underworld, waters [and mountains,] (4) cause the *ba*-spirit of the Osiris Sheshonq to live."

Rhodes 1997, p. 5 = 1994, p. 5:
"O God of the Sleeping Ones[40] from the time of the creation. O Mighty God, Lord of heaven and earth, of the hereafter, and of his great[41] waters, may the soul of the Osiris Shishaq be granted life.[42]"

Rhodes 1977, p. 4:
"O God of the Sleeping Ones from the time of the Creation. O Mighty God, Lord of Heaven and Earth, the Netherworld and his Great Waters, grant that the soul of Osiris Sheshonk, may live."

---

[36] Again, garbled traces of [p]f ꜥꜣ from register 1 have been recopied to fill the end of Smith's section 9 (far left), shown empty in "Valuable Discovery," p. 13. For the standard restoration, see Erman and Grapow 1957, vol. V, p. 415/10; and the example in Daressy 1903, p. 55.

[37] The badly copied "s" of sꜥnḫ may be my "give": "give life (to) the *ba*-spirit."

[38] The personal name may be spelled either with or without an "n" (whence the spellings Sheshonq vs. Shishaq), but the earlier "Valuable Discovery" copy retains clear traces of the n before the final q and seated man determinative.

[39] Literally, "first occasion."

[40] Rhodes wrongly read sḏr.w, confusing Gardiner Sign-List A55 with the lower portion of Sign-List A 50.

[41] Rhodes wrongly read mw=f ꜥꜣ.

[42] Rhodes read tỉ-ꜥnḫ, which is possible, but does not fit the copy.

Smith's Explanations/Translations:
Fig. 8. Contains writings that cannot be revealed unto the world; but is to be had in the Holy Temple of God.
Fig. 9. Ought not to be revealed at the present time.
Fig. 10. Also.
Fig. 11. Also. If the world can find out these numbers, so let it be. Amen.

VIII. Text of four horizontal columns (Smith's Figs. 12, 13, 14 and 15). The beginning of each line is lost and has been restored wrongly in later editions by the insertion of hieratic text from the Breathing Permit of Hôr and the Book of the Dead of Ta-sherit-Min, copied upside down and backwards to the direction of the hypocephalus text.[43] The traces are too inexact for secure translation, and the following bits are only suggestions.

(1) [...] y n (2) [...] n rd.wy ... (3) [...] Rᶜ ỉ (4) [...].w=f
(1) ... (2) [...] on the feet ... (3) [...] Re. O (4) [...] his (divine) [words(?)].[44]

Smith's Explanation/Translation:
Figures 12, 13, 14, 15, 16, 17, 18, 19, 20, and 21 will be given in the own due time of the Lord.

IX. A vignette of deities (Smith's Figs. 5, 6 and 7) drawn inversely to the first two registers. The text of Book of the Dead 162 stipulates that images in this register are the most significant. Hathor as the heavenly cow[45] strides in the center, followed by a goddess whose head is a disk with the

---

[43] The breaks and remaining text are clear in "Valuable Discovery," p. 13; see Heward and Tanner 1968, pp. 96–97. The inserted text from The Breathing Permit of Hôr, col. II/4 reads: (Smith fig. 15) šᶜy.t (Smith fig. 14) snsn (Smith fig. 13) ỉr n nty "Breathing Document, being what." The inserted text in Smith fig. 12 is not identified by Heward and Tanner, but appears to be an incomplete writing of Ta-sherit-Min's mother's name: [Ns]-Ḫn[s]w. For a further possible garbling of this name in the "restored" hypocephalus, see section III = Smith's fig. 3 (text in inverted, i.e. correct, direction).

[44] The signs indicate a plural number of entities determined by a man-with-hand-to-mouth and the sign for god.

[45] The cow is labeled ỉh.t wr.(t) ms(.t) Rᶜ "the great cow who gave birth to Re" in Gestermann 2001, p. 104 (fig. 1).

Wedjat-Eye and who extends a water lily.[46] Before the Hathor cow stand the mummiform four sons of Horus and a trigram for the sun god in his three manifestations: srp.t mȝỉ sr "Lily, Lion, Ram."[47] Behind (and facing away from) Hathor and the goddess appears the enthroned and ithyphallic Min-Amon, in half human and half bird form, raising his arm with a flabellum. The ithyphallic serpent deity Nehebkau stands before Min-Amon, offering the Wedjat-Eye.[48] This register of figures is closely paralleled by examples in Brussels, London and Leiden.[49]

Smith described Hathor (fig. 5) as a planet supposedly named in Egyptian "Enish-go-on-dosh," yet another pseudo-Egyptian phrase of gibberish. In keeping with Smith's interpretation of the hypocephalus as an astronomical document, he explains the four sons of Horus (fig. 6) as simply "the earth in its four quarters." While any group of four can have directional relevance, that is hardly the pivotal significance of these protectors of the embalmed viscera (lungs, liver, stomach and intestines). Smith's statement that Amon (fig. 7) is "God sitting upon his throne" was an easy guess,[50] but the deity is not revealing "Key-words of the Priesthood," and neither he nor Nehebkau is a dove.[51]

Smith's Explanations/Translations:

Fig. 5. Is called in Egyptian Enish-go-on-dosh; this is one of the governing planets also, and is said by the Egyptians to be the Sun, and to borrow its light from Kolob through the medium of Kae-e-vanrash, which is the grand Key, or, in other words, the governing power, which governs other fixed planets or stars, as also Floeese or the Moon, the Earth and the Sun in their annual revolutions. This planet receives its power through the medium of Kli-flos-is-es, or Hah-ko-kau-beam, the stars represented by numbers 22 and 23, receiving light from the revolutions of Kolob.

---

[46] Conventionally (but wrongly) called a lotus.

[47] See Ryhiner 1977, pp. 125–37.

[48] Cf. Haslauer 2001, pp. 176 and 178.

[49] Cf. Brussels No. 6319, formerly in the collection of Lady Meux, in Varga 1961, pp. 237–38, and Freeman 1974, plate 5 (noted on p. 9, n. 22); BM 8445c, in Varga 1961, pp. 244 and 246; and Leiden No. AMS 62, in Varga 1998, p. 30.

[50] Also used in the explanation of the intrusive "Fig. 3."

[51] Clear images of the deities appear in the citations in n. 49, above.

Fig. 6. Represents the earth in its four quarters.
Fig. 7. Represents God sitting upon his throne, revealing through the heavens the grand Key-words of the Priesthood; as, also, the sign of the Holy Ghost unto Abraham, in the form of a dove.

X. Text of two horizontal columns oriented inversely to the first two registers (Smith's Figs. 17 and 16, numbered by him in reverse order as he could not recognize that the script was upside down).

(1) ḥꜣ(?)[52] th ḥꜣ nn th tw (2) nn th.tw bꜣ pn ḥnꜥ nb=f m dwꜣ.t ḏ.t
"Back, injury, back[53]! There is none who attacks[54] you. (2) This *ba*-spirit and his lord will not be attacked in the underworld forever."

Rhodes 1997, p. 5 = 1994, p. 5:
"May this tomb never be desecrated,[55] and may this soul and its lord never be desecrated in the hereafter."

Rhodes 1977, p. 4:
"May this tomb never be desecrated, and may this soul and its possessor never be desecrated in the Netherworld."

---

[52] The hand copy in "Valuable Discovery" copies nn (crossed out and with otiose "t" and house determinative) in what appears to be a damaged area. The nn may have been restored by Smith on the basis of the line below. Later editions place the sign ḥꜣ "back (of the head)" at the beginning of the passage, moving it from its earlier position below the center of line 1. This translation restores the initial ḥꜣ, following the preserved signs, and also maintains the second instance of the word in the middle of the line. Other hypocephali combine ḥꜣ and th in varying ways in this position; see Varga 1961, p. 244, fig. 5: ḥꜣ th n ỉtrw "Back, injury of the river …"; and Daressy 1903, p. 55: ḥꜣ th.t n.t nṯr.w nb.w "Back, injury of all the gods … !" The translation of ḥꜣ as "Back!" (Erman and Grapow 1957, vol. III, pp. 8–10) seems preferable to "grave" or "portico" (Erman and Grapow 1957, vol. III, pp. 12 and 16). The word choice puns upon the position of the hypocehpalus "back of the head." Cf. also Charron 2002, p. 110, no 47: ḥꜣ=k ḫfty{.w} "Back, you, enemy!"

[53] As explained in the previous note, the initial sign of ḥꜣ "back (of the head)" appears below the line here in "Valuable Discovery," while the determinative and an otiose "t" are above it.

[54] The term can also mean "lead/go astray," which is equally possible in this context. For th tw as older thỉ ṯw, see Erman and Grapow 1957, vol. V, p. 320.

[55] Rhodes (1997 and 1994, p. 5, n. 23) disregarded parallels as "garbled" and emended the text to nn th.tw ḥꜣ.t tn. For the initial nn in "Valuable Discovery," see n. 52, above.

Freeman 1974, p. 6:
"the cavern of the passage of the waters."[56]

Smith's Explanation/Translation:
Figures 12, 13, 14, 15, 16, 17, 18, 19, 20, and 21 will be given in the own due time of the Lord.

[56] Freeman's translation implies tpḥ.t snỉ mw or similar, but the traces do not suit this interpretation.

BIBLIOGRAPHY

Adams, Henry

1952 "Charles Francis Adams Visits the Mormons in 1844," *Proceedings of the Massachusetts Historical Society* 68, pp. 267–300.

Allen, T. G.

1960 *The Egyptian Book of the Dead Documents in the Oriental Institute Museum at The University of Chicago,* OIP 82, Chicago: The University of Chicago.

1974 *The Book of the Dead or Going Forth by Day,* SAOC 37, Chicago: The University of Chicago.

Anderson, Devery S., and Gary James Bergera, eds.

2005 *The Nauvoo Endowment Companies, 1845–1846: A Documentary History,* Salt Lake City: Signature Books.

Anderson, Lavina Fielding, ed.

2001 *Lucy's Book: A Critical Edition of Lucy Mack Smith's Family Memoir,* Salt Lake City: Signature Books.

Ashment, Edward H.

1979 "The Facsimiles of the Book of Abraham: A Reappraisal," *Sunstone* 4 (December), pp. 33–48.

2000 "Joseph Smith's Identification of 'Abraham' in Papyrus JS 1, the 'Breathing Permit of Hôr'," *Dialogue: A Journal of Mormon Thought* 33/4 (Winter), pp. 121–26.

2001 "Abraham in the Breathing Permit of Hôr (pJS1)," *Mormon Scripture Studies: An E-Journal of Critical Thought:* http://mormonscripturestudies.com/.

Aufrère, Sydney H.

2000 *Le propylône d'Amon-Rê-Montou à Karnak-Nord,* Mémoires publiés par les Membres de l'Institut Français d'Archéologie Orientale du Caire 117, Cairo: Institut Français d'Archéologie Orientale.

Baer, Klaus

1968 "The Breathing Permit of Hôr. A Translation of the Apparent Source of the Book of Abraham," *Dialogue: A Journal of Mormon Thought* 3/3 (Autumn), pp. 109–34.

Barney, Kevin L.

2005 "The Facsimiles and Semitic Adaptation of Existing Sources," in John Gee and Brian M. Hauglid, eds., *Astronomy, Papyrus, and Covenant,* Provo: The Foundation for Ancient Research and Mormon Studies (FARMS), pp. 107–30.

Barney, Ronald O.

2005 *The Mormon Vanguard Brigade of 1847: Norton Jacob's Record,* Logan, UT: Utah State University Press.

Bell, Lanny

2008 "The Ancient Egyptian 'Books of Breathing,' the Mormon 'Book of Abraham,' and the Development of Egyptology in America," in Stephen P. Thompson and Peter Der Manuelian, eds., *Egypt and Beyond: Essays Presented to Leonard H. Lesko upon His Retirement from the Wilbour Chair of Egyptology at Brown University, June 2005,* Providence: Brown University, pp. 21–39.

Bergera, Gary James, ed.,

1990 *Line upon Line: Essays on Mormon Doctrine,* Salt Lake City: Signature Books.

Bleeker, Claas J.

1929 *De beteeken van de Egyptische Godin Ma-a-at,* Leiden: Ijdo.

Bonechi, Marco.

1993 *I nomi geografici dei testi di Ebla,* Repertoire Géographique des Textes Cunéiformes 12/1, Wiesbaden: Ludwig Reichert Verlag.

Bonnet, Hans

1952 *Reallexikon der ägyptischen Religionsgeschichte,* Berlin: Walter de Gruyter.

Brodie, Fawn M.

1945 *No Man Knows My History: The Life of Joseph Smith,* New York: Alfred A. Knopf [second edition 1971].

Brovarski, Edward

1984a "Sobek," in W. Helck and E. Otto, eds., *Lexikon der Ägyptologie,* Wiesbaden: Otto Harrassowitz, vol. V, cols. 995–1031.

1984b "Sokar," in W. Helck and E. Otto, eds., *Lexikon der Ägyptologie,* Wiesbaden: Otto Harrassowitz, vol. V, cols. 1055–74.

Brunner-Traut, Emma, and Hellmut Brunner

1981 *Die Ägyptische Sammlung der Universität Tübingen,* Mainz: Philipp von Zabern.

Cauville, Sylvie

1997 *Le temple de Dendara: Les chapelles osiriennes,* Dendara 10, Cairo: Institut Français d'Archéologie Orientale.

Charron, Alain, ed.

2002 *La mort n'est pas une fin,* Musée de l'Arles: Arles.

Chassinat, Émile

1966 *Le mystère d'Osiris au mois de Khoiak,* vol. I, Cairo: IFAO.

Church Educational System

2000 *The Pearl of Great Price: Student Manual Religion 327,* Salt Lake City: Church of Jesus Christ of Latter-day Saints.

Clarysse, Willy

1981 *Prosopographia Ptolemaica IX. Addenda et Corrigenda au Volume III (1956),* Studia Hellenistica 25, Louvain: Fondation Universitaire de Belgique.

Coenen, Marc

1995 "Books of Breathings. More Than a Terminological Question?" *Orientalia Lovaniensia Periodica* 26, pp. 29–38.

1998a "The Dating of the Papyri Joseph Smith I, X and XI, and Min Who Massacres His Enemies," in W. Clarysse, et al., eds., *Egyptian Religion: The Last Thousand Years.* vol. II, OLA 85, Leuven: Peeters, pp. 1103–15.

1998b "An Introduction to the Document of Breathing Made by Isis," *Revue d'Égyptologie* 49, pp. 39–47.

1999a "Horos, Prophet of Min Who Massacres His Enemies," *Chronique d'Égypte* LXXIV, no. 148, pp. 257–60.

1999b "A Remarkable Judgement Scene in a *Document of Breathing made by Isis:* Papyrus Florence 3665 + 3666 and Papyrus Vienna 3850," *Orientalia* n. s. 68, pp. 98–103.

2000 "The Funerary Papyri of the Bodleian Library at Oxford," *Journal of Egyptian Archaeology* 86, pp. 87–94.

2001 "On the Demise of the Book of the Dead in Ptolemaic Thebes," *Revue d'Égyptologie* 52, pp. 69–84.

2003 "The Funerary Papyri of Horos Son of Estneteretten in the Kunsthistorisches Museum in Vienna," *Zeitschrift für ägyptische Sprache und Altertumskunde* 130, pp. 160–69.

Coenen, Marc, and Jan Quaegebeur

1995 *De papyrus Denon in het Museum Meermanno-Westreenianum, den Haag of Het Boek van het Ademen van Isis,* Monografieën van het Museum van het Boek 5, Leuven: Peeters.

Cook, Andrew W.

2012 "Formulas and Facts: A Response to John Gee," *Dialogue: A Journal of Mormon Thought* 45/3 (Fall), pp. 1–10.

Cook, Andrew W., and Christopher C. Smith

2010 "The Original Length of the Scroll of Hôr," *Dialogue: A Journal of Mormon Thought* 43/4 (Winter), pp. 1–42.

Copenhaver, Brian P.

1992 *Hermetica,* Cambridge: Cambridge University Press.

Crapo, Richley H.

1970 "Emic and Etic Studies: The Proper Approach to the Book of Abraham," *Book of Abraham Symposium. April 3, 1970,* Salt Lake: The Salt Lake Institute of Religion and the Latter-Day Saint Student Association, pp. 25–35.

Crapo, Richley, and John Tvedtnes

1968 "A Study of the Hor Sen-Sen Papyrus," *Newsletter and Proceedings of the Society for Early Historic Archaeology* 109 (25 October), pp. 1–6.

1969 "The Hor Sen-Sen Papyrus as a Mnemonic Device: A Further Study," *Newsletter and Proceedings of the Society for Early Historic Archaeology* 114 (2 June), pp. 6–13.

Crum, Walter E.

1939 *A Coptic Dictionary,* Oxford: Oxford University Press.

Daressy, Georges

1903 *Textes et Dessins Magiques,* (CGC), Cairo: IFAO.

Davies, Norman De Garis

1953 *The Temple of Hibis in El Khargeh Oasis. Part III: The Decoration,* New York: Metropolitan Museum of Art.

Dawson, Warren R., Eric P. Uphill and Morris L. Bierbrier

1995 *Who Was Who in Egyptology,* 3rd revised edition, London: Egypt Exploration Society.

De Keersmaecker, Roger O.

2010 *Thebes: The Ramesseum,* Travellers' Graffiti from Egypt and the Sudan IX, Mortsel (Antwerp): Graffito-Graffiti.

Devauchelle, Didier

1978 "À propos du papyrus de Genève D 229," *Enchoria* 8/2, pp. 73–75.

Devéria, Théodule

1881 *Catalogue des manuscrits égyptiens écrits sur papyrus, toile, tablettes et ostraca en caractères hiéroglyphiques, hiératiques, démotique, grecs, coptes, arabes et latins, qui sont conservés au Musée égyptien du Louvre,* Paris: Charles de Mourgues Frères.

Edzard, Dietz Otto, Gertrud Farber and Edmond Sollberger
1977 *Die Orts- und Gewässernamen der präsargonischen und sargonischen Zeit,* Repertoire Géographique des Textes Cunéiformes 1, Wiesbaden: Ludwig Reichert Verlag.

Ehat, Andrew F., and Lyndon W. Cook, eds.
1980 *The Words of Joseph Smith: The Contemporary Accounts of the Nauvoo Discourses of the Prophet Joseph,* Provo, UT: Religious Studies Center, Brigham Young University.

Erichsen, Wolja
1954 *Demotisches Glossar,* Copenhagen: Ejnar Munksgaard.

Erman, Adolf, and Hermann Grapow, eds.
1957 *Wörterbuch der ägyptischen Sprache,* 2nd edition, 7 vols., Berlin and Leipzig: Akademie Verlag and J. C. Hinrichs.

Evans, Elaine A.
2002 "A Magical Papyrus Fragment Speaks," (McClung Museum) *Research Notes* 24 (July), pp. 1–4.

Fabretti, A., F. Rossi and R. V. Lanzone
1882 *Regio Museo di Turino, Antichità egizie,* Turin: Paravia.

Faulkner, Raymond O.
1985 *The Ancient Egyptian Book of the Dead,* revised edition, New York: Macmillan Publishing Company.

Faulring, Scott H., Kent P. Jackson and Robert J. Matthews, eds.
2004 *Joseph Smith's New Translation of the Bible: Original Manuscripts,* Provo, UT: Religious Studies Center, Brigham Young University.

Fowden, Garth
1986 *The Egyptian Hermes,* Cambridge: Cambridge University Press.

Frayne, Douglas
1993 *Sargonic and Gutian Periods (2334–2113 BC),* Royal Inscriptions of Mesopotamia, Early Periods Vol. 2. Toronto/Buffalo/London: University of Toronto Press.

Freeman, G. E.
1974 "The Osiris-Shoshenq Hypocephalus," *SSEA Newsletter* (reissued as *SSEA Journal*) vol. V/2 (December), pp. 4–9.

Gardiner, Alan H.

1957 *Egyptian Grammar,* 3rd edition, Oxford: Griffith Institute.

Gee, John

1992 "A Tragedy of Errors," *Review of Books on the Book of Mormon* 4, pp. 93–119.

1996 "Telling the Story of the Joseph Smith Papyri," *FARMS Review of Books* 8/2, pp. 46–59.

1998 "The Hagiography of Doubting Thomas," *FARMS Review of Books* 10/2, pp. 158–83.

2000a *A Guide to the Joseph Smith Papyri,* Provo: The Foundation for Ancient Research and Mormon Studies (FARMS).

2000b "Eyewitness, Hearsay, and Physical Evidence of the Joseph Smith Papyri," in Stephen D. Ricks, Donald W. Parry, and Andrew H. Hedges, eds., *The Disciple as Witness: Essays on Latter-day Saint History of Doctrine in Honor of Richard Lloyd Anderson,* Provo, UT: Foundation for Ancient Research and Mormon Studies (FARMS), Brigham Young University, pp. 175–217.

2001 "Towards an Interpretation of Hypocephali," in *Mélanges offerts à Edith Varga,* Bulletin du Musée Hongrois des Beaux-Arts Supplément, Budapest, pp. 325–34.

2003 "One Side of a Nonexistent Conversation," *FARMS Review* 15/1, pp. 81–85.

2004 "S3 mỉ-nn: A Temporary Conclusion," *Göttinger Miszellen* 202, pp. 55–58.

2005 "Facsimile 3 and Book of the Dead 125," in John Gee and Brian M. Hauglid, eds., *Astronomy, Papyrus, and Covenant,* Provo: The Foundation for Ancient Research and Mormon Studies (FARMS), pp. 95–105.

Gee, John, Michael D. Rhodes and Hugh Nibley, eds.

2005 The Collected Works of Hugh Nibley, vol. 16: Hugh Nibley, *The Message of the Joseph Smith Papyri: An Egyptian Endowment,* second edition, Salt Lake City: Deseret Book Company.

Gestermann, Louise

2001 "'Gegrüßet seiest Du, Schöngesichtiger'—Zur Bonner Mumienmaske des Imhotep," in *Mélanges offerts à Edith Varga,* Bulletin du Musée Hongrois des Beaux-Arts Supplément, Budapest, pp. 101–12.

Gordon, Cyrus H.

1958 "Abraham and the Merchants of Ura," *Journal of Near Eastern Studies* 17, pp. 28–31.

1963 "Abraham of Ur," in D. Winton Thomas and W. D. McHardy, eds., *Hebrew and Semitic Studies Presented to Godfrey Rolles Driver in Celebration of His Seventieth Birthday, 20 August 1962,* Oxford: Clarendon Press, pp. 77–84.

1977 "Where is Abraham's Ur?" *Biblical Archaeological Review* 3/2, pp. 20–21, 52.

Gordon, Scott

2003 "Anti-Mormon Video Reaches National Television Audience," *Meridian Magazine:* http://ww.meridianmagazine.com/ideas/030528anti.html (accessed 7/17/06).

2005 "Leaving the Saints or Leaving Reality?" *FAIR* Book Review: http://fairlds.org/authors/gordon-scott/leaving-the-saints-or-leaving-reality.

Goyon, Jean-Claude

1972 "Les livres des respirations," in idem, *Rituels funéraires de l'ancienne Égypte,* Littératures anciennes du Proche-Orient 4, Paris: Les Éditions du Cerf, pp. 183–317.

Green, Doyle L.

1968 "New Light on Joseph Smith's Egyptian Papyri. Additional Fragment Disclosed," *The Improvement Era* 71/2 (February), p. 40.

Green, Tamara

1992 *The City of the Moon God: Religious Traditions of Harran,* Religions in the Graeco-Roman World 114, Leiden/New York/Köln: E. J. Brill.

Griffith, F. Ll., and Herbert Thompson

1904 *The Demotic Magical Papyrus of London and Leiden,* vol. 1, London: H. Grevel & Company.

1921 *The Demotic Magical Papyrus of London and Leiden,* vol. 3, Oxford: The Clarendon Press.

Haslauer, Elfriede

2001 "Hypocephali in Wien und im Asasif," in *Mélanges offerts à Edith Varga,* Bulletin du Musée Hongrois des Beaux-Arts Supplément, Budapest, pp. 173–84.

Hastings, James, F. C. Grant and H. H. Rowley

1963 *Dictionary of the Bible,* revised edition, New York: Charles Scribner's Sons.

Haynes, Stephen R.

2002 *Noah's Curse: The Biblical Justification of American Slavery,* New York: Oxford University Press.

Herbin, François-René

1999 "Trois manuscrits originaux du Louvre porteurs du Livre des Respirations fait par Isis (P. Louvre N 3121, N 3083 et N 3166)," *Revue d'Égyptologie* 50, pp. 149–239.

2008 *Books of Breathing and Related Texts,* Catalogue of the Books of the Dead and Other Religious Texts in the British Museum IV, London: The British Museum.

Heward, Grant S., and Jerald Tanner

1968 "The Source of the Book of Abraham Identified," *Dialogue: A Journal of Mormon Thought* 3/2 (Summer), pp. 92–98.

Hölscher, Uvo

1939 *The Temples of the Eighteenth Dynasty. The Excavation of Medinet Habu II,* Oriental Institute Publications 41, Chicago: The University of Chicago Press.

de Horrack, Philippe-Jacques

1875 "The Book of Respirations," in S. Birch, ed., *Records of the Past,* IV, London: S. Bagster and Sons, pp. 121–28 (reprinted in *Oeuvres diverses,* pp. 99–107).

1907 “Le Livre des Respirations d’après les manuscrits du Musée du Louvre,” *Oeuvres diverses,* Bibliothèque égyptologique 17 (Paris: Ernest Leroux, 1907), pp. 109–37 (reprinted from Paris: Klincksieck, 1877).

Houlihan, Patrick F.
1986 *The Birds of Ancient Egypt,* Cairo: American University in Cairo.

Howard, Richard P.
1968 “A Tentative Approach to the Book of Abraham,” *Dialogue: A Journal of Mormon Thought* 3/2 (Summer), pp. 88–92.

1995 *Restoration Scriptures: A Study of Their Textual Development,* 2nd revised edition, Independence, MO: Herald Publishing House.

Howe, Eber D.
1834 *Mormonism Unvailed* [*sic*], Painesville, OH: Printed and Published by the Author.

Janák, Jiří
2003 “Journey to the Resurrection. Chapter 105 of the Book of the Dead in the New Kingdom,” *Studien zur altägyptischen Kultur* 31, pp. 193–210.

Jessee, Dean C., ed.,
1992 *The Papers of Joseph Smith: Journal, 1832–1842,* vol. 2, Salt Lake City: Deseret Book Company.

2002 *Personal Writings of Joseph Smith,* revised edition, Salt Lake City: Deseret Book Company/Provo, UT: Brigham Young University Press.

Jessee, Dean C., Mark Ashurst-McGee and Richard L. Jensen, eds.
2008 *The Joseph Smith Papers: Journals, Volume 1: 1832–1839,* Salt Lake City: Church Historian’s Press.

Johnson, Benjamin F.
1947 *My Life’s Review,* Independence, MO: Zion’s Printing and Publishing Company.

Junker, Hermann
1917 *Die Onurislegende,* Vienna: Alfred Hölder.

Kadish, Gerald E.

1979 “The Scatophagus Egyptian,” *Journal of the Society for the Study of Egyptian Antiquities* 9, pp. 203–17.

Keller, Roger R.

2001 “Episcopalian Bishop Franklin S. Spalding and the Mormons,” *Utah Historical Quarterly* 69 (Summer), pp. 232–46.

Kenney, Scott G., ed.

1983–85 *Wilford Woodruff’s Journal,* Typescript, 9 vols., Midvale, UT/Salt Lake City: Signature Books.

Kimball, Stanley B.

1983 “New Light on Old Egyptiana: Mormon Mummies, 1848–71,” *Dialogue: A Journal of Mormon Thought* 16 (Winter), pp. 72–90.

Kobayashi, Yoshitaka

1992 “Haran,” in David Noel Freedman, ed., *The Anchor Bible Dictionary,* New York: Doubleday, vol. 3, pp. 58–59.

Kriéger, Paule

1960 “Note concernant les numéros d’inventaire des objets conservés au Départment des antiquités égyptiennes du Musée du Louvre,” *Revue d’Égyptologie* 12, pp. 94–96.

Kurth, Dieter

2004 *Edfou VII,* Wiesbaden: Harrassowitz Verlag.

2007 *Einführung ins Ptolemäische,* Teil 1, Hützel: Backe-Verlag.

Larson, Charles M.

1992 *... By His Own Hand upon Papyrus: A New Look at the Joseph Smith Papyri,* Grand Rapids MI.: Institute for Religious Research [revised edition of 1985].

Larson, John A.

1994 “Joseph Smith and Egyptology,” in D. Silverman, ed., *For His Ka: Essays Offered in Memory of Klaus Baer,* Studies in Ancient Oriental Civilization 55, Chicago: The Oriental Institute, pp. 159–78.

Leonard, Glen M.

2002 *Nauvoo: A Place of Peace, A People of Promise,* Salt Lake City: Deseret Book Company/Provo, UT: Brigham Young University Press.

Lepsius, Richard

1842 *Das Todtenbuch der Ägypter nach dem hieroglyphischen Papyrus in Turin,* Leipzig: Georg Wigand.

Lüddeckens, Erich, et. al, eds.,

1996–2000 *Demotisches Namenbuch,* Wiesbaden: Dr. Ludwig Reichert Verlag, vol. 1/1–18.

Margueron, Jean-Claude

1992 "Ur," in David Noel Freedman, ed., *The Anchor Bible Dictionary,* New York: Doubleday, vol. 6, pp. 766–67.

Mariette, Auguste

1873 *Dendérah,* vol. IV, Paris: Librarie A. Franck.

Marquardt, H. Michael, ed.

1981 *The Joseph Smith Egyptian Papers,* Cullman, AL: Printing Service.

1999 *The Joseph Smith Revelations: Text and Commentary,* Salt Lake City: Signature Books.

2000 *Literary Dependence in the Book of Mormon: Two Studies,* Grand Rapids, MI: Institute for Religious Research.

2007a *Early Patriarchal Blessings of The Church of Jesus Christ of Latter-day Saints,* Salt Lake City: Smith-Pettit Foundation.

2007b *The Four Gospels According to Joseph Smith,* Longwood, FL: Xulon Press.

Matthews, Rodger, and Cornelia Roemer

2003 "Introduction: The Worlds of Ancient Egypt—Aspects, Sources, Interactions," in R. Matthews and C. Roemer, eds., *Ancient Perspectives on Egypt,* London: Institute of Archaeology, University College London, pp. 1–20.

McCarter, P. Kyle

1999 "The Patriarchal Age," revised by Ronald S. Hendel, in Hershel Shanks, ed., *Ancient Israel: From Abraham to the Roman Destruction of the Temple,* revised edition, Washington, DC: Biblical Archaeology Society, pp. 1–31.

de Meulenaere, Hermann

1955 "Quatre noms propres de Basse Époque," *Bulletin de l'Institut Français d'Archéologie Orientale du Caire* 55, pp.141–48.

Millard, Alan R.

2001 "Where Was Abraham's Ur? The Case for the Babylonian City," *Biblical Archaeological Review* 27/3, pp. 52–53, and 57.

Möller, Georg

1912 *Hieratische Paläographie,* vol. 3, Leipzig: J. C. Hinrichs'sche Buchhandlung.

Mormon History, "Joe Smith's Egyptian Mummies—1857" www.truthandgrace.com/1857mummies.htm

Mormon Quotes, "Book of Abraham," www.mormonthink.com/QUOTES/boaquotes.htm.

Morris, Larry E.

2004 "The Book of Abraham: Ask the Right Questions and Keep on Looking," *The FARMS Review* 16/2, pp. 355–80.

Muhlestein, Kerry

2005 "The Book of Breathings in Its Place," *The FARMS Review* 17/2, pp. 471–86.

Naville, Édouard,

1886 *Das aegyptische Todtenbuch der XVIII. bis XX. Dynastie aus verschiedenen Urkunden zusammengestellt und herausgegeben,* 3 vols., Berlin: A. Asher & Company (reprinted Graz, 1971).

Nelson, N. L.

1913 "An Open Letter to Bishop Spalding," *The Improvement Era* 16/6 (April), pp. 603–610.

Nibley, Hugh

1968 "Phase One," *Dialogue: A Journal of Mormon Thought* 3/2 (Summer), pp. 99–105.

1968–70 "A New Look at the Pearl of Great Price," *The Improvement Era* 71/1 (January), pp. 18–25; 71/2 (February), pp. 14–21; 71/3 (March), pp. 16–22; 71/4 (April), pp. 64–69; 71/5 (May), pp. 54–57; 71/6 (June), pp. 18–22; 71/7 (July), pp. 48–55; 71/8 (August), pp. 53–64; 71/9 (September), pp. 66–80; 71/10 (October), pp. 73–81; 71/11 (November), pp. 36–44; 72/1 (January 1969), pp. 26–33; 72/2 (February), pp. 64–67; 72/3 (March), pp. 76–84; 72/4 (April), pp. 66–72; 73/5 (May 1970), pp. 82–94.

1971 "The Meaning of the Kirtland Egyptian Papers," *Brigham Young University Studies* 11 (Summer), pp. 350–99.

1975 *The Message of the Joseph Smith Papyri: An Egyptian Endowment,* Salt Lake City: Deseret Book Company.

Otto, Eberhard

1967 *Ancient Egyptian Art: The Cults of Osiris and Amon,* New York, Harry N. Abrams.

Parker, Richard A.

1968a "The Joseph Smith Papyri: A Preliminary Report," *Dialogue: A Journal of Mormon Thought* 3/2 (Summer), pp. 86–88.

1968b "The Book of Breathings (Fragment 1, the 'Sensen' Text, with Restorations from Louvre Papyrus 3284)," *Dialogue: A Journal of Mormon Thought* 3/2 (Summer), pp. 98–99.

Peterson, H. Donl

1995 *The Story of the Book of Abraham: Mummies, Manuscripts, and Mormonism,* Salt Lake City: Deseret Book Company.

Phelps, Leah Y.

1942 "Letters of Faith from Kirtland," *The Improvement Era* 45 (August), p. 529.

Pinches, T. G.

1909 "Ur of the Chaldees," in James Hastings, ed., *A Dictionary of the Bible,* New York: Charles Scribner's Sons, vol. 4, pp. 835–37.

Pomponio, Francesco, and Paolo Xella

1997 *Les dieux d'Ebla: Étude analytique des divinités éblaïtes à l'époque des archives royales du IIIe millénaire,* Alter Orient und Altes Testament 245, Münster: Ugarit-Verlag

Porter, Bertha, and Rosalind L. B. Moss

1939 *Topographical Bibliography of Ancient Egyptian Hieroglyphic Texts, Reliefs and Paintings,* vol. VI: Upper Egypt Chief Temples, Oxford: Griffith Institute.

Preisendanz, Karl

1941 *Papyri Graecae Magicae,* vol. III, Teubner, Leipzig.

Quack, Joachim F.

1996 "Zwei demotische Ausdrücke zur Bezeichnung des Charakters," *Zeitschrift für ägyptische Sprache und Altertumskunde* 123, pp. 62–69.

2004 "Fragmente Memphitischer Religion und Astronomie in semidemotischer Schrift," in F. Hoffmann and H. J. Thissen, eds., *Res Severa Gaudium,* Leuven: Peeters, pp. 467–96.

2009 "Der Schlußparagraph des Buches vom Atmen, das Isis machte," *Die Welt des Orients* 39, pp. 72–76.

Quaegebeur, Jan

1982 "VIII. Demotic Inscriptions on Wood from the Tomb of ʿAnch-Hor," in Manfred Bietak and Elfriede Reiser-Haslauer, *Das Grab des ʿAnch-Hor,* vol. 2, Vienna: Österreichischen Akademie der Wissenschaften, pp. 259–66.

1990 "La stèle Brooklyn 71.37.2 reconsidérée," *Göttinger Miszellen* 119, pp. 73–89.

1994 "Le papyrus Denon à La Haye et une famille de prophètes de Min-Amon," in M. Minas and J. Zeidler, eds., *Aspekte spätägyptischer Kultur: Festschrift für Erich Winter zum 65. Geburtstag.* Mainz am Rhein: Philipp von Zabern, pp. 213–25.

1995 "À la Recherche du Haut Clergé Thébain à l'Époque Gréco-Romaine," in S. P. Vleeming, ed., *Hundred-Gated Thebes,* Papyrologica Lugduno-Batava 27, Leiden: E. J. Brill, pp. 139–61.

1997 "Books of Thoth Belonging to Owners of Portraits? On Dating Late Hieratic Funerary Papyri," in M. L. Bierbrier, ed., *Portraits and Masks: Burial Customs in Roman Egypt,* London: The British Museum, pp. 72–77.

Ranke, Hermann

1935 *Die ägyptischen Personennamen,* vol. 1, Glückstadt: J. J. Augustin.

Remy, Jules

1860 *Voyage au Pays des Mormons,* 2 vols., Paris: E. Dentu.

Remy, Jules, and Julius Brenchley

1861 *A Journey to Great Salt Lake City,* London: W. Jeffs.

Reynolds, George

1879 *The Book of Abraham. Its Authencity Established as a Divine and Ancient Record,* Salt Lake City: Deseret News and Publishing Establishment.

Rhodes, Michael D.

1977 "A Translation and Commentary of the Joseph Smith Hypocephalus," *Brigham Young University Studies* 17 (Spring), pp. 259–74.

1992 "Facsimiles from the Book of Abraham," in Daniel H. Ludlow, ed., *Encyclopedia of Mormonism: The History, Scripture, Doctrine and Procedure of the Church of Jesus Christ of Latter-day Saints,* New York: Macmillan Publishing Company, vol. 1, pp. 135–37.

1994 *The Joseph Smith Hypocephalus . . . Seventeen Years Later,* Provo, UT: FARMS, 14 pp., online at http://www.lightplanet.com/response/BofAbraham/jshypo.htm.

1997 *The Joseph Smith Hypocephalus . . . Twenty Years Later,* Provo, UT: FARMS, 14 pp., online at: http://home.comcast.net/~michael.rhodes/JosephSmithHypocephalus.pdf.

2002 *The Hor Book of Breathings. A Translation and Commentary,* Provo: The Foundation for Ancient Research and Mormon Studies (FARMS).

Ritner, Robert K.

1981a "Hermes Pentamegistos," *Göttinger Miszellen* 49, pp. 73–75.

1981b "Additional Notes to Hermes Pentamegistos," *Göttinger Miszellen* 50, pp. 67–68.

1993 *The Mechanics of Ancient Egyptian Magical Practice,* Studies in Ancient Oriental Civilization 54, Chicago: The Oriental Institute.

1994 "Denderite Temple Hierarchy and the Family of the Theban High Priest Nebwenenef: Block Statue Oriental Institute Museum 10729," in D. Silverman, ed., *For His Ka: Essays Offered in Memory of Klaus Baer,* Studies in Ancient Oriental Civilization 55, Chicago: The Oriental Institute, pp. 205–26.

1998 "The Wives of Horus and the Philinna Papyrus (PGM XX)," in W. Clarysse, A. Schoors and H. Willems, eds., *Egyptian Religion: The Last Thousand Years. Studies Dedicated to the Memory of Jan Quaegebeur, Part II,* OLA 85, Leuven: Peters Press, pp. 1027–41.

2000 "Book of the Dead 125 (The "Negative Confession")," in W. W. Hallo and K. L. Younger, eds., *The Context of Scripture,* Volume II, Leiden: E. J. Brill, pp. 59–64.

2002 "The 'Breathing Permit of Hôr' Thirty-four Years Later," *Dialogue: A Journal of Mormon Thought* 33/4 [Winter 2000], pp. 97–119.

2003a "The 'Breathing Permit of Hôr' among the Joseph Smith Papyri," *Journal of Near Eastern Studies* 62/3, pp. 161–80.

2003b "The Bentresh Stela," in W. K. Simpson, ed., *The Literature of Ancient Egypt,* 3rd edition, New Haven: Yale University, pp. 361–66.

2009 *The Libyan Anarchy: Inscriptions from Egypt's Third Intermediate Period,* Writing from the Ancient World 21, Atlanta: Society of Biblical Literature.

2010 "Two Third Intermediate Period Books of the Dead: P. Houston 31.72 and P. Brooklyn 37.1801E," in Zahi Hawass and Jennifer Wegner, eds., *Millions of Jubilees, the Festschrift for David P. Silverman,* Supplément aux Annales du Service des Antiquités de l'Égypte, vol. 39/2, pp. 167–83.

Rochemonteix, Maxence de Chalvet Marquis de

1894 "Le temple d'Apet ou est engendré l'Osiris thébain," *Bibliothèque égyptologique,* vol. 3, Paris: Leroux.

Rochmonteix, Maxence de Chalvet Marquis de, and Émile Chassinat

1897 *Le Temple de Edfou,* vol. 1, Mémoires publiés par les Membres de la Mission Archéologique Française au Caire 10, Paris: Ernest Leroux.

Russmann, Edna R.
2001 *Eternal Egypt*, London: The British Museum.

Ryhiner, Marie-Louise
1977 "À propos de trigrammes panthéistes," *Revue d'Égyptologie* 29, pp. 125–37.

Satzinger, Helmut
1994 *Das Kunsthistorische Museum in Wien, Die Ägyptisch-Orientalische Sammlung,* Zaberns Bildbände zur Archaölogie 14, Mainz: Verlag Philipp von Zabern.

Seeber, Christine
1976 *Untersuchungen zur Darstellung des Totengerichts im Alten Ägypten,* Münchner Ägyptologische Studien 35, Munich: Deutscher Kunstverlag.

Seixas, Joshua
1834 *A Manual Hebrew Grammar for the Use of Beginners,* 2nd edition, Andover: Gould and Newman.

Seyffarth, Gustavus
1860 "A Remarkable Papyrus-Scroll, written in the Hieratic character about 1050 B. C.," *The Transactions of the Academy of Science of St. Louis,* vol. I 1856–1860, St. Louis: George Knapp & Co., pp. 527–69.

Shanks, Hershel
2000 "Abraham's Ur: Is the Pope Going to the Wrong Place?," *Biblical Archaeological Review* 26/1, pp. 16–19, and 66–67.

Smith, Brian L.
1997 "A Book of Abraham Research Update," *Religious Studies Center Newsletter* (Brigham Young University), (May), pp. 5–8.

Smith, Joseph Jr.
1830 *The Book of Mormon,* Palmyra, NY (revised edition 1952).

1851 *The Pearl of Great Price,* Liverpool (2nd edition Salt Lake City, 1878).

1995 *The Essential Joseph Smith,* Classics in Mormon Thought 4, Salt Lake City: Signature Books.

Smith, Joseph Jr., et al.

1978 *History of the Church of Jesus Christ of Latter-day Saints. Period 1,* Brigham H. Roberts, ed., revised and enlarged, 6 vols., Salt Lake City: Deseret Book Company.

Smith, Mark

1987 *The Mortuary Texts of Papyrus BM 10507,* London: British Museum.

2009 *Traversing Eternity: Texts for the Afterlife from Ptolemaic and Roman Egypt,* Oxford: Oxford University Press.

Spalding, Rt. Rev. F. S.

1912 *Joseph Smith, Jr., as a Translator,* Salt Lake City: The Arrow Press.

Steindorff, Georg

1946 *Catalogue of the Egyptian Sculpture in the Walters Art Gallery,* Baltimore: Walters Art Gallery.

Stenhouse, Thomas B. H.

1873 *The Rocky Mountain Saints: A Full and Complete History of the Mormons,* New York: D. Apppleton and Company (reprinted London 1874 and 1878, New York 1900, and Salt Lake City 1904).

Stevenson, Joseph Grant, ed.

1991 *Richards Family History,* Provo, UT: Stevenson's Genealogical Center.

Tanner, Jerald, ed.

1966 *Joseph Smith's Egyptian Alphabet and Grammar* [Microform], Salt Lake City: Utah Lighthouse Ministry.

Tanner, Jerald, and Sandra Tanner

1992 "Solving the Mystery of the Joseph Smith Papyri," *Salt Lake City Messenger* 82 (September).

Thissen, Heinz J.

1989 *Die demotischen Graffiti von Medinet Habu,* Demotische Studien 10, Sommerhausen: Gisela Zauzich Verlag.

Thompson, Stephen E.

1995 "Egyptology and the Book of Abraham," *Dialogue: A Journal of Mormon Thought* 28/1, pp. 145–48.

Times and Seasons
1839– 6 vols., Nauvoo, IL.

Todd, Jay M.
1968 "Background of the Church Historian's Fragment," *The Improvement Era* 71/2 (February), pp. 40·A–40·I.

1969 *The Saga of the Book of Abraham,* Salt Lake City: Deseret Book Company.

Tolk, Norman, Lynn Travers, George D. Smith Jr., and F. Charles Graves
1967 "An Interview with Dr. [Henry G.] Fischer," *Dialogue: A Journal of Mormon Thought* 2 (Winter), pp. 55–64.

Trigger, Bruce
1995 "Egyptology, Ancient Egypt, and the American Imagination," in Nancy Thomas, ed., *The American Discovery of Ancient Egypt,* Los Angeles: Los Angeles County Museum of Art, pp. 21–35.

Tvedtnes, John
1970 "The Use of Mnemonic Devices in Oral Traditions, as Exemplified by the Book of Abraham and the Hor Sen-Sen Papyrus," *Newsletter and Proceedings of the Society for Early Historic Archaeology* 120 (April), pp. 2–10.

Urrurtia, Benjamin
1969 "The Joseph Smith Papyri," *Dialogue: A Journal of Mormon Thought* 4/2 (Summer), pp. 129–34.

Vallogia, Michel
1979 "Le Papyrus Lausanne No. 3391," in Jean Vergotte, ed., *Hommages à Serge Sauneron,* vol. 1, Bibliothèque d'Étude 81/1, Cairo: IFAO, pp. 285–304.

2001 "Les manuscrits hiératiques et hiéroglyphiques de la Bibliotheca Bodmeriana," in J. L. Chappaz and S. Vuilleumier, eds., *Sortir au jour. Art égyptien de la Fondation Martin Bodmer,* Cahiers de la Société d'Egyptologie, Genève 7, Geneva: Société d'Egyptologie; Genève: Musées d'art et d'histoire de la Ville de Genève; et Munich: K. G. Saur Verlag, pp. 135–46.

Van Orden, Bruce A., ed.
1993 "Writing to Zion: The William W. Phelps Kirtland Letters (1835–1836)," *Brigham Young Studies* 33, pp. 542–93.

Vandier, Jacques

1961 *Le Papyrus Jumilhac,* Paris: CNRS.

Varga, Edith

1961 "Les travaux préliminaires de la monographie sur les hypocéphales," *Acta Orientalia Academiae Scientarium Hungaricae* 12, pp. 235–47.

1998a *Napkorong a fej alatt,* Budapest: Akadémiai Kiadó.

1998b "Les Hypocèphales," *Acta Orientalia Academiae Scientarium Hungaricae* 50, pp. 29–41.

Vergote, Jozef

1959 *Joseph en Égypte,* Orientalia et Biblica Lovaniensa III, Louvain/Leuven: Université de Louvain/Universiteit te Leuven.

Verhoeven, Ursula

1993 *Das saitische Totenbuch der Iahtesnacht,* 3 vols., Bonn: Dr. Rudolf Habelt.

2001 *Untersuchungen zur späthieratischen Buchschrift,* Orientalia Lovaniensia Analecta, vol. 99, Leuven: Peeters.

Vogel, Dan, ed.

1996– *Early Mormon Documents,* 5 vols., Salt Lake City: Signature Books.

Webb, Philip R.

2005 "Mystery of the Mummies: An Update on the Joseph Smith Collection[:] Interview with Brian L. Smith by Philip R. Webb," *Religious Studies Center Newsletter* (Brigham Young University), 20/2, pp. 1–5.

Webb, Robert C. [pseud. J. E. Homans]

1915 *The Case against Mormonism,* New York: L. L. Walton.

West, William S.

1837 *A Few Interesting Facts Respecting the Rise, Progress and Pretensions of the Mormons,* Warren, Ohio: self-published.

Westendorf, Wolfhart
1980 "Luft (Luftgott)," in W. Helck and E. Otto, eds., *Lexikon der Ägyptologie*, Wiesbaden: Otto Harrassowitz, vol III, cols. 1098–1102.

Westergren, Bruce N., ed.
1995 *From Historian to Dissident: The Book of John Whitmer*, Salt Lake City: Signature Books.

Williams, Stephen
1991 *Fantastic Archaeology*, Philadelphia: University of Pennsylvania.

Wilson, John A.
1964 *Signs and Wonders upon Pharaoh*, Chicago: The University of Chicago Press.

1968 "The Joseph Smith Egyptian Papyri, Translations and Interpretations: A Summary Report," *Dialogue: A Journal of Mormon Thought* 3/2 (Summer), pp. 67–85.

1972 *Thousands of Years*, New York: Charles Scribner's Sons.

Wilson, Luke P.
2006 "Did Joseph Smith Claim His Abraham Papyrus Was an Autograph?" http://bib.irr.org/did-joseph-smith-claim-his-abraham-papyrus-was-autograph.

Wilson, Penelope
1997 *A Ptolemaic Lexikon*, Leuven: Peeters.

de Wit, Constant
1958–62 *Les inscriptions du temple d'Opet à Karnak*, 2 vols., Brussels: Fondation égyptologique Reine Élisabeth.

Wolfe, S. J., and Robert Singerman
2009 *Mummies in Nineteenth Century America*, Jefferson, NC: McFarland & Company.

Wright, David P.
1993 "'In Plain Terms that We May Understand': Joseph Smith's Transformation of Hebrews in Alma 12–13," in Brent Lee Metcalfe, ed., *New Approaches to the Book of Mormon: Explorations in Critical Methodology*, Salt Lake City: Signature Books.

2002 "Isaiah in the Book of Mormon: Or Joseph Smith in Isaiah," in Dan Vogel and Brent Lee Metcalfe, eds., *American Apocrypha: Essays on the Book of Mormon,* Salt Lake City: Signature Books.

Wright, Lawrence
2002 "Secrets of the Mummies," pp. 51–53, in "Lives of the Saints," *New Yorker* (January 21), pp. 40–57.

Wyl, W. [pseud. Wilhelm Ritter von Wymetal]
1886 *Mormon Portraits or the Truth about Mormon Leaders from 1830 to 1886,* Salt Lake City: Tribune Printing and Publishing Company.

Zucker, Louis C.
1968 "Joseph Smith as a Student of Hebrew," *Dialogue: A Journal of Mormon Thought* 3/2 (Summer), pp. 41–55.

REJOINED FRAGMENTS OF P. JS 1 AND 2

Plate I. Overview of P. JS 1: consecutive Fragments I, XI and X.

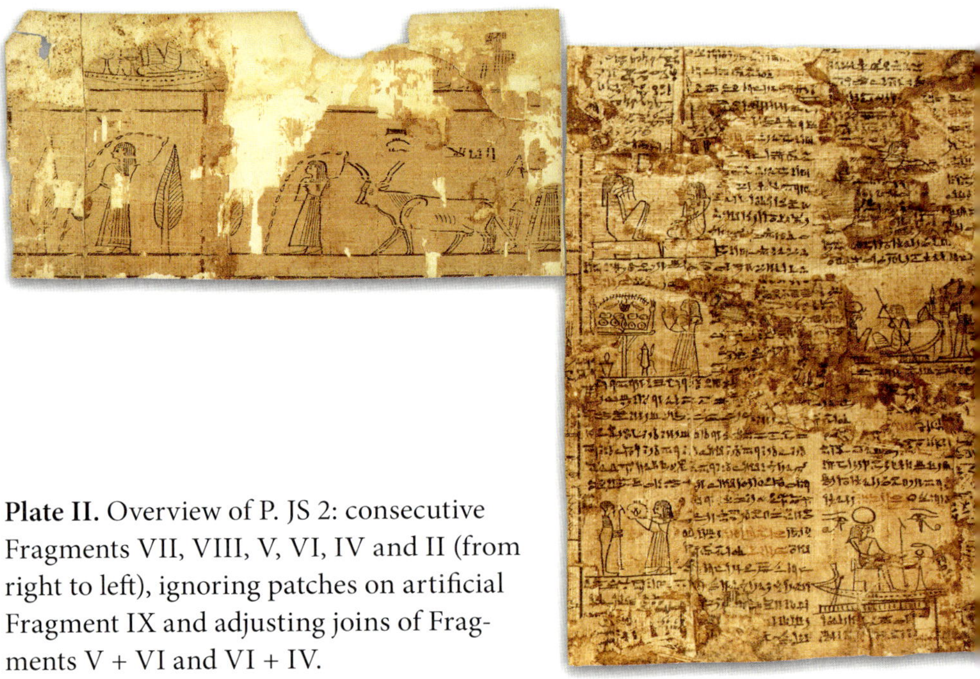

Plate II. Overview of P. JS 2: consecutive Fragments VII, VIII, V, VI, IV and II (from right to left), ignoring patches on artificial Fragment IX and adjusting joins of Fragments V + VI and VI + IV.

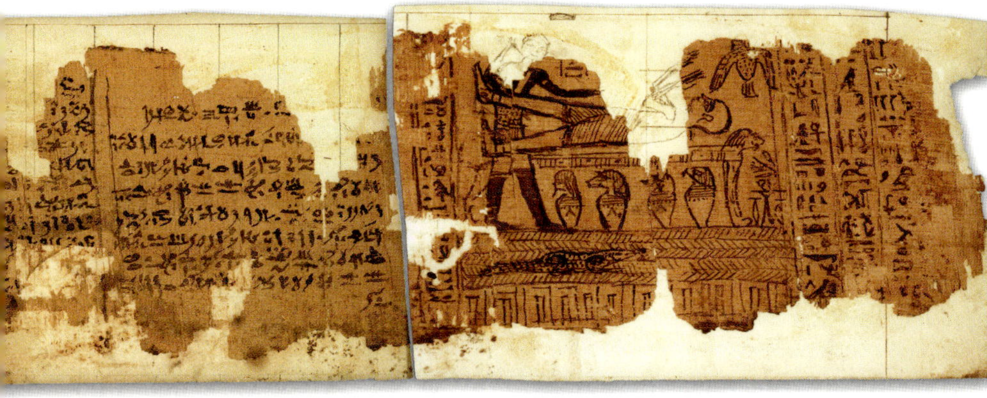

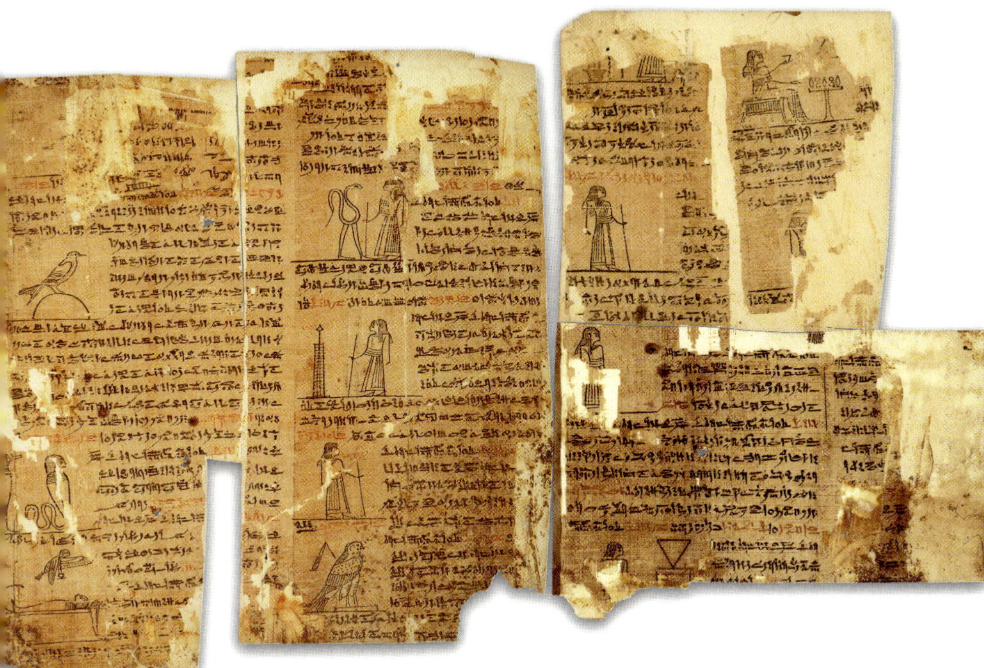

INDIVIDUAL PLATES

Plates IV, V, VI, VII, VIII, IX, X, XI, XIII, XIV, XV, XVI, XVII, XVIII, XIX, XX, XXI, and XXIII appear courtesy of the Smith-Pettit Foundation; Plate XII appears courtesy of the Institute for Religious Research.

For the page numbering of "Valuable Discovery," see above p. 95, n. 9.

A FACSIMILE FROM THE BOOK OF ABRAHAM

No. 1

Explanation

Fig. 1. The Angel of the Lord.
Fig. 2. Abraham fastened upon an altar.
Fig. 3. The idolatrous priest of Elkenah attempting to offer up Abraham as a sacrifice.
Fig. 4. The altar for sacrifice by the idolatrous priests, standing before the gods of Elkenah, Libnah, Mahmackrah, Korash, and Pharaoh.
Fig. 5. The idolatrous god of Elkenah.
Fig. 6. The idolatrous god of Libnah.
Fig. 7. The idolatrous god of Mahmackrah.
Fig. 8. The idolatrous god of Korash.
Fig. 9. The idolatrous god of Pharaoh.
Fig. 10. Abraham in Egypt.
Fig. 11. Designed to represent the pillars of heaven, as understood by the Egyptians.
Fig. 12. Raukeeyang, signifying expanse, or the firmament over our heads; but in this case, in relation to this subject, the Egyptians meant it to signify Shaumau, to be high, or the heavens, answering to the Hebrew word, Shaumahyeem.

Plate III. Facsimile 1 as published in Joseph Smith's Book of Abraham.

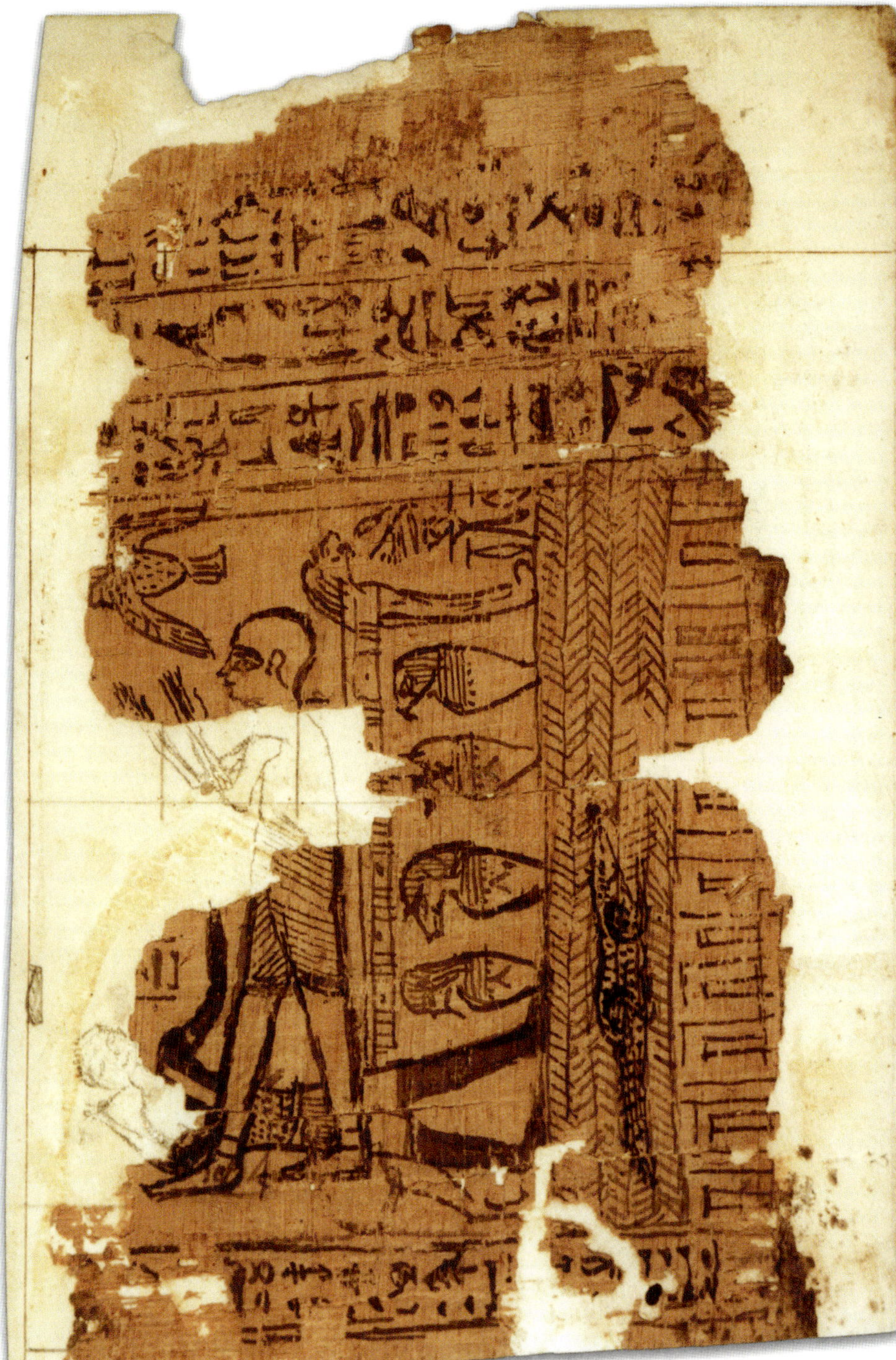

Plate IV. P. JS 1.1 = Fragment I.

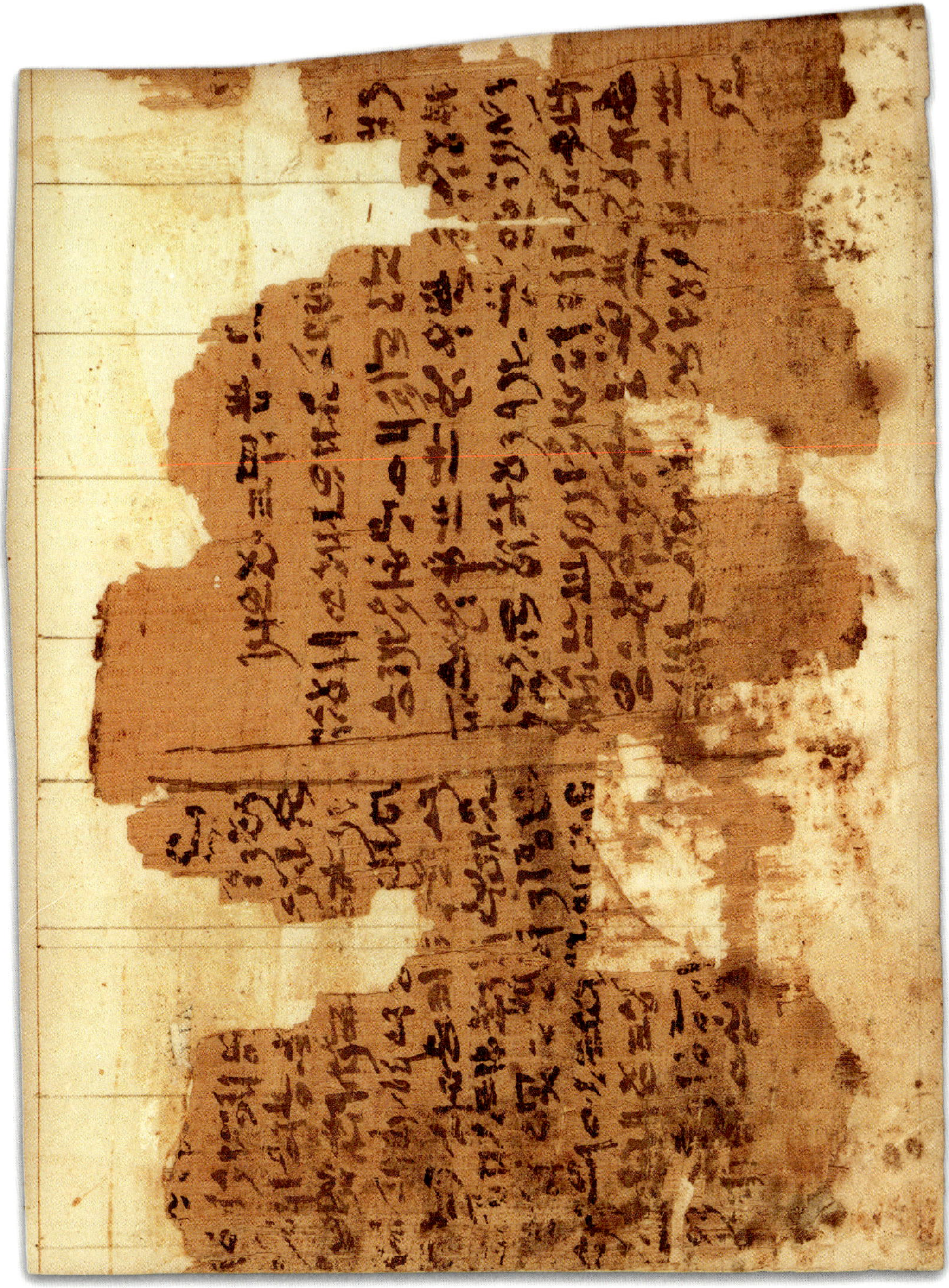

Plate V. P. JS 1.2 = Fragment XI.

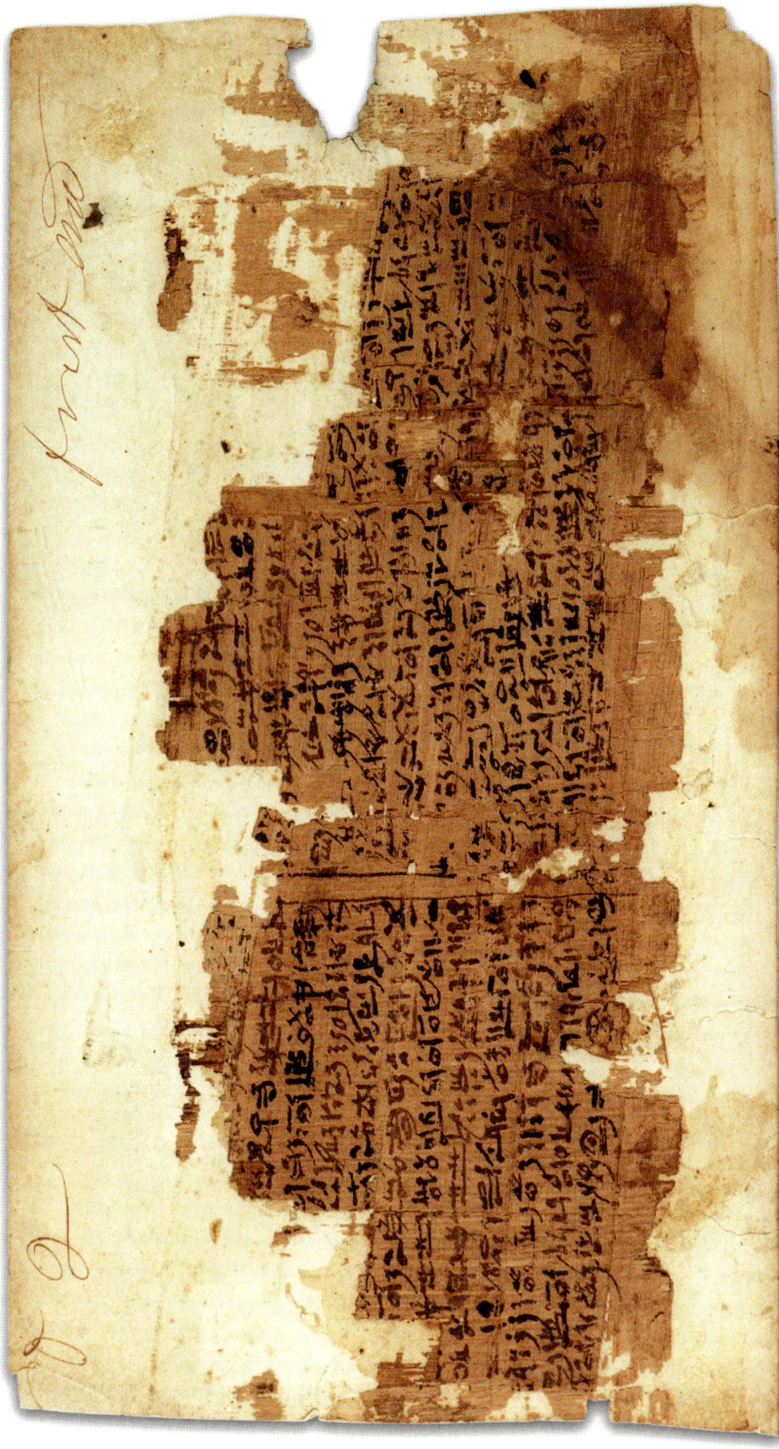

Plate VI. P. JS 1.3 = Fragment X.

A FACSIMILE FROM THE BOOK OF ABRAHAM

No. 3

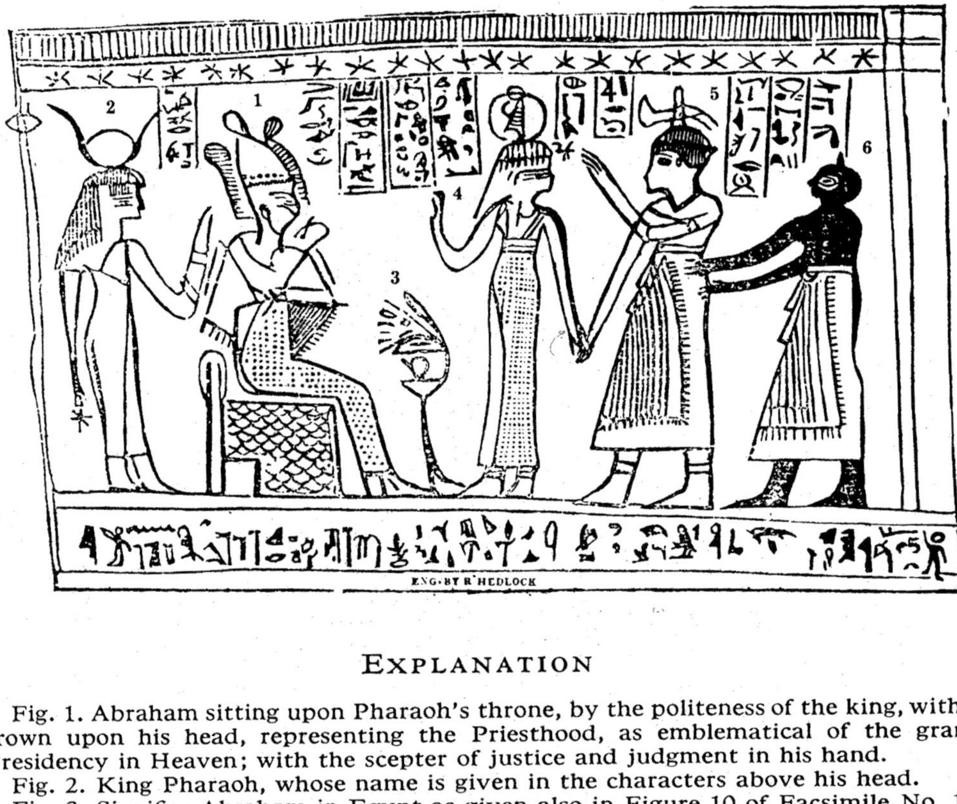

Explanation

Fig. 1. Abraham sitting upon Pharaoh's throne, by the politeness of the king, with a crown upon his head, representing the Priesthood, as emblematical of the grand Presidency in Heaven; with the scepter of justice and judgment in his hand.

Fig. 2. King Pharaoh, whose name is given in the characters above his head.

Fig. 3. Signifies Abraham in Egypt as given also in Figure 10 of Facsimile No. 1.

Fig. 4. Prince of Pharaoh, King of Egypt, as written above the hand.

Fig. 5. Shulem, one of the king's principal waiters, as represented by the characters above his hand.

Fig. 6. Olimlah, a slave belonging to the prince.

Abraham is reasoning upon the principles of Astronomy, in the king's court.

Plate VII. Facsimile 3 as published in Joseph Smith's Book of Abraham.

Plate VIII. P. JS 2.1 = Fragment IX, consisting only of arbitrarily grouped patches.

Plate IX. P. JS 2.2 = Fragment VII.

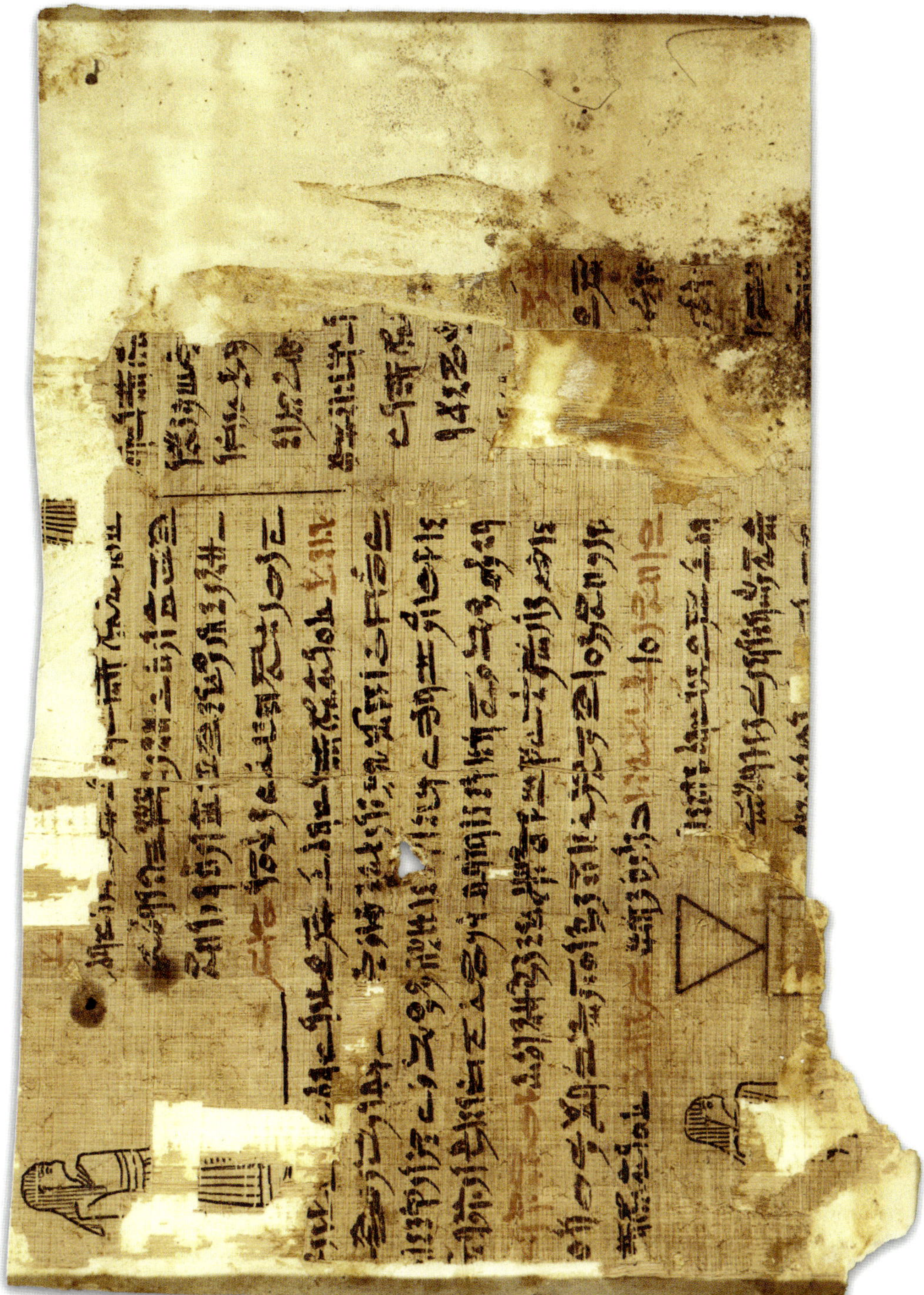

Plate X. P. JS 2.3 = Fragment VIII.

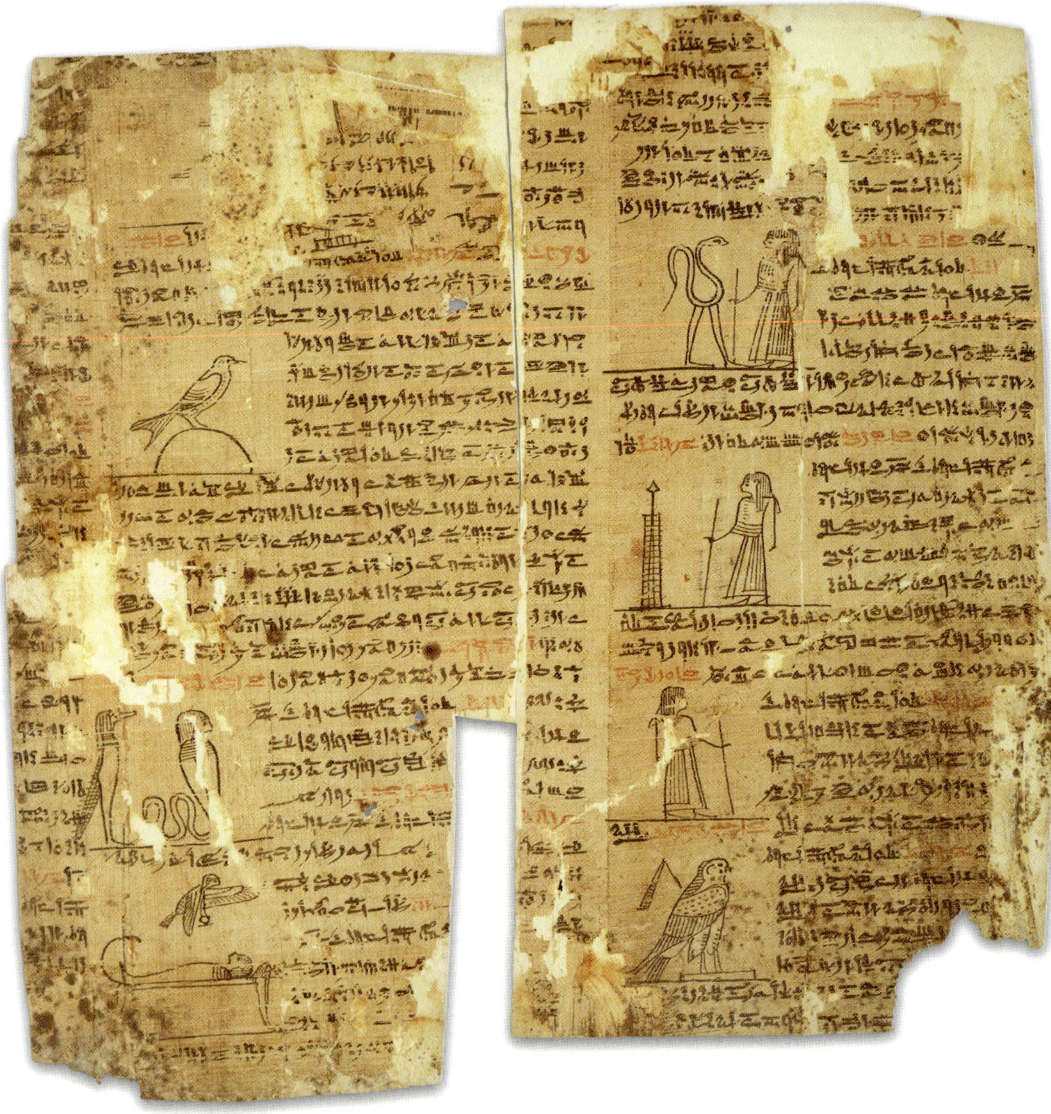

Plate XI. P. JS 2.4–5 = Fragments V (right) and VI (left), adjusted for proper alignment.

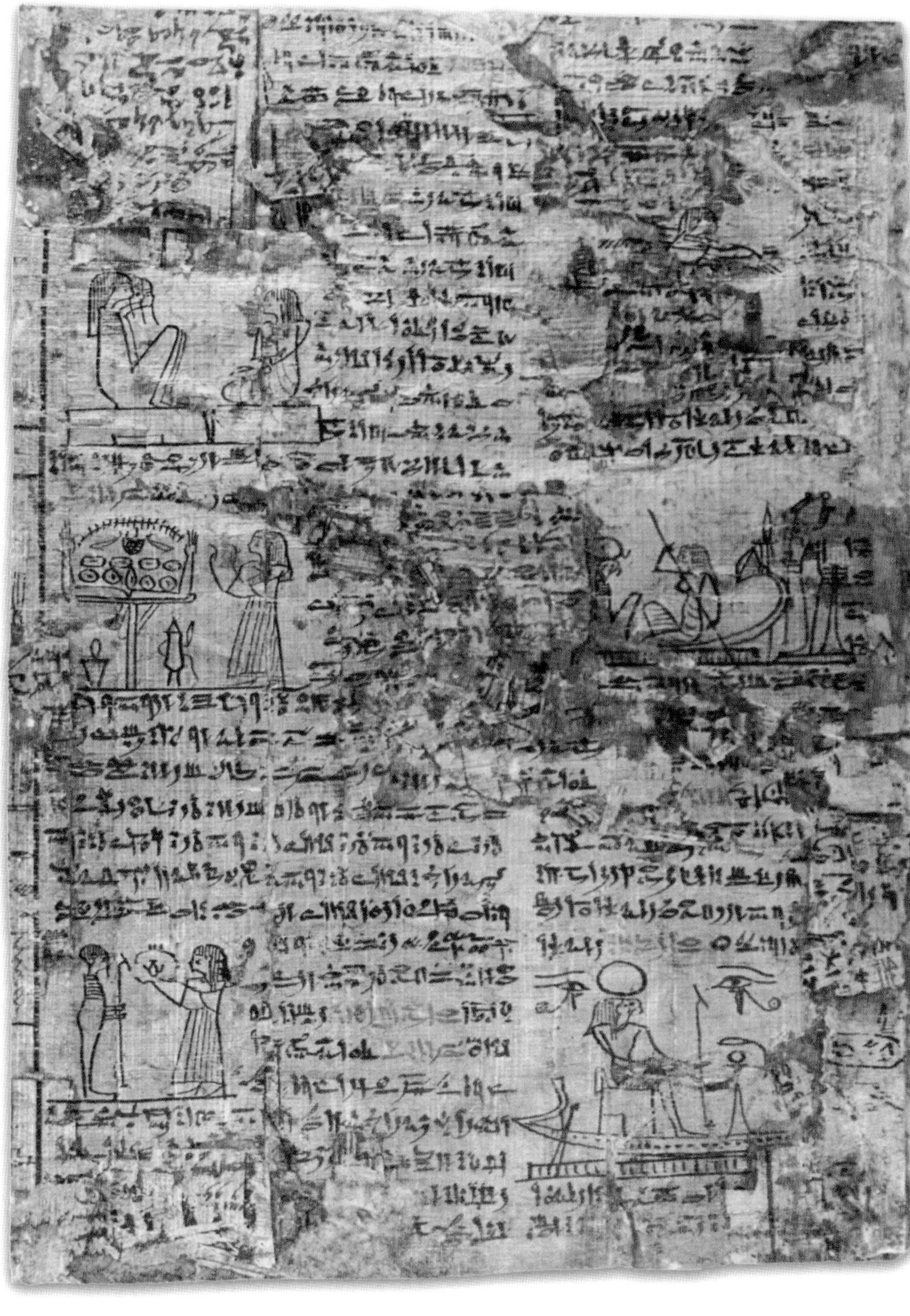

Plate XII. P. JS 2.6 = Fragment IV. (Institute for Religious Research)

Plate XIII. P. JS 2.7 = Fragment II.

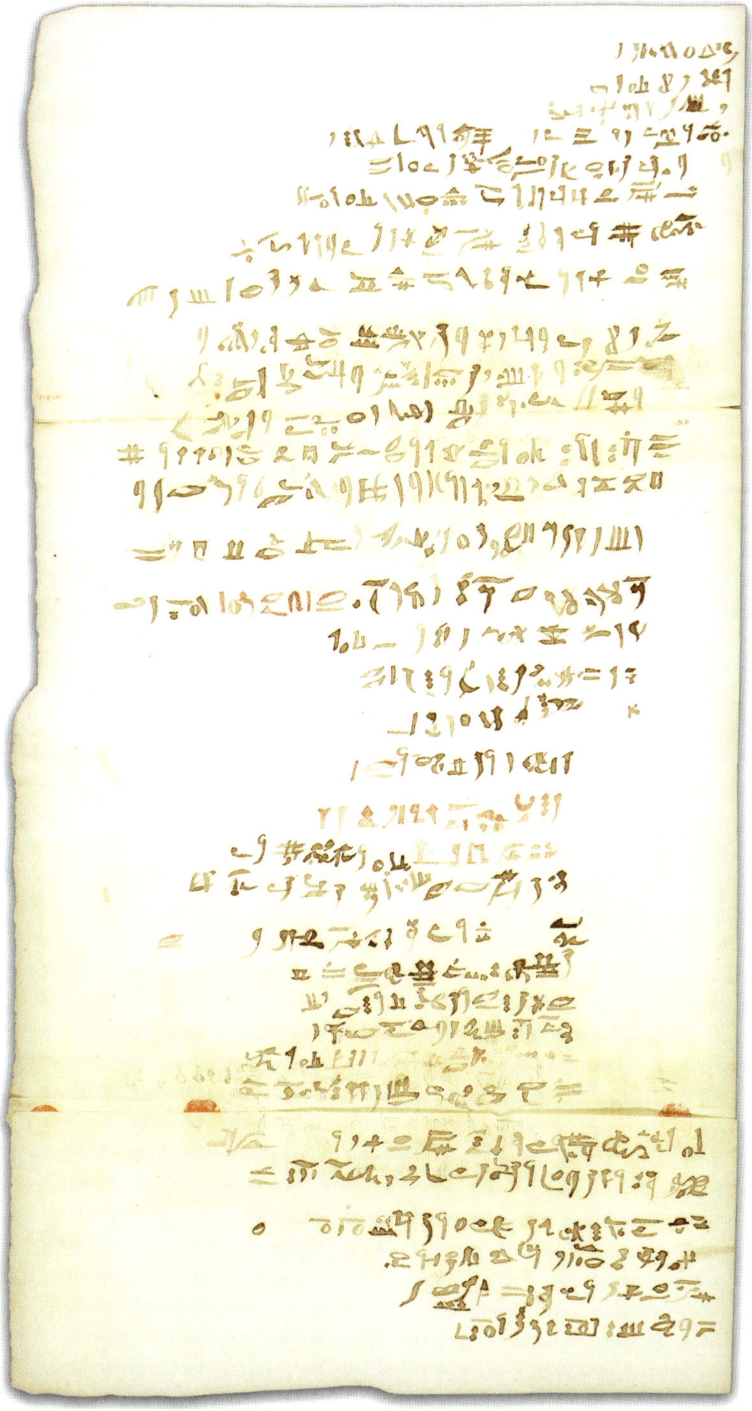

Plate XIV. Joseph Smith's "Valuable Discovery" hand copy, p. 12.

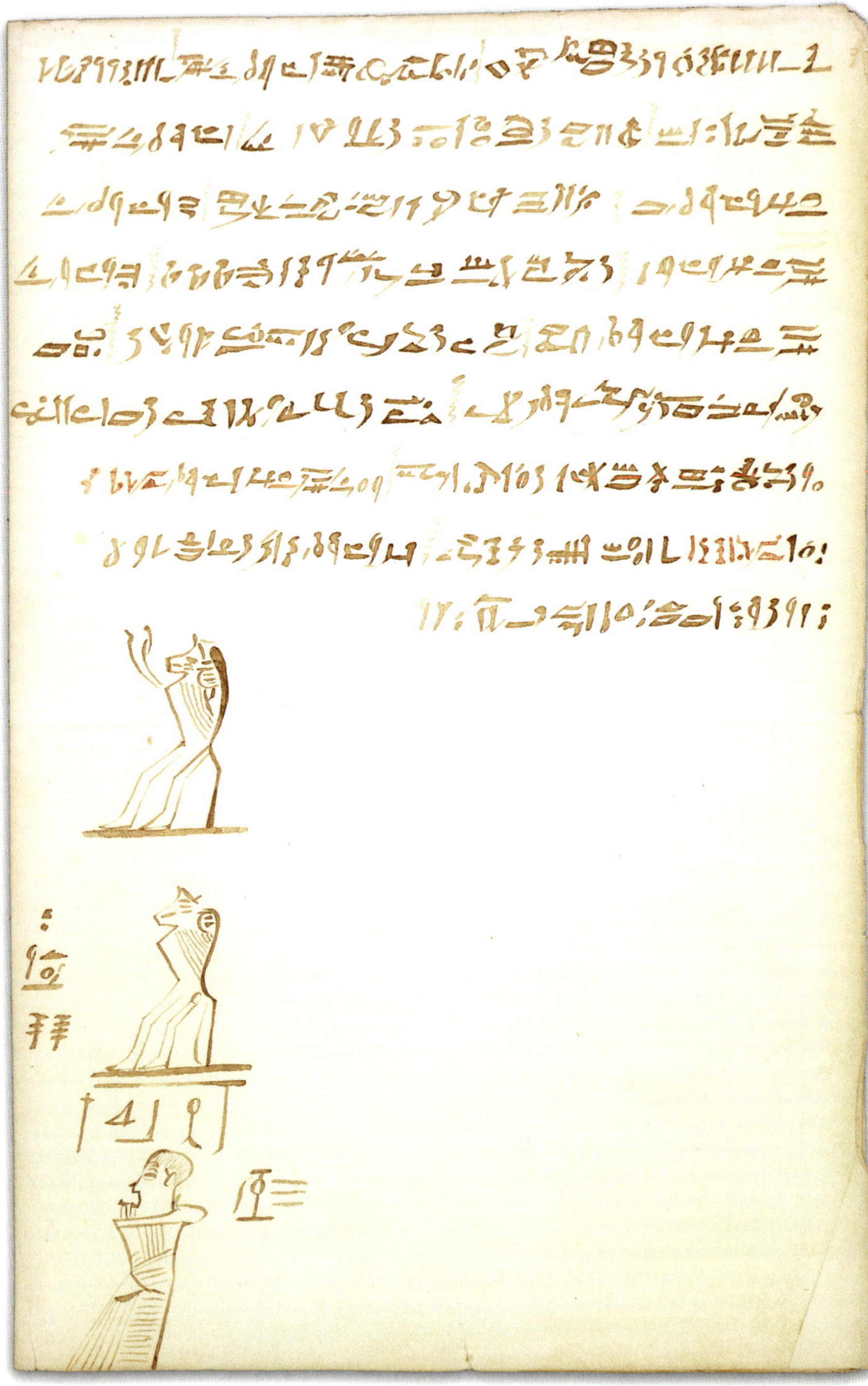

Plate XV. Joseph Smith's "Valuable Discovery" hand copy, p. 14.

Plate XVI. P. JS 3 = Fragment III/A-B.

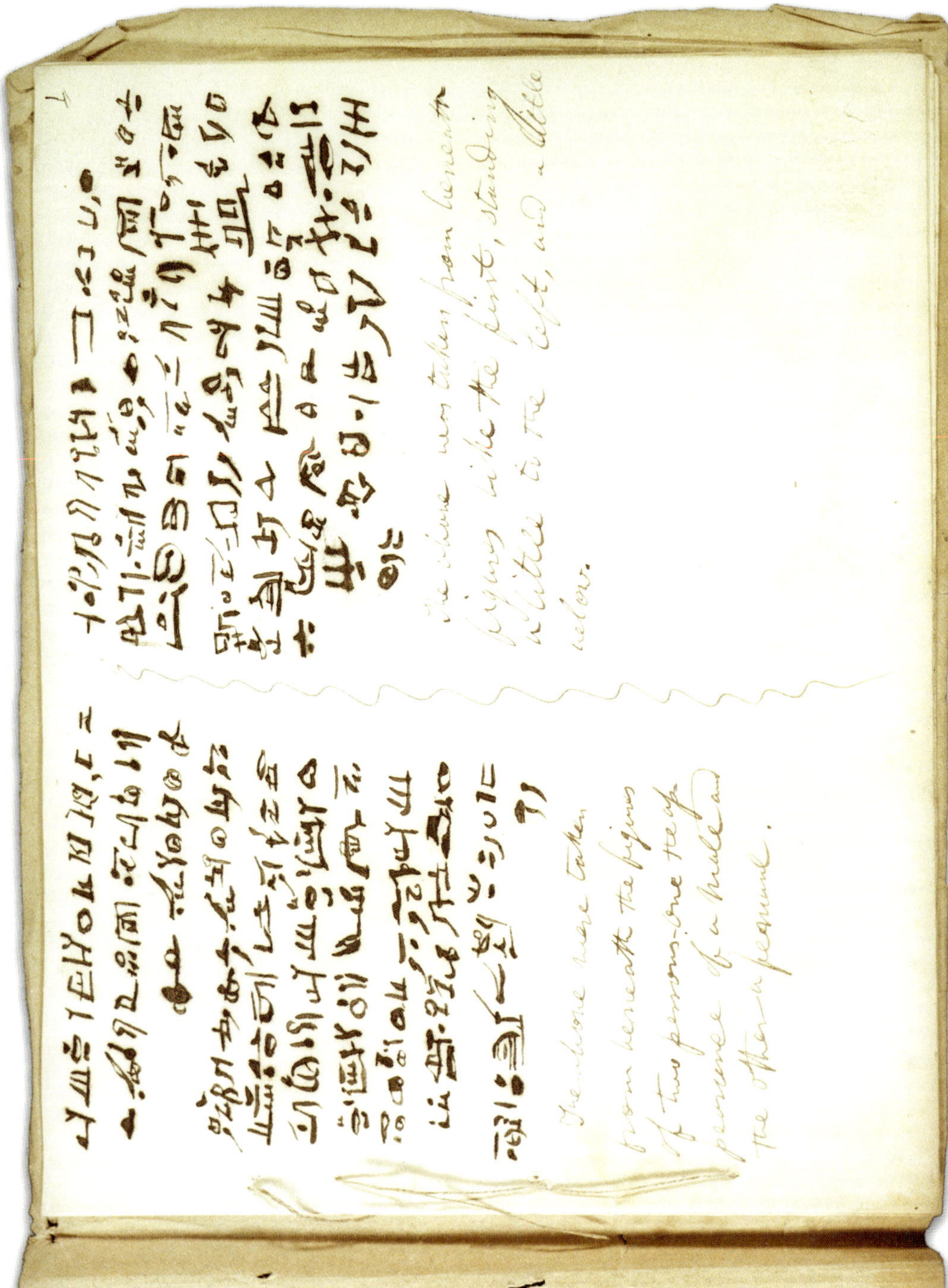

Plate XVII. P. JS 4 = Joseph Smith's "Valuable Discovery" hand copy, p. 2.

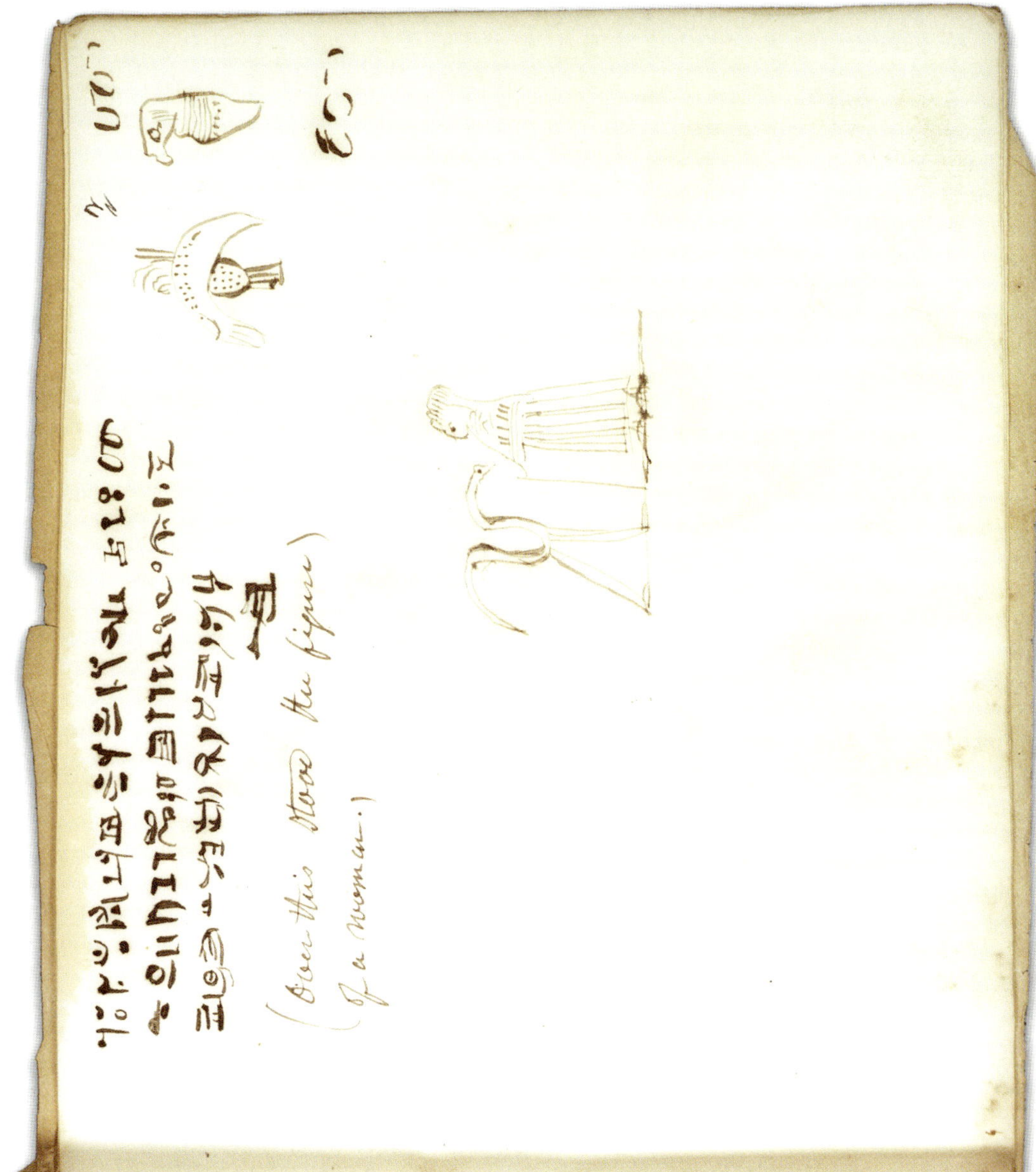

Plate XVIII. P. JS 4 = Joseph Smith's "Valuable Discovery" hand copy, p. 6.

Katumin, Princess, daughter of On-i-tas king of Egypt, who began to reign in the year of the world 1962.

Katumin was born in the 30th year of the reign of her father, and died when she was 28 years old, which was the year 3020.

Plate XIX. P. JS 4 = Joseph Smith's "Valuable Discovery" translation, p. 4.

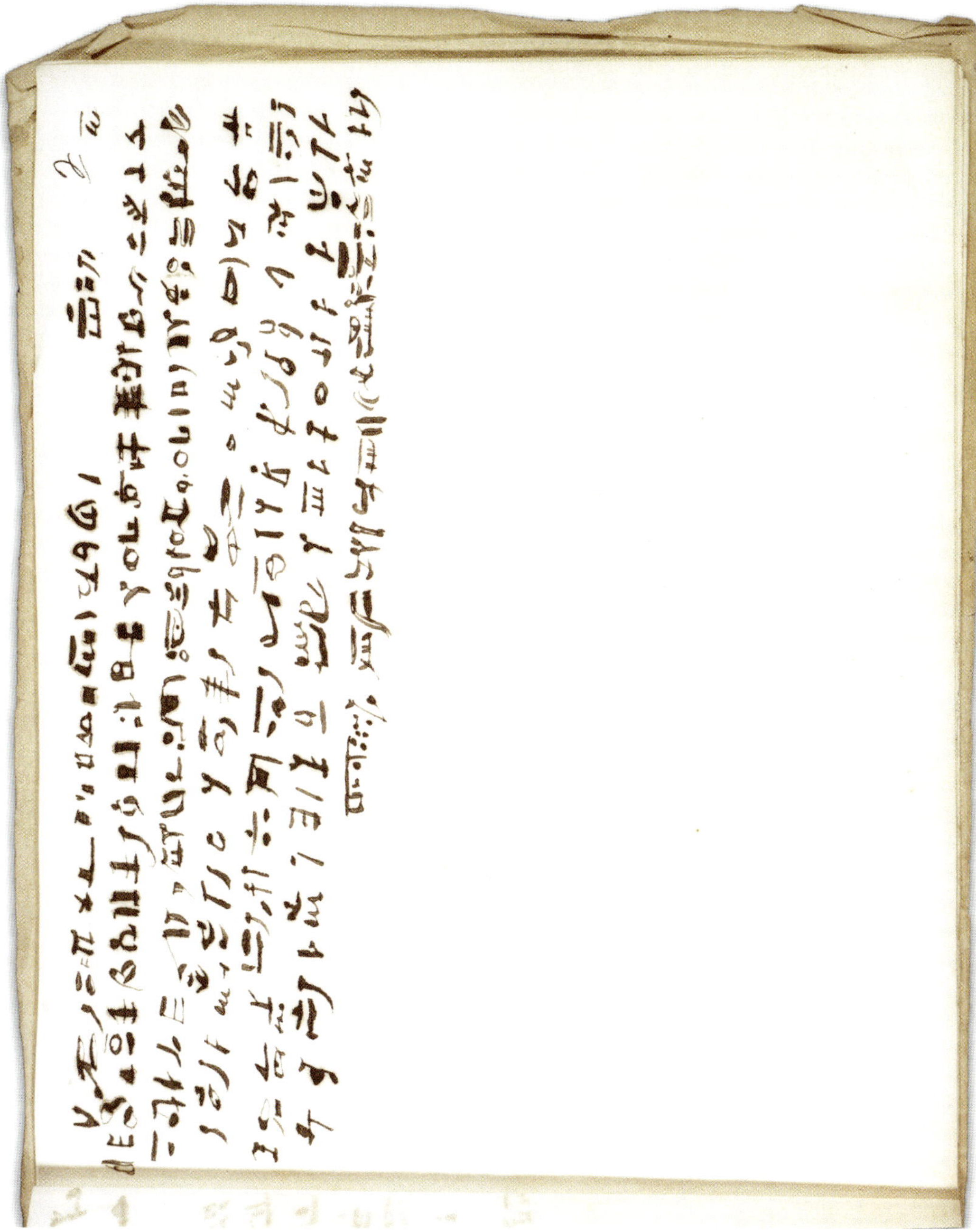

Plate XX. P. JS 4 = Joseph Smith's "Valuable Discovery" hand copy, p. 3.

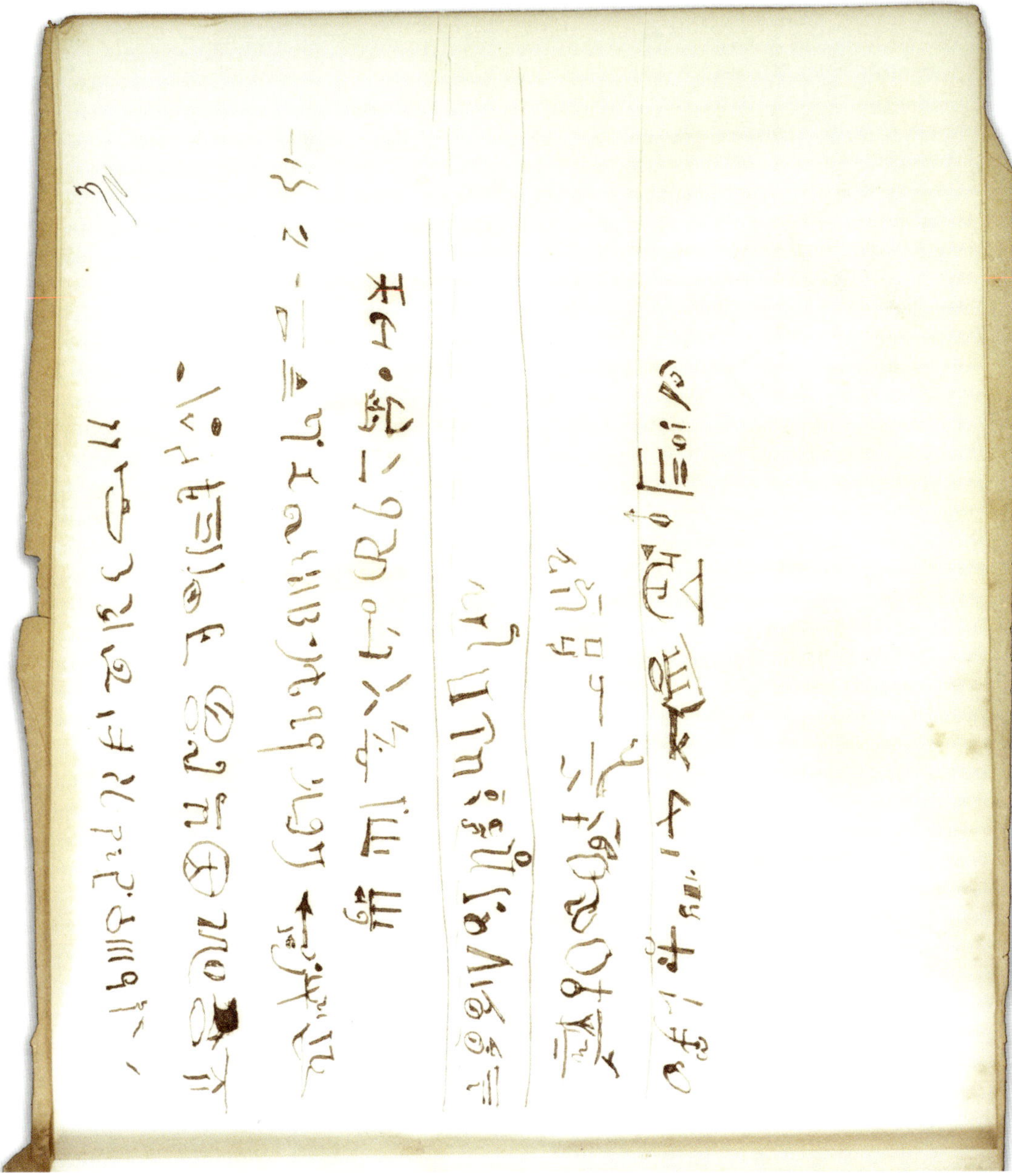

Plate XXI. P. JS 4 = Joseph Smith's "Valuable Discovery" hand copy, p. 7.

HYPOCEPHALUS OF SHESHONQ

A FAC-SIMILE FROM THE BOOK OF ABRAHAM, NO. 2.

EXPLANATION OF THE ABOVE CUT.

Fig. 1. Kolob, signifying the first creation, nearest to the celestial, or the residence of God. First in government, the last pertaining to the measurement of time. The measurement according to celestial time; which, celestial time, signifies one day to a cubit. One day, in Kolob, is equal to a thousand years, according to the measurement of this earth, which is called by the Egyptians Jah-oh-eh.

Fig. 2. Stands next to Kolob, called by the Egyptians Oliblish, which is the next grand governing creation near to the celestial or the place where God resides; holding the key of power also, pertaining to other planets; as revealed from God to Abraham, as he offered sacrifice upon an altar, which he had built unto the Lord.

Fig. 3. Is made to represent God, sitting upon his throne, clothed with power and authority; with a crown of eternal light upon his head; representing, also, the grand Key words of the Holy Priesthood, as revealed to Adam in the Garden of Eden, as also to Seth, Noah, Melchisedek, Abraham and all to whom the Priesthood was revealed.

Fig. 4. Answers to the hebrew word Raukeeyang, signifying expanse, or the firmament of the heavens: also, a numerical figure, in Egyptian, signifying one thousand: answering to the measuring of the time of Oliblish, which is equal with Kolob in its revolution and in its measuring of time.

Fig. 5, Is called in Egyptian Enish-go-ondosh; that is one of the governing planets also; and is said by the Egyptians to be the Sun, and to borrow its light from Kolob through the medium of Kae-e-vanrash, which is the grand Key, or in other words, the governing power, which governs fifteen other fixed planets or stars, as also Floeese or the Moon, the earth and the Sun in their annual revolutions. This planet receives its power through the medium of Kli flos-is-es, or Hah-ko-kau-beam, the stars represented by numbers 22, and 23, receiving light from the revolutions of Kolob.

Fig. 6, Represents this earth in its four quarters.

Fig. 7, Represents God sitting upon his throne, revealing, through the heavens, the grand Key words of the Priesthood; as, also, the sign of the Holy Ghost unto Abraham, in the form of a dove.

Fig. 8, Contains writing that cannot be revealed unto the world; but is to be had in the Holy Temple of God.

Fig. 9, Ought not to be revealed at the present time.

Fig. 10, Also.

Fig. 11, Also.—If the world can find out these numbers, So let it be, Amen.

Figures 12, 13, 14, 15, 16, 17, 18, 19, and 21, will be given in the own due time of the Lord.

The above translation is given as far as we have any right to give, at the present time.

Plate XXII. Facsimile 2 as published in Joseph Smith's Book of Abraham. Image above from *Times and Seasons* 3, no. 10 (Nauvoo, Illinois; March 15, 1842): folded insert placed between pp. 720 and 721.

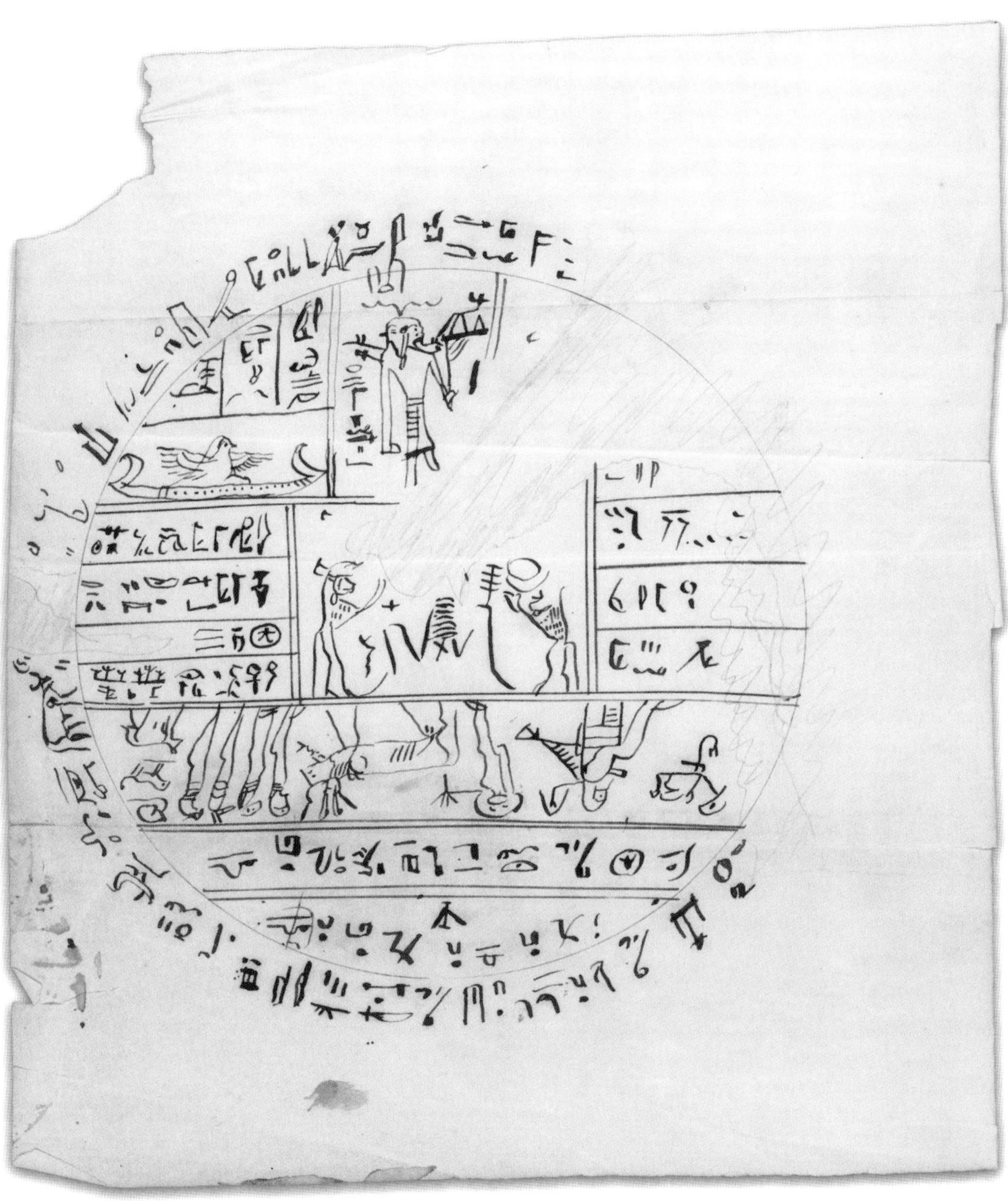

Plate XXIII. Hypocephalus = Joseph Smith's "Valuable Discovery" hand copy, p. 13.

FINDING LIST OF PATCHES IN P. JS 1 AND 2

This numbered list represents the most significant patches. Other smaller patches exist.

Patch 1 (belonging in P. JS 1, Paragraph I)
Now located in Fragment IV.2, upper left corner.

Patch 2 (belonging in P. JS 1, Paragraphs II and III)
Now located in Fragment IV.1, below ba-bird vignette of Chapter 91.

Patch 3 (belonging in P. JS 1, Paragraph III)
Now located in Fragment X.1, upper right.

Patch 4 (belonging in P. JS 1, Paragraphs IV and V)
Now located in Fragment IV.2, left of the vignette for Chapter 100.

Patch 5 (belonging in P. JS 1, Paragraph VI)
Now located in Fragment X.1, over hole in lines 9 and 10.

Patch 6 (belonging in P. JS 1, Paragraphs IX and X)
Now located in Fragment IV.1, above ba-bird vignette (below patch 12).

Patch 7 (belonging in P. JS 2, Chapters 3, 4, 5 and 6)
Now located in Fragment IX, middle of the second artificial column.

Patch 8 (belonging in P. JS 2, Chapters 10, 11, 12 and 13)
Now located in Fragment IX, middle of the left artificial column.

Patch 9 (belonging in P. JS 2, Chapter 16)
Now located in Fragment IX, in the right artificial column.

Patch 10 (belonging in P. JS 2, Chapter 16)
Now located in Fragment IX, in the right artificial column.

Patch 11 (belonging in P. JS 2, Chapter 16)
Now located in Fragment IX, in the upper left artificial column.

Patch 12 (belonging in P. JS 2, Chapters 59? and 72)
Now located in Fragment IV.1, upper right corner.

Patch 13 (belonging in P. JS 2, Chapters 75, 76 and 77)
Now located in Fragment VIII.1, lower right corner.

Patch 14 (belonging in P. JS 2, Chapter 83)
Now located in Fragment V.2, upper left corner.
Patch 15 (belonging in P. JS 2, Chapter 91)
Now located in Fragment IV.1, left of the ba-bird vignette of Chapter 91.
Patch 16 (belonging in P. JS 2, Chapter 91)
Now located in Fragment IV.1, left of the ba-bird vignette of Chapter 91 (above patch 15).
Patch 17 (belonging in P. JS 2, Chapters 100 and 105)
Now located in Fragment VI.1, upper right, below patch 18.
Patch 18 (belonging in P. JS 2, Chapters 100 and 105)
Now located in Fragment VI.1, upper right.
Patch 19 (belonging in P. JS 2, Chapter 100)
Now located in Fragment IV.1, below the vignette for Chapter 100.
Patch 20 (belonging in P. JS 2, Chapter 103)
Now located in Fragment IV.2, left of patch 12.
Patch 21 (belonging in P. JS 2, Chapter 103)
Now located in Fragment IV.2, below patches 23 and 36.
Patch 22 (belonging in P. JS 2, Chapters 104 and 105)
Now located in Fragment IV.1, right of patch 21.
Patch 23 (belonging in P. JS 2, Chapter 105)
Now located in Fragment IV.2, below patch 4.
Patch 24 (belonging in P. JS 2, Chapter 110)
Now located in Fragment IV.1, right of the vignette for Chapter 101.
Patch 25 (belonging in P. JS 2, Chapter 110)
Now located in Fragment IV.1, below and to the right of the vignette for Chapter 101.
Patch 26 (belonging in P. JS 2, Chapter 110)
Now located in Fragment IV.2, behind the head of Ptah in the lowest vignette.
Patch 27 (belonging in P. JS 2, Chapter 125)
Now located in Fragment IX, top of the middle artificial column.
Patch 28 (belonging in P. JS 2, unplaced)
Now located in Fragment VIII.2, upper right corner.
Patch 29 (belonging in P. JS 2, unplaced)
Now located in Fragment V.2, upper left (at x+3).
Patch 30 (belonging in P. JS 2, unplaced)
Now located in Fragment V.2, above the vignette for Chapter 74.
Patch 31 (belonging in P. JS 2, unplaced)
Now located in Fragment VI.1, upper right corner.

Patch 32 (belonging in P. JS 2, unplaced)
Now located in Fragment IV.1, above and to the right of the vignette for Chapter 101.

Patch 33 (belonging in P. JS 2, unplaced)
Now located in Fragment IV.1, above and to the right of the vignette for Chapter 101 (right of patch 32).

Patch 34 (belonging in P. JS 2, unplaced)
Now located in Fragment IV.1, above and to the right of the vignette for Chapter 101 (below patches 32 and 33).

Patch 35 (belonging in P. JS 2, unplaced)
Now located in Fragment IV.1, right of the vignette for Chapter 101.

Patch 36 (belonging in P. JS 2, unplaced)
Now located in Fragment IV.1, below and to the left of the vignette for Chapter 100.

Patch 37 (belonging in P. JS 2, unplaced)
Now located in Fragment IV.1, left of the vignette of Chapter 105.

Patch 38 (belonging in P. JS 2, unplaced)
Now located in Fragment IX, middle artificial column.

Patch 39 (belonging in P. JS 2, unplaced)
Now located in Fragment IX, bottom of middle artificial column.

Patch 40 (belonging in P. JS 2, unplaced)
Now located in Fragment IX, left artificial column, between patches 11 and 8.

Patch 41 (belonging in P. JS 2, unplaced)
Now located in Fragment IX, right artificial column, below baboons.

Patch 42 (belonging in P. JS 2, unplaced)
Now located in Fragment IX, middle artificial column, below patch 7.

Patch 43 (belonging in P. JS 2, unplaced)
Now located in Fragment IX, middle artificial column, below patch 39.

Patch 44 (belonging in P. JS 2, unplaced)
Now located in Fragment IX, top of right artificial column.

Patch 45 (belonging in P. JS 2, unplaced)
Now located in Fragment IX, right artificial column, right of patch 44.

Patch 46 (belonging in P. JS 2, unplaced)
Now located in Fragment IX, right artificial column, below patch 44.

Patch 47 (belonging in P. JS 2, unplaced)
Now located in Fragment IX, right artificial column, below patch 46.

Plate XXIV. Patches in Fragment X (nos. 3 and 5).

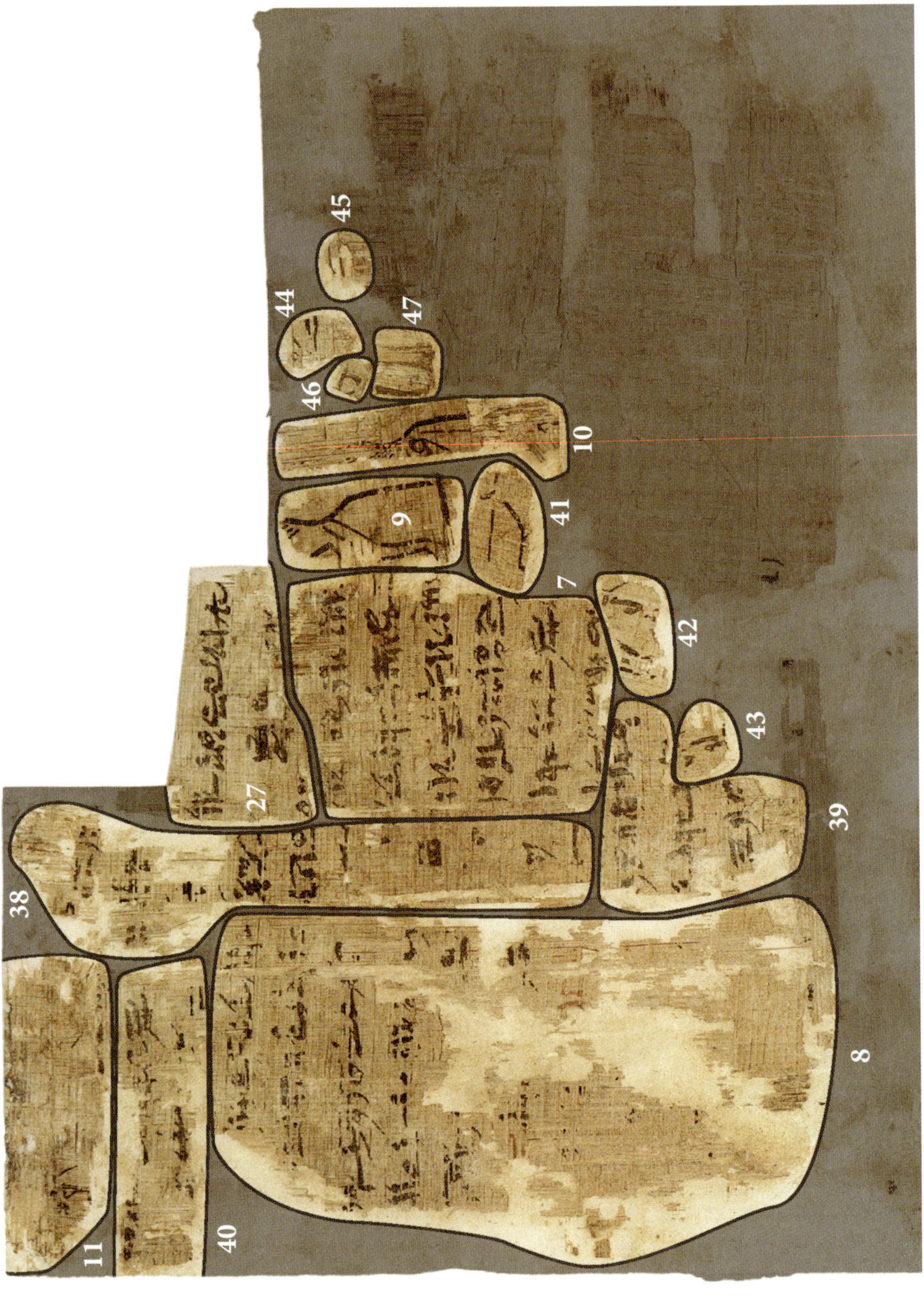

Plate XXV. Patches in Fragment IX (nos. 7-11, 27, 38-47).

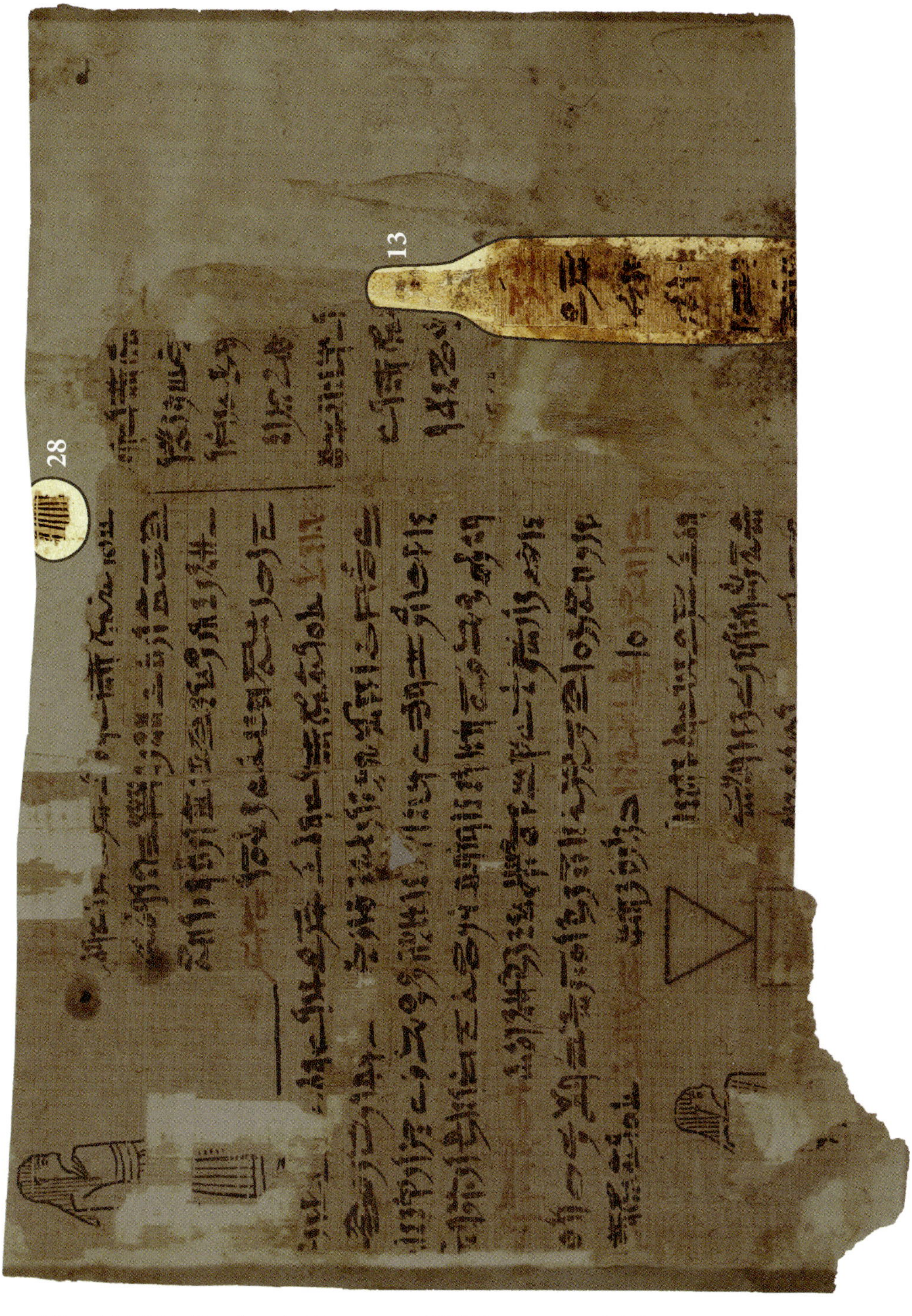

Plate XXVI. Patches in Fragment VIII (nos. 13 and 28).

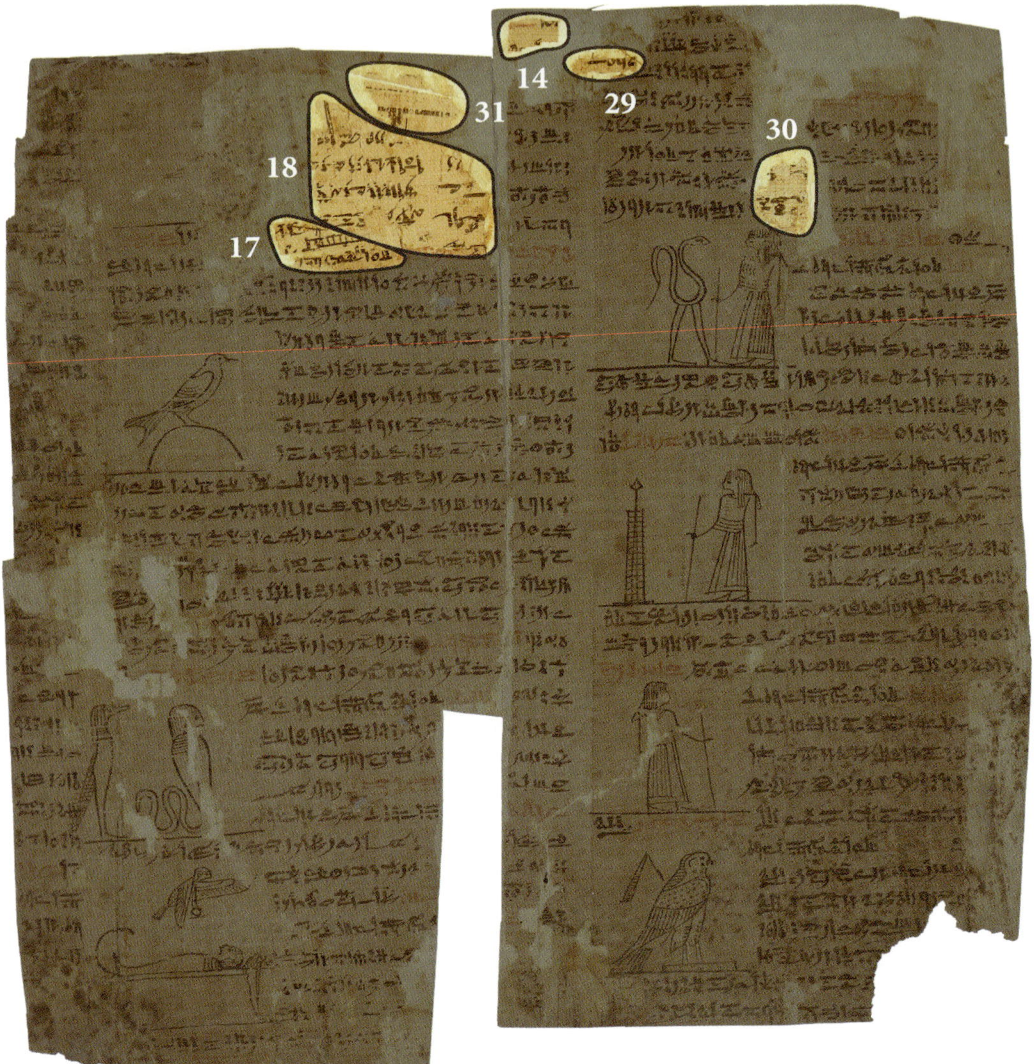

Plate XXVII. Patches in Fragments V (nos. 14, 29-30) and VI (nos. 17, 18, 31).

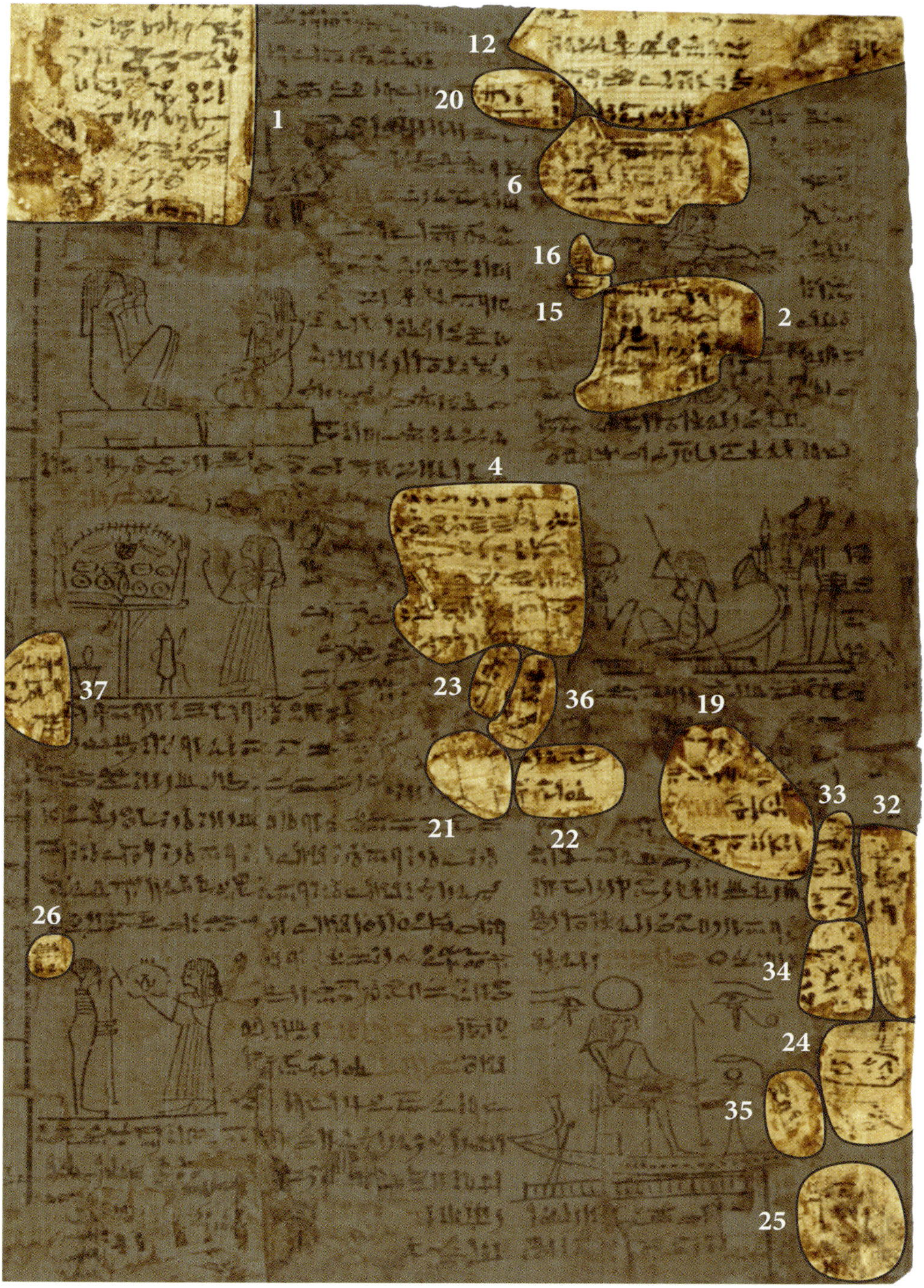

Plate XXVIII. Patches in Fragment IV (nos. 1, 2, 4, 6, 12, 15, 16, 19-26, 32-37).

ABOUT THE AUTHOR

Robert K. Ritner is Professor of Egyptology in the Oriental Institute, Department of Near Eastern Languages and Civilizations, Program on the Ancient Mediterranean World in the Department of Classics, and in the College, The University of Chicago, Illinois. He was formerly on the faculty of Yale University (1991–96), and has been a visiting lecturer/professor at L'Ecole Pratique des Hautes Etudes, Sciences Religieuses, Paris, and at the University of Pennsylvania. His research interests include Egyptian religion and magic, language, and social history, with over a hundred publications on these and related topics. His most recent monographs are *The Libyan Anarchy: Inscriptions from Egypt's Third Intermediate Period* (2009) and *The Mechanics of Ancient Egyptian Magical Practice* (1993). He is a contributing editor and/or translator to *The Literature of Ancient Egypt* (2003), *The Context of Scripture* (1997–2002), and *The Greek Magical Papyri in Translation* (1986). His publications at press or in progress include *Libya in Egypt: The Impact of Tribalism on Dynasties 19 through 26, A Catalogue of the Egyptian Objects in the Museum of Fine Arts (Houston),* and *The Hynes Papyrus (OI 25389): A Roman Mortuary Compendium.* He regularly conducts tours of Egypt sponsored by the Oriental Institute.